China and English

CRITICAL LANGUAGE AND LITERACY STUDIES
Series Editors: Vaidehi Ramanathan, *University of California, USA*;
Bonny Norton, *University of British Columbia, Canada*; and Alastair Pennycook,
University of Technology, Sydney, Australia

Critical Language and Literacy Studies is an international series that encourages
monographs directly addressing issues of power (its flows, inequities, distributions
and trajectories) in a variety of language- and literacy-related realms. The aim with
this series is twofold: (1) to cultivate scholarship that openly engages with social,
political and historical dimensions in language and literacy studies and (2) to widen
disciplinary horizons by encouraging new work on topics that have received little
focus (see below for partial list of subject areas) and that use innovative theoretical
frameworks.

Full details of all the books in this series and of all our other publications can be
found on http://www.multilingual-matters.com, or by writing to Multilingual
Matters, St Nicholas House, 31–34 High Street, Bristol, BS1 2AW, UK.

Other books in the series

Collaborative Research in Multilingual Classrooms
Corey Denos, Kelleen Toohey, Kathy Neilson and Bonnie Waterstone
English as a Local Language: Post-colonial Identities and Multilingual Practices
Christina Higgins
The Idea of English in Japan: Ideology and the Evolution of a Global Language
Philip Seargeant
Language and HIV/AIDS
Christina Higgins and Bonny Norton (eds)

CRITICAL LANGUAGE AND LITERACY STUDIES
Series Editors: Vaidehi Ramanathan, Bonny Norton and
Alastair Pennycook

China and English

Globalisation and the Dilemmas of Identity

Edited by
Joseph Lo Bianco, Jane Orton and
Gao Yihong

MULTILINGUAL MATTERS
Bristol • Buffalo • Toronto

Library of Congress Cataloging in Publication Data
A catalog record for this book is available from the Library of Congress.
China and English: Globalisation and the Dilemmas of Identity/
Edited by Joseph Lo Bianco, Jane Orton and Gao Yihong.
Critical Language and Literacy Studies
Includes bibliographical references and index.
1. English language--Social aspects--China. 2. English language--Study and
teaching--China. 3. English language--Globalization. 4. Language and
culture--China.
I. Lo Bianco, Joseph. II. Orton, Jane. III. Yihong, Gao.
PE3502.C54C45 2009
427'.951–dc22 2009033462

British Library Cataloguing in Publication Data
A catalogue entry for this book is available from the British Library.

ISBN-13: 978-1-84769-229-0 (hbk)
ISBN-13: 978-1-84769-228-3 (pbk)

Multilingual Matters
UK: St Nicholas House, 31–34 High Street, Bristol BS1 2AW, UK.
USA: UTP, 2250 Military Road, Tonawanda, NY 14150, USA.
Canada: UTP, 5201 Dufferin Street, North York, Ontario, M3H 5T8, Canada.

The policy of Multilingual Matters/Channel View Publications is to use papers
that are natural, renewable and recyclable products, made from wood grown in
sustainable forests. In the manufacturing process of our books, and to further
support our policy, preference is given to printers that have FSC and PEFC Chain
of Custody certification. The FSC and/or PEFC logos will appear on those books
where full certification has been granted to the printer concerned.

Typeset by Techset Composition Ltd., Salisbury, UK.
Printed and bound in Great Britain by Short Run Press Ltd.

Contents

Part 3: Landscapes and Mindscapes

Part 4: Narratives

Part 5: English for China in the World

Contributors

Joseph Lo Bianco is Professor of Language and Literacy Education and Associate Dean (Global Relations) at the Graduate School of Education, University of Melbourne. He is author of Australia's first comprehensive language policy, the National Policy on Languages, 1987. In 2007 he produced a Special Issue of the journal *Language Policy* entitled *The Emergence of Chinese*. His email address is j.lobianco@unimelb.edu.au

Jane Orton is an Honorary Senior Fellow in the Graduate School of Education at the University of Melbourne, where she has researched, taught and supervised for many years in the area of international English, language teaching and culture, and non-verbal communication. Her email address is j.orton@unimelb.edu.au

Gao Yihong is Professor in the English Department, School of Foreign Languages, Peking University, and Director of The Association of Chinese Sociolinguistics. Her major research interest lies in the social psychology and social context of language learning. Her email address is gaoyh@pku.edu.au

Bian Yongwei is Associate Professor in the Department of Language and Literature of the University of International Relations, China. She is a PhD candidate in the English Department, School of Foreign Languages, Peking University. Her research addresses identity and language learning, intercultural communication and discourse analysis. Her email address is tongbianca@163.com

Li Jingyan received her Doctor of Education degree from the Graduate School of Education at the University of Melbourne and is a staff member at the Harbin Institute of Technology in China. She is an experienced EFL teacher and an associate professor at the College of Foreign Languages, Harbin Institute of Technology in China. Her email address is lijingyan.622@163.com

Liu Yi is a Doctor of Philosophy candidate in the School of Foreign Languages at Peking University and specializes in applied linguistics. Liu Yi has published on language assessment, systemic functional linguistics, EFL teaching methodologies and EFL teachers' professional identities. Her email address is daphneliu3@hotmail.com

Li Yuxia is a Doctor of Philosophy candidate in linguistics and culture studies in the School of Foreign Languages at Peking University. Her research and published work have focused on second language learning, discourse analysis and sociolinguistics. At present, her research interest lies in EFL learner identities. Her email address is mortalbird@126.com

Li Zhanzi received her PhD in linguistics from the English Department of Peking University. She is now a Professor of English in Nanjing Normal University and her research interests include functional grammar, discourse analysis and language-learning autobiographies. Her email address is lizz402@hotmail.com

Xu Hongchen is a Doctor of Philosophy candidate in the School of Foreign Languages at Peking University, majoring in sociolinguistics. His research covers bilingual education in China, language and identity, and intercultural communication. His email address is michaelhongchenxu@yahoo. com.cn

Zhou Qingsheng is Director of Department of Southern China Minority Languages at the Institute of Ethnology and Anthropology of the Chinese Academy of Social Sciences. A volume of the *Annual Report of the Language Situation in China 2005* (Volume 1) edited by him was published in 2006 and of the *Annual Report of the Language Situation in China 2006* (Volume 1) edited by him was published in 2007. His email address is qshzhou@163bj.com

Preface

As editors of this series, we were very interested to read the proposal on China and English, forwarded to us by Joe Lo Bianco, Jane Orton and Gao Yihong. For a number of years, we have observed the dramatic changes in the relationship between China as a nation, and English as a language, and were intrigued to see how diverse scholars would frame and analyse China's complex linguistic landscape. We were not disappointed. Drawing on a range of innovative research, the authors in this edited volume have given readers a window into the multiple ways in which Chinese speakers are negotiating the English language at a time of great sociopolitical change, and how issues of identity at individual and national levels are implicated. Of particular interest is how the editors have been able to accomplish this ambitious project, and what themes the authors of individual chapters have considered the most salient.

How the editors have accomplished this task speaks to the nature of much international collaborative research conducted in the academic world in this era of globalisation, where the internet has facilitated research relationships between scholars separated by thousands of miles, and air travel has made regular face-to-face collaboration possible. In the great sweep of history, it was not that long ago when international collaborative research was constrained by a laborious mail system and cumbersome sea travel (Leavitt, 2007). Modern technologies have enabled Lo Bianco and Orton of the University of Melbourne in Australia to collaborate with Gao of Peking University in China, to produce a research-based volume that indexes a unique set of mutual interests and investments. These interests are centrally concerned with interculturalism, and indeed arise from exemplary intercultural collaboration. Interculturalism is thus both the medium and the message of this volume, and authors have engaged in what Orton calls 'mutual self-exploration' in productive new ways. Clearly, such relationships need to be supported by a scholar's institution, which in turn reflects wider priorities at national levels, an issue of great interest to language planners and policy-makers (Spolsky, 2004).

Interestingly, the very technologies that have made international collaborative research possible are also associated with the increasing dominance of the English language internationally, and with respect to China in particular. Crystal (2006) documents the extent to which the internet and world wide web are dominated by the English language, though recent research has suggested that while English language use may be increasing, its proportional representation on the internet is decreasing as more languages are used (Danet & Herring, 2007; Graddol, 2006). Nonetheless, the publishing industry, and scientific publication in particular, remains English-dominated. Small wonder then that China's English language planning has been particularly intense in recent years. Indeed, Lo Bianco argues that recent developments in China's language planning have, in some cases, and in parallel with similar trends elsewhere in the world, begun to shift English from object of instruction to medium of instruction. This forms part of the context to this book: English dominates communication in many domains, and yet the growing international significance of China is giving Chinese languages, cultures and identities an increasingly important role in this mix.

Such shifts in language policy and use have considerable implications for how identity is understood and negotiated, particularly with respect to what Orton calls China's 'narrative of self-identity'. This question has a long history in China – as it has for many other countries in the world – from early relations with missionaries and colonial powers, through the turbulent 20th century and the strong antipathy to Western knowledge and culture, and on to the more accommodatory stance of more recent years. As Chen (1995) makes clear, China's relation to and construction of the Occident has to be seen as a counterpoint to the Orientalist constructions of China. It is in this context that many of the concerns of this book need to be understood: how can Chinese speakers negotiate a productive relationship with English, and Western ideas more broadly, without sacrificing Chinese cultural identity? As Gao notes in Chapter 2:

> One issue that Confucius and his contemporaries did not have to worry about was the learning of languages other than the native. It has been left for generations of their descendents to respond to the central threat to the integrity of Chinese identity posed by the rituals embedded in another language. (p. 59)

This complex question is taken up in all five sections of the book, which include research in diverse traditions, from historical analysis (Lo Bianco, Orton, Zhou) and narrative (Li Yuxia, Li Zhanzi, Liu) to quantitative study (Bian) and survey research (Lo Bianco, Orton). Themes investigated include relations between China and Western societies (Gao, Lo Bianco, Orton); legitimacy of identity research (Gao); language pedagogy (Li Jingyan); teacher identity (Liu); and bilingual education (Xu).

The fundamental question of cultural identity in relation to language use raises two second-order series of questions: What is a language, and who owns it? With respect to the nature of language, applied linguistics in the West varies between structuralist orientations that take the position that language is a neutral medium of communication, characterised by a systematic set of rules, structures and vocabulary (Saussure, 1966), and more poststructuralist orientations that view language as a complex social practice that engages the identities of learners in diverse and often contradictory ways (Block, 2007; Norton, 2000; Pavlenko & Blackledge, 2004; Toohey, 2000). Readers of this volume learn that the Chinese distinction between *yong* (Chinese learning as essence) and *ti* (Western learning as utility), as discussed by Gao, is highly paradoxical with respect to debates on the nature of language. On the one hand, the notion of *ti* seems to suggest that it is possible to learn a language as a neutral set of structures, leaving cultural identity intact; on the other hand, the notion of *yong* suggests that any learning (and this must include the learning of a language) is integral to cultural identity. These paradoxes around identity underscore for us ways in which identities are constructed within discourses, as produced by particular historical contingencies, modes of teaching, institutional sites of learning and individual proclivities. As the various chapters attest, identities emerge within fluid circulations of power, which defy notions of identity as seamless and unified.

The question of who owns English – and the notion of ownership may vary substantially across different political and cultural systems – is another important theme in this volume. In the field of applied linguistics, early distinctions between English as a Second Language and English as a Foreign Language, while seeking to address the importance of context in relation to the learning of English, nevertheless reinforced the notion that learners of English were newcomers to the language, and that the goal of English language learning was to approximate the native speaker. The work of scholars such as Canagarajah (1997) Pennycook, (1994, 2007), and Ramanathan (2002, 2005) has begun to shift the grounds of this debate, challenging common-held assumptions about English language teaching internationally. Most recently, as the European Union grapples to accommodate its multilingual population (Phillipson, 2003), scholars such as Jenkins (2007) and Seidlhofer, Breitender, and Pitzl (2006) are becoming advocates for an understanding of English as a Lingua Franca. Similarly in the Asian context, the notion of English as a Lingua Franca, as a language that is no longer tied to the cultural baggage of either native or nativized varieties of English, as a language produced in the communicative marketplace of an expanding, diverse and vociferous Asia, has been the subject of much debate (Kirkpatrick, 2006; Tupas, 2008). If, as many scholars have suggested, the non-native speaker of English needs far greater recognition (Braine, 1999; Kachru, 1986; Norton, 1997), or indeed the very nature of the native/nonnative distinction is an untenable one, particularly in the context of global Englishes (Rajagopalan, 2004), then Chinese speakers of English are an important stakeholder in this increasingly crowded linguistic marketplace (Norton & Gao, 2008). In this view, learning English will not necessarily compromise the cultural identity of Chinese speakers, but render it more complex and multifaceted.

We conclude with a note on the genealogy and dissemination of ideas. It is evident from this volume that ideas, like international collaborative research projects, do not exist in a vacuum, but index complex histories, sets of relationships, and access to resources. While Lo Bianco, Orton, and Gao are all senior scholars at the University of Melbourne and Peking University, all of the other contributors, with the sole exception of Zhou, have been trained as PhD candidates at these two institutions. What this suggests is that many ideas, theories, and research projects have genealogies that reflect a discursive history between established and emerging scholars. This is not to suggest that the relationships are uni-directional, or that the theories are static. Rather, the extent to which theories are shared, generated, and possibly resisted takes place within networks, which themselves are part of wider sets of relationships. It is sobering to consider what opportunities are available to emerging scholars who have little access to such valuable material and symbolic resources; equally troubling is to reflect on the impact of this volume if it were published in a lesser-known language than English. Such concerns aside, we appreciate that globalization has created the conditions necessary for us to access an exciting array of scholarship from a region of the world that is making a significant impact on applied linguistics.

Bonny Norton, Vaidehi Ramanathan and Alastair Pennycook
June 2009

References

Block, D. (2007) *Second Language Identities*. London: Continuum.
Braine, G. (1999) *Non-Native Educators in English Language Teaching*. Mahwah, NJ: Lawrence Erlbaum.

Canagarajah, S. (1999) *Resisting English Imperialism in Language Teaching*. Oxford: Oxford University Press.

Chen, Xiao-Mei (1995) *Occidentalism: A Theory of Counter-Discourse in Post-Mao China*. New York: Oxford University Press.

Crystal, D. (2006) *Language and the Internet*. Cambridge: Cambridge University Press.

Danet, B. and Herring, S.C. (eds) (2007) *The Multilingual Internet: Language, Culture, and Communication Online*. New York: Oxford University Press.

Graddol, D. (2006) *English Next: Why Global English May Mean the End of 'English as a Foreign Language'*. London: British Council.

Jenkins, J. (2007) *English as a Lingua Franca: Attitude and Identity*. Oxford: Oxford University Press.

Kachru, B. (1986) *The Alchemy of English: The Spread, Functions, and Models of Non-Native Englishes*. Champaign, IL: University of Illinois Press.

Kirkpatrick, A. (2006) Which model of English: Native-speaker, nativized or lingua franca? In R. Rubdy and M. Saraceni (eds) *English in the World: Global Rules, Global Roles* (pp. 71–83) London: Continuum.

Leavitt, D. (2007) *The Indian Clerk*. New York: Bloomsbury.

Norton, B. (1997) Language, identity, and the ownership of English. *TESOL Quarterly* 31 (3), 409–429.

Norton, B. (2000) *Identity and Language Learning: Gender, Ethnicity and Educational Change*. Harlow: Longman/Pearson Education.

Norton, B. and Gao, Y. (2008) Identity, investment, and Chinese learners of English. *Journal of Asian Pacific Communication* 18 (1), 109–120.

Pavlenko, A. and Blackledge, A. (eds) (2004) *Negotiation of Identities in Multilingual Contexts*. Clevedon: Multilingual Matters.

Pennycook, A. (1994) *The Cultural Politics of English as an International Language*. Essex: Longman.

Pennycook, A. (2007) *Global Englishes and Transcultural Flows*. London: Routledge.

Phillipson, R. (2003) *English only Europe? Challenging language policy*. London: Routledge.

Rajagopalan, K. (2004) The concept of 'World English' and its implications for ELT. *ELT Journal* 58 (2), 111–117.

Ramanathan, V. (2002) *The Politics of TESOL Education: Writing, Knowledge, Critical Pedagogy*. London: Routledge.

Ramanathan, V. (2005) *The English-Vernacular Divide: Postcolonial Language Politics and Practice*. Clevedon: Multilingual Matters.

Saussure, F. de (1966) *Course in General Linguistics*. W. Baskin (trans.). New York: McGraw-Hill.

Spolsky, B. (2004) *Language Policy*. Cambridge: Cambridge University Press.

Seidlhofer, B., Breitender, A. and Pitzl, M-L. (2006) English as a lingua franca in Europe: Challenges for applied linguistics. *Annual Review of Applied Linguistics* 26, 3–34.

Toohey, K. (2000) *Learning English at School: Identity, Social Relations, and Classroom Practice*. Clevedon: Multilingual Matters.

Tupas, R. (2008) Anatomies of linguistic commodification: The case of English in the Philippines vis-à-vis other languages in the multilingual marketplace. In P. Tan and R. Rubdy (eds) *Language as Commodity: Global Structures, Local Marketplaces* (pp. 89–105). London: Continuum.

Introduction

JOSEPH LO BIANCO

The Volume

The idea for this volume arose from a series of research projects on Chinese learners' acquisition of English and from research conducted on the experiences of Chinese learners in Australian education. Also relevant have been wider considerations about effective teaching and learning of languages in general, such as Chinese in Australian education. These experiences stimulated reflection on a range of theoretical and practical issues concerning identity change, educational adjustment and cultural consequences of the encounter with difference and otherness represented by rapidly integrating global education.

The roots of the volume are ultimately in our individual encounters with diverse learners and the simultaneous transformation of the disciplines of applied linguistics and comparative education under the influence of critical perspectives, rapid globalisation of education markets and the emergence of highly competitive and interacting knowledge economies in the Asia Pacific region (Marginson, 2007). Foremost among these is China with its extensive investment in English language-mediated education, and therefore its deep interest in effective teaching and learning of English, not to mention research and publishing efforts, which increasingly rely on English. These considerations have influenced our choice of title for the volume, *China and English: Globalisation and Dilemmas of Identity*. The locus of the writing is China, overwhelmingly in relation to its encounter with English under contemporary conditions of more rapidly enmeshed globalisation. All these raise some issues and dilemmas related to identity at national or collective levels and for individuals.

This volume is the outcome of an extended interaction among the writers. Our essential aim has been to capture something of the flavour of many conversations that have informed this work, conversations extended over several meetings, mostly in China, between a largely stable grouping of Australian and Chinese scholars thinking, writing and teaching about the intersection, problems and dilemmas of contemporary language education. The volume as it appears therefore is the outcome of a long gestation of the independent research trajectories of the participants and of our collective discussions and encounters.

The Collaboration

The writers are individual researchers, teachers and teacher educators located in Australian and Chinese institutions who have engaged in conversation around questions of language and identity. These interactions led to a formal agreement between the University of Melbourne and Peking University to facilitate and support the evolving collaboration.

The endeavour envisaged in this institutional accord was a highly productive eight-institution Roundtable held at Peking University in October 2005. In preparation for the Roundtable, the editors of the volume, Lo Bianco, Orton and Gao, supported by Dr Margaret Kumar, prepared a literature review of Chinese and Western understandings of the culture and identity consequences of language learning and provided this to participants of the Roundtable. The fruitful discussions that followed were incorporated into papers written by the participants and were published in the *Journal of Chinese Sociolinguistics*[1] in December 2005, a rapid turnaround, which is testament to the success of the collaboration.

In December 2006 a number of Roundtable participants presented papers at the 5th International Conference of Chinese Sociolinguistics in Beijing. In May 2007 'the team' once again came together, this time running a well-attended symposium entitled *English: Language and Identity in China* during the 5th International Congress of the China English Language Education Association, jointly held with the 1st Congress of the Chinese Applied Linguistics Association.

As a result of these activities, the collaboration and the ideas that inform it have been field tested and the research areas have formed a relatively coherent and holistic enterprise, although studied from a diverse array of perspectives. These perspectives illuminate what is empirically a very complex field and so no attempt has been made to restrict, limit or direct the specific approaches, methods or theoretical assumptions brought to bear on the problem of English learning and identity issues in China.

English: Expanding and Extending in Education

China's English language planning has been particularly intense since 2000. While the expansion of English in Chinese education has been continuous since the late 1980s, the coincidence of the country's admission to the World Trade Organisation on 11 December 2001, Beijing's hosting of the Olympic Games in 2008 and Shanghai's successful bid to host the 2010 World Expo have meant that the first decade of the third millennium has seen a major acceleration of provisions and planning on behalf of foreign languages in general and English in particular. Most of these measures aim to extend the reach of English throughout Chinese education and some aim to raise competency outcomes, but others point to new directions and new reasons as to why English is allocated a prominent role in Chinese education, and therefore in Chinese society (Wen & Gao, 2007).

In January 2001, the Chinese Ministry of Education issued a document entitled 'Guidelines for Promoting English Teaching in Elementary Schools' (Ministry of Education, 2001a), which stipulated that the threshold of compulsory English learning be lowered by four years, from the first year of junior high school to Grade 3 in elementary school. Significantly, the Guidelines replaced the general focus of the 1999 curriculum on receptive language skills, like reading, with a new emphasis on the productive use of English for interpersonal communication. In some large cities and in the private and non-formal sectors, English study begins earlier. Shanghai is a good case in point. Local authorities have moved to develop internationally competitive foreign language teaching programmes with the explicit aim of supporting the wider municipal goal of positioning Shanghai as a competitive international metropolis (Shanghai Education Commission, 1999: 3). One component is an expanded role for English, now used to teach arts and ballet, mathematics and some sciences, especially the computer sciences, and information technology. Subjects that are not presently taught in English and for which it appears that there are no current plans to teach in English, such as physics, chemistry, history and politics, are not immune from English influence, since in these learning areas technical terms, laws, translations of key concepts and other glossing from English are promoted. This approach of including English labels and information within Chinese-medium courses (Shanghai Education Commission, 2002–2003) suggests a new role for English, that of semantic accompaniment to material and concepts primarily mastered in Chinese.

This inclusion of English within Chinese-taught subjects underscores the wide set of roles and expectations of bilingual functioning in Chinese contexts, differentiated according to levels of competence, purpose and audience. These might range from basal recognition of romanised or pinyin-rendered Chinese, to English equivalence recognition, to basic translation knowledge, to receptive skills of reading and listening, all the way through to productive skills of speaking and interacting, and, maximally, high-level academic writing production. The situation is dynamic and, depending on levels of preparation and resourcing, is likely to expand further in the coming decade.

A new English language curriculum for senior secondary schools was published in the People's Education Press in April 2003 (Ministry of Education, 2003). This too is significant because it modifies the traditional aims of English education, adding a 'humanistic' goal to the longstanding 'instrumental' rationale (Wang, 2006), thereby reinforcing moves away from compartmentalisation of English language knowledge as simply an exercise in gaining extraneous utilitarian skill to advance culturally uninterrupted Chinese national interests. In August of 2001, the Ministry of Education (2001b) issued university-level language of instruction guidelines. Entitled 'Guidelines for Improving Teaching for University Undergraduate Students', this document facilitated an increase in the use of English as an alternative medium of instruction at the tertiary level by suggesting that 5–10% of all undergraduate teaching should be imparted through a foreign language.

The collective effect of these laws has been to shift English from the object of instruction to the medium of instruction, although admittedly still at low levels, to widen the purposes from strictly utilitarian to officially 'humanistic', and to expand sectors from high school down to elementary school and up to undergraduate and post-graduate provision.

The Chapters

The volume is influenced by these policy moves and our collaborative initiatives and aims to apply Western and Chinese understandings of the notion of identity as it takes shape in and through language. The varied professional backgrounds of the writers ensure that a multi-methodological approach complements its multiple disciplinary perspectives. As a result, we present this as a genuine collaboration between Chinese and Australian researchers, teachers and students, jointly exploring issues of identity from multiple angles.

Part 1: Western Dreams, Chinese Quests – Habitus and Encounter

Three chapters establish the foundations of the volume, providing a platform for the broad consideration of key ideas and issues. These chapters trace a wide terrain in the cultural and civilisational exchange that is ultimately involved in interactions between China and Western societies.

The opening chapter by Lo Bianco takes as its theme the sequence of intercultural encounters immediately prior to the historical domination of English in China's engagement with the rest of the world. Its focus is the late Ming and early Qing courts at which scientifically literate and technologically capable Jesuit missionaries established an extensive and mutually influencing interaction with Chinese literati and court officials. This particular West that engaged in interaction with China, from the arrival of Matteo Ricci at Beijing in 1598, is a totally different entity from 'the West' dominating China's relationships during the mid-19th and early 20th centuries. The interactions between China and the West had, by this later period, been forever transformed by a diminished and subjugated China, dominated by the devastating effects of gunboats and opium, which forced open Chinese space to British and other imperial trading interests and catapulted the Chinese imperial system to collapse, leading to upheaval, foreign invasion, warlordism and revolution in the early 20th century. The violent transition from the Ming to Qing dynasties was no less tumultuous, but the indigenous imperial system was conserved.

This chapter discusses the complicated relationships that emerged as competing interests in China and Europe struggled to understand, influence and interpret each other as they pursued their own ends. The discussion shows the reverberating effects that knowledge of and about China had when relayed into post-Reformation and Enlightenment Europe, and the transformative effects of Western knowledge injected into Chinese public life and conceptual systems.

Focusing on a period before English became the main language of China–Western interaction and in which religion, even more than trade, was the dominant modality of exchange, the chapter shows how a long-term project of mutual re-constitution has been at the heart of the 'Western' encounter with China. Ironically, much of this encounter weakens the dominant maxim by which the encounter itself has been conducted, that is the distinction between preserving an unchanged cultural essence while interacting in a utilitarian way with a skilled and powerful other. Assumptions of essential core and utilitarian engagement with the other are abstractions that are difficult to sustain in practice. Ricci's mission of scholarship began and remained a mission of evangelisation, a complex, ambiguous and problematical project requiring a simultaneous investment in 'knowing the other', irretrievably changing the knower into a version of the other. Like many such encounters, it destabilises comforting beliefs that engagement can be totally without effects.

Encounters with China have often produced 'confounding essentialisation' but also self-serving usage of other knowledge, surprising kinds of fused cultural forms and examples of personal hybridity that post-colonial usage of this term might not have imagined. The Christian encounter with China turns out to be reciprocated in a Confucian encounter with the West: each motivated to absorb elements of the other, shaped by the context and purposes of the interactants. One of the aims of the chapter is to underscore the longevity, depth and persistence of the intercultural encounter, the mutuality of the China–Europe interaction, each impacting on core value systems in often unrecognised ways, as a prelude to discussions of contemporary globalisation and English.

Chapter 2 by Gao Yihong describes the Confucian construction of a *habitus* (Bourdieu, 1993) of learning, resting on a binary distinction between an intrinsic, growth-enhancing orientation in human beings contrasted with an extrinsic, utilitarian orientation. This tradition is the starting point for a discussion that shows how, centuries after its consolidation, this Chinese traditional disposition towards learning had to accommodate to a different *habitus* embodied in the English language being sought as part of China's modernisation.

How to manage the relationship between different cultural *habita* so as to benefit from Western learning without losing the native cultural identity has become a central issue underlying China's education policies and learners' goals for over 150 years.

The dominant principle throughout has been 'Chinese learning as essence (体 *ti*); Western learning as utility (用 *yong*)', and hence instrumental motivation has been strongly fostered in foreign language learning. Yet an unresolved tension between the two forces has always been present. While the contemporary shift from planned to market economy opens up new possibilities of identity construction, it also intensifies the *ti–yong* tension.

Gao concludes her chapter by pointing out that in the contemporary climate where English is increasingly seen as a world language associated with an imagined global community, rather than the 'target culture' of native speakers, the recurring theme of cultural identity conflict, deeply rooted in China's social historical context, will continue to challenge Chinese education policy makers, language educators and learners.

The third chapter is by Jane Orton, who discusses 'the Chinese quest', locating its origin in China's response to the British invasion of the mid-19th century. Essentially the response was to 're-skill' (Giddens, 1991), and thus the Chinese set out to develop defences in order to meet the foreign power with equal strength. The power was perceived to be a new type of knowledge, and English was considered the transparent window by which this knowledge could be accessed. The new knowledge was seen as something separate from much of Chinese knowledge, which could be learned but quarantined by a person and a society already educated in Chinese knowledge. As Giddens has pointed out, however, decisions to re-skill tend to refract back upon, and be mobilised to develop, the narrative of self-identity. In this way, Orton's analysis continues and extends the other two chapters in this section by underlining reciprocal and un-confineable consequences of engagement across cultural differences, which launches processes whose reverberations cannot be easily predicted or held in check. Orton's chapter presents a piece of Giddens' narrative process from the perspective of a native speaker of English who has been involved in China's interactions over the past 25 years. It constitutes part of an ongoing attempt both to ponder the issues and to re-negotiate the commonly assigned identity of the native English speaker in China from a source of authentic language and meta-linguistic knowledge, to one which recognises, with Giddens, that 'only linked processes of self-exploration and the development of intimacy with other' can achieve the goal.

In such a spirit of mutuality, some recent developments are discussed in which the teaching, learning and use of English in China are seen to have entered a new phase, perhaps even a new era, in the re-skilling quest.

Part 2: Learners, Identities and Purposes

Four chapters make up Part 2 of the volume. These comprise four complementary but radically dissimilar approaches to understanding and documenting the intersection between language learning and identity.

Gao's chapter traces the state of the art of research on foreign language learning and identity in China and exemplifies the issues involved through a debate on the legitimacy of this field of research. This debate arose in the course of the Roundtable meeting in Beijing in October 2005 during which the outline of the present volume was discussed. The debate constituted a challenge to the very legitimacy of identity research in what are essentially foreign language contexts for English in China. In response to the problems raised by this challenge, Gao summarises empirical studies carried out in the past decade on English language learning and cultural identity changes in China, and traces the related theoretical debates.

The challenge to the legitimacy of identity research arose because English in China is principally taught as a foreign language, and to some researchers this seems to negate the relevance of research on learners' identity construction. Gao discusses this debate by contrasting a social constructivist perspective to language learning with a structuralist–essentialist approach in what is traditionally perceived to be English as a foreign language (EFL) context. She points out that the concerns and criticisms of identity research in Chinese EFL settings are well accommodated by China's social historical tradition of making a distinction between *ti–yong* orientations in learning. The implication the constructivist view offers for future research is also discussed.

For most practical purposes English will long remain a foreign language for most Chinese, and yet issues of identity and culture arise. The vast scale and depth of penetration of English in China's education make this likely, but so too does the global nature of English, confounding attempts to tie it directly to American or British interests alone. Government plans for wide-ranging English-knowing bilingualism for Chinese link therefore to future employment and careers that will be influenced by global knowledge economies, each carrying their own distinctive identity repercussions, beyond associations with nation, locality or tradition.

Li Zhanzi's chapter is a discussion of a comparative reading of two language-learning narratives. These are different in many ways, a Chinese and an international cosmopolitan text, but both are about learner experiences, identity shifts, and engagement with communities of speakers of the target language and with the practice and process of language learning.

Li discusses the role of language-learning autobiographies, which are attracting increasing interest in that they enable us to study the discursive process of identity construction. The two texts under discussion are Zhang Haidi's *Beautiful English* and Natasha Lvovich's *The Multilingual Self*. *Beautiful English* explores the relationship between English learning and identity construction in a specific generation of Chinese youth, represented by the author Zhang Haidi, a youth model in China during the 1980s, known for her tenacious willpower and desire to make herself useful to society. Natasha Lvolvich is a professional language teacher who migrated from Russia to the United States.

Li uses concepts drawn from critical pedagogy, such as ownership and imagined community, to inform her analysis of these two writings, and shows how autobiography, with its emotional, personal and narrative qualities, traverses the terrain that occupies the interest of learners who engage with the imagined community offered to them and constructed by them in English learning. In this discussion, we can recognise the wider questions of identity and English as explored empirically in other chapters in the personal, interpersonal and imaginative realm of learners and authors who write for learners. Whatever government policy documents might require, expect or anticipate for language learning and its reasons, an independent and vast marketplace of ideas about personal growth, imaginative identity and being in a cosmopolitan and less bounded world carry identity change and challenge into all classrooms.

Orton's chapter looks at educational systems as official bodies with tasks to carry out on behalf of the local, often national, society, one of which is to establish school curricula that fit and serve society's goals. Principal among these goals is the passing on of the best from the past and, at the same time, education of the current generation to improve on that past. In all societies there is an inherent tension involved in managing these two objectives. Similarly, subjects offered on the curriculum reflect community regard for those fields of study, and members expect this to be made clear to their children. On the other hand, within the formal education system, at least, there will be strong community expectation that the curriculum designed by the educational system will not present matters that unduly challenge community norms. Yet introduction to certain areas – a new language and society, for example – inevitably offers the risk of introducing considerable variations to local moral, cultural and economic values and practices. Textbooks and other pedagogical materials are ideological tools that serve multiple functions, but in the contemporary world in which information circulates more rapidly and with fewer controls, they must negotiate their place and effects with other media that help frame the views and attitudes of learners. The particular agendas that official texts and programmes carry have a continuing importance as indicators of state and public agendas, but their traction and effects within institutions of teaching and certification are now refracted in more complex ways as student mobility, information flows and transnational cultural formations influence attitudes and behaviours as well.

By contrast, Bian Yongwei's chapter reports the findings from a longitudinal research examination of Chinese non-English majors' English learning identity in an English-oriented arts university. She describes changes in the students' positive and negative self-confidence and finds that their subtractive identity reached levels of significance. Generally speaking, the students' positive self-confidence decreased and negative self-confidence increased in the process of their college English learning, and on their way to feeling and exploring more fully English language and its culture(s).

The shifts in student identification can be considerable, as some began to identify more with the language, culture(s) and relevant community(ies). The author shows how it is possible to interpret the temporary loss of self-confidence and the relative distance that language learning produces in relation to the native language and culture in positive ways, in the specifically foreign context of learning, as a restructuring of self. In this way she goes on to argue that this distancing is a natural process of personal growth. This chapter underscores both how the diverse kinds of experiences within English learning, that is, the modes in which English is present in Chinese institutions, are itself a factor influencing identity relations and how this variegated presence of English speaks of the multiple professional and academic relationships that learners are expected to have with English. While English is therefore, to all intents and purposes, a sociologically foreign language in China, it is less so within its institutions of education and training.

Part 3: Landscapes and Mindscapes

This section of the volume contains four chapters, which provide an account of the linguistic landscape in geographical and imagined space within which the China, English identity analysis occurs.

Setting the widest framework is the first chapter by Zhou Qingsheng, which focuses our attention on formal processes of ethnic identification and their historical stipulation.

The author discusses the relations between language, ethnicity and identity through an examination of the ethnic identifications in the 1950s and 1960s. An outcome of ethnic identification marked the formation of the final pattern of the Chinese nation: 1 (ethnic Han as majority) + 55 (ethnic minorities). This is a central issue in the relationship between language and ethnicity, whether the majority of an ethnic group is able to use their native language or not.

The author identifies three models of the language–ethnicity correspondence. The 'one ethnicity, one language' model is the basic, stable and major model, and 70% of all ethnic groups belong to this. The two other models of 'one ethnicity, plural languages' and 'plural ethnicities, one language' reflect the variability and/or the non-conformity of language, ethnicity and ethnic identity. These correspondences are secondary, changing and non-mainstream. Ethnic groups belonging to the latter two models make up about 30% of all ethnic groups in China. In this chapter, the author reports the maximum official record of state thinking about the key ideas of this volume. The repertoire of current ways to understand and view attachments that individuals and groups have to languages is a long continuum. One point of this continuum addresses the situated and post-colonial hybridity that is the lived world of millions for whom state administration and scholarly abstractions are distant worlds. Another point of this continuum refers to the continuing commitment of state authorities to organise and determine both the nomenclature and content of designated identities. In US census policy, such as the 22nd administration in 2000, race, ethnicity and ancestry ascriptions are provided on the forms that citizens fill out, and this has been criticised for not permitting mixed or self-identification possibilities. Zhou's chapter reveals the world's largest exercise in identity ascription and the thinking underlying it in its current and past administrations. Self-identification and other-identification are in intimate correspondence.

Xu Hongchen's chapter continues this theme of ethno-linguistic diversity within China's population, specifically as this applies to Chinese ethnic minorities in bilingual education programmes in a process of identity formation at the point where the local intersects with the global, which he identifies with the term 'glocalisation'.

Xu's review draws on Norton's account of imagined community (2001) and Dornyei's L2 motivational self system (2005) to explain the development of ethnic minority students' identity while learning *Putonghua* and their own ethnic languages. He argues that Chinese ethnic minority students' learning of *Putonghua* as a second language aims to realise their Ideal L2 Selves (a national identity as a Chinese). The case under discussion is that of a fluent user of *Putonghua* in interaction with other members from the same imagined community. This imagined community is all the people from the diverse different ethnic groups that comprise China, whose learning of their own ethnic languages is a method to maintain their Ought-to L2 Selves (an ethnic identity as a member of their own ethnic groups). Bilingual education is already a concession from a state operating with an official language charter that domestic linguistic demography varies from its legal depiction. Rather than addressing the contingent and political nature of much of identity formation and selfhood commonly found in much contemporary writing about these matters, Xu approaches the issue from the angle of psychological selfhood. He shows that global level arguments for the utility of English are mirrored at the national level for *Putonghua*; however, at neither level can such complementarity be seen as either equal or smooth. Instead at both levels there operates a hierarchy of opportunity, support and reward. The mental processes of a learner's engagement with these 'out there' worlds are a finer point of analysis from global, glocal, local to personal.

In his chapter, Lo Bianco links the effects of mass English teaching on minority ethnicities in China, the emergence of English as the preferred foreign language in education systems worldwide, and the recent official project for the expansion of the Chinese language abroad. These three elements of communicative planning result in an interdependent project of trilingualism for Chinese ethnic minorities, bilingualism for the Han majority and promotion of Chinese as a foreign language abroad.

The chapter begins with a review of the status of English as the first foreign language in curricula across the world showing that what is taken for granted is in fact a rather recent development, English having displaced German, French and Russian. His review of the effects of compulsory English teaching in China draws on research studies that fail to show a single pattern of effects on minority communities, although in general obligatory English is found to impose considerable extra learning demands on such communities (trilingualism, accompanied by citizen loyalty) compared to the bilingual expectation for the majority community. Identifying emergent local reward systems for English, suggesting the growth of Chinese domestic contexts for its use, he raises a series of questions about how far the bond of utilitarian attachment between Chinese national, economic and political interests extends into the lives and interests of ordinary Chinese doing Chinese things in China. This imagined communicative load for English is tied to an imagined place for Chinese in the world in recognition of the rise of China's power and importance.

The final chapter in this section is by Li Jingyan, where she discusses one of the most radical and popular English training programmes in China. Crazy English learners declare that the method heightens their motivation and generates positive learning. Academics, on the other hand, have been critical of Crazy English's unorthodox teaching practices, extravagant claims of learning outcomes and unabashed pursuit of commercial success, one of whom questions whether a person can learn the theory of relativity by repeatedly screaming $E = MC^2$? Yet a decade on, Crazy English is clearly more than just a passing phenomenon. Indeed, it seems that Crazy English has become a subculture in China, suggesting that it has entered the mindscape of Chinese life promising to effect improved learning via the changes in attitude it suggests are needed.

The chapter discusses three learners in terms of their motivation and responses to the distinctive pedagogy of Crazy English and raises issues that go well beyond its methodological specificities related to stimulating learner motivation and its specific modes of operation as a pedagogy to ask about the imagined community it assumes and produces. As such the chapter debates what is essentially an example of the domestication of English in China. In so doing it brings into sharp relief some key ideas of the volume about the inseparability of domains of language, identity, culture, nation and personhood in a globalising context in which English is a key factor and producer of the flows of culture, economy and opportunity.

Part 4: Narratives

Three narrative chapters linked by their attention to personal and professional dimensions of identity and identity behaviour are discussed. The first chapter concerns a reflective researcher contemplating the significance and Chinese application of 'teachering' or professional autobiography of acts of teaching, linking actual New York and imagined China. The second chapter debates and reports the subjective life of learners engaged in resistant behaviour. The third chapter explores a continuous multi-thread narrative of English specialists within Chinese society. Li Zhanzi's chapter is a reflection on and an interpretation of Frank McCourt's novel *Teacher Man*. McCourt has written about the life and experiences of a teacher in a New York school. Li questions what this book has to say about teaching and teachers in general and Chinese teachers and English teaching in particular. What is the effort in which they are engaged, in whose interests and with what understandings?

By analysing narrative and identity, Li uses recent studies in discourse and identity to suggest that while there are striking consequences when identity is constructed from major conceptual categories such as race and ethnicity, 'minor aspects' of identities also contribute significantly to our sense of ourselves. She uses the much-praised narrative *Teacher Man* to illustrate how we can reconstruct identity formations by appealing to stages, experiences, interpretations and emotions in a personal or professional account of life. The relationship between narrative and identity is explored with reference to the book's multi-positioning, and how McCourt engages, reproduces and resists the traditional discourse of teaching. Li suggests that for English teachers in China to understand themselves in a more flexible and enlightening way when they are called upon to serve national interests and advance the project of global interconnectedness, teacher narratives need to be elicited and analysed to support their endeavour and success. In this way, Chinese English teachers will contribute to the ways in which they are socially positioned. The ways in which China's English teachers see themselves, as Teacher Women and Teacher Men, raises critical issues of interests served and roles played.

Li Yuxia's chapter draws on ideas about situated learning and communities, and reflexively organised self-identity, to analyse the biographical narratives of three 'unsuccessful' college English learners. Specifically she is interested in how these learners negotiate self-identity through participation and non-participation in English learning practice.

The chapter reveals contradictions and tensions that the focal learners experienced in the context of China's economic reforms and global opening up. What does it mean to be 'unsuccessful' as a foreign language learner in a context where being successful is a required or expected competency in the modern world? What do such learners suggest about the vast enterprise of English teaching and learning in contemporary China? The space of participation and resistance is debated as the writer throws light on the processes through which a learner's personal agency comes into being in refusing to go along with what society might choose, require or reward. If English in China is to be a mass and obligatory language, an experience and an objective for all, the experiences, views, feelings and outcomes for those who are 'unsuccessful' in this engagement become a vital point of reflection and contemplation about the whole activity itself.

Liu Yi's chapter is concerned with the notion and relevance of narrative. It concerns the construction of teachers' professional identities in Chinese tertiary settings. Liu Yi analyses how such narrative studies blossomed in the field of general education during the 1980s and are now taken up in second language research studies, coinciding with a move from an exclusive focus on learners to include attention to teachers' development. Drawing on data from interviews with two college English teachers in China who have experienced the deep changes in attention to English and its place in Chinese society, she aims to explore how professional identities of Chinese English teachers are embedded in personal narrative. The chapter takes a multiple narrative perspective weaving the voices of students, family, authorities and other social objects, to align the teacher's professional identities in a continuous multi-thread narrative with professional trajectories, critical incidents, identity metaphors, uncertainties and doubts, and dilemmas. The study sheds light on the significance of exploring the evolution of a professional identity for the category of specialist English language agent within Chinese society.

Part 5: English for China in the World

Two chapters linked by a common survey database make up the final part of the volume. A small survey of tertiary teachers' judgments of the positive and negative effects of the vast penetration of English into Chinese education provides a springboard for policy-related reflections on historic questions of language and national purpose.

Orton shows how, originally conceived as a transparent window to the Western technical knowledge needed to strengthen China against foreign domination, English in China has today become inextricably mobilised in the development of the country's 'narrative of self-identity'. The chapter shows that English is not only a dynamic entity for change inside China, but also, in a radical development, valued as the means of presenting China to the world for mutual benefit. The slogan of those advocating this move is global 'Easternisation'. This is a reversal of the centuries-long movement of Western thought and learning, and is gradually permeating the East.

This new role for English is discussed in terms of China's original quest for Western learning and some principles of Confucian tradition. It is suggested that the move to share their heritage through English and through encouraging foreigners to learn Chinese may lead the Chinese to transcend their age-old 'essence–utility' (体–用 *ti–yong*) split. In the course of this, the need for dialogue over essence, identity and the constitutive power of language could lead to very rich global conversations.

Lo Bianco concludes this section and the volume with reflections on the role of influence in language education. Influence is both informal and institutional. The Chinese state has moved in recent years to institutionalise and formalise its organisation of influence, using English, and increasingly also Chinese, to enter the world of globally projected 'soft power'. In such an enterprise, language education planning and intercultural communication in English and Chinese at the micro-level instantiate wider ambitions. Inherited images of 'China' and the 'West' are recognisably undergoing historic reformation to which many of China's English teachers feel palpably connected as agents as well as observers of historically unprecedented transformations of power in the domains of economics, education and culture.

The question of China's ancient civilisation is associated even with the learning and teaching of English within tertiary institutions in China, by Chinese teachers and for Chinese learners. But what they desire to do with its inheritance, and what role China's distinctiveness will play in the global re-emergence of China, only time will tell.

The volume responds to conditions of citizenship and transnationality, which insinuate themselves into the lives of increasing numbers of people in the world and which through globalisation forge links across space, time and culture. Chinese learners of English, the Chinese state and the idea of 'China' are all linked to others, English speakers, users, learners across the world, and both enthusiasts and those who question, probe or criticise the global role of English. In Aihwa Ong's (1999) terms, these are the *logics of transnationality*. She proposes interesting labels to allow us to speak in a more nuanced way of the flow, hybridity and indeterminacy of contemporary citizenships, identity and language that these logics impose on us. Pre-eminent among these is 'flexible citizenship', which works to dismantle the ready co-relation between language and nation.

In various ways the chapters in this volume are all contributions to an ongoing reflection on how to understand the dynamic processes of ideological and cultural change, the subtle economies of mind, culture and identity that co-vary with the obvious globalisation of finances and trade that our contemporary age brings to attention. Ordinary living today exposes us all to the obvious globalisation. The consequences of the financial lending policies adopted by American and British institutions reverberate rapidly to all parts of the world. In the wake of global economic turmoil, there is conflict over which group and number of sovereign nations will be admitted to the conversations in order to determine policy responses: the G7, the G8 or the G20? Is it ultimately, in realpolitik terms, a numerically more anaemic but politically more realistic G2, America and China?

Macro-economic change matters because of its micro-economic devastation: farms, families and factories in all parts of the globe disrupted, unemployment rising and social tension stoked. We all have a more or less articulated awareness of the eroding boundaries of concepts and institutions our education taught us to conceive with fixity and clarity. Sociologists and anthropologists alike (Appadurai, 1996; Taylor, 2007) look to processes of culture and social imagination that accompany and help produce the palpable integration of local and global realities. These imaginaries are a fertile terrain for charting and predicting shifts and flows of a world that, despite its multiple trajectories, highlights a broad flow of economic and political influence from the West to the East. Political scientists and economists seek to depict this new age according to such underlying patterns and flows, a dawning but unnamed new era: Is it the multi-polar world? Is it the Pacific Age? The Asian century? China's century? Or is it, against the flow of much current belief, not America's decline but the signal of its new ascendancy (Friedman, 2009)?

All simplifications are abstractions and all ultimately are encountered in local particularities, in education, social life and economic activity. The contributors to this volume are fellow travellers who offer ideas, themes and accounts of the flexible citizenships that shared experience imply. The shared focus is the intersection of English, as global medium, and China, as the emergent superpower. English and China are two already preformed and immense constructions, internally differentiated by the many readings of insiders and outsiders alike, but whatever depiction of future worlds are produced both will play determinative roles.

Conclusion

For 60 years the British Broadcasting Corporation, recently through Radio 4, has run a series of annual lectures. The 2008 edition was devoted to China and delivered by the eminent China historian Jonathan Spence, author of many scholarly and popular works on Chinese imperial and contemporary history. Spence's four lectures, collectively entitled *Chinese Vistas*, reflected on the history and current understanding of the encounter between China and the West. Designed for an English-speaking American and British audience and understanding 'the West' as the United Kingdom and the United States, the lectures traverse only the most recent phase of what is a much more ancient encounter, the past two centuries being those in which American and British interests have been prominent in relations with China. Pointing to the long history of utilitarianism underlying language learning, Spence notes the firm position of successive Chinese governments who were unwilling to let foreigners learn Chinese.

Today of course this is reversed in China's creation of a large network of Confucius institutes around the world, precisely to promote the learning of Chinese among foreigners and in foreign places.

The second lecture, English Lessons, broadcast from St. George's Hall, Liverpool, on 10 June 2008 (http://www.bbc.co.uk/radio4/reith2008/transcript2.shtml), ties language learning to commerce and interests, admiration and violence, trade and conflict. While Spence dates English learning in China from 1620, on any major scale it followed the decisive events allied to British commercial intrusion there from the early 19th century, rupturing Chinese control over people movement, residential location and the conduct of trade, and hence the context for English learning has always been marked by a strong commercial element. Nevertheless he asks 'who is the pupil, who is the teacher' in such lessons and, in this conundrum of influence and effects, raises the complex nature of intercultural interaction. This observation resonates with the central purpose of this volume, the reciprocal effects of encounters with difference, taken up in diverse ways in all the chapters, effects that are not always intended by those who permit or design the teaching and learning of languages spoken by foreign others.

The third lecture, American Dreams (http://www.bbc.co.uk/radio4/reith2008/transcript3.shtml), was recorded at the Asia Society in New York and broadcast on 17 June 2008. Spence (2008) concludes American Dreams as follows:

> And I want to end with ... English as a weapon, which is being cele-brated in China now by the apparently very charismatic teacher called Li Yang ... Li Yang's language institutes are all over China, backed by large business machinery ... and a huge amount of offices and staff ... the actual banner ... over some of these classes ... a thousand or more people ... some ... held in ... soccer stadiums and games stadiums, and the huge banners read 'Conquer English to make China stronger'.

English is more often called a tool than a weapon, a special kind of tool with an unambiguous purpose, but even weapons can have purposes and effects different from those anticipated by their designers or can have their intended purposes subverted. Globalisation has been accompanied by and mediated through English, and so the language tied to the national and cultural interests of America and Britain now takes on a wider global facilitative role as Chinese weaponry.

As the chapters in this book reveal, at the heart of research on aspects of identity and language, specifically English, has been the constant questioning of native speaker knowledge in relation to China's historical quest to use English to develop economic equality with the West. Authorised versions of why specific foreign languages are admitted to national class-rooms and training centres, certification procedures and examination practices, research labs and publishing ventures might structure the activity of teaching and learning but they also set off more diffuse and ambiguous possibilities.

These possibilities are ultimately in the hands of learners and teachers, the human agents of the process of China's engagement with an English that is no longer the exclusive national possession of its originating and diffusing states. As a key tool of globalisation in its lingua franca role, contemporary English scrambles these past associations, especially the assumed organic and even romantic link between the language and 'the native speaker', and the more problematical notion of native speaker knowledge as a discrete set of skills, dispositions or know-how.

Beyond what policy might stipulate as legitimate reasons or expect as reasonable outcomes, and beyond authorised justifications for mass compulsory learning of English, there remains a wide space available to teachers, learners and researchers in questioning cultural influences through language learning at interpersonal, professional, institutional and societal levels.

Acknowledgement

Every effort has been made to trace the copyright holder for permission to quote from Collani, C. von (1994) Charles Maigrot's Role in the Chinese Rites Controversy, pp. 149–184 in D. E. Mungello, editor, *The Chinese Rites Controversy*. Nettelala: Steyler Verlag. In Chapter 1 by Lo Bianco and from the People's Education Press of China to quote the three lines in Orton, Chapter 6.

Note

1. We gratefully acknowledge the *Journal of Chinese Sociolinguistics* for giving us permission to publish revised versions of earlier papers by Gao Yihong (Chapter 2), Li Zhanzi (Chapter 5), Jane Orton (Chapters 3 and 6) and Zhou Qingsheng (Chapter 8). Similarly, we thank *Intercultural Communication Studies* for permission to publish Gao Yihong's revision of her 2007 paper in the journal XVI (1); (Chapter 4).

References

Appadurai, A. (1996) *Modernity at Large: Cultural Dimensions of Globalization.* Minnesota: University of Minnesota Press.

Bourdieu, P. (1993) *Sociology in Question.* (R. Nice, trans.). London: Sage.

Dornyei, Z. (2005) *The Psychology of the Language Learner: Individual Differences in Second Language Acquisition.* Mahwah, NJ: Lawrence Erlbaum Associates.

Friedman, G. (2009) *The Next 100 Years, A Forecast for the 21st Century.* New York: Doubleday.

Giddens, A. (1991) *Modernity and Self-identity: Self and Society in the Late Modern Age.* Stanford: Stanford University Press.

Marginson, S. (2007) *Prospects of Higher Education: Globalization, Market Competition, Public Goods and the Future of the University.* Sense Publishers: Rotterdam.

Ministry of Education (2001a) 《全日制义务教育普通高级中学英语课程标准 (实验稿)》 [Quanrizhi yiwu jiaoyu putong gaoji zhongxue yingyu kecheng biaozhun (shiyangao)]. Standard of English courses for 9-year compulsory education and general senior high schools (for experiment). On WWW at http://www.tefl-china.net/2003/ca13821.htm.

Ministry of Education (2001b) 关于加强高等学校本科教学工作提高教学质量的若干意见》 [Guanyu jiaqiang gaodeng xuexiao benke jiaoxue gongzuo tigao jiaoxue zhiliang de ruogan yijian]. Guidelines for Improving Teaching for University Undergraduate Students. On WWW at http://www.cuc.edu.cn/highedu/law/4th.htm.

Ministry of Education (2003) 《普通高中英语课程标准 (实验)》 [putong gaozhong yingyu kecheng biaozhun(shiyan)]. Standard of English courses for general senior high schools (for experiment). Beijing: People's Education Press. On WWW at www.sxbjjy.com/upload/200741317124048074.doc.

Norton, B. (2001) Non-participation, imagined communities and the language classroom. In M.P. Breen (ed.) *Learner Contributions to Language Learning* (pp. 159–171). Harlow: Longman.

Ong, A. (1999) *Flexible Citizenship: The Cultural Logics of Transnationality*. Durham, NC: Duke University Press.

Spence, J. (2008) English Lessons; American Dreams. Lectures 2 and 3, BBC Radio, UK. On WWW at http://www.bbc.co.uk/radio4/reith2008/index.shtml.

Shanghai Education Commission (Curriculum and Materials Reform) (1999) *Facing the 21st Century: Research Report on Principles for Action in Shanghai Primary and Secondary Foreign Language Education Reform*. Shanghai Education Commission Office of Pedagogical Research, Shanghai: Shanghai Education Press. [上海中小学课程教材改革委员会办公室、上海市教育委员会教学研究室 1999《面向21世纪上海市中小学外语学科教育改革行动纲领（研究报告）》,上海：上海教育出版社。]

Shanghai Education Commission (2002–2003) 上海教育委员会 2002–2003 http://www.shmec.gov.cn如, http://www.shmec.gov.cn/web/news/show_article.php?article_id=6732,http://www.shmec.gov.cn/web/news/show_article.php?article_id=1778, http://www.shmec.gov.cn/web/news/show_article.php?article_id=19186.

Taylor, C. (2007) *Modern Social Imaginaries*. Durham, NC: Duke University Press.

Wang, W. (2006) Teacher beliefs and practice in the implementation of a new English language curriculum in China. In J. Huang, M. Gu and P.K.E. Cheung (eds) *Research Studies in Education* (Vol. 4) (pp. 198–208). Hong Kong: University of Hong Kong.

Wen, Q. and Gao, Y.H. (2007) Dual publication and academic inequality, viewpoint. *International Journal of Applied Linguistics* 17 (2), 221–225.

Part 1

Western Dreams, Chinese Quests – Habitus and Encounter

Chapter 1

Intercultural Encounters and Deep Cultural Beliefs

JOSEPH LO BIANCO

Introduction

Although it now looks decidedly redundant, the most recent grand
claim for human universalism, Francis Fukuyama's (1992) triumphant
declaration that the end of the Cold War and the collapse of centrally
planned state economies represented 'the end of history', underscores a
distinctively Western universalism relevant to the global expansion of
English, and especially its penetration into the institutional life of China.
Fukuyama's belief that Western liberal democracy was the final form of
human governance and that capitalist market economics the most reasonable and efficient mode of ordering economic life proclaims both economic–
political virtues but also cultural and ideological ones. More recently,
Headley has called the human rights and democracy elements of Western
universalism the *Europeanization of the World* (2008).

Some trace of this can be found in the universalistic inclination in
Western political practice since ancient times, most dramatically in the
year 212 and the Edict of Caracalla, granting all free men admission to
Roman citizenship (Pagden, 2008: 99), which is part of 2500 years of often
tense interaction between various manifestations of the cultural 'West'
and the cultural 'East'. This chapter discusses culture and identity issues
arising from mass English learning in China in reference to such questions
of universalism and particularism around three deep beliefs: capitalism,
Christianity and Confucianism. As China domesticates English, enshrin-
ing a historically unprecedented level of linguistic accommodation and
appropriation, this chapter looks to an older civilisational encounter
between the West and China, a period much more richly reciprocal than

is often supposed. The chapter pursues a line of questioning on these three big Cs as a kind of exploration of difference, a feature of exchanges between the interpreters of civilisation in China and various Western powers. If global English today does presage a world civic community as many suppose, it is preceded by an ancient history in which few people have doubted the deep cultural and ideological consequences of language learning.

Changing China

In his speculation about China's future, former *Time* magazine reporter David Aikman (2005) claims that over the next three decades up to 30% of China's population will become Christian, with many of China's cultural and political leaders espousing Christian principles. He imagines an 'Augustinian' impact on China's foreign relations, asking whether 'the Chinese dragon' will be 'tamed by ... the Christian lamb?' (Aikman, 2005: 292). Apparently believing that restraint, justice and reason have characterised the foreign policies of 'the two Anglo Saxon' empires, Aikman supposes that these virtues, derived from St. Augustine's fourth-century treatise City of God, will be transferred to Christianised China. What this implies about the millennial Chinese state, which some consider 'the most open, flexible, fair, and sophisticated system of government' (Leys, 1997: xxvii), is controversial to say the least.

Whether Aikman's conversion calculation is empirically tenable cannot be assessed, nor would that affect the main point of its inclusion here, nor is it my purpose to examine or critique his biases – other than to mention Spence's (1998) survey of the never-ending Western dreams projected onto Chinese realities. Aikman, however, opens a door onto the ignored but central role of belief in relations between China and the West. Contemporary secularism makes understanding religion- and belief-based international relations difficult and strange, and yet religion was fundamental to Western political and social history from the 313 Edict of Milan and Emperor Constantine's Christian conversion to the 1500-year tortuous process of separation of Church and State that followed. During this long period, cultural and imperial China 'met' cultural and imperial Europe frequently, often under religious guise, a mode of encounter continued in China's relations with America and its Protestant missions from the 19th century.

This chapter addresses religion–belief encounters of the 17th and 18th centuries because these differ from current relations in crucial ways. While all intercultural meetings contain curiosity, comparison, admiration and repudiation, this pre-industrial and pre-colonial encounter is a veritable phase of comparative civilisation, remarkable for the intensity of its focus on deep cultural beliefs. Despite being well documented it is rarely cited today, perhaps because few English speakers were involved and because in contemporary secular scholarship religion-based interculturalism is more condemned than studied.

Three substantial overviews address relations between China and the West over large sweeps of time. Jonathan Spence (1998) calls these encounters 'sightings', David Mungello (1999) 'borrowings' and Harry Gelber (2007) 'relationships'. Spence discusses 48 'sightings' over 700 years, from the problematical Polo in 1253 to the celebrated Calvino in 1985. Mungello's time frame is more restricted but his treatment is more detailed and reciprocal, discussing states, individuals and institutions engaged in mutual influence analysed from multiple perspectives. Gelber's volume is the most extensive: a narrative spanning more than three millennia of relations between 'the dragon and the foreign devils'.

Separate or Linked?

Aikman reflects a school of thought linking Christianity, liberalism and capitalism as locomotives of scientific and technological history. The most recent instalment, Rodney Stark's *Victory of Reason* (2006), accounts for European global pre-eminence by its 'faith in reason' attributed to Christian rational theology. On this account, capitalism was invented on medieval monastic estates, but was stifled by absolutist monarchies in France and Spain threatened by independent wealth, flourishing only in the independent Italian city republics. Here a new merchant citizenship emerged, producing responsive states, generating wealth, fuelling the Renaissance, secular humanism and modern science.

When squashed by foreign invasion this commercial civic culture had already been introduced to northern Europe and England, from whose fertile base science, capitalism and personal freedoms were transported to North America by Puritan émigrés, there yielding the individualism, capitalist success and political triumph of contemporary America. This meta-narrative of personal and political liberty associates economic and technological advancement with a facilitative commitment to reason derived from Christianity, establishing an ancient authorisation for capitalism and American ascendancy. Although overturning the timing and location of capitalism's origins espoused by sociologist of modernity Max Weber, the narrative retains his famous claim of religious propulsion underlying capitalism through a spirit of deferred consumption and belief in linear worldly progress. Historians of large-scale social and economic change, such as Fernand Braudel, Carlo Cipolla and Henri Pirenne, also locate essential elements of capitalism and its enabling conditions of relative liberalism in the pre-Reformation period. But, like Aikman, Stark invokes the centrality of Christianity, claiming that Chinese scholars share his view. He declines to explain how his thesis is not scrambled by a China, atheist and communist, adopting capitalist market economics while adopting neither religion nor democracy.

China's rise has given birth to re-interpretive literature, including polemical Sino-triumphalism (Hobson, 2004) resembling the Western triumphalism it excoriates (Duchesne, 2006). More considered exposes of Euro-centric historiography (Blaut, 2000; Frank, 1998), however, provide evidence of interdependent economic development, rather than discrete and separated centres of commercial civilisation, even when the accounts assume Western economic pre-eminence (Landes, 1998). The interdependency thesis has multiple origins. Early in the 20th century land-mass interdependency was proposed repeatedly in the voluminous Tibeto-Indian-Western Chinese historical researches of Italy's pre-eminent 'oriental' scholar Giuseppe Tucci, who coined the term Eurasia to account for interlinked commercial and cultural developments. Tucci even posited a coherent historical unity across the vast Eurasian landmass (Tucci, 1958).

Du (1996, 2000) offers a contemporary version from Chinese standpoints. Addressing the 1990s assertion of unique 'Asian values' by Singapore's Lee Kuan-Yew to explain Asian economic success, Du takes a multi-civilisation approach to account for modernity and proposes Confucian humanism 'as the basic value system underlying East Asian political economy' (2000: 258). While repudiating the implied excusing of authoritarianism in the 'Asian values' movement, Du's explorations identify a process of 'creative adaptation' in Eastern projects of modernity and in struggles against colonialism, both Western and Asian (1996). This creative adaptation offers future 'transformative potential' for the recovery of Confucian traditions by 'cultural China', and in this way Du also makes faith, belief and spirit central to projects of economic modernisation.

This chapter shifts Du's idea of 'creative adaptation' towards 'motivated adaptation' to write an account of interculturalism differing from technical–descriptive anthropology and from the position-taken approach characteristic of West-critical post-colonialism. It is acknowledged that the former promises a de-centring stance when researching human differences and the latter critiques the self-serving character of some Western scholarship on historical progress. However, the first is inappropriate because the present work is based on secondary sources rather than original fieldwork, and the second overcorrects and becomes guilty of the deficiencies it condemns.

Protagonists

The present discussion is of a series of meetings between Ming and Qing elites with various European entities: national states, monarchies, counter-reformation religious orders and many individuals. At the centre are the Jesuit missions. This diverse array of interests and agents suggests that the totalised West is a term of limited coherence that demands deconstruction; in some ways the term China also obfuscates persistent internal differences. Both categories assume cohesion, sequence, continuity and stability of worldview and cultural norms that deserve problematisation, something that can only be noted rather than pursued here.

Temple, synagogue and mosque

Eurasia in Jesuit garb was not an anomaly. In a 'detour' via synagogue, mosque and temple, Zürcher (1994) assembles archaeological and documentary evidence for ancient examples of accommodation and interaction in projects of seeking souls. Each of several marginal religions entering Chinese space had to negotiate the *wulun*, the five social relations of Confucianism, and the interpretation of sacrificial rites indigenous to Chinese traditions.

Citing Jewish passages inscribed on steles from a synagogue courtyard at Kaifeng dated 1489, 1512 and 1663, Zürcher shows how these try to reconcile Chinese observances and introduced doctrines, noting differences, analogies and precedents. Memorial inscriptions express Judaism in Confucian terms, making links to China's most distant past in which Adam is identified with Pan Gu (Shan hai jing), a mythical being whose dead body was transformed into heaven and earth, and with Fu Xi and Yu, saintly rulers of the highest antiquity.

Noticing the different, calibrating distances, seeking analogies or identifying incommensurability are intercultural processes also pursued by Islam and Buddhism in what Zürcher calls a pattern of 'conciliation and adaptation'. Also preceding the Jesuits were two Christian arrivals on Chinese cultural terrain who also engaged in 'conciliation and adaptation': Syriac Nestorians in the middle of the first millennium and Italian Franciscans in the early 12th century.

Ricci and the Catholics

Counter-reformation Catholics were the main religious explorers between 1500 and 1800. The intensity of their engagement remains unequalled in Chinese–Western interaction for the close proximity of foreigners to elite Chinese cultural life, especially with the astronomical, calendrical and literary activity of the imperial court. The first Protestant missionary Robert Morrison was present in China only from 1807 when '...westerners again knocked on the door of China. This time ... with gunboats as well as the bible' (Xu, 2001: 449).

Among the Jesuits, Matteo Ricci (Li Madou, 1552–1610), 'Perhaps the most brilliant of a group ... characterised by brilliance'[1] (Mungello, 1977: 12), looms large because he established the paradigm within which the engagement proceeded. Eminent China historian Jonathan Spence (1994) has written: 'From the first moment I went to China as a student, the one Chinese name of a Westerner that I found recognized by everyone was Li Madou ... To say that I was interested in Li Madou evoked smiles and nods all over China ... [he] has a kind of special resonance in the hearts of the Chinese even now in the 1990s...' (Spence, 1994: 16). Ricci failed to convert a Chinese Emperor but he '....converted the historians', including the towering British figure of Chinese science and civilisation studies, Joseph Needham, who described Ricci as 'one of the most remarkable and brilliant men in history' (Cummins, 1993: 2).

Some readings criticise the Jesuits as prefiguring European expansion or as manipulative dissemblers, but few deny their sincere admiration of China. Several developed a fused identity containing Confucian, Christian, European and Chinese elements, encapsulated in verse as self-and-other mutuality in Ricci's famous *Treaty on Friendship* (Ricci, 1595/2003), a text in which, through friendships, individuals fuse identities and swear obligations of assistance, forging synthetic categories that transcend differences (Mignini, 2003b). This Chinese text is perhaps his most recognised work today (Bollettino I; Ricci, 1598–2003; Cronin, 1999). Despite China's '...political-cultural antipathy to organized religion' (Uhalley & Wu, 2001: 3), identified as early as the Tang dynasty (Witek, 2001), organised religion and trade have been characteristic modalities of its encounter with non-China.

Churching China

The Portuguese Francis Xavier (1506–1552), 'pioneer of all missionaries in Asia' (Young, 1983: 9), devised a distinctive approach to Japan and

China premised on learning 'native customs and rites' to meet another culture 'on its own terms' (1983: 9). Xavier, apparently astonished by Japanese 'reverence for reason' and 'European superiority in science', was affected by a Japanese challenge that if Christianity really were the 'one true religion' surely the 'intelligent Chinese' would have known, giving Chinese conversion a specifically charged importance.

Xavier died before entering China but on his entry Ricci discovered a fundamental error in Xavier's plan of targeting the imperial court. Unlike Buddhist Japan, the prevailing intellectual system at the late Ming Chinese court was neo-Confucianism, a synthesis of Confucianism, religious Daoism and sinified Buddhism (Bresciani, 2001; De Bary, 1991a, 1991b; Tucci, 1922; Xu, 2001). Xavier's immediate successor Alessandro Valignano (1539–1606) became the architect of the Jesuits' mission philosophy; believing that East Asians were 'gente bianca', white people, with cultures equal to those of Europe, he bequeathed the mission its initial ethos (Mungello, 1977). For well over a century the Jesuits represented the bulk of intellectual exchange between China and the West. They were not simply priests bent on conversion, but also highly educated men skilled in abstract reasoning, literature and poetry, science and mathematics, technology and mapmaking, languages and music (Mignini, 2003a). Although they became useful in the service of imperial governance, the long duration of their presence in China, and the depth of their influence, made them vulnerable to alienation from their source institutions and to resentment from rival groups among their hosts.

What reflections for interculturalism and cross-cultural studies can be drawn from peculiar, extensive and early encounters such as these? This question will be addressed through a Controversy and the approach of motivated adaptation.

Entering Chinese Spaces

Entry to China required two movements, into Chinese territory and into Chinese concepts. Misled by Xavier, Ricci discarded his Jesuit dress and physically entered China dressed as a Buddhist monk. Gaining access to the mental universe of the literati involved harder barriers than entering geographic space, a movement imposing more of 'its own terms'. To effect this move Ricci again changed dress, to that of the Chinese scholar, as depicted in surviving portraits. This dressing is an external marker of mental transitions through space and ideology, because local dress is both a constitutional requirement (Rule, 1999) and a depiction of identity (Jensen, 1997).

Physical entry signified overcoming the tribute system controlling movement and residential location, but Ricci's overcoming of the second shifted history, inaugurating a reverberating conceptual intercultural project. His Christian presence in China impacted on local space and thought, and then his account of Confucian natural philosophy reverberated back into Christian Europe, where Confucian possibilities were exploited in local struggles of ideas and politics; still later Westernised Confucianism reverberated back into China, re-appropriated by Westernising Chinese, as transformed images of Chinese wisdom reinhabiting their native land. The conceptual synthesis that Ricci's entry into China produced was a creation with the imprint of many hands, in the dress of different conceptual interpreters, shaped by the interests of diverse and contesting forces.

The project of conversion depended on entry to China, and entry was predicated on acceptance. Facilitating entry and acceptance were Ricci's scientific literacy, mathematical skill and prodigious memory. His cartographic talents added particularly to his value at court as he revealed 'Europe and America to the Chinese for the first time' (Cummins, 1993: 50). As Xu expresses it: 'Ricci ... informed Chinese intellectuals of a whole array of western knowledge including: mathematics, physics, chemistry, astronomy, cartography and philosophy' (Xu, 2001: 447).

Contemporary understandings of cultural fusion and hybridity rely on notions of the personal self that emphasise its multiple or unstable character and the situated nature of identity formations. Ricci was to undergo a personal evolution that sheds unconventional light on these ways to view identity and self-hood, as the ultimate failure of his mission also sheds light on how essentialist ideas of belonging are imposed on liminal personalities. In post-colonial theorising about relations between the rest-of-the-world and the West-of-the-world, how is the strange intercultural hybridity of this European hegemonic project to be understood? Theorising hybridity within the frame of post-colonial studies would seem to exclude its manifestation in pre-colonialism, but its historic presence is undeniable.

Neo, new and no Confucianism

Ricci was dressed for the Ming literati, for whom a pre-existing neo-Confucianist synthesis dominated thought. In neo-Confucianism (*Daoxue*, teaching the way; *Lixue*, the teaching of principle) *li* is essentially characterised by a concern for rational order in the universe and its moral consequences. This connection between universal reasoned order and moral behaviour was decisive in attracting external fascination with the traditional Chinese worldview. Although inherent in the classic texts of 3rd–4th century BCE, a 9th-century repudiation of Buddhism reinvigorated the canon eventually bringing forth neo-Confucianism (Bresciani, 2001). The provoking incident was mass hysteria caused by relocation of a Buddha image. The social upheaval this implied was lamented in Han Yu's 819 anti-Buddhist polemic. Combined with anti-foreigner sentiment, a divide between educated, aristocratic elites and conservatism among ordinary people intent on veneration of sacred objects was exposed. By the 12th century a neo-Confucianist synthesis had emerged under Zhu Xi, building on 11th-century scholar predecessors. An ambition of these *jinshi* or scholar bureaucrats, graduates of civil service examinations, had been to understand the Great Ultimate. This quest for the sense of the universe and the nature of time was systematically linked to gleaning lessons from the transcendent for behavioural ethics.

By Zhu Xi's time the project of philosophical reconstitution divided into two broad streams: one stressing statecraft and ethical conduct, and the other stressing the rational principle *li* and *xin*, intuition or mind. The most well-known intuitionist or idealist was Lu Xianshan (1139–1191), whose subjectivism produced a self-referential ethics, encapsulated in the aphorism 'the universe is my mind and my mind is the universe' (De Bary, 1991a, 1991b).

The most distinguished rationalist was Zhu Xi (1130–1200), sometimes dubbed the completer of Confucianism. Suffering exile for his heretical interpretation of 'original' Confucianism, Zhu achieved political and intellectual exoneration and returned to exercise influence and prestige. Twentieth-century Communist Party propaganda criticised Zhu, alleging culpability in diffusing obscurantism and cultural stultification, judged the cause of China's decline after the Middle Ages. Zhu's influential work downplayed the supernatural in human affairs but extolled it in 'high' pursuits, such as wisdom, happiness and ethical social life. The pre-established harmony of the world can be recovered by individuals who approach perfection by behaving in conformity with nature's inherent pattern. This system postulates two ultimate forces or entities in the universe, the Supreme Ultimate and *li*; the former involves the existence of matter and the latter is ontology, the form and development of matter. A benevolent, self-renewing or regenerative capability pervades nature, *ren* (仁), a force offering individuals a principled and ethical existence (Ching, 1993; De Bary, 1991a, 1991b).

This symmetrical alignment between natural universal entities and human personal and social conduct linked Zhu's innovations with classical thought. The display of authenticity established authority for his synthesis. In *Dao Tong*, the Transmission of the Way, he discusses the origins of his ideas using links with native antiquity to mark the Buddhist canon as foreign, mystical and otherworldly, despite its long presence on Chinese soil (De Bary, 1991a, 1991b). Zhu's compilation of the Four Books, *Lun Yu* (Analects of Confucius), *Mengzi* (Mencius), and two chapters from the Book of Rites called *Daxue* (Great Learning) and *Zhongyong* (Doctrine of the Mean), comprised the bulk of the standard curriculum for civil service examinations until its 1905 abolition.

Immediately preceding the Jesuits' arrival, a further reformulation, guided by Ming idealist Wang Yangming's (1472–1529) rejection of 'vulgarisation' (Ching, 1976, 1993) of essential Confucian precepts, was underway. This eventually produced a School of Mind version of neo-Confucianism, in which cultivation of mind–heart *xin*, and teaching of mind–heart (*Xinxue*), stressed intuition, *knowledge as action* or innateness in knowledge. This stood in contrast to the School of Li, or principle of *knowledge for action*, which had evolved from Zhu, but itself changed over the intervening centuries and through its recognition by the Ming court. Wang's reaction was partly against the accumulation and display of knowledge manifest in civil service examinations and curricula, rather than knowledge pursued principally for self-awareness. Wang Yangming therefore becomes a crucial Confucian theoriser and reformer, a denier of the rationalist dualism of Zhu Xi and its 'degeneration' into forms designed for administration and public service.

Confucianism was to be subject to more 'invention', even by the Jesuits who favoured the archaic *ru* or scholar class, over the contemporary neo-Confucian manifestations (Jensen, 1997: 80). Under the Qing (1644–1911) a reaction against the speculative character of both Zhu and Wang's neo-Confucianisms took place in a movement called *hanxue*, calling for a more grounded or evidentiary basis for belief, behaviour and morality. And, later still, 'new' Confucianisms emerged in the extreme circumstances of the May 4th movement finding 20th-century revitalised form as *xin rujia*, in dialogue now with Western philosophy, including Jesuit-influenced Westernised conceptions of the great sage and his wisdom. The 'neo' and the 'new' became 'no' Confucianism under communist repudiation. Maoist thought dispatched all traditions, schools and streams of Confucian philosophy, rejected as 'left-over venom from feudalism' (Bresciani, 2001: 419; Ching, 1993), replacing them with atheistic governance premised on the dictatorship of proletarian and peasant classes, buttressed by historical materialism.

Early in an encounter

An early phase in intercultural encounter involves display. One of Ricci's was demonstration of the Greco-Roman, but recently revived, ars memoria. The memory arts involve cultivation of prodigious feats of recall perfected through advanced memorisation techniques. On Ricci's use of ars memoria, Spence (1984: 1) writes: 'In 1596 Matteo Ricci taught the Chinese how to build a memory palace .... to provide storage spaces for the myriad concepts that make up the sum of our human knowledge'.

The skill is impressive but also practical and made Ricci popular because mnemonics helped exam-cramming literati memorise large tracts of the Confucian classics. Prodigious recall supported the idea that ever vaster knowledge could be accumulated by talented individuals bolstering personal cultivation and advancement in competitive promotions. What is involved here is more than trickery or mere dramaturgical display, more even than culture, since, as Chen (1979) has argued, though writing mostly about a later period, 'science and technology were the first territories Confucian traditionalists conceded to the West' (Chen, 1979: 174).

Rites and names

The Chinese Rites and Names Controversy is the name given to a dispute arising within this Catholic–Chinese encounter. It was to last 350 years, involving nine popes, two emperors, three kings, two papal legates, *Propaganda Fide*, Chinese literati and Enlightenment polymaths (Malatesta, 1994; Mungello, 1994). According to Voltaire the dispute proceeded from a 'monks' quarrel' to a 'philosopher's concern' (Cummins, 1993: 7; Witek, 1994) with 'political interference on both sides' (Xu, 2001: 452).

Rule (1994) notes that it lacks a definitive history, due to its 'sprawling' nature, and that the primary documentation and secondary literature are in Chinese and Manchu, Latin, Portuguese, Spanish, Italian, French and some German, and the original source materials are dispersed across China, Italy, France, Portugal, Spain, Germany and England, and elsewhere in Europe plus Japan and the Philippines, and even in the United States and Australia (Rule, 1994: 251). The controversy was mostly an internal Catholic argument about the meaning of Chinese devotional rituals, complicated by the rivalry among the Catholic monarchies, especially France, Portugal, Spain and several states on Italian soil, some undergoing Reformation loyalty shifts. Opposing Jesuit 'leniency' were Spanish Dominican Friars who feared the reverberations back onto Catholic religious practice from the syncretism the Jesuits were promoting.

The Jesuits had followed Ricci's interpretation that ancestral rites honouring Confucius were essentially civil rather than religious (Mignini, 2004; Ricci, 1953) and that the ancient Chinese terms *Shangdi* or *Shang-ti* (上帝, King-on-High, Above Emperor) and *Tian* or *T'ien* (天, Heaven) were the correct translations of God and Heaven. Opponents insisted the rites were religious and that the Christian God required an original label to mark conceptual innovation, favouring *Tianzhu* (天主, Lord-of-Heaven).

Chinese Christian literati became embroiled after a 44-day missionaries' conference at Guangzhou (December 1667 to January 1668) debating rites and names. Their liminal status, simultaneously Christian and Confucian, gave the converts a special mediating role to explain, refine and elaborate names and concepts. Sometimes they argued a Christian and sometimes a Confucian interpretation. Regarding ancestor rites the converts took the Confucian side, but were not always understood because of their 'complicated state of mind and dual identity' (Jinshi, 1994: 82) and while they wanted Christianity to spread throughout China they did not want China 'transformed into a Western culture' (1994: 82). In a mirror image of their dilemmas, several Europeans who embraced Confucian ethics and philosophy through Jesuit mediation experienced cultural and political tension, exemplified by the Sinophile Christian Wolff, expelled from his pietist German university charged with foreign atheism and Jesuit sympathy (Lach, 1953). If reconciling Confucian natural philosophy with the revealed belief of Christianity appeared feasible in private study, creative imagination or personal effort, in real-world institutions and political struggle it often proved impossible for both Chinese Christians and European Confucians.

The meticulous nature of the questions that occupied the Controversy's antagonists is highlighted by the 30 years of research of Joseph Prémare. Prémare lived in China between 1698 and 1736, specialising in philological interpretation of the Book of Changes (*Yijing* or *I Ching*), the Book of Songs and the Book of History, producing his main work *Notitia Linguæ Sinicæ*, which discussed 'the problem of the proper name of God in Chinese' (Lundbaek, 1994: 129). 'Correct' meanings of *Tian* and *Shangdi* were critical to prove Prémare's belief that the Chinese had always known 'the true God'. The framing of this question indicates its intended audience, 'to explain that the concept of a judging god could be found in Confucianism' (Xu, 2001: 446).

But God's Chinese names already had a history, even among the Catholics. Before Prémare, Michele Ruggeri had introduced *Tianzhu* (天主 Heavenly Lord) to mean Our Lord in Heaven. *Tianzhu* was retained by Ricci (Xu, 2001: 446, claims Ricci created it) and adopted by Pope

Clement XI and is still used by Chinese Catholics today; however, others rejected *Tianzhu*, favouring more 'straightforward' *Tian* and *Shangdi* which were already used throughout China. Heading straight for the central symbolic figures in the two cosmologies Ricci had earlier tried to find sense equivalents in Latin between Chinese and Christian terms. Ricci's suggestion was that God in Chinese should be *Tianzhu Shiyi*. His religious rivals in China and in Rome agreed, and then disagreed. Ricci's extensive written reflections on the problems of writing and reading Chinese (Battaglini, 2003), and of finding sense equivalents and translation terms between Chinese and European languages (Ricci, 2003) reveal a self-conscious process of documenting ancient words and meanings with extrapolations to current applications in new settings. This forms a rich learners' journal grappling without guidance with the mental universe of another culture to map its contours via points of connection and incommensurability. It, and the story so far, endorses the claim of mutual change in this motivated encounter.

Rome, Spain and the Catholic orders

During the early 16th century, 'China .... sat apart in solitary grandeur, self-sufficient, proud and unaware that .... she was under holy siege as Jesuit and Friar gazed longingly towards the empire, the one from India, the other from Mexico' (Cummins, 1993: 48). Attempts to make converts in Ming and Qing China produced the Mandarin-Missionaries, a group of hybrids beginning with Ricci, 'Wise Man from the West' rather than clergyman (Cronin, 1999). Dress signified definitive choice; Ricci permanently discarded his monk's robes and 'assimilated' (Spence, 1984); all portraits depict a literatus rather than a priest. Admitted in 1582, he never left China, dying in 1610. He is buried in a specially sanctioned imperial plot in Peking, his many writings an invaluable account of mission and interculturalism (Ricci, 1953).

The aim Ricci inherited (*Convert Emperor*) suggests ambitious institutional overreach but 'The missions [Ricci] established in Nanjing and Beijing thrived to such an extent that by 1650 there were 150,000 converts and by 1700, 300, 000' (Borthwick, 1998: 80). And, as it turned out, his successor Jesuit at court Schall von Bell (1592–1666) brought the young Kangxi (r. 1662–1722) Qing Emperor close to personal conversion. Revealing the depth of influence wielded by the court missionaries is the first-person narrative reconstructed by Spence from Emperor Kangxi's writings (1661–1772). The brutal Qing conquest had won the Manchu foreigners the imperial throne but even by 1644, the commencement of their dynastic calendar and despite a subjugated Beijing, bloodshed and massacre continued (Spence & Wills, 1979). Spence's 'self-portrait' of Kangxi conveys some of the reasoning and strategising of the imperial hosts vis-à-vis the Jesuit interlopers and some of the domestic interests they served. Spence has him say (1974: 81), 'I told the Westerners that they must follow Ricci's interpretation of the Chinese Rites', and then sketches an intended conversation with the Pope, the imagined 'other' power in the world. But the powerful Chinese Emperor and his imagined counterpart in power, the 'European' pope, represented barely comprehending civilisational universes whose communication was dependent on mediators, themselves interested and embittered with rivalry.

The Controversy is ultimately understandable only from within Western religious–political parameters. The primary rivalry was between religious orders, the Jesuits and Dominicans, occasionally also Franciscans, attempting to negotiate the prevailing, and shifting, Chinese worldview as Chinese elites in turn sought to understand and respond to European intrusion. The Jesuit approach was to conduct their encounter through science, technology and cultural accommodation, an approach that changed them and their hosts, thwarted by papal denunciation of the revolutionary science of Galileo, and eventually by papal refusal of Ricci's interpretation of the customary meaning of Chinese ancestor veneration. While most Jesuits followed the policy of syncretic accommodation, Dominican friars became agitated about the compromise it implied, eventually necessitating papal adjudication.

As each side advocated its case Rome became the de-facto (and first) European centre of Sinology, even of Asian studies, called upon to interpret Chinese cosmology, classic texts and ritual practices, a role later shared with Spain in its Italian capital of Naples. Between 1724 and 1732 the artist priest Matteo Ripa founded the *Collegio dei Cinesi* at Naples, training 108 Chinese priests along with interpreters and glossators for 'oriental texts' and introduced Hindi, Urdu and Chinese language teaching. The *Collegio* remained until its transformation in 1888 into the Oriental Studies unit of the University of Naples. However, under Spanish rule and influenced by the activist Friar Navarrete, the Dominicans developed implacable hostility to accommodation despite living with Jesuit priests during more than four years of their persecution in Beijing in the early 1600s.

The four main religious orders were divided by national origins. The Dominicans (the most loyally Roman and Catholic congregation) and the Jesuits (dedicated to saving Europe from Protestantism and defending incumbent Popes) both emerged from Spain, but in China represented the supra-nationalism of Catholic orthodoxy among the learned upper reaches of Chinese society. On the other hand, the two originally Italian congregations, Benedictines and Franciscans, were confined to work among traders and commoners in the countryside and southern seaports, especially Macao, and these different audiences conditioned their views and actions. The rivalry between Jesuits and Dominicans was compounded by wider religious conflict in late Renaissance Europe. For Spain the religious orders were embedded in its exploding world role, including in Europe, and even in Rome. In 1527 Spanish troops and German mercenaries under Charles V looted, burned and destroyed much of Rome, after the Vatican, France, Venice and Milan had forged the Treaty of Cognac to halt Spanish expansion in Italy and elsewhere in Europe. For these reasons the Controversy was political and Spanish, as well as intercultural, religious and Chinese. It later became French and German, and even English, when the early Jesuits were followed by French, but also Dutch, Belgian and German priests, who informed European intellectuals of Chinese philosophy, ethics, cosmology and governance. As mediators between an aloof China and a turbulent Europe, Jesuit interpretations of Chinese civilisation filtered into the intensive reconstitution of European thought at the hands of enlightenment intellectuals, inserting unpredictable fragments from a dissonant worldview.

Meanings in the signs

Preparation for work in China required the priests to learn Chinese, and study of characters invited curiosity, speculation and, as shown below, even exposed a papal legate to imperial ridicule. Ricci offered an early pragmatic interpretation. In his Journals (1953) he notes the utility of character-based writing: 'If this were universally true, we would be able to transmit our ideas to the people of other countries in writing, though we would not be able to speak to them' (Ricci, 1953: 446).

However, others saw much more meaning in characters, indeed too much. Some looked to find evidence of the original human language, source speech or remnants of universal communication; some even imagined characters were a source of religion itself, beyond any specific forms of faith. Especially prominent in such questioning was a group of French Jesuits later called the Figurists who, between the end of the 17th and early 18th centuries, after initially keeping faithfully to Ricci's interpretations of ancient texts, went on to seek evidence of a shared religion of God and a link to the Judeo-Christian tradition. Their contribution to the Controversy was to incorporate Chinese rites directly because at some point in antiquity they imagined that Chinese history belonged to all human cultures, even imagining traces of the biblical Flood. The link with post-deluge Noah, whose son Shem had washed up in the Far East, suggested the intriguing possibility that some secret knowledge about Adam would be revealed, or ideas preserved in pure original forms would be uncovered.

This language-centred speculation recalls Eco's *Search for the Perfect Language*, an enduring European dream of seeking lost perfection (Eco, 1997: 91, 284–287), provoked by disappointment with the 'fallen' present and yearning to recover past utopia. Some Figurists thought Chinese characters depicted actual biblical figures and might reveal messages about the anticipated arrival of the Messiah, and some even imagined that the Chinese literary canon had foreshadowed the birth of Jesus. These speculations were destabilising and provoked strong opposition from anti-Western literati as well as antagonising various European interests. The Figurists were bitterly divided among themselves and their whole project was dogged by intractable problems of translation fidelity between critical Chinese and Latin concepts.

The main Figurist was Joachim Bouvet (1656–1732), Prémare's teacher, who made a distinctive contribution to the idea of China as a kind of 'noble savage' injecting information and interpretations into European discourses about the origins of Chinese civilisation that reverberated within enlightenment writing on human nature, governance, modernity and otherness. The work of one of his converts, Shao Fuzhong's *Tianxue Shuo*, 'On the Heavenly Learning', a mathematical–mechanical logical system linking Immaculate Conception, Trinity and other Christian concepts to classical Chinese texts and the Great Commentary of the *Yijing* was introduced to German polymath Gottfried Leibniz, inaugurating a remarkable effort of cultural calibration and wide-ranging intellectual synthesis (Mungello, 1977). Leibniz devoted considerable time to the interpretation of the Yijing, Mungello (1977) declaring him the first serious European intellect to closely research Chinese civilisation. Leibniz admired Chinese natural reasoning recommending the Confucian ethical tradition to European intellectuals, and conducted mathematical calculations on synchronous relations between Chinese characters and his *Universal Characteristic*. He also identified in the hexagrams that comprise the divination system of the *Yijing* a sequence of binary numbers ranging from 0 to 111111, interpreting this as early evidence of the philosophical–mathematical system he advocated.

An 'ecumenical Lutheran' Leibniz was seeking various kinds of intellectual and practical reconciliation, an accord (Mungello, 1977) between

Chinese civilisation and Europe, between Christianity and Confucianism: a search for concord and harmony that he hoped would also reunite Rome and North German Protestants. But Leibniz was only one major European intellectual for whom Chinese knowledge informed and invigorated a personal intellectual quest.

Ricci's search for credible equivalences and Bouvet's quest for profound symmetry were religious equivalents of Leibniz's wider project of intellectual reconciliation of East and West. The rapid pace of diffusion of Chinese ideas across national boundaries and disciplinary fields is remarkable. It is impossible to imagine this speed and depth of penetration, from contact between Chinese intellectuals and Jesuit intellectuals at court, to Church officials, to philosophers and public figures across Europe, without the mediating role of Latin. It was the shared language of European scholarship, located within the 'Republic of Letters' (Ostler, 2007), but apparently also a republic of interculturalism as well. In having a supranational literate form, Europe resembled China more in the 17th century than it has since.

But a shared means of communication and a common culture could not prevent intellectual overreach. Bouvet's most extreme construction was to believe that the *Yijing* and the Bible were essentially the same and, using Chinese sources (*Ma Duanlin's Wenxian Tongkao* of 1224), that there were in early antiquity literary linkages between China and Rome. This association between Old Confucianism and Catholicism or even Pagan Europe was a mystical vision upsetting to both Chinese and Europeans, accompanied by political flattery about the inevitability of the Kangxi Emperor and the French Sun King ruling the earth. Eventually Bouvet was undermined by fellow Jesuits who found such claims untenable, even absurd. Although such 'correlative cosmology' has Chinese precedents (Smith, 2001), Chinese literati were equally offended at Bouvet's extreme appropriations of their literary canon.

Imperial instruction

A series of excerpts from the recorded encounter between the Kangxi Emperor and papal delegate Charles Maigrot, drawn from Collani (1994: 161–166), highlights the intimate relations that had developed between the Jesuits and the imperial court, which the Figurist over-interpretations jeopardised and which eventually the Controversy destroyed. A feature of these discussions is the importance of display around formally correct language skills, representing personal credibility as much as skilled literacy.

Emperor: Am I right that you cannot quote two words of the Confucian Four Books?

The delegate lived down to the Emperor's surmise and managed to fail other 'high stakes language tests' (McNamara & Roever, 2006), including inability to identify the four characters above the imperial throne or distinguish between original and later Confucian writings. These failures brought imperial reproach.

Emperor: Why do you not mention anything about that which you once disapproved and condemned as being ill-natured? ... the characters *jingtian* ... the reverence for Confucius ... the tablets of the ancestors ... What are your objections to the characters *jingtian*?

Maigrot: *Tian* does not mean the Lord of Heaven.

Emperor: I am very surprised at you. Did I not already state that *Tian* is a much better expression for the Lord of Heaven than *Tianzhu* (Lord of Heaven) and *tiandi wanwu zhizhu* (Lord of Heaven and Earth and ten-thousand things)? *Fo Tian* universally means the Lord of Heaven and the ten-thousand things. Tell me, why do the people call me *wansui* (ten-thousand years)?

Maigrot: To indicate that they wish Your Majesty innumerable years.

Emperor: Learn from that: the true meaning of Chinese words does not always coincide with their literal meaning.

But Maigrot had an official duty to perform, to communicate the authoritative adjudication of the far-away Pope on the rites and names. It did not go down well with the here-and-now Emperor. Collani reports the Emperor's response, paraphrased and abbreviated below:

Two hundred years and more have elapsed since the times of Father Ricci, when the Europeans came to China to cultivate virtue. Up to now they have not broken the public peace ... You came ten years ... ago ... and I declare that you do not know the Chinese teachings, and even less have you learned the literal sense or the usual manner of speaking ..... You cannot write (in Chinese) yourself, but you are asking other persons to write for you .... you add the European phonetic transcription and the meaning with your own letters when writing Chinese characters, and then you send them to Europe....

Although Maigrot replies that 'most things in the Chinese books' are 'extraordinarily good and in harmony with Christianity', he declares '... in my opinion, there are some things which are opposed to Christianity'. Charles Maigrot's meeting with the Emperor transposed the internal Catholic conflict into an issue for the Chinese court. The Controversy escalated in 1693 after Maigrot's order for the exclusive use of *Tianzhu* and the Papal Bull *Ex Illa Die* of 1715 'which ... brought feelings of the missionaries in China and people in Europe to boiling point' (Lundbaek, 1994: 133; see also Spence, 1994). On 20 December 1722 the Jesuit-favouring Kangxi Emperor died, and was succeeded by his fourth son, the missionary-mistrusting Yongzheng, who feared a Chinese sect was plotting against the government. Things deteriorated rapidly. In Fujian province in June 1723, a Christian literatus denounced the missionaries; the Emperor restricted their work and closed churches. In July 1724 all were expelled to Canton save some doing needed work at the Peking Court, ultimately being confined to Macao. In 1742 Benedict XIV condemned Jesuit policy and in 1773 Clement XIV suppressed the Jesuits altogether (McBrien, 1997: 437).

Controversy's end

In late 1939, a decree from Rome put a formal end to the Controversy by annulling the anti-rite oath stipulated by the Papal Bull of 1742 *Ex Quo Singulari* and recognised the civil nature of ancestor veneration and other related Chinese rites. This belated vindication of the Ricci stance completed in formal terms what had been finished in reality some 200 years earlier.

Young (1994) points out that the formal conclusion of the Controversy encouraged some more Chinese writing on the issue, and cites Hou Wailu[2] writing in the 1950s and 1960s who criticises Ricci's tolerance of Chinese rites as self-serving and strategic, a forerunner of 19th-century colonialism that characterised China's dealings with Western powers. In this interpretation early converts were also being strategic, some aiming to use Christian conversion only to dislodge Buddhist influence at court. Hou Wailu also rejects ancestral honouring and Confucian rites as totally meaningless in Marxist-Leninist China, believing them to be superstitious rituals.

The Supreme Ultimate and Anthropomorphic God

Any meeting featuring the Supreme Ultimate (*Taiji*) of the Confucian cosmological order and the Christian anthropomorphic God should command attention in discussions of intercultural encounter. Yet this sprawling engagement with deep cultural concepts and ideational differences is often ignored.

The encounter that forms the basis of the present discussion involved foreigners admitted for extended periods in a society that had taken more than 1000 years to 'sinicise' Indian-introduced religion. They participated in the indigenous civil service and spread technical expertise. Young (1983) cites Liang Ch'i Ch'ao, who claims it is 'still widely held today' that science was used 'as a lure, since the Chinese lacked science' to attract Chinese interest in 'preaching Christianity' because the Chinese 'did not like religion of extreme superstition' but himself judges the encounter positively concluding, 'Such a method was carried out for years, and both sides were satisfied' (Young, 1983: 5 and endnote 14: 129).

Liang endorses Zhang Zhidong's (1837–1909) much-cited maxim [*Chinese learning for essence (体 ti); Western learning for utility (用 yong)*], a traditional binary about China and the West, in which Christian conversion, like learning English today, might be regarded as instrumentally useful, temporary, connected to unaltered Chinese essences that would draw knowledge and skill from the learning but would endure, largely unchanged. Young dissents from this view, applying the dichotomy retrospectively to outline a wider range of reactions among Chinese literati, those interested in both Western *ti* (Christianity) and Western *yong* (i.e. science); some only in *ti*, others only in *yong* and still others who wanted the Jesuits evicted altogether.

The first anti-Christian movement took place six years after Ricci's death, and marked the beginning of Christian persecution (Young, 1983: 6). For Young a different question was central, a view endorsed in most of the reading that has informed this chapter: the encounter of this period gravitated around the central question of how to calibrate, name and organise the idea of God. The Controversy was essentially a struggle to name and constitute this set of ideas. That it occurred within a wider project of European hegemony conditions assessments of its character, achievements and limits. Chinese literati, converts and anti-converts, shaped how the question was posed, even when it was intended as a closed conversation among Christian Westerners. But the conversation was continually extended to new categories of participants, in China and in Europe, each modifying its terms and effects. Secularising Western intellectuals turned to China for support from the Confucian notion of the Supreme for their anti-religious campaigning in Europe, a line of questioning that endangered Western adherents in the face of intolerant believers, but which in turn changed the terms in which the question itself was framed.

Ricci's access was facilitated because he possessed technical skills of practical use in an agricultural society, specifically the Emperor's mediating function between heaven and earth and the practical consequences that flowed from it. A reliable and properly functioning calendar is vital for irrigation, forecasting ideal sowing, harvesting and cultivation times. Ming founder Zhuan Yuanzhang had established an astronomical observatory in 1368 and inherited Chinese and Muslim astronomy bureaus from the Mongols. But limitations in Ming astronomical knowledge were producing major calendar discrepancies with failure to predict solar and lunar eclipses.

Technical skill was the utilitarian equivalent of the gaining of expertise, but could the encounter that allows the sharing of skill or expertise stimulate a deeper engagement? And, given that Ricci was no mere purveyor of skills, would his entry into Chinese physical and cosmological space lead to a synthesis of Chinese and Western conceptual systems? Converts 'seemed to have arrived at a synthesis of Christianity and Confucianism' according to Young (1983: 128), but did it rest on solid or shallow foundations? He concludes that even without the Controversy, Chinese literati would have stifled any synthesis of cultural and conceptual forms, a failure attributed to the 'moral absoluteness of the Confucian tradition, supported by a Neo-Confucian metaphysical base' because, despite the Figurists' fantastic constructions, Young's belief is that Confucianism and Catholicism are 'irreconcilable'.

Reciprocity, Fusion or Synthesis?

In his discussion of the first 'native' Protestant churches, Chen (2004) puts forward various possible interpretations of the meeting of Christianity and modern China. He argues that indigenisation is not primarily about 'recasting the Christian message into Chinese terms or forms' (Chen, 2004: 3) like the 'accommodationism' of the Jesuits and the 1920s 'Protestant apologetical formulations'. Instead he proposes 'indigenisation' and 'ecclesiastical devolution', evoking a franchise-like metaphor to produce an account of American Protestant missions, arguing that Catholic understanding stresses 'inculturation', while Protestants prefer 'contextualisation'. The multi-denominational basis of Christian evangelisation produces this distinctive lexicon attuned to denomination-specific work, each a permutation of *ti/yong* frameworks.

A wide-ranging reflection of such religious 'indigenisation' appears in a 1999 San Francisco ecumenical conference. Co-sponsored by the Ricci Institute for Chinese–Western Cultural History, the conference commemorated the 1692 Edict of Toleration issued by the Kangxi Emperor through the Board of Rites permitting Chinese to embrace Catholicism and inaugurating the intercultural encounter around deep cultural beliefs that continues. Uhalley's introduction to the published papers (Uhalley & Wu, 2001) describes the Chinese-Christian story as a 'longstanding and continuing drama of epic proportions'. Taking an explicitly 'Chinese perspective' Zhang (2001) sees 'the story' as 'transplantation', observing that 'normal cultural communication is a two-way interactive process' (Zhang, 2001: 29) and pushes the encounter into the deep past, noting that 'it has been over 1300 years since Christianity first spread into China' (see also Mignini, 2003b).

In light of this claim Zhang surveys Chinese scholarship on Christianity in China and finds three dominant interpretations, 'encounter', 'mutual influence' and 'impact', but notes arrested effort at understanding because between 1949 and 1976 Chinese scholarship became 'woeful' with 'only one pamphlet written directly related to the history of Christianity' (Zhang, 2001: 31).

In contrast to Aikman's confident forecast of robust growth, Zhang suggests little penetration of Christianity in China, a position endorsed by Standaert (2001: 86) who compares the 'success' of Buddhism's penetration with Christianity's 'failure': two proselytising styles he calls clouds and clocks. Addressing the same contrast Zhang rejects both European and Chinese 'essentialisms' that pervade 'the story' and suggests instead that the encounter involved a robust mutual transmission of cultural information and practices, linking thought and society between China and Europe.

Less reciprocal and more absorptive is Li's (2001) interpretation. He estimates utilitarian Western influence as particularly deep, approvingly citing the philosopher, constitutional reformer and moderniser Liang Ch'i Ch'ao's (1873–1929) belief that '...the Chinese renaissance was strongly influenced by Jesuit missionaries, and Chinese translation of Western works, very much as the Italian Renaissance was influenced by the works of Asian cultures' (Li, 2001: 117). Applying to China terms conventionally associated with European history periods, Reformation, Enlightenment and Renaissance, Li offers an image of a profound and lasting impact, to the extent that the specific 'outlook' of the Chinese Renaissance was dependent on Jesuit influence, and develops this reasoning through vignettes of the lives of the key figures: for example, Ricci, Aleni, Schall and Brancati, whom he describes as 'Chinese Jesuits' who used Chinese names, wrote in Chinese and '... understood Chinese culture even better than many contemporary Chinese'. The fusion proclaimed here by Li gives '...Confucianism a modern definition' but insists the encounter was reciprocal.

Li claims longstanding recognition among Chinese intellectuals for the idea that China's early modernity was promoted by the Jesuits citing especially approvingly a famous 1932 lecture at the University of Chicago by moderniser and Westerniser Hu Shi called 'The Chinese Renaissance' (2001: 125). For Li different academic disciplines interpret the roles played by the Catholics at the Chinese court in divergent ways: 'Historians tend to treat Jesuits as foreigners and often forget that they lived in China for many years. Some of them (such as Ricci) knew Chinese better than the Chinese, and many of them respected Chinese culture more than their own ... Most ... were humanists ... the sons of the Italian Renaissance. They were pro-Confucian both inside and outside China...' (Li, 2001: 126). This view is endorsed by Zhuo (2001), in whose words the assimilation of the early Jesuits transformed their faith as well as their culture into 'Cultural Christians': a view endorsed in Italian (Mignini, 2003a), Irish (Cronin, 1999) and French (Dreyfus, 2004) scholarship on the transformation ripples of the Ricci mission.

The many terms used to express the encounter between the religious orders, their converts and the non-Christian Chinese imply that the encounter itself has many forms and contradictory aspects. This seems appropriate since the Controversy itself revolved around terms: what things are called, how Chinese entities and concepts are rendered in European languages and, reciprocally, how Western faith concepts are attached to equivalences in the Chinese cosmological system. In this respect Westerners and Chinese engaged in cultural calibration, finding correspondences and differences, giving their encounter significance for general intercultural studies.

From Sinophile heights to Sinophobe depths

However, deterioration was imminent. From the admiring idealisations of the 17th century religious, and 18th century secular, intellectuals (e.g. the French philosophes and physiocrats Voltaire, Du Halde, Rousseau, Quesnay and Turgot and the British David Hume and Oliver Goldsmith), cultural imagery and esteem declined. In Chen's (1979) assessment China had served domestic ideological or political interests, so that French reformers criticising the established social and political order were now subject to changing personal influence. The deterioration exposes a self-serving component of the original embrace and the disappointing domestic traction the embrace produced.

One especially revealing case concerns the German mathematician and philosopher Christian Wolff, 'one of the foremost architects of German rationalism' (Lach, 1953: 561). On 12 July 1721 Wolff delivered a famous speech, *De Sinarum Philosophia*, practically a eulogy to Chinese civilisation, at Halle University. Some of Wolff's colleagues planned to send missions to the Chinese court to compete with the Jesuits. Despite being dependent on Jesuit interpretations for his knowledge of Confucius, Wolff praised the 'practical philosophy' of China, finding great utility in Confucian principles drawn from nature rather than revelation. For Wolff the 'rationalism' of Chinese morality was consonant with his interpretations of Plato's idealisation of benevolent rule by philosopher kings, both of which he endorsed as superior to Europe's contemporary mode of organising moral reasoning.

Refracting the standpoints in evidence here, varieties of Western Christian practice and Western secularising philosophy, with diverse Confucianisms, are a fascinating angle from a 'Japanese Confucian' standpoint by Kanamori (1997). He points to Wolff's pivotal role in the growth of the German conception of social sciences, especially political science and psychology, suggesting its dependence on forms of reasoning that are inclined to find phenomena explained in non-transcendental ways. Kanamori notes that Wolff's eventual expulsion from the pietist University that hosted his provocative lecture was because of the charge of atheism, compounded, perversely, by claims that he was a 'friend of the Jesuits' (Lach, 1953).

The repudiation of Wolff brings into sharp relief the brilliant, if temporary, reputation of China, the array of interests that used Chinese knowledge in European debates and the ambiguous effects of introducing external modes of reasoning into conceptual systems under challenge. Wolff's contemporary, French political philosopher Montesquieu bitterly denounced Chinese 'despotism', breaking ranks with the prevailing Sinophilia. This denunciation was part of a Sinophobia beginning to overturn the prevailing admiration. This esteem collapse owes much to political transformations in America and France, and political reforms in Britain.

Britain and America

As these societies democratised, at least ideologically, a new rationality based on liberalism, progress and science came to allege the superiority of the contemporary 'modern' West. Exemplifying this was the 'apostle' of liberalism, John Stuart Mill, with a withering assessment of China as an oriental despotic state in which superhuman emperors managed the entire affairs of a passive population. In writings from the early 1830s Mill begins to use images of China as a stagnant civilisation in an 'Asian parable' (Kurfirst, 2001), a warning to Britain of the despotism that would follow should it allow its embrace of individualism and political pluralism to wane.

In this new narrative, China was demonised as oppressive despite its impressive ancient past. Descent into severe racial stereotyping was rapid, reaching a point of cruel infantilisation of Chinese as people who threw 'temper tantrums' (Chen, 1979: 41) and were 'depraved and dense' (1979: 47). However even as Chen documents what was to become an unrelenting hostility in high culture, he notes how others could struggle to account for China's glorious history and its fallen present state, and points out that popular culture could rescue some images. Memory was critical to either fate. China's image of the West, starting with Ricci's permission to proceed to Peking and present his map of the world to Emperor Wanli who learned of five continents and their races/cultures, was '... information ... largely forgotten by ... 1839' (Chen, 1979: 47).

The Chinese vigorously reciprocated the stereotyping engaging in massive national character generalisations of physically hideous and socially repulsive Westerners driven only by greed. Defeat at the hands of a derisory force of 10,000 British in 1839–1842 caused the Chinese to elevate the British to the superior Westerners. Accounting for their domination many Chinese internalised outsiders' critiques of China, a process intensified through the 19th century in a series of national humiliations, continuing after the overthrow of the Qing and the imperial examination systems, into the dramatic events of the early 20th century. A quest for explanation followed, exemplified by the provocative question, 'How did Europe achieve its magnificence and splendour?' (Chen, 1979: 71), posed by co-founder of the Chinese Communist Party and editor of the monthly *Youth Magazine*, later *New Youth* (1916–1919), Peking University Professor Chen Duxiu. This influential periodical circulated radical new nationalist and anti-traditional ideas of the New Culture and May 4th movements. The answer to the question was fatal for Confucian practice: Western success was due to cultural and personal restlessness, the reverse of passivity and reticence, the opposite of the Confucian injunction for order and harmony.

During the late Qing, ascendancy had long passed from the Catholic countries, with their deference to and domination of Rome, to the English-speaking nations, including newly born America, and while religion remained prominent, it had a new 'style' not so closely linked to cultural exchange, inventions and literature, but to commerce, 'free' trade and liberal political ideology. Most important though the change came with new judgments of China and its culture, and in turn China had cause to re-evaluate 'Westerners'.

Even new styles of interaction came up against old style ritual obstacles. Chinese dignity had always demanded outward acknowledgment of sovereignty. By the early 1900s, it was political rites rather than ancestor rites that lit a fuse of controversy, in collision not with Catholic observance but with British 'national standing' (Gelber, 2007: 182). Courtly culture demanded an obsequious display of hierarchy; British 'national standing' deplored the implied humiliation. Chinese insistence on ritual obeisance, especially the *koutou* (nine times prostration), infuriated both English and American legates (Spence, 1998). The Controversy was left behind but new controversies took its place.

The England that ruled the waves, aligned with precocious America, altered dramatically the nature of relations between China and the West. In these ways the China that the Protestant missionaries encountered was much weakened in both power and reputation, and made vulnerable because increasing numbers of American, English and French intellectuals expressed scepticism about the value or portability of its natural philosophy judged against new democratic yardsticks. Even as early as the 1830s the Qing empire 'had neither any clearly defined boundaries based on international agreements . . . . nor a law of nationality based on either *jus sanguinis* or *jus soli*' . . . a nation that could only be defined in cultural terms (Chen, 1979: 25).

The Taiping theocracy

An immense upheaval between 1850 and 1864 epitomises *in extremis* the volatile potential of cultural transfers whose new host soil differs radically from what it absorbs, in this case combining explosive political conflict with economic revolution, and underscores China's chaotic and reduced state.

Hong Xiuquan, convinced he was Jesus's younger brother requested by God to rid China of the foreigners (the Manchu rulers not the Westeners), styled his loyal followers the Taiping Heavenly Army. By 1853 he had seized Nanjing and created the Taiping New Jerusalem, holding out till 1864. In Spence's (1997) estimation nearly 20 million died before Hong's army itself perished. Sometimes unaccounted for because of its bizarre compound forms, the Taiping (uprising/rebellion/revolution) invites questions about culture, language, religion and violent political change. This extremely bloody uprising ushered in changes that defy consensus of interpretation. The history department of Fudan University and Shanghai Teacher's College (1976) in a *History of Modern China* volume offers what reads like an approved version. After the 1840 aggressive intrusion of 'foreign capitalism', the 'old feudal oppression' under imperial rule was compounded by the dealing in Opium during which 'the British invaders did a lot of looting and extorting' (Fudan University, 1976: 17), lauding Hong Xiuquan's opposition to Qing corruption as a nationalist rebellion of resistance. It quotes Mao Zedong approvingly on Hong as one of China's earliest progressives, and, incredibly, the text feels a need to explain who Confucius was, citing Hong's repudiation of the sage and treating his Christian conversion as dissembling and partial, essentially a preparation for the revolutionary cause of 'killing the evil to protect the righteous' and 'wiping out injustice among men' (Fudan University, 1976: 16).

This image of Hong as a rebel against capitalist-imperial aggression is much disputed. In Deng's reading (1971) Taiping was a destructive civil war led by a fanatical religious leader engaged in ethnic revolution, although he does acknowledge nationalist elements as noted by Sun Yat Sen. Deng cites Hu Shi's more muted evaluation: 'This Rebellion, led by a few peasant converts to some form of Protestant Christianity, was a curious mixture of peasant revolt, an anti-Manchu revolution, and a religious crusade of most terrible Christian iconoclasm', which aimed to overthrow the Qing and preach Christianity. According to Xu (2001) it was 'Chinese folk millennialism in a cloak of Christianity' (2001: 449).

For Spence (1997) the Taiping has two distinct phases: 'The first half … (1851–6) …. marked a proletarian revolutionary movement to overthrow the Manchu regime and replace it by a new nationalist government with a radical economic, social and cultural program'; the second half resembled a peasant rebellion for land with little knowledge of Christianity and slogans such as 'land to the tiller', 'down with Manchu devils' and 'language simplification'. Internal dissension, new leadership, betrayal and corrupt luxurious lifestyles led to the alienation of peasants, anti-Confucian slogans antagonised the scholar official class and strong nationalism alienated Western powers.

Motivated Adaptation

Perhaps the Taiping qualify as an example of catastrophic intercultural connections. According to Mungello (1999), intercultural connections are not devoid of such consequences; he argues for a continuous mutuality of the Chinese–West encounter in the 1500–1800 years, and documents this period for its political sectarian interests but claims that it remains a superior precedent for future China–West interaction to what followed. This judgment is largely due to the quality of reciprocation, adaptation and learning that the 1500–1800 encounters contain.

The mutuality of interests, in Mungello's estimation, involved Chinese literati who used Christianity to try to eject Buddhist and Daoist ideas from neo-Confucianism, and Enlightenment thinkers who used Confucianism to contest Christianity in European society and politics. He divides the European participants into three groups and assesses the seriousness of their engagement with China and the effects of their actions, a series of judgements consistent with Jensen's account (1997).

Missionaries: The most serious in study of China and depth of understanding, and quality of relations they forged. They were the most respectful of China's traditions and attained the most profound understanding of its traditions, owed largely to the mission philosophy of Valignano and its enactment by Ricci, later perverted by Bouvet and the Figurists.

Proto-Sinologists: A less focused interest among individuals located in Europe and dependent on the missionaries for information. These people had an eclectic interest and approach to China. They were the most disparate in their engagement: combining some superficial with many serious scholars.

Popularisers: The shallowest approach to China, using China to bolster domestic political and intellectual interests and agendas. Mungello locates the *philosphes* Voltaire and Diderot, here, as exploiters of available China knowledge to 'push barrows'.

The incursions and penetration of Chinese territory by militant trading powers produced recipes for rapid Westernisation. This is well represented by the controversial Hu Shi (1891–1962), prominent philosopher and writer, key language reformer and famous liberal, and active in the New Culture and May 4th movements. Influenced by the pragmatism of John Dewey while studying in US universities, he advocated major changes such as vernacular in place of classical Chinese and a general commitment to breaking the 'tyranny of the classics' (Fairbank, 1979). Hu Shi's Westernising claims disturb and antagonise not only cultural purists, but they also signify return into Chinese hands and agency of native, if hybridised, cultural constructions. At least this is the thesis of perhaps the most radical among the versions of this genre of conceptual interculturalism, Jensen's (1997) claim that the missionaries, and particularly Ricci, through use of translations and interpretations of the ancient *ru* scholar tradition, invented the presumably historical persona, since then globally endorsed and celebrated as China's pre-eminent ethicist and sage, Confucius. In this invention, Jensen believes, was manufactured Confucianism.

This 'over-interpretation', according to Rule (1999), is a radical extension of the underlying claim of the present chapter that emphasises the inseparability of motivation, and therefore of mutual influence in intercultural encounters. Jensen traces the mechanism of the manufacture of Confucius and the Jesuits' positioning of themselves as native proclaimers of his teaching: in effect transforming understandings of the repercussions of the missionary encounter. In this singular interpretation of the encounter, Chinese intellectuals, several in the 19th and several, especially Hu Shi, in the early 20th century, reconstituted a cosmopolitan culture for a new China by drawing on the Jesuitical depiction of Confucianism and Confucius.

Such appropriation and re-appropriation appears scandalous to cultural purists. Surely, though, its effects on post-colonial theorising, in which the sources and agents of cultural hybridity are not typically imagined to be proselytising Christian missionaries from a pre-industrial past, are as radical. Jensen's provocative thesis is that Ricci's substantive exploration of *ru* constructed a Chinese/Western joint entity, in a process of mutual interpretations and representations of traditional beliefs, which forged synthetic new forms for new audiences in new 'markets'. In this analysis, Ricci, 'the principal inventor of Confucius' (1997: 87), invented name and category, persona and teaching, for consumption and recognition of an alien tradition.

Other hands in other dress, Europeans and Chinese, religious and secular, politicians and philosophers, extended, elaborated and continued the manufacture, effecting a composite project of universal civilisation. To accomplish this Jensen must repudiate any view of the missionaries as guilty of inserting subversive or destabilising foreign doctrines into Chinese conceptual systems, asserting instead their essential status as a hybrid community (Jensen, 1997: 79–80) constructing an indigenous tradition for themselves, acting as 'native Chinese sectarians and as European men of science'.

Conclusion

In this depiction of a dialectical encounter of invention, appropriation and re-appropriation, inherited cultural designs are re-designed even in the process of comprehension, and they are transformed and confirmed with newly assigned meanings as they are applied to current circumstances and purposes. This kind of cultural authorship requires that Ricci become Chinese and relinquish much of the faith he had '*gone to China to propagate*' (Jensen, 1997: 282–283).

The purpose of this tale in an account of China today and its national investment in English is that intercultural meetings, and interpretations of their meaning, serve interests even in the process of gaining recognition, and engage in advocacy, even as they pursue understanding. The allegation of self-serving motivations is both true and beside the point, since all encounters spring from some measure of the self, and if they are sustained produce multidirectional influence. Specifically here we have seen how extended encounter with the deep cultural beliefs of others forged distinctively Chinese kinds of Western religiosity and in turn produced distinctively Western representations of Chinese moral science.

Serious language learning can resemble this kind of deep cultural practice, calling on and requiring personal meanings, identity formations and also social domains and institutions for the use and deployment of the learned communicative forms. These in turn circulate and validate the distinctive meanings of the learned system, its underlying signifiers (Wierzbicka, 2006), but in their applications, the signs that are made in discourse can be transformed and made local.

Obligatory and universal learning of English in today's China requires local settings for its use, produces domestic discourses for its understanding and stimulates local norms for its comprehension. The settings and institutions for the accomplishment of a Chinese domestication of English are analogous to the intercultural encounter around deep questions of belief that has been discussed here, and will quite probably generate similarly deep reverberating effects on its participants, teachers and learners, Chinese users and non-Chinese interlocutors.

Notes

1. *Life Magazine* ranks Ricci among the 'Top 100 People' of the 2nd millennium, placing him in the 68th position http://www.life.com/Life/millennium/people/01.html.
2. Young footnote p. 107: Hou Wailu, *Zhongguo sixiang tongshi*, A General History of Chinese Thought. Beijing, 1959–1960, IV, no 2, 1226–1240.

References

Aikman, D. (2005) *The Beijing Factor: How Christianity is Transforming China?* Oxford and Grand Rapids, MI: Monarch.
Battaglini, M. (2003) 'E finalmente ...': Matteo Ricci e La Tradizione Libraria Cinese. In F. Mignini (ed.) *Padre Matteo Ricci: L'Europa all Corte dei Ming* (pp. 47–57). Milan: Edizioni G. Mazzotta.

Blaut, J.M. (2000) *Eight Eurocentric Historians*. New York: Guildford.

Bollettino I. (n.d.) P. Matteo Ricci, S.J., Fondatore delle Missioni Cattoliche in Cina, Macerata, Italy Misericordiae.

Borthwick, M. (1998) *Pacific Century* (2nd edn). Boulder, CO: Westview Press.

Bresciani, U. (2001) *Reinventing Confucianism: The New Confucian Movement*. Taipei: Ricci Institute.

Chen (Ch'en), J. (1979) *China and the West*. Bloomington: Indiana University Press.

Chen, Y. (2004) *Christianity in Modern China*. Leiden and Boston: Brill.

Ching, J. (1976) *To Acquire Wisdom: The Way of Wang Yang-ming*. New York: Columbia University Press.

Ching, J. (1993) *Chinese Religions*. London: Macmillan.

Collani, von, C. (1994) Charles Maigrot's role in the Chinese rites controversy. In D.E. Mungello (ed.) *The Chinese Rites Controversy* (pp. 149–184). Nettelala: Steyler Verlag.

Cummins, J.S. (1993) *A Question of Rites: Friar Domingo Navarrete and the Jesuits in China*. Aldershot Hants: Scolar Press.

Cronin, V. (1999) *The Wise Man from the West*. London: Harvill.

De Bary, W.T. (1991a) *The Trouble with Confucianism*. Cambridge, MA: Harvard University Press.

De Bary, W.T. (1991b) *Learning for One's Self: Essays on the Individual in Neo-Confucian Thought*. New York: Columbia University Press.

Deng (Teng), S.Y. (1971) *The Taiping Rebellion and the Western Powers*. Oxford: Clarendon Press.

Dreyfus, P. (2004) *Mattèo Ricci: Le Jésuite qui Voulait Convertir la Chine*. Paris: Editions du Jubilé.

Du (Tu), W-M. (ed.) (1996) *Confucian Traditions in East Asian Modernity*. Cambridge: Harvard University Press.

Du (Tu), W-M. (2000) Multiple modernities … inquiry into the implications of East Asian modernity. In L.E. Harrison and S.P. Huntington (eds) *Culture Matters* (pp. 256–268). New York: Basic Books.

Duchesne, R. (2006) Asia first? *Journal of the Historical Society* 6 (1), 69–91.

Eco, U. (1997) *The Search for the Perfect Language*. London: Fontana.

Fairbank, J. (1979) *The United States and China*. Cambridge: Harvard University Press.

Frank, A.G. (1998) *ReOrient: Global Economy in the Asian Age*. Berkeley: University of California Press.

Fudan University (1976) *The Taiping Revolution 1851–1864*, History Department and Shanghai Teachers' College, Shanghai: People's Publishing House.

Fukuyama, F. (1992) *The End of History and the Last Man*. New York: Avon.

Gelber, H.G. (2007) *The Dragon and the Foreign Devils*. London: Bloomsbury.

Headley, J. (2008) *The Europeanization of the World; On the Origins of Human Rights and Democracy*. Princeton, NJ: Princeton University Press.

Hobson, J.M. (2004) *The Eastern Origins of Western Civilisation*. Cambridge: Cambridge University Press.

Jensen, L. (1997) *Manufacturing Confucianism*. Durham: Duke University Press.

Jinshi, L. (1994) Chinese literati and the rites controversy. In D.E. Mungello (ed.) *The Chinese Rites Controversy* (pp. 65–82). Nettelal, Germany: Steyler Verlag.

Kanamori, S. (1997) Christian Wolff's speech on Confucianism. *European Journal of Law and Economics* 4 (2–3), 299–304.

Kurfirst, R. (2001) John Stuart Mill's Asian parable. *Canadian Journal of Political Science* 34 (3), 601–619.
Landes, D. (1998) *The Wealth and Poverty of Nations*. New York: W.W. Norton.
Lach, D. (1953) The Sinophilism of Christian Wolff (1679–1754). *Journal of the History of Ideas* 14 (4), 561–574.
Leys, S. (1997) *The Analects of Confucius*. New York: Norton.
Li, T. (2001) *Chinese Renaissance*. In S. Uhalley and X. Wu (eds) *China and Christianity* (pp. 117–127). Armonk, NY: M.E. Sharpe.
Lundbaek, K. (1994) *Joseph Prémare and the name of God in China*. In D.E. Mungello (ed.) *The Chinese Rites Controversy* (pp. 129–149). Nettelal, Germany: Steyler Verlag.
McBrien, R.P. (1997) *Lives of the Popes*. San Francisco: Harper Collins.
McNamara, T. and Roever, C. (2006) *Language Testing: The Social Dimension*. London: Blackwell.
Malatesta, E.J. (1994) A fatal clash of Wills. In D.E. Mungello (ed.) *The Chinese Rites Controversy* (pp. 211–248). Nettelal, Germany: Steyler Verlag.
Mignini, F. (2003a) L'Europa di Matteo Ricci e l'Altro Mondo della Cina. In F. Mignini (ed.) *Padre Matteo Ricci: L'Europa all Corte dei Ming* (pp. 9–19). Milan: Edizioni G. Mazzotta.
Mignini, F. (ed.) (2003b) *Padre Matteo Ricci: L'Europa all Corte dei Ming*. Milan: Edizioni G. Mazzotta.
Mignini, F. (2004) *Matteo Ricci: Il Chiosco Delle Fenici*. Ancona, Italy: Il Lavoro Editoriale.
Mungello, D.E. (1977) *Leibniz and Confucianism*. Honolulu: University of Hawaii Press.
Mungello, D.E. (1994) *The Chinese Rites Controversy*. Nettelala: Steyler Verlag.
Mungello, D.E. (1999) *The Great Encounter of China and the West* (pp. 1500–1800). Lanham: Rowman and Littlefield.
Ostler, N. (2007) *Ad Infinitum: A Biography of Latin*. London: Walker.
Pagden, A. (2008) *Worlds at War: The 2,500 – Year Struggle between East and West*. Oxford: Oxford University Press.
Ricci, M. (1953) *China in the Sixteenth Century: The Journals of Matthew Ricci 1583–1610*. New York: Random House.
Ricci, M. (1598–2003) *Trattato Sull'Amicizia, Nanciam 1598* La Redazione, 0733.230660, July. Macerata, Italy: Bollettino Misericordiae.
Ricci, M. (2003) Le Religioni della Cina. In F. Mignini (ed.) *Padre Matteo Ricci: L'Europa all Corte dei Ming* (pp. 19–29). Milan, Italy: Edizioni G. Mazzotta.
Rule, P. (1994) Towards a history of the Chinese rites controversy. In D.E. Mungello (ed.) *The Chinese Rites Controversy* (pp. 249–267). Nettelal, Germany: Steyler Verlag.
Rule, P. (1999) Manufacturing Confucianism by Lionel M. Jensen, review article. *Journal of Chinese Religion* 27, 105–111.
Smith, R. (2001) Jesuit Interpretations of the Yijing … City University of HK and Beijing University, 13–16.10.2001. On WWW at http://cohesion.rice.edu/Humanities/asia/emplibrary/Jesuits%20and%20Yijing%20article%20061003.pdf. Accessed November 2007; March 2008.
Spence, J.D. (1974) *Emperor of China: Self-Portrait of K'ang-hsi*. London: Jonathan Cape.
Spence, J.D. (1984) *The Memory Palace of Matteo Ricci*. London: Faber.

Spence, J.D. (1997) *God's Chinese Son*. London: Flamingo (HarperCollins).

Spence, J.D. (1998) *The Chan's Great Continent, China in Western Minds* London: Penguin.

Spence, J.D. (1994) Claims and counter-claims, the Kangxi Emperor and the Europeans (1661–1722). In D.E. Mungello (ed.) *The Chinese Rites Controversy* (pp. 15–30). Nettelal, Germany: Steyler Verlag.

Spence, J.D. and Wills, J.E. (1979) *From Ming to Ching*. New Haven: Yale University Press.

Standaert, N. (2001) Christianity in late Ming and early Qing. In S. Uhalley and X. Wu (eds) *China and Christianity* (pp. 81–116). Armonk, NY: M.E. Sharpe.

Stark, R. (2006) *Victory of Reason: How Christianity Led to Freedom, Capitalism and Western Success*. New York: Random House.

Tucci, G. (1922) *Storia della Filosofia Cinese Antica*. Bologna, Italy: Zanichelli.

Tucci, G. (1958) *Le Grandi Vie di Comunicazione Europa-Asia*. Torino: Edizioni Radio Italiana. On WWW at http://www.giuseppetucci.isiao.it/index.cfm?ID=scritti.

Uhalley, S. and Wu, X. (eds) (2001) *China and Christianity*. Armonk, NY: M.E. Sharpe.

Wierzbicka, A. (2006) *English: Meaning and Culture*. Oxford: Oxford University Press.

Witek, J.W. (1994) Eliminating misunderstanding. In D.E. Mungello (ed.) *The Chinese Rites Controversy* (pp. 185–210). Nettelal, Germany: Steyler Verlag.

Witek, J.W. (2001) Christianity and China. In S. Uhalley and X. Wu (eds) *China and Christianity* (pp. 11–27). Armonk, NY: M.E. Sharpe.

Xu (Hsu), C-Y. (2001) Chinese encounters with other civilisations. *International Sociology* 16, 438–454.

Young, J.D. (1983) *Confucianism and Christianity: The First Encounter*. Hong Kong: Hong Kong University Press.

Young, J.D. (1994) Chinese views of rites and the rites controversy, 18th–20th centuries. In D.E. Mungello (ed.) *The Chinese Rites Controversy* (pp. 83–110). Nettelal, Germany: Steyler Verlag.

Zhang, K. (2001) Chinese perspective. In S. Uhalley and X. Wu (eds) *China and Christianity* (pp. 29–39). Armonk, NY: M.E. Sharpe.

Zhuo, X. (2001) 'Cultural Christians' in China. In S. Uhalley and X. Wu (eds) *China and Christianity* (pp. 283–300). Armonk, NY: M.E. Sharpe.

Zürcher, E. (1994) Jesuit accommodation and the Chinese cultural imperative. In D.E. Mungello (ed.) *The Chinese Rites Controversy* (pp. 31–64). Nettelal, Germany: Steyler Verlag.

Chapter 2
Sociocultural Contexts and English in China: Retaining and Reforming the Cultural Habitus

GAO YIHONG

Introduction

This chapter examines the development of English language learning in the People's Republic of China as part of the country's modernization process. The focus is on explicating the basic drives and dilemmas of English language learning considered in its sociocultural context. This development is traced from the establishment of the Confucian tradition of learning, through the introduction of foreign language education as part of 19th-century reform and the twists and turns of the 20th century, to the current situation at the beginning of the 21st century. The primary theoretical concepts drawn upon in this investigation are Bourdieu's notion of *habitus*, *capital* and *field*.

Bourdieu uses the term *habitus* to symbolize the system of durable, generative dispositions, which is historically acquired and embodied in the individual. The linguistic *habitus* is one of the forms of *habitus*.

> The linguistic *habitus* is a sub-set of the dispositions which comprise the *habitus*: it is that sub-set of dispositions acquired in the course of learning to speak in particular contexts (the family, the peer group, the school, etc.). These dispositions govern both the subsequent linguistic practices of an agent and the anticipation of the value that linguistic products will receive in other fields or markets. (Thompson, Introduction to Bourdieu, 1991: 17)

It is important to note that *habitus* is not a pure individual trait; it is always associated with a *field*. A field or *market* may be seen as a structured space of positions (Thompson, Introduction to Bourdieu, 1991: 17); it is the specific social context in which individuals act. A field is always the site of struggle in which people seek to maintain or alter the distribution of specific forms of *capital*. Bourdieu's notion of capital is an expansion on that of Marx, and includes the following forms: (1) the traditional type of economic capital; (2) social capital, referring mainly to institutional affiliation and relations; (3) cultural capital, which can be embodied (such as skill and knowledge); objectified (such as published books and articles) or institutional (such as degrees and qualifications; and (4) symbolic capital, which is an overarching category, an institutionally recognized and legitimated authority and an entitlement requisite for the exchange and conversion of cultural, economic and social capital. This can be prestige, status and reputation (Bourdieu, 1986). Taken together, the linguistic *habitus* is not a trait of 'competence'. As acquired dispositions, it is a response to its field or specific social context. At the same time, it is a form of embodied cultural capital, which can be transformed into other forms of capital, in a specific field or market.

While aware of the postmodernist assertion that basic sociolinguistic constructs such as 'language' and 'speech community' are 'invented' in an essentialist manner, ignoring the great variation within such terms (Makoni & Pennycook, 2007; Pennycook, 2007), such a radical stance has its own restricting as well as liberating influences (Walker, 2008). It is the author's view that concepts such as 'east' and 'west' cannot be easily dismissed as if they had no existence. A social constructivist perspective may still look at how material, institutional and psychological factors interact to construct cultural realities, while recognizing stable and general tendencies as well as changeability and variation. The discourses about languages, including widely adopted slogans, language policies, and academic and public discussions, with their embedded language ideologies (Blommaert, 2006), constitute part of such cultural realities for examining such phenomena. When applied to the concept of *habitus*, they provide great insight.

The chapter begins with a brief description of the Confucian tradition of learning and a historical review of foreign language education as part of China's modernization process, and then focuses on the current situation from the late 20th century to the first decade of the 21st century, presenting some issues of concern and controversy among government officials, scholars and the public. The learning of a foreign language involves acquiring a *habitus* that may be perceived to clash with the learners' first language *habitus*, and in the course of this review, it will be shown how this has generated prolonged identity anxiety among Chinese involved in learning English. The solution to easing this anxiety has been to nominate Western learning as *yong* (utility) only and thus to focus on the economic value of the language as capital. Yet, because there is always cultural *ti* (essence) embedded in linguistic *habitus*, attempts to separate *yong* from *ti* in the learning of English and other languages have not solved the problem. Instead, there has been a recurring *ti–yong* tension, which has highlighted the fundamental identity dilemma in China's English language education. Furthermore, in contemporary China, where English language education itself has developed into a semi-autonomous field in the context of globalization, the persistent *ti–yong* dilemma has acquired increased intensity and complexity. Thus the *ti–yong* relation is crucial to understanding Chinese cultural identities, language policies and language pedagogy.

The Confucian *Habitus* of Learning

The predominant school of thought in Chinese culture, and particularly education, for over 2000 years, Confucianism proposes a natural predisposition towards both external and internal learning functions or drives. The external refers to pragmatic acquisition of essential knowledge, whereas the internal refers to a natural drive towards the cardinal Confucian virtue 'benevolence' (仁 *ren*) – becoming the most genuine, sincere and humane self possible (Li, 2003; Li & Yue, 2004). These two forces coexist in the Confucian tradition, although their centrality in Confucian thought is not equal. To Confucius, to be truly human is to reach the internal state of *ren*, and this is what it means to become 'a sage' (君子 *junzi*), the highest level of being human. Learning is the pathway to sagehood and, in this sense, the process of learning is intrinsically rewarding. While internal moral cultivation remains the locus and focus of Confucian virtue, it is not in conflict with the external functions that learned people perform in society. Indeed, ideally, a person should become 'a sage within and a king without' (内圣外王 nei sheng wai wang).

In the centuries following Confucius' death, the Chinese nation was gradually consolidated, and by the start of the Han dynasty in 220BC, there was a great need for learned men to run the empire. At this time, learning in the form of study of the Confucian classics was institutionalized in a Civil Service Examination system, which lasted for over 2000 years before its abolition at the beginning of the 20th century. Open to scholars from all backgrounds, Confucian learning for these examinations created the conditions for social mobilization.

Foreign Language Learning in China: *Ti* versus *Yong*

Language education, essentially first language literacy, was perceived as important in the Confucian tradition mainly for its instrumental function in moral cultivation. The learning required to reach the state of *ren* was called 'the great learning' (大学 *daxue*), while the study of Chinese in its written form was called 'the small learning' or 'elementary learning' (小学 *xiaoxue*), most likely because language skills were what children first learned when they started their schooling. The commonly understood purpose of language study was to 'comprehend the classics and put their teaching into practice' (通经致用 *tongjing zhiyong*).

In Confucian learning, the external social aspect of 'governing the country' and the internal aspect of moral cultivation come together in the practice of rituals (礼 *li*). Rituals constitute part of a person's *habitus*, and the language functions and rhetorical practices in the rituals form part of their linguistic *habitus*. As people regulate their linguistic behaviour, aligning it with the forms acquired, they perfect their character, harmonize interpersonal relationships and achieve social stability. Thus language was a significant component of the Confucian *habitus*, as rhetoric carrying important moral and sociopolitical value and as excellence in writing, instrumentally essential for passing the Civil Service Examination.

One issue that Confucius and his contemporaries did not have to worry about was the learning of languages other than the native. It has been left for generations of their descendants to respond to the potential threat to the integrity of Chinese identity posed by the rituals embedded in another language.

Social Historical Context for Foreign Language Learning in China: *Ti* versus *Yong*

'The linguistic market is the site of forms of domination' (Bourdieu, 1991: 83). And, indeed, the initial impetus for China's learning of foreign languages came from the military, political and economic domination by foreign powers. It was set in motion by the Opium Wars (1840–1842), when the nation was invaded by Britain. Having considered China as the centre of the world for a long time, the government of the late Qing Dynasty had to realize painfully the nation's inferiority to the West, and the consequent necessity of learning from the West.

The initial result was the *Self-Strengthening Movement* (洋务运动 *yangwu yundong*) gradually launched between the 1860s and 1890s. As part of the movement, the government established an interpreter training institution, the 京师同文馆 *Jingshi Tongwenguan*, in 1862. From 1872, students were sent abroad to study science, technology and diplomacy. The goal of these initiatives is spelled out clearly in the *Historical Notes of the Qing Dynasty*:

> Facing the threat of solid ships and powerful canons of foreign powers, there is an urgent need for training specialists in translation, ship building, and the preparation of ground and naval forces. The first thing to do now is to establish schools for such purposes, including *Jingshi Tongwenguan*, …. (cited in Cheng, 2008)

The linguistic *habitus*, however, is not a simple 'competence' or production of utterances, but the product of social conditions (Bourdieu, 1993). Hence the linguistic *habitus* of native English speakers is shaped in its own cultural context. This *habitus* cannot be comfortably transported from its original field to a new field. While responding to the dominating Western cultures by learning their languages, a conflict between cultural identities was invoked, from which there emerged a strong need to defend the Chinese cultural identity. Following the Chinese tradition of separating internal essence and external utility, the government adopted the principle proposed by the official, Zhang Zhidong (1837–1909), 'Chinese learning for essence (*ti*); Western learning for utility (*yong*)'.

With China's defeat in the Sino-Japanese war of 1995, however, the formal Self-Strengthening Movement came to an end. In 1898, the *Jingshi Tongwenguan* was merged into the newly established 京师大学堂 *Jingshi Daxuetang* (the Supreme College of the Capital City), predecessor of the present Peking University. Courses taught at the *Daxuetang* included applied natural sciences, foreign languages and law. In this first modern university, applied disciplines took precedence over basic disciplines. Thus, despite efforts to keep the *yong* of foreign languages subordinate to the Chinese *ti*, the first 50 years of modernization ended with *ti* being overtaken by *yong* (Cheng, 2008: 8).

However, the *ti–yong* tension did not disappear. Instead, it has become a central issue in China's foreign language education in various historical periods. As description of China's English language education history has already been provided by many (Adamson, 2002; Hu, 2003; Lam, 2002; Wen & Hu, 2007; Yang, 2000; Zhao & Campbell, 1995), details will not be discussed here. Table 2.1 summarizes major historical periods concerning the status of English in China (adapted from Adamson, 2002: 233; Lam, 2002: 246).

Despite superficial differences in various periods, the *ti–yong* relationship recurs as a fundamental issue. With the exception of the revolutionary

Table 2.1 The historical status of English language in China

Period	Time	Historical background	Status of english	Ti–Yong relation	Characteristics of English education
Late Qing Dynasty	1861–1911	The two Opium Wars (1940s–1960s) brought great challenge and humiliation to China's ability of protecting itself against Western invasion	English as a vehicle for gaining access to Western science and technology; 'Learning the enemies' strengths in order to defeat them'	'Chinese learning for *ti* (essence); Western learning for *yong* (utility)'. Technological utility only	On the curriculum of institutions set up to facilitate transfer of scientific knowledge; after 1903, included on the curricula of secondary and tertiary institutions
The New Cultural Movement	1911–1923	The New Cultural Movement (1917–1923) launched criticism of the Confucian tradition and introduced various 'isms' from abroad; linguistic reform from classical Chinese to modern Chinese	English as a vehicle for exploring Western philosophy and other ideas	Western *ti* (schools of ideas/'isms') entered the scene of China's sociocultural transformation	On the curricula of secondary and tertiary institutions
The Republican Era	1924–1949	China aligned more with the West against Japan. The ruling party Guomindang sought for support from the US and followed the model of US education system	English as a vehicle for diplomatic, military and intellectual interaction with the West	Primarily *yong* (military, diplomatic, political utilities)	On the curricula of secondary and tertiary institutions

Continued

Table 2.1 Continued

Period	Time	Historical background	Status of english	Ti–Yong relation	Characteristics of English education
PRC before the Cultural Revolution	1949–1960	In the early 1950s, China was closely aligned with the Soviet Union against the West, but the Sino–Soviet relationship broke in the late 1950s	The status of English declined while that of Russian was boosted. The trend was reversed in the late 1950s	Status of *yong* fluctuated. English fell out of favour for political reasons; later considered valuable for modernization	On the curricula of very few secondary and tertiary institutions in the 1950s. Promoted on the curricula of secondary and tertiary institutions in the early 1960s
PRC during the Cultural Revolution	1966–1976	A radical political movement to re-establish class struggle. Education in general suffered greatly	English was associated with imperialism and capitalism; Western learning was repudiated	If any *yong* at all, as an instrument of political propaganda	Removed from the curricula of secondary and tertiary institutions; later restored rather sporadically
PRC Reform Era	1978 onwards	Economic reform and development; transformation from planned economy to market economy; China entered WTO	English seen as an essential instrument for modernization	Great value of *yong*; as an instrument for economic development	Strongly promoted on the curricula of secondary and tertiary institutions. Commonly adopted in urban elementary schools

period of The New Cultural Movement in the early part of the last century (the evaluation of which has generated continuous debate), government concern during most periods has been to promote the instrumental value of foreign languages and to attempt to keep out the foreign essential cultural values to the greatest extent possible. Decision-making concerning foreign language education policy has centred around the specific purposes the instrument serves at the time – military, political, economic or technical.

The particular foreign language favoured and the extent of resources put into its acquisition varied accordingly. Yet there is an underlying conceptual framework throughout, which holds language learning as dual in nature – involving a *yong* that is separable from the *ti*. Conceived thus, it was reasoned that foreign languages could be imported for practical purposes without their cultural essence being involved, and hence the language learning would not cause cultural *ti* conflict or identity loss. Through years of continual enactment, the *ti–yong* dualism and the valorization of *yong* over *ti* have been internalized and have become a fundamental disposition of the Chinese foreign language learning *habitus*.

Yet what has not been fully realized or willingly acknowledged by the Chinese government at least is that *ti* is embodied in the dispositions that make up a linguistic *habitus*. Anyone learning a language for any reason is bound to respond to the dispositions contained within it. Thus the clash in *ti* between China and the West has been tacitly but painfully felt by the Chinese government, teachers and learners alike and has become a haunting issue in the field of foreign language education.

The *Ti–Yong* Dilemma in English Education in Today's Market Economy Society

In the contemporary era of reform, where the *yong* is geared particularly to economic needs and the value of English as a form of economic capital is highlighted, the *ti–yong* dilemma persists. China's current economic reform started in the late 1970s, by which time the national matriculation examination was also restored. In the early 1980s, a pass in final year high school English became a prerequisite for university entrance. Since 1999, Chinese tertiary education has been expanding and the number of undergraduate students has increased at a rate of 8% each year. The competition among college graduates in the job market has subsequently intensified.

Among graduates who obtained employment in 2005, three kinds of enterprises involving foreigners – foreign enterprises, joint ventures and cooperatively run enterprises (三资企业*san zi qiye*) – offered the highest starting salaries (Yang, 2006). Graduating students with competence in their own discipline plus good English skills are more likely to find employment than those who lack such skills. Attracted by the chance to get a job, and by the high salaries in foreign-related enterprises, students are motivated to achieve a good command of English, especially in listening and speaking.

Too Much Time, Too Little Efficiency

At a 1996 conference in Beijing on the teaching of English in China, the Vice Premier of the State Council, Li Lanqing, stated that urgent improvement in the English proficiency of Chinese people in general was not an *educational* issue per se, but an issue pertaining to China's modernization. In a similar vein, in 1998, the Ministry of Education official in charge of foreign language education, Cen Jianjun, spelled out the economic significance of English education in the eyes of the Chinese government:

> Foreign language teaching is not a simple issue of teaching. It bears direct influence on the development of China's science, technology, and economy, and the improvement of the quality of reform. (Cen, 1998, cited in Cai, 2006: 3–4)
>
> If a nation's foreign language proficiency is raised, it will be able to obtain information of science and technology from abroad and translate it into the native language. Ultimately this will be turned into production force. (Cen, 1998, cited in Cai, 2006: 3)

Determined to turn the cultural capital of English knowledge and skills into economic capital, the Chinese Government has since then constantly increased its investment in English education. In January 2001, in its document 'Guidelines for Promoting English Teaching in Elementary Schools', the Ministry of Education stipulated that the threshold of compulsory English learning be lowered by four years, from the first year of junior high school to grade 3 in elementary school. In August 2001, the document 'Guidelines for Improving Teaching for University Undergraduate Students' was issued, which called for a gradual increase of English as an alternative medium of instruction at tertiary level.

In his 1996 speech, Vice Premier Li [a fluent speaker of English himself] had also said that it was a common problem with English language education in China that it was 'taking too much time and achieving fairly low efficiency'. Two years later, Cen Jianjun raised the problem that, despite the government's zeal, China's English language education was not producing the hoped for goods:

> The disparity between China's foreign language education and development of the economy, science and technology is becoming increasingly great every year. … The speed of reform is seriously hampered due to the overly low foreign language proficiency of our university students. (Cen, 1998, cited in Cai, 2006: 3–4)

Encapsulated in the phrase 'too much time, too little efficiency' (费时低效*feishi dixiao*), Li Lanqing's charge has impacted heavily on China's English language education circles and has generated considerable heated and unresolved debate to this day among government officials, scholars, teachers and learners over the quality of English language teaching and learning in China.

Evaluation of English Education in China: Efficient or Inefficient?

The debate over proficiency and efficiency in the practice of English teaching began immediately after Vice Premier Li's conference statement, appearing in the official intellectual newspaper, 光明日报 *Guangming Daily*.

In March 1999, another official newspaper *China Youth Daily* published a group of articles written by English educators, which supported the government view and compared English education in China to 'a kettle of half-warm water that cannot be brought to the boil' (Jing, 1999). Top academic journals such as *Foreign Language Teaching and Research, Foreign Language World* and *Foreign Languages* also joined in the discussion (Guan & Wei, 2003; Pang *et al.*, 2002). 'Too much time, too little efficiency' became established as a fact, based on which efforts were then made to search for causes and solutions. Among the targets, the 'Band 4' and 'Band 6' College English Tests – national standards required for a bachelor degree in any subject other than English as a major – came in for a great deal of criticism, as did 'College English' teaching centred on these standard tests (e.g. Su, 2004; Wang, 2004; Zhu & Yang, 2004). It was claimed that such tests have tied learners to mechanical multiple-choice skills, but failed to direct their attention to communicative competence, resulting in job seekers who have only 'deaf and dumb English'.

However, at a forum on 'College English Reform' held in 2003 by the Research Association of College Foreign Language Teaching, China's English education specialists made a strong claim that the College English teaching and learning of the past 20 years had been a great success and that the 'deaf and dumb' charge was unfair (Zhu & Yang, 2003, Summary Report). Statistics and detailed facts were provided to show the 'substantial developments' and 'extraordinary achievements created under extremely hard conditions' (Zhu & Yang, 2003, Summary Report: 7–8). These showed, for example, that the sole College English standard of the 1970s was a reading rate of approximately 17 words per minute, whereas 20 years later standards comprised a reading rate of 70–90 words per minute, plus skills in listening, speaking, writing and translating (Zhu & Yang, 2003, Summary Report: 7–8).

The experts involved held that reform in English language teaching (ELT) had to follow two principles: first, contextual reality has to be taken into consideration, such as the great linguistic difference between Chinese and English, the lack of target language culture in the learners' environment and the shortage of teaching resources compared with social demands. Second, ELT is a science. Those so-called visions for the future that overlooked reality were not 'scientifically based perspectives'. 'Pedagogical principles based on such views can never meet their claimed goals. Indeed, they could create chaos and bring damage to English education at the tertiary level' (Zhu & Yang, 2003, Summary Report: 7). Formal papers stating these views were also published in major journals (e.g. Hu, 2002), and were praised in ELT academic circles as 'independent thinking' and 'not just following the trend' (Hu Wenzhong in the preface to Hu Zhuanglin, 2008: viii).

The question of 'efficient' or 'inefficient' teaching is only meaningful when made relevant to specific goals. In China's context, the goal was for all university students to master English as an instrument for economic modernization or, in terms of Bourdieu, for the accumulation of economic capital. To some such as this author, the 'too much time and too little efficiency' blame has overtones of the slogan 'greater amount, faster speed, better quality, and less expenditure' (多快好省 *duo kuai hao sheng*), a principle for building socialism proposed in the Great Leap Forward Movement in the late 1950s, the goal of which turned out to be ridiculously unrealistic. The eagerness for quick success and immediate profits in contemporary English teaching and learning is very similar.

Objective of English Teaching and Learning: Utilitarianism or Humanism?

Before the 1980s, the objective of English language education at the tertiary level was quite simple and clear, that is, to train those people with good skills in listening, speaking, reading, writing and translating so as to undertake practical tasks such as translation and interpretation. In the

1980s, this objective underwent a change, as the developing economic needs required people who could directly work in English, without a translator or interpreter. As it was joked about at that time, it took three people to write an international newspaper story: one to do the writing, one to drive the car and the other to interpret the language. The moral of the story was that China's ELT should produce three-in-one learners, where the practical roles of reporter, chauffeur and interpreter could be played by a single individual, 'for economy and efficiency' (Xu, 1985/1990: 6). When addressing the 1996 conference in Beijing, Vice Premier Li Lanqing stated that the objective of English language education was to produce 'composite talents' (复合型人才 *fuhexing rencai*), which meant a combination of English language skills plus knowledge in specific fields such as business, law and medicine. Under this official guideline, many universities started to develop programmes and courses that were 'composite' in nature, such as 'Business English' and 'International Law'. Some universities were restructured and renamed institutions of 'foreign languages and international trade'. The composite-programme development was particularly popular in southern cities such as Guangzhou and Shanghai, which took the lead in China's economic growth.

Yet the composite programmes encountered practical difficulties as well as intellectual resistance. For one thing, due to limited time span and the shortage of personnel competent in both English and other disciplines, some 'composite programmes' turned out to be half-cooked and fell short of their claimed objectives. For another, the instrumental nature of English in the 'composite' was resented by scholars, who held that language learning should be a part of 'liberal education'. Such intellectual resistance was particularly strong in some universities in Beijing, where 'culture' was a big concern in general, and English education had a literary-oriented tradition.

Hu Zhuanglin (2002), previous Dean of the English Department at Peking University, challenged the curriculum reform of English majors by asking such very pointed questions as: 'Where will interpreters for government officials and the UN come from? Who will translate the works of Shakespeare, Dickens and Mark Twain into Chinese? Who will translate the works of Li Bai, Du Fu and Lao She into English?' His younger colleague Cheng Zhaoxiang (2002), department Dean at the time, argued in a more formal and conceptualized paper published in *World Englishes* that English departments in Chinese universities should foster 'humanistic education'.

Likewise, in an article entitled 'Utilitarianism and humanism in foreign language education', Zhang Zhongzai (2003), a senior scholar from Beijing University of Foreign Studies, criticized the tendency of foreign language education in contemporary China for focusing on 'instrument making' rather than the 'education of persons'. While both Japan and China sent students abroad to study in the late 19th century, according to Zhang, Japanese students learned humanities as well as natural sciences, whereas Chinese students concentrated on technical subjects only. This resulted in 'Japan's gradual prosperity and China's gradual decline'. Zhang warned that 'China will pay dearly for ignoring the humanistic nature of education'.

'Composite talent' can be seen as the expression of extreme utilitarian-ist, or *yong*-centred disposition. The embodied cultural capital of English skills, included in the compartmentalized 'talent', is to be quickly converted to economic capital. However, the oppositional 'liberal' or 'humanistic' English education is yet to be scrutinized. It seems to the present author that, in principle and practice, 'liberal' or 'humanistic' English has been very much modelled on English education in Britain and the United States, where Chinese culture has little place. This can be seen from the curriculum design of English majors in most Chinese universities, where few, if any, courses on Chinese culture are offered when compared with the large number of courses concerning English-speaking cultures.

'Liberal' or 'humanistic' English also shows up in various institutional discourses, mostly less formal than published academic works, such as discussions of departmental meetings on curriculum and teaching eval-uation. The potential clash between or integration of Western *ti* and Chinese *ti* has not been properly resolved, nor even seriously addressed in China's ELT.

English Learning and Chinese Identity: National Shame or Patriotism?

The issue of cultural identity largely unattended to by scholars is enthu-siastically picked up by ordinary learners. One such public outcry was the call for rejection of Christmas celebrations made by 10 young PhD candi-dates from top Chinese universities, who in December 2006 wrote an arti-cle entitled 'Transcend Cultural Collective Unconscious, and Promote the Agency of Chinese Culture – Our view of Christmas celebrations', which was posted on various major news websites.

It said:

> In China, the status of Western culture has changed from a drizzle to a tempest, and its most prominent manifestation is the gradual popu-larization of Christmas celebrations. … This phenomenon reveals the Chinese have fallen into a cultural collective unconscious, … and its fundamental reason is Chinese culture's loss of subjectivity and degra-dation of agency.

When interviewed, one leading proponent said they meant to 'awaken the Chinese people to resist the expansion of Western culture' (新民 Xinmin website, 2006). Public response to this call was mixed. A poll on sina.com shows that among 17,334 respondents, 54% agreed that celebrating Christmas was a sign of the invasion of Western culture, 30% thought that it was only a lifestyle for relaxation that had nothing to do with cultural invasion and 17% did not care (新民 Xinmin website, 2006).

Debates on English learning have also been carried out on internet forums. Mostly using pseudonyms, netizens have expressed contradictory feelings and attitudes. There have been attacks launched against the perceived 'learning of English by the entire nation'. Apart from the complaint that the learning consumes too many resources, there is the claim that English learning reduces the national self-esteem of the Chinese. Some have held that English learning reveals a Chinese national characteristic of self-despising.

> Only slaves need to learn their masters' language! It seems that the slave character traits (of the Chinese) have not changed! (Jianke)

> Foreign language – a language that subjugates our nation. (Zhoubapi)

Among those who hold counter-arguments, there are some who take a radical cultural stance but an instrumental view of the nature of language, citing those from the Westernization Movement of the 19th century:

> Learning English is a necessary path for the vitalization of our nation. This is because one has to understand his rivals in order to conquer them. 'Learning the strengths of the enemies so as to conquer them' – this is true by all means!!!! (Chengaogong)

Adapting a speech by Gao Zhendong, a university president from Taiwan once wrote:

> The learning of English by Chinese people is a national shame; it is the most lamentable behavior in China. However, we cannot afford not to learn, because we are behind others; we are overpowered by the cannon and sciences of our 'enemies.' ... Therefore, we should learn English with clenched teeth! (Hubiantongzhi)

Still there are others who embrace an open attitude:

> I have studied English for 20 years. ... Now I've become fully aware that learning the English language is only a means and a process, the

essence of which is learning a new culture, just as in Tang Dynasty, people from other countries came to China to learn Chinese culture.

I don't think the craze for English learning in the entire nation is bad in any sense, if that learning is out of people's own will. In every historical period, there are bound to be some movements that draw the passion of the entire populace. This is a normal phenomenon in any existing culture. (Can't be true)[1]

The above issues of debate are informative about China's English language education in several respects. First of all, they provide a glimpse of the intensified *ti–yong* clash. While the claim of 'inefficiency' and the aim for 'composite talents' imply an obsession with the utility of the language as economic capital, 'learning English with clenched teeth' reveals the cultural psychological complex that is deeply rooted in a nation whose modernization process started from foreign invasion. Secondly, the debates reveal the increased degree of autonomy of China's ELT as a 'field'.

Compared to the beginning stage of the Tongwenguan, when foreign language education was entirely submerged in macro-level social needs, China's contemporary ELT has gained more autonomy as a mediating space, where forces from the government are transferred, buffered or resisted. Distinct sub-fields have been formed, including state-owned mainstream education as against the private commercial enterprises, the academic versus the official, formal school setting versus the learner public gathered via the new media such as internet forums.

This field is a site of struggle where multiple voices compete and are in dialogue. Thirdly, perhaps paradoxically, although the principle of 'Chinese learning as *ti*, Western learning as *yong*' persists, the cultural themes that are under discussion and targets of reference are mostly Western in the conventional sense. The position variations are mainly for or against such given propositions or facts, how closely given standards are followed, as shown in scholars' call for 'humanistic education' and learner resistance to Christmas celebrations. The development of an agency in forming China's autonomous field of ELT still has a long way to go.

Yu Minhong's Story: 'Godfather for Studying Abroad'

In China's field of ELT, the identity transformations of some in the younger generation, or the public perception of such transformations, deserve special attention. For them, the process of English learning and use is assumed to involve instrumental motivation on the one hand, and the strengthening of native cultural identity on the other. In other words, they seem to incarnate the *ti–yong* ideal in a contemporary manner. In the author's opinion, however, this seeming integration conceals unsolved cultural identity conflicts. The case to be analysed in this section is that of Yu Minhong, director of a private English teaching enterprise, The New Oriental School.

Yu Minhong used to be a poor peasant boy. His sole dream was to get out of the countryside and obtain an 'iron rice bowl', or guaranteed income. After failing twice in the college entrance exams, he managed to pass and gained admission to Peking University in the early 1980s; and on graduation he was recruited to the faculty of the University's English Department. Yu was not able to obtain a visa for going abroad, and so in order to realize this dream in the future, in his spare time he started teaching English to those wanting to take the American university entrance Test of English as a Foreign Language (TOEFL). Failing to reach agreement with his department over his use of university equipment and each party's share of profit from his training programme, Yu resigned from the university and started up on his own. He began teaching for free, and after a while began charging fees. The story goes that he walked from street to street in the freezing cold carrying a bucket of paste for putting up posters for his first English classes.

In 1993, his 'New Oriental School' was formally established, with fewer than 30 students. By the end of 1995, however, the number of students trained by New Oriental had reached 15,000, and by the end of 2006, the number had soared to 4 million (New Oriental website). New Oriental's courses expanded from TOEFL and the American postgraduate entry test, the Graduate Record Exam to local tests such as the Band 4 and Band 6 College English tests, and included consultations on going abroad and running kindergarten English courses. In 2004, the School began taking over the teaching of Band 4 in some universities, which had usually only been undertaken within the college English framework (Benla, 2004). Indeed, the New Oriental became the largest and richest non-state-owned English training institution in China. In a media-run public survey, Yu was named one of the 'Top 10 People Who Have Influenced Chinese Society in the 21st Century' and earned the title of 'godfather for studying abroad' (Zhou, 2003).

Yu Minhong has gone through a number of major transformations: from a peasant boy in a remote Jiangsu village whose biggest dream was to change his peasant identity and obtain an 'iron bowl,' to the president of a famous school; from a poor university instructor, to a private enterprise owner resigned from the university, and then to being 'godfather for studying abroad' with tens of thousands of students over China, Europe and North America; from a small training class with two students and a room of 10 square meters, to a 'foreign language training aircraft carrier' constituting 80% of the market in Beijing and 50% of the market in China; from a private school with investment less than 200 thousand *yuan*, to an educational enterprise with a total capital as high as 50 billion *yuan*. While creating the 'legend of the New Oriental', Yu Minhong has also created his own legendary life. (Zhou, 2003: 8)

Moral of the Stories: Accumulation of Capital and Enhancement of Self-esteem

In the eyes of Chinese English learners, Yu demonstrates that learning English means the accumulation of various kinds of capital (Bourdieu, 1991). First, he is seen as a successful learner of English, thereby embodying the cultural capital of English skills. Second, he has accumulated a great deal of economic capital by developing an English teaching enterprise. Third, he is perceived as possessing an enormous amount of symbolic capital – prestige, status and reputation as a high achiever rapidly moving up the social ladder. In a sense, his story parallels the Abraham Lincoln log cabin to White House myth. Through such models – another would be Li Yang of 'Crazy English' fame, reported in Chapter 11 of this volume – Chinese learners perceive the possibility for their dreams of personal success to come true.

Yu's transformed identities – from failure to success, from poor peasant boy to billionaire – are characteristic of a 'self-esteem personality' (Xu, 1999). Matching Maslow's theory of basic human needs with a Marxist classification of social development, Xu claims that while China undergoes the social change from planned to market economy, the personality for the majority is being transformed from a 'belonging personality' centred on belonging needs to a 'self-esteem personality' centred on self-esteem needs. The latter is characterized by an 'enterprising life attitude, independence and awareness of human rights, competitive spirit, a strong sense of efficiency, and cooperative work style' (Xu, 1999: 3). The first four of these are typically seen in Yu Minhong's 'New Oriental Spirit', which exhorts learners to 'seek the extraordinary, challenge the limit, find hope amid despair, create a glorious life!' (The New Oriental School, 2003: 91). As English examinations have become a powerful mechanism of social stratification, overturning the egalitarianism in the pre-reform era (Yan, cited in Xu, 2004), English learning provides tangible opportunities for upwards social mobility. As a symbol of success, Yu has, indeed, achieved great efficiency and wasted no time, yet he has done this primarily by transforming English skills into economic capital, rather than through acquiring the skills themselves. For individual learners, the accumulation of various forms of capital constitutes their development towards a 'self-esteem personality' or success-driven self.

Problem of the Stories: Carriage of the Orient – the Cow or the Horse?

Yu appeals to his followers with calls for patriotic English learning (as does Li Yang of Crazy English). His English school is named 'The New Oriental' and is well known for its campus humour such as 'When China becomes powerful, we will use a Chinese TOEFL to test Americans' and 'Announcement of change – those who take the Chinese TOEFL will have to do it using the Chinese [calligraphy] brush' (Huang *et al.*, 2004; Lu, 2002). When the Chinese embassy in the former Yugoslavia was bombed by NATO in 1999, some university students withdrew from their pre-paid TOEFL tests and classes at the New Oriental as a patriotic act of protest. The New Oriental then put up a 'small character poster' on Peking University campus, among an ocean of protesting posters. It urged students to go back to English classes and tests because 'only when you have mastered English can you make China strong!'

As is evident, the 'self-esteem' of the individual is to be associated with a group identity – the esteem of being a Chinese. Using instrumental mastery of English as an index of self-esteem, or cultural capital, is simple, reasonable and clever, yet the potential clash between different *habita* and the basis for their reconciliation are notably absent from the ideas propagated by the New Oriental. This may explain why, compared to a large general pool of Chinese university students, New Oriental students manifested higher changes in both 'self-confidence' and 'cultural identity split' when surveyed (Huang *et al.*, 2004).

In the foreword of a book about its history, the New Oriental is portrayed as an 'Oriental horse-drawn carriage' (东方马车 *dongfang mache*):

> China is a clumsy, strolling cow; the West is a vigorous, galloping horse. In learning from the West, it is not enough for China just to import the horse's hooves. Only when the brains, eyes, and bones ... of the horse are all acquired, can China – the carriage of the Orient – complete its voyage of modernization on bumpy roads. (Lu, 2002)

Here the carriage – China as well as its epitome, The New Oriental School – returns to its recurrent yet intensified *ti–yong* dilemma. The image of a cow adopting the organs of a horse captures the difficulty of *habitus* transformation. Yet what is not visualized is the identity the cow will have acquired once the brain, eyes, bones as well as the hooves of the horse have been attached to its body. The economic success of Yu Minhong was so efficient on the ELT market, and the 'patriotic' jokes so hearty, while satisfying esteem needs and helping in the discharge of nationalistic sentiment, that the unresolved *ti* conflicts tend to be concealed. The English learners perceived to be high-achieving and patriotic may yet be left struggling to plant their feet on any cultural base.

Conclusion

China has never been a 'language free community' (Makoni & Pennycook, 2007: 14). On the contrary, languages are at least perceived to have essential roles to play in cultural identity maintenance and change. English language education has been influenced by Chinese cultural traditions, historical contact with the West and the contemporary socioeconomic transformation from planned to market economy. The Confucian *habitus* of learning embraced the tension between external and internal functions of learning. Throughout history, this tension has been retained and manifested in the field of ELT as a *ti–yong* dilemma and, for individual learners, as cultural identity conflicts. Such dilemmas are intensified in contemporary China, as the need for English skills increases with economic growth.

China's modern history, and hence English language education, began with the nation's semi-colonization, which was a great social psychological trauma as well as a political one. The national identity was violently shaken, but not completely shattered. The *ti–yong* conceptualization was intended to empower the nation and restore identity integrity while facing the 'solid ships and powerful cannons' of the West. Sociohistorically situated, the *ti–yong* tension has embedded in it a profound inferiority–superiority complex, which has become a part of the Chinese *habitus* and generates repeated practice.

Embedded in the *ti–yong* conceptualization is a fixed, essentialistic view of culture, which might have become outdated. Such a disposition explains the persistent ambivalence in attitudes towards English learning, and the lack of true mutuality when relating to other cultures as already noted (Orton, 2005). Had China never been invaded by the West and not fallen into a semi-colonial state, English learning in China would probably embrace the target culture of its language learning with a more open heart and mind.

On the other hand, had China been entirely occupied and become a full colony of the West, the struggle for linguistic and cultural identity would probably have developed along the lines of full resistance to the colonizer's language, or resulted in a local variety of English becoming established, as in countries within the 'outer circle' of world English (Kachru, 1992). In either case, the *ti–yong* tension might not have been so acute.

The identity dilemma of China's English education may have some broader implications. Second language education around the globe in a post-colonial and post-modern era has perceived English as a 'world language' with variations in different circles (Kachru, 1992). From a social constructivist perspective in particular, learners in conventional 'EFL' contexts will mostly aim at membership in varied global communities rather than in a fixed target culture of native speakers (Ryan, 2006).

The essentialist cultural *ti* can be critically deconstructed, and a multiplicity of new identities can be shaped. Some have even argued that English is altogether a 'post-identity language' (see Lo Bianco, 2005). These visions certainly open up new possibilities for identity development in second language education. Nevertheless, the haunting issue of the cultural identity dilemma cannot be readily dissolved by these new possibilities. It should be kept in mind that a *habitus* is grounded in its sociohistorical context and is durable; it will not easily diminish as the power disparity between nations remains. Transformations can be brought about, but within limits (Bourdieu, 1993).

For the Chinese, the *ti–yong* dilemma, the recurrent themes of a clash between *ti* and ambivalent attitudes towards English are deeply rooted in history, and have formed a psychological complex transmitted down through generations. Current and future generations of Chinese language policy makers, educators and learners are destined to struggle for creative solutions to this persistent identity dilemma.

Acknowledgments

Special thanks to Dr Peter Gu and Dr Guangwei Hu, whose suggestions initiated this chapter, and to Dr Jane Orton, Dr Jin Li and Professor Gao Yuan for their insightful comments. An earlier version of the chapter was published in *The Journal of Chinese Sociolinguistics* 2005 (2), 60–83.

Note

1. The above citations of internet discussion are from the forum Guantian Chashe at Tianya Xuni Shequ, www.tianyaclub.com, 2004.

References

Adamson, B. (2002) Barbarian as a foreign language: English in China's schools. *World Englishes* 21 (2), 231–243.

Benla (2004) 大学英语教学嫁接英语培训 Daxue yingyu jiaoxue jiajie yingyu peixun [College English teaching married with English training]. 新京报 *Xin Jing Bao (New Beijing Daily)*, 17 March.

Blommaert, J. (2006) Language policy and national identity. In T. Ricento (ed.) *An Introduction to Language Policy: Theory and Method* (pp. 238–254). Malden: Blackwell.

Bourdieu, P. (1986) The form of capital. In J.G. Richardson (ed.) *Handbook of Theory and Research for the Sociology of Education* (pp. 241–258). New York: Greenwood Press.

Bourdieu, P. (1991) *Language and Symbolic Power* (J.B. Thompson, ed.; G. Raymond and M. Adamson, trans.). Cambridge: Cambridge University Press.

Bourdieu, P. (1993) *Sociology in Question* (R. Nice, trans.). London: Sage.

Cai, J.G. (2006) 大学英语教学：回顾、反思和研究 *Daxue Yingyu Jiaoxue: Huigu, fansi he yanjiu [ELT at Tertiary Level in China: Review, Reflection and Research].* Shanghai: Fudan University Press.

Cheng, Z.X. (2002) English departments in Chinese universities: Purpose and function. *World Englishes* 21 (2), 257–267.

Cheng, Z. (2008) Plenary speech at the Symposium on the Development of Foreign Language Education Programs in Peking University, Beijing, 4 January.

Guan, X.H. and Wei, Z.Z. (2003) 大学英语教学效率研究 Daxue yingyu jiaoxue xiaolu yanjiu [Research on teaching efficiency of college English]. 辽宁工学院学报 *Liaoning Gongxueyuan Xuebao [Journal of Liaoning Institute of Technology]* (2003) (5), 49–53.

Hu, W.Z. (2003) A matter of balance – reflections on China's language policy in education. In W.Z. Hu (ed.) *ELT in China 2001* (pp. 107–127). Beijing: Foreign Language Teaching and Research Press.

Hu, Z.L. (2002) 中国英语教学中的 "低效" 问题 Zhongguo yingyu jiaoxue zhong de 'dixiao' wenti [The 'low efficiency' issue in China's ELT]. 国外外语教学 *Guowai Waiyu Jiaoxue [Foreign Language Teaching Abroad]* (4), 3–7.

Hu, Z.L. (2008) 英语教育自选集 *Yingyu Jiaoyu Zixuanji [Self-Selected Essays on ELT].* Beijing: Foreign Language Teaching and Research Press.

Huang, Q.H., Zhou, L. and Gao, Y.H. (2004) "新东方" 学员英语学习动机与自我认同变化 'Xindongfang' xueyuan yingyu xuexi dongji yu ziwo rentong bianhua [Motivation types and self-identity changes among New Oriental School trainees]. 中国社会语言学 *Zhongguo Shehui Yuyanxue [Journal of Chinese Sociolinguistics]* 3, 51–63.

Jing, S.H. (1999) 英语教学是壶烧不开的水 Yingyu jiaoxue shi hu shaobukai de shui. ELT is a kettle of half-warm water that cannot be brought to the boil. 中国青年报 *China Youth Daily*, 10 March.

Kachru, B. (1992) *The Other Tongue: English across Cultures* (2nd edn). Urbana: University of Illinois Press.

Lam, A. (2002) English in education in China: Policy changes and learners' experiences. *World Englishes* 21 (2), 245–256.

Li, J. (2003) The core of Confucian learning. *American Psychologist* 58, 146–147.

Li, J. and Yue, X.D. (2004) Self in learning among Chinese children. *New Directions for Child and Adolescent Development* 104, 27–43.

Lo Bianco, J. (2005) No longer a (foreign) language: The rhetoric of English as a post-identity language. *The Journal of Chinese Sociolinguistics* (2), 17–40.

Lu, Y.G. (2002) 东方马车-从北大到新东方的传奇 *Dongfang Mache – Cong Beida Dao Xindongfang de Chuanqi* [*The Oriental Carriage – The legend from Peking University to the New Oriental*]. Beijing: Guangming Daily Press.

Makoni, S. and Pennycook, A. (2007) *Disinventing and Reconstituting Languages*. Clevedon: Multilingual Matters.

The New Oriental School (2003) 新东方精神 *Xindongfang Jingshen* [*The New Oriental Spirit*]. Training handbook for students of the New Oriental School.

Orton, J. (2005) English and identity in China: An engaged native speaker's perception. *The Journal of Chinese Sociolinguistics* (2), 41–59.

Pang, J.X., Zhou, X. and Fu, Z. (2002) English for international trade: China enters the WTO. *World Englishes* 21 (2), 201–216.

Pennycook, A. (2007) *Global Englishes and Transcultural Flows*. London: Routledge.

Ryan, S. (2006) Language learning motivation within the context of globalization: An L2 self within an imagined global community. *Critical Inquiry in Language Studies: An International Journal* 3 (1), 23–45.

Su, D.F. (2004) 外语教学改革: 问题与对策 *Waiyu Jiaoxue Gaige: Wenti yu Duice* [*FLT in China: Problems and Suggested Solutions*]. Shanghai: Shanghai Foreign Language Education Press.

Walker, D. (2008) Postmodernism in intercultural rhetoric: Problematizing the deconstruction of an academic discipline. *Asian Journal of English Language Teaching* 18, 123–142.

Wang, T.J. (2004) 四六级考试及大班授课带来的潜在心理影响 Siliuji kaoshi ji daban shouke dailai de qianzai xinli yingxiang [Hidden psychological effects of Band 4, Band 6 tests and large-size classes]. 黔南民族师范学院学报 *Qiannan Minzu Shifan Xueyuan Xuebao* [*Journal of South Guizhou Normal University for Ethnic Minorities*] (1), 87–92.

Wen, Q.F. and Hu, W.Z. (2007) History and policy of English education in mainland China. In Y.H. Choi and B. Spolsky (eds) *English Education in Asia: History and Policies* (pp. 1–32). eduKL, Seoul: AsiaTEFL.

Xu, G.Z. (1985/1990) China's modernization and its English language needs. In G.Z. Xu (ed.) *ELT in China: Papers presented at the International Symposium on Teaching English in the Chinese Context, Guangzhou, China, 1985* (pp. 2–10). Beijing: Foreign Language Teaching and Research Press.

Xu, J.L. (2004) 等级社会是如何再生产的-再论考研变高考 Dengji shehui shi ruhe zaishengchan de – zailun kaoyan bian gaokao [How a hierarchical society gets reproduced – a continued discussion on the phenomenon of MA/PhD candidate selection turning into undergraduate entrance exam]. On WWW at http://www.acriticism.com/. Accessed 23.10/.04.

Xu, J.S. (1999) 活出最佳状态-自我实现 *Huochu Zuijia Zhuangtai – Ziwo Shixian* [*To Reach the Best State of Life – Self-Actualization*]. Beijing: Xinhua Press.

Yang, D.P. (ed.) (2006) 2005年中国教育发展报告 *2005 Nian Zhongguo Jiaoyu Fazhan Baogao* [*The Development Report of China's Education*]. Beijing: Social Sciences Academic Press.

Yang, Y. (2000) History of English Education in China. ERIC, ED441347.

Zhang, Z.Z. (2003) 外语教育中的功用主义和人文主义 Waiyu jiaoyu zhong de gongyong zhuyi he renwen zhuyi [Utilitarianism and humanism in foreign language education]. 外语教学与研究*Waiyu Jiaoxue yu Yanjiu* [*Foreign Language Teaching and Research*] (6), 453–457.

Zhao, Y. and Campbell, K.P. (1995) English in China. *World Englishes* 14 (3), 377–390.

Zhou, C. (2003) "留学教父" "俞敏洪的传奇人生" "Liuxue jiaofu" Yu Minhong de chuanqi rensheng [The legendary life of Yu Minhong, "godfather for studying abroad"]. 现代交际*Xiandai Jiaoji* [*Modern Communication*] (7), 8–10.

Zhu, L.Z. and Yang, A.X. (2003) "大学英语教学改革座谈会" 纪要 "Daxue yingyu jiaoxue gaige zuotanhui" jiyao (Summary report: A forum discussion on the reform of College English teaching), 外语界 *Waiyujie* (*Foreign Language World*) 2003 (2), 7–11.'

Zhu, L.Z. and Yang, A.X. (2004) 走火入魔的英语 *Zouhuorumo de Yingyu* (*The Madness of English Learning*). Changsha: Hunan People's Press.

Chapter 3
English and the Chinese Quest

JANE ORTON

Introduction

> During the Ming dynasty in the 15th and 16th centuries, The College of
> Interpreters [会同馆*Huitong Guan*] was the official residence for all
> foreign envoys in Peking. ... The Chinese imposed limitations on their
> freedom of movement. They could neither travel freely around the city
> nor meet with individual Chinese without permission. There were,
> however, compensations for these restrictions. The envoys received
> provisions from the Chinese court and servants catered for their needs.
> The emperor invited them to several banquets; one of them held during
> the New Year festivities was attended by all the foreign envoys in
> China. The lavish entertainment consisted of music, acrobatics and
> dancing. ... The Court assigned a number of individuals and agencies
> to deal with foreigners. Those Chinese who had the most intimate
> associations with foreigners frequently occupied the least prestigious
> positions in the government. (Rossabi, 1975: 17, 64–65)

I first read the passage above in 1981 while sitting in my apartment in
the Beijing Friendship Hotel complex. In the other room the maid swept
the floor and on the road outside my driver sat in the car listening to a
radio serial. On the table lay coupons for lunch and an invitation from the
Chairman of the Central Committee of the Chinese Communist Party, Hu
Yaobang, to join the Politburo and hundreds of high-ranking Chinese in
the Great Hall of the People for a grand celebration of the 100th anniversary of the birth of Lu Xun. A phone call from the person assigned by the
university to look after me said my permit to travel to Xi'An had come
through, and later that day a student said she and a classmate had received
permission from the university authorities to visit us on Saturday.

The similarity of my situation to that of foreign envoys to Beijing some 500 years ago was remarkable and also challenging, as it suggested aspects of identity both positive and negative that did not match well the sense of self in China that I and many in similar positions felt. On the one hand, we were treated with much greater consideration than we were used to, starting with our label of 'foreign expert', and, on the other, as something often to be kept at arms' length. Nowhere was this more clearly illustrated than at the Lu Xun memorial event. Addressing a hall packed with Chinese officials and all the foreigners working in Beijing education and publishing, the Chairman warmly welcomed his compatriots and the 'foreign friends' of China. He then extolled at length the talent and virtue of the great Chinese author we were there to celebrate, and railed equally strongly and at length against the evils of Western bourgeois liberalism.

Despite our clear links to the evil system in which we had been educated, we foreign friends were welcome because we were seen to have an essential role to play in China's quest for the knowledge that constitutes the power of the West. In this chapter, some enduring themes in the play of constructs pertaining to that knowledge and its relation to language are considered, as they have emerged since the quest began some 150 years before that meeting in the Great Hall, and in this era of globalisation, 27 years after it. In light of these considerations, recent developments in the teaching, learning and use of English in China are seen to mark a radical new era in its realisation.

The Chinese Quest

Inception

The Chinese ambiguity in attitude towards foreigners – and most especially towards native English speakers – was not new 27 years ago. As Rossabi shows, it pre-dates Western contact, although it became considerably more specifically directed at English speakers once British gunboats arrived in Chinese waterways in the mid-19th century. Adamson (2002: 231) calls it 'ambivalence' and explains it as 'a strategy' to deal with the consequences of the foreign invasion. Major among these were a threat to the quintessential Confucian belief in the superiority of Chinese culture in a naturally hierarchical world, and the fundamental preference of the Chinese for national insularity (Liu, 1998: 106–108). From this perspective, the arrival of the armed invaders can be seen to have faced the Chinese with what Giddens (1991: 142) calls 'a fateful moment': a transition point where consequential decisions to launch out into something new, once taken, have an irreversible quality, or at least it will be difficult thereafter to revert to the old paths (1991: 114).

The eventual Chinese response to their fateful moment was a decision to 're-skill' (Giddens, 1991: 141), and thus they set out 'to learn the superior skills of the barbarians in order to control them' (Wei Yuan, 1842, in Teng & Fairbank, 1954: 30). The means to this end were 'a controlled and selective appropriation' (Adamson, 2002: 231) of the source of the foreigners' power. The source was a new type of knowledge, clearly separate from much of Chinese knowledge, which they believed could be learned and still kept separate by those already educated in Chinese knowledge. Thus the framework for learning was to be 'Chinese ethics and Confucian teachings ... as an original foundation ... supplemented by the methods used by the various nations for the attainment of prosperity and strength' (Feng Guifen, 1861, in Teng & Fairbank, 1954: 52), a position later encapsulated in the phrase 'Chinese learning for moral principles (or *essence*), Western learning for practical application (or *utility*)' 中学为体, 西学为用 *Zhong xue wei ti, Xi xue wei yong*] (Zhang, 1898). As Giddens, however, points out, while deciding to re-skill may allow learning about the options available, decisions on what to choose from among the new options are more difficult to make. Furthermore, these are not simply behavioural options: they tend to refract back upon, and be mobilised to develop, the narrative of self-identity (Giddens, 1991: 140–141). And, indeed, from the start of the quest, options taken did refract back upon the Chinese narrative of self-identity, one consequence of which was that the perceived source of foreigners' power would then shift. To this day the targeted source remains elusive in definition, and never more so than in its relationship to language.

The initial period

China began re-skilling by appropriating the immediately perceivable elements of foreign knowledge, arsenals and shipyards. But while 'what we have to learn from the barbarians is only the one thing, solid ships and effective guns' continued to be the objective, by 1860, in light of failures to develop as hoped for through technical learning, language was also seen to play a central role in the endeavour. The new requirement for those selected to study translation of scientific sources was that they be 'brilliant students', not just volunteer 'rascals' (Feng Guifen, c. 1860, in Teng & Fairbank, 1954: 53). Feng's view that language proficiency was a key to success in the quest was then endorsed by a senior military commander and by the co-founder of Shanghai's Kiangnan Arsenal:

> If we have really mastered the Western languages and, in turn, teach one another, then all their clever techniques of steamships and firearms can be gradually and thoroughly learned. (Li Hongzhang, 1863, in Teng & Fairbank, 1954: 75)

In addition a school should be established in which to learn translation, because translation is the foundation for manufactures ... It is
simply because the languages are mutually incomprehensible that,
even though every day we practise on their machines, after all we do
not understand the principles underlying their manufacture and
operation. (Zeng Guofan, 1865, in Teng & Fairbank, 1954: 65)

By the end of the century, however, the Qing Court edicts of 1901 were
suggesting that the principles being sought lay elsewhere:

In recent years the study of Western methods has been limited to
languages and technical skills – the superficial aspects of Western
arts, not the underlying sources of Western knowledge. (In Grieder,
1981: 139)

If the direction of the quest at that time seemed doubtful, half a century
of seeking the knowledge needed to re-skill had nonetheless mobilised
development of the Chinese narrative of self-development in no uncertain
terms, culminating in 1905 with abolition of the imperial examination
system as it had existed for nearly 2000 years, in favour of a more 'modern'
educational model, which included science, mathematics and English. Yet
even before this result, some had begun to feel that just changing the educational curriculum would never lead to the essence of Western power:

What you mean by foreign matters are things you have seen such as
steamships, telegraph lines, trains, guns, cannon, torpedoes, and
machines for weaving and for metallurgy; that's all. You have never
dreamed of or seen the beauty and perfection of Western legal systems
and political institutions ... All you speak of are the branches and foli-
age of foreign matters, not the root. ... (Tan Situng, 1898, in Teng &
Fairbank, 1954: 158)

And a decade after the introduction of modern education, and some
five years after the entire imperial system of government had also been
abolished, still spurred by a sense of vulnerability, this line of thinking
was again proposed by one of the most active intellectuals of the day.

If we want to build a new society according to the Western model in
order to survive in this world, the basic task is to import the foundation of the Western society, that is, the new belief in equality and
human rights. (Chen Duxiu, 1916, in Spence, 1982: 144)

Summing up the outcome of the initial re-skilling period a few years
later, in his *Review of China's Progress 1873–1922*, the great reformer Liang

Qiqiao found that there had been some improvement, citing especially the abolition of the imperial examination system and the gradual opening of scholars' minds. Reflecting on the shift in quest direction, from first perceptions that mechanical objects were the source of power, to a focus on 'the world of thought' and the consequent reform of civic institutions, he noted the then current further shift to reform of the social culture and 'a re-awakening of the whole psychology'. Despite this progress, however, Liang was essentially negative about the true goal of the quest having yet been found:

> Let us ask our scientists, do we have one or two things that might be considered inventions of world importance? Ask our artists, do we have one or two productions which can be offered for world appreciation? And in our publication circles, do we have one or two books which are important works of the world? Alas, we had better wait until after the third period and see what it may bring. (Liang, 1922, in Teng & Fairbank, 1954: 269–272)

The modern period

In the time that has elapsed since the early years of the Republic, China has continued its quest for the knowledge that would bring parity with the West. In the first half of the period, this was done by working closely with American and other foreign friends, and then for 25 years China turned away from them, initially to collaborate with the Soviet Union and finally to stand alone. By the centenary of the birth of Lu Xun, however, Westerners were once more being invited to be partners in the endeavour. Nonetheless, a further 21 years later, and 80 years after Liang's review, the goal of the quest for power to strengthen the country was still being newly defined. This time the source was identified as *creativity*, and its attainment was seen to lie through change to 'experimental "Western style" science classes' (Zhao, 2002). To this end, in words that echo the same passion and purpose of reformers from a century ago, contemporary Chinese educators such as Zhao Zixiu, Professor of Psychology at The Chinese Academy of Sciences, have been advocating sweeping change:

> The entire concept of education must change, from top to bottom, if you want to nurture creativity in kids. If kids' thinking becomes rigid then it will be impossible to have a flourishing, developed country. (Zhao, 2002: 26)

When the movement to re-skill began, the crushing need was to make China strong enough to protect its cultural identity and territorial integrity from foreign invasion. The goal was clear, the quest seemed finite and for more than a century, in government rhetoric and in much of individual rhetoric, the momentum for China's development continued to be drawn from that historical base. Little was said about the time ahead: about how the destination once arrived at would be recognised, or what might happen then. These matters, and even at what cost the quest should be pursued, were usually left undiscussed by the proponents of various positions, or if made the focus of debate, as they were at times, in the end were left unresolved.

Throughout this course of re-skilling, English has been constructed as no more than a tool, the transparent window through which the sought-after knowledge might be accessed. In this modern era, after many swings in the intervening decades away from and back towards promoting the learning of English, the role of language in the quest is again seen as paramount:

> To develop world-class foreign language teaching programs in Shanghai is a prerequisite for turning the municipality into a world-class international metropolis. (Shanghai Curriculum and Teaching Materials Reform Commission, 1999: 3)

'Foreign language' programmes in the plans of the Shanghai Education Commission overwhelmingly means 'English language' programmes. To develop these, in no small number of Shanghai primary and secondary schools the scope of the window provided by English has recently been considerably broadened:

> English is used to teach mathematics, science, biology, computer science, arts, ballet, IT, and a few other subjects. For subjects not taught in English (e.g. physics, chemistry, history, and politics) technical terms, formulas, laws and definitions are presented in both Chinese and English. (Hu, 2002: 33–34; Shanghai Education Commission, 2002–2003)

Furthermore, in the course of the present decade, the Chinese–English bilingual education programme in Shanghai schools is being expanded so that, in addition to the above, it will include

> Creation of a bilingual environment within schools, communities and other public places; 'English Corner', 'English Square', 'English Park', etc. established to meet the demand of English learning by students

and citizens. [在学校内和社区及其他公共场所营造双语环境，建立英语角、英语广场、英语公园等，适应学生和市民学外语的需要。]

Bilingual decoration of schools using English posters, English quotations from famous people and English wall newspapers; setting up English radio programs and closed-circuit TV, regularly organizing 'English Day/Week/Month Festivals', English competitions, and exhibitions of English proficiency. [学校要实现环境布置双语化，张贴英语标语、名人名言及英语园地、墙报、建立英语广播、闭路电视；经常举办英语日 (周、月、节)，英语竞赛和能力展示。] (Shanghai Education Commission Teaching and Research Section, 2000: 67–68.) [Author's translation]

While this massive undertaking in the production of language resources and training of staff is still framed largely in the language of the 19th-century Chinese quest, in fact, it expresses part of a radically further developed narrative of self-identity, one in which English is projected as part of the social capital of China's 21st-century modern citizen, someone still thoroughly patriotic, but also internationally competent. President Jiang Zemin set the ball rolling in the 1990s by being shown on Chinese and international television chatting comfortably with world leaders and joking with the world's press, all in English; and recent high school texts for the first time show Chinese people from the Mainland living in English-speaking societies and learning what is necessary to fit in there. The emergence of both the local bilingual education movement and the global Chinese presence is evidence of a new step in the re-skilling endeavour. Henceforth, the quest is to be for knowledge not only to protect China physically and culturally, but also, and in its own right, to make China modern, prosperous and global.

In considering this latest shift, two factors appear particularly salient with respect to success. One concerns the nature of the constantly elusive source of Western power; the other concerns the still prevailing view that 'English, after all, is only a tool to know the world' (Yu, 2004).

The Source

Locating 'it'

The Chinese government rhetoric of 1981 positioned native English-speaking teachers working in China as people valuable in the Chinese quest – foreign experts and friends of China – but it also *im*-positioned them as little more than respected sources of authentic English language and meta-linguistic knowledge; and this was largely how they were treated by the groups of students and teachers they worked with. Texts of all kinds were deconstructed into turns of phrase and linguistic structure which they were to explain, but the thrust of their content as grist for thought was ignored, and attempts to attend to this level of meaning positively resisted. There was, it seemed, little interest in what the English speakers knew and valued about themselves and their societies and cultures, or in what they were critical about or worried about with regard to them. It was as if, having found a ship anchored along a river bank, people wanted to seize the vessel and dismantle it into decking planks, brass door handles, pieces of steel hull, etc. to be stored for later use. There was no interest in the sailors' stories of the risks and joys of voyages at sea, and no awareness at all of the human curiosity and spirit of adventure that had led to the ship being built in the first place. Yet these are aspects of the essential knowledge of those who create and sail ships, and by its nature cannot be grasped if ships are treated as static objects, to be dismantled into parts. Likewise, in language learning, appreciation of the discursive intent in an author's choice of topic and arrangement of words and structures involves essential knowledge, which, by its nature, cannot be discovered by treating those who understand the language simply as walking dictionaries of linguistic systems. Indeed, for learners to acquire it ever is difficult, because much of it may lie outside their ken.

Accessing knowledge one cannot yet recognise as such is possible only with the help of an insider; and if any help offered is to be usable, the insider will need the seeker's assistance. For both parties, the task thus requires a partnership of mutuality with a co-operative and critical other. Or, as Giddens would put it, the narrative of self-identity that China seeks to develop through its contact with English speakers cannot be affirmed and developed simply by 'recognising the other', however respectfully. Instead, it can only be negotiated through linked processes of self-exploration and the development of intimacy with the other (Giddens, 1991: 97). This means, among other things, that to play their part in such a relationship, Westerners need to ponder very much as their own the conundrum faced by modern Chinese in pursuit of the quest: How much, in fact, must Chinese in search of the knowledge and skills of Western society understand of Western people's sense of identity in order to be successful?

Naming 'it'

Research by this author and others on intercultural issues in the teaching of English in China (e.g. Muehl & Muehl, 1993; Orton, 1991, 1996) and on the relationships between Westerners and Chinese working together in commercial ventures (e.g. Clissold, 2004; Orton, 2000, 2004; Yang, 1994) has contributed some useful information on this matter. In brief, the results show that in appropriating Western technical knowledge, in both the classroom and at work, the visible and tangible parts of the Western world (the teaching methods and the linguistic forms, the bricks and mortar, the technology and machinery – in short, the ships) have been quite readily appropriated and adapted to fit Chinese views and practices. In the course of doing this, however, some key aspects of the essence as English speakers perceive it – the systems of relating and practices needed to successfully conduct voyages at sea – have often been overlooked or actually resisted, and thus the value of what has been appropriated has at times been neutralised – or so it often seems to the Westerners involved.

Difficulties in successfully transferring what they see as some essentials in their work to Chinese colleagues they usually both like and admire have pushed many expatriates to deep reflection on what actually constitutes the expertise they own. In answering, most point to their *dynamic structures and relationships*, by which they mean specifically (1) the thought to anticipate outcomes beyond the immediate results of an action, (2) the sense of individual responsibility to do something about a problem although outside one's own immediate area and (3) the assumed joint commitment to truth, which accords one a right and duty to confront error in another's work whatever the formal relationship structures. These, they say, are essential matters most needing to be appropriated by their Chinese colleagues and workers in order to run a wide variety of businesses successfully. But, in fact, whether talking to executives or truck drivers, these are the points they find the hardest to get across, the most resisted and those most commonly found at the heart of any dispute. For their part, the Chinese colleagues and workers in these businesses are every bit as aware of the same points of difficulty, but frame the situations in different language: 'I did my best. How was I to know they [the client] would do that until it happened?', 'It's not my job to do that. He is the Manager, *he* should manage that problem' and 'He shouldn't expect the workers to do that on their own accord, he should *make* them do it'. In a similar vein, Western teachers in awe of their Chinese students' diligence, nonetheless, lament their lack of overt curiosity and initiative. Chinese students echo their compatriots above in complaints about foreign teachers, saying that they do not take the responsibility to prepare thoroughly to provide them with all they should know about a subject, but just ask questions and even evade giving answers when asked directly.

The view of expatriates in business in China, and of Western teachers of Chinese students inside and outside China, that the essence of the 'it' being sought lies in their social and dynamic processes, reflects an important difference from the Chinese primary focus on seeking knowledge and products. Yet something further illuminates why transfer at this level so rarely succeeds, and when it does, only with great difficulty. This is because imported processes are not just the essentials of *modern* management and teaching practices, but of *Western* practices. That is, not only are they new, they are culturally different, driven by different beliefs and values. Furthermore, at the core, these beliefs and values are so different that they contradict some key Chinese beliefs and values.

Action design

Like the layout of buildings designed to house them, Western work processes are in large part the predictable realisations of a culture that, in its social structures and relationships, routines of practice and language, stresses individual identity and will, privileges causal relationships and seeks personal achievement and fulfilment through action. They are practices that have emerged from an educational system in which the core goal is to develop the individual to his or her fullest potential so that he or she can live successfully in a society where the core value is to stand on one's own feet. The basic belief that supports these fundamentals sees life as

> … a series of situations in which one has to learn to think for oneself, to solve problems on one's own, and even to discover new problems for which creative solutions are wanted. (Gardner, 1989: 5)

The successful English-speaking child – which the contemporary expatriate professionals in China, virtually by definition, all were – has been taught that he or she is an individual, one who has a right, even a duty, to be an agent in the world, one who can and should introduce change (for the better) through his or her own action. Socialisation into such a way of perceiving and behaving starts at least as early as the first week after birth, when, for example, a baby born into an English-speaking family is left to sleep in its own cot, in its own room, and even at times allowed to cry there alone (to the intense distress of any Chinese visitor); the process is continually if casually fostered by parents and teachers, who do not simply command obedience – 'Put that down!', 'Look at this' and 'I will do that for you' – but present the world as a series of interrelated, causal events in which the child is one of the active agents – 'If you ask Mrs Jones nicely, I am sure she would let you play with the dolls', 'If you touch that, you'll get hurt!', 'If you look at it carefully, I am sure you can work out where it goes' and 'Which one would you like to choose?' The focus is generally on macrolevel learning – problem solving – rather than items of information, and error and minor injuries are accepted as inevitable and useful elements in the process of growth.

These fundamental social practices in child rearing are not typically found in China (Bond, 1991; Ho, 1986: 11–19; Li & Yue, 2004; Ran, 2001), and reflect a central difference between the beliefs and values of the two societies that goes back through the ages. In traditional Chinese thinking there is no concept of the human being who knows good but is free to choose evil. As one modern Confucian wrote: 'No ethics of any kind would allow freedom to do evil' (Xie, in Moore, 1966: 321). But in the foundation text of Judeo–Christian–Islamic civilisations, an all-loving, all-knowing and all-powerful God does exactly that (Genesis II). And centuries later, that same concept of self as an individual of free will is maintained as a core belief by the reformers of the Enlightenment, while, as Grieder points out,

> in a fundamental way … Rousseau would have remained entirely an enigma to … Confucian thinkers. They could not have comprehended that side of him which strove to reconcile 'freedom' to the claims of 'sovereignty' … for these were categories quite extraneous to their minds. (Grieder, 1981: 46)

The notion of the free and sovereign self is held just as firmly by Westerners at the beginning of the 21st century, as expatriates in China show in their work processes; and it can just as entirely remain an enigma for contemporary Chinese, as an error in the 1987 Chinese translation of Rousseau's *Emile* shows, where the passage, 'Conscience! Conscience! … sure guide for a creature ignorant and finite indeed, yet intelligent and free' (Rousseau, 1964: 378), is rendered, 'Conscience! Conscience! … you are the reliable guide of an ignorant and limited creature; *you* are intelligent and free'. [良心！良心！你是一个无知而且狭隘的生物的可靠的领导；你是理智而且自由的。] [emphasis added] (Beijing University Philosophy Dept., 1987: 86.) [Author's translation.]

The significance of this difference is not an incidental matter but, as the eminent 20th-century Confucian philosopher, the late Professor Tang Junyi, says, a clear conflict at the core, as a result of which:

> Our two forms of self-assertion each imply that the other is pathological. … Western individualism with its clearly bounded ego unabashedly pursuing direct gratifications, distorts human experience and

blocks *chengji* [成己], the Confucian goal of completion of the self. *Chengji* is properly reached through a mental act of 'holding onto' [执著 *zhizhuo*] rationalised egotistic desires which otherwise cut into and interrupt the natural 'flow' of empathy. (In Metzger, 1977: 43–45)

In such a world, the Chinese impose a responsibility on the superordinate to take care of and train the subordinate:

> Those who are elder brothers, they on their part, must tenderly love their younger brothers. Be their age what it may, they should simply be treated as children. (Emperor Kangxi, Baller trans. 1892: 10)

And the result, in the words of a young Chinese man today, is that

> We're brought up in a home where your dad tells you what to do. You just shut up your whole life. ... We follow instructions, we don't voice our opinions, we show respect. (Nicholas Ling, in *The Age* newspaper, Melbourne: 19-9-05: 14)

But in Western eyes, mature moral orientations and the criteria that underlie dominance and submission patterns are always in a contradictory relationship (Wilson *et al.*, 1981: 10). Congruently, the *rights* to be taken by the Western self are accompanied by a concomitant *responsibility* as an essential co-part of self-construction. Hence behaviour that may appear in Confucian terms to be an unjustifiable *privileging of self* [优越感], in terms of the other will often mean *taking responsibility for oneself* [责任感], a central element in Western moral education and in good Western work practices, including teaching.

These contradictions at core mean that the theory of action by which each form of self-identity is realised in the modern world is very different. The result is not only that the practices are often antagonistic, but that the resulting surface clashes are hard to resolve because the beliefs, values and action strategies of the theory they cohere in are often known only tacitly by the person acting on them, and are simply invisible – even unimaginable – to an interactant raised according to a different set. In this predicament, certain aspects of Chinese re-skilling can only involve a binary struggle between, on the one hand, total lamination by imported practices, laying the new over the old so as to all but suffocate what lies below – a process, not surprisingly, often resisted, or, on the other, a 'sinicising' of the new to make it fit more comfortably with the old – a move that, in fact, robs it of the very power it was borrowed to create. Rarely in the contested areas is there sufficient clarity about what is at stake to develop the *graft*, which any hope of success would require.

Process of interchange

Routine Western knowledge and practices can be, and quite evidently have been, adopted and made to flourish in China as elsewhere, and many innovations have been incorporated into a changed China. But appropriation of Western processes, especially the creative processes that generate new knowledge – Liang Qiqiao's 'works of world importance', and of the now sought-after patents and Nobel Prizes – requires recognition of the difference at core, and a valuing of it precisely for its role as critical reflector. Embrace of the difference could allow creative resolution of the binary struggle in the emergence of a new form. But this transcendence of difference, as Giddens says, can only be accomplished through linked processes of self-exploration.

Bakhtin describes this learning from other as a process of mutuality:

> In the realm of culture, outsideness is a most powerful factor in understanding ... A meaning only reveals its depths once it has encountered and come into contact with another, foreign meaning: they engage in a kind of dialogue, which surmounts the closedness and one-sidedness of these particular meanings, these cultures. We raise new questions for a foreign culture, ones that it did not raise itself; we seek answers to our own questions in it; and the foreign culture responds to us by revealing to us its new aspects and new semantic depths ... Such a dialogic encounter of two cultures does not result in merging or mixing. Each retains its own unity and open totality, but they are mutually enriched. (Bakhtin, 1979; trans. 1986: 7)

It is a view not unknown in China. Yue Daiyun, for example, has warned of systems confined to their borders 'sealing off and growing old'. Drawing on Habermas's proposed 'mutual subjectivity', like Bakhtin, she asserts:

> The only way out of this contradiction is 'communicating', which means finding another frame of reference and re-examining oneself in the light of this other frame of reference, 'alienated' eyes. ... The contact between and convergence of two cultures does not mean the dispelling of the differences ... nor the transplanting of identical contents. On the contrary the co-existence of these differences maintains the tension and richness. (Yue, 1991: 2–5)

Cheng (2002: 262) argues similarly, albeit from the Chinese perspective only:

> As part of the training for good citizens, students should be ... liberal-minded through exposure to cultures with different value systems.

> They will understand the ways of thinking of different peoples ... and should contribute to their own culture by injecting 'foreign' elements into it, and shaking it out of a rut.

While these writers illuminate the process that needs to be taken, there has been no systematic identification of the contradictions involved in realising it for today's Chinese and Westerners working together and hence little progress in dealing with them. The shift in China's educational goal towards a Western style *being creative* can, nonetheless, be seen to constitute a quite radical new move in the quest. In particular, the goal is qualitatively different from the earlier focus on *knowledge of*, for example, skyscraper construction or the blueprints for an electronic circuit. It moves the source of power from a noun to a verb, and thus targets *doing* as the key factor in Western learning. This seems a productive move, as an orientation to doing has been identified as a fundamental Western attribute by interculturalists for decades (e.g. Condon & Yousef, 1975; Chen & Starosta, 1998; Kluckhohn & Strodtbeck, 1961). It is an attribute that is also consonant with the view of the Chinese linguist Shen Xiaolong (1985/1997: 38) that the verb is the focus in the Western mode of thinking – in contrast to that of the Chinese, which, he claims, is more diffuse. But perception of action as the goal, without perception also of the moral and intellectual force to link principle with practice that actually drives the action, is a hard process to copy.

Even so, just understanding the point allows interpretation of the quest of 'Western learning for practical application' [西学为用] as no longer primarily focused on 'acquiring "Western knowledge" [西方的 "知识"]', but on 'operating Western "learning processes" or "practices" [西方的 "学法"or "做 法"]'. This is a view strongly congruent with the beliefs of Western business expatriates about themselves, and it also fits the findings of research pinpointing mismatches in basic Chinese- and English-speaking educational goals (e.g. Li & Yue, 2004: 37–38; Ran, 2001: 326).

If the source and nature of 'being creative' seem clearer, the depth and polarisation of the cultural contradictions revealed in the studies mentioned above immediately raise the questions: Can it be done? Or will local ways and values transform *learning processes* [学法] into the more familiar *knowledge* [知识] as they are appropriated and thus, inadvertently, stifle their creative nature? Alternatively, if it can and is done in even a small number of schools, the question Gardner (1989) posed at the end of his large comparative study of art education in the United States and China immediately arises: Can China develop schoolchildren through creative learning without the devastating waste often incurred by such methods in the

West, that is, without losing much in China now that is of value? Western educators will watch the new developments in Chinese classrooms with interest and hope.

The English Language

Just a tool

The decision to pursue re-skilling by using English in regular classes in Shanghai schools establishes a relationship to the language, and to what it is used to learn, that is also fundamentally new. Earlier schools where teaching content was conducted in English were almost all missionary and other foreign-run establishments. It seems a momentous decision, one that has a potentially irreversible quality, to start using English in otherwise totally Chinese environments. Of particular significance in terms of the quest is the apparent assumption that when their common language is usurped by English as the medium of instruction in their mathematics and other classrooms, children in the top schools of the country's major city will somehow be able to maintain development of their narrative of self-identity in Chinese: 'the root we grow from' – while English will remain additional to and separate from it: just 'a tool to know the world' (Yu, 2004).

Giddens (1991: 1) reminds us that 'the transmutations introduced by modern institutions interlace in a direct way with individual life and therefore with the self', and that when these confront individuals and create anxiety, it is the individual actors who 'mobilize their efforts ... and ultimately bring about social change' (Giddens, 1984: 134–135). This new era of Shanghai schoolchildren will not only face challenges unknown to those who set them, but will need to deal with them at a much younger age, and for a much longer time than those who have come before. What social change may emerge when so much that will be new to these Chinese children conceptually is met first, and perhaps only, in English, when Chinese reality even in the park needs to be annotated in English? The relationship of language to meaning – to naming and framing reality – is such that it is hard to believe they could develop intellectually as intended and yet keep English separate and subordinate to their Chinese self and Chinese reality.

Future period

For more than a century, the Chinese government and people have made clear their aspiration to avoid being the victims of cultural imperialism.

Yet what immersion in the English language might offer – indeed, even demand of – a successful Chinese learner beyond access to the facts of subject content is not discussed. The Shanghai Education Commission's programme thus appears to ignore the constitutive role of language in the formation of self-identity, and the fact that engagement with the knowledge and social practices available through English, and even embedded in the language itself, will involve learners in a potentially transformative experience. In light of fundamental contemporary understandings of language, learning and education, in which such forces are acknowledged, this new programme would seem likely to produce considerably more than just the desired knowledge outcomes. In addition, they suggest, the self-identity of the interculturally competent, modern, creative, bilingual Chinese graduate of the next decade is likely to reflect a hybridity that is not present in any monolingual Chinese, or even in older Chinese who have mastered English under very different circumstances.

Conclusion

The contradiction at heart between Chinese ethics and teaching and Western technical know-how was clear to the 19th-century Chinese reformers. Yet they believed that both could be learned in relative harmony by one person. What they only gradually came to realise was that the technical expertise they sought was not simply the result of knowledge of a neutral physics, but the active manifestation of a system of basic beliefs and values that was in part at odds with, even antagonistic to, their own. There have been many twists and turns in their subsequent efforts to handle inherent contradictions in acquiring the desired knowledge. Chinese society has developed and changed as a result and, as Giddens suggests will happen, perception of the target has also shifted. Thus the quest remains alive today, with the structures and relationships that frame modern work practices, and a spirit of intellectual curiosity, now the targets.

In all this, English has largely been regarded as no more than a transparent medium for realising the quest. Just how (like work routines and child rearing practices) it, too, constitutively both manifests and shapes beliefs and values is still rarely acknowledged. It is only very recently that the transformative power of coming to own English has been the subject of Chinese scholarly attention (see Gao, this volume, Chapter 2), and of mutual self-exploration by both sides, as for example in this book. Both kinds of activities are needed to generate the process of healthy graft that Bakhtin proposes would allow each to retain its own unity and open totality, but be mutually enriched.

Note

1. I am grateful to Chen Jianai for pointing out this discrepancy.

References

Adamson, B. (2002) Barbarian as a foreign language: English in China's schools. *World Englishes* 21 (2), 257–267.

Bakhtin, M.M. (1979 and 1986) Response to a question from the *Novy Mir* Editorial Staff. M.M. Bakhtin. In C. Emerson and M. Holquist (eds) *Speech Genres & Other Late Essays* (V. McGee, trans.) (pp. 1–7). Austin: University of Texas Press.

Bond, M.H. (1991) *Beyond the Chinese Face: Insights from Psychology*. New York and Hong Kong: Oxford University Press.

Chen, G.M. and Starosta, W.J. (1998) *Foundations of Intercultural Communication*. Boston: Allyn and Bacon.

Cheng, Z.X. (2002) English departments in Chinese universities: Purposes and function. *World Englishes* 21 (2), 231–243.

Clissold, T. (2004) *Mr China*. London: Robinson; Sydney: Random House Australia.

Condon, J.C. and Yousef, F. (1975) *An Introduction to Intercultural Communication*. Indianapolis: Bobbs-Merill.

Gardner, H. (1989) *To Open Minds: Chinese Clues to the Dilemmas of Contemporary Education*. New York: Basic Books.

Giddens, A. (1984) *The Constitution of Society: Outline of the Theory of Structuration*. Berkeley: University of California Press.

Giddens, A. (1991) *Modernity and Self-identity: Self and Society in the Late Modern Age*. Stanford: Stanford University Press.

Grieder, J.B. (1981) *Intellectuals and the State in Modern China: A Narrative History*. New York: The Free Press.

Ho, D.Y.F. (1986) Chinese patterns of socialization. In M.H. Bond (ed.) *The Psychology of the Chinese People* (pp. 1–37). New York: Oxford University Press.

Hu, G.W. (2002) Recent important developments in secondary English-language teaching in the People's Republic of China. *Language, Culture and Curriculum* 15 (1), 30–49.

Kangxi, Emperor of China (1654–1722) The sacred edict. In *The Sacred Edict, with a Translation of the Colloquial Rendering, Notes and Vocabulary* (F.W. Baller, trans. (1892)). Shanghai: American Presbyterian Mission.

Kluckhohn, F. and Strodtbeck, F. (1961) *Variations in Value Orientations*. Evanston, IL: Row, Peterson.

Li, J. and Yue, X.D. (2004) Self in learning among Chinese children. In M. Mascolo and J. Li (eds) *Culture and Developing Selves: Beyond Dichotimization* (pp. 27–43). San Francisco: Jossey Bass, Pub.

Liu, Y.Y. (1998) Chinese attitudes towards English. In K. Parry and X.J. Su (eds) *Culture, Literacy, and Learning English Voices from the Chinese Classroom* (pp. 106–108). Portsmouth, NH: Heinemann.

Metzger, T.A. (1977) *Escape from Predicament: China's Evolving Political Culture*. New York: Columbia University Press.

Moore, C. (1966) *The Chinese Mind: Chinese Philosophy and Culture*. Honolulu: East-West Centre Press, University of Hawaii Press.

Muehl, L. and Muehl, S. (1993) *Trading Cultures in the Classroom*. Honolulu: University of Hawaii Press.

Orton, J. (1991) Educating the reflective practitioner in China: A case study in teacher education. PhD thesis, School of Education, La Trobe University, Bundoora, Australia.

Orton, J. (1996) Perceiving education. Author: China education. In A. Milner (ed.) *Australia in Asia: Comparing Cultures* (pp. 69–103). Melbourne: Oxford University Press.

Orton, J. (2000) *Keys to Successful Intercultural Communication in Australian–Chinese Joint Ventures*. Melbourne: The Australia China Business Council (Vic. Branch).

Orton, J. (2004) Australia–China relations in business – an intercultural perspective. In N. Thomas (ed.) *Re-Orienting Australia–China Relations* (pp. 110–125). London: Ashgate.

Peking University Philosophy Department Foreign Philosophy History Teaching and Research Office (eds & trans.) (1987), *Selected Readings of Western Philosophy*. Beijing: The Commercial Press. [北京大学哲学系外国哲学史教研室 编译 1987 《西方哲学原著选读》, 北京：商务印书馆。]

Ran, A. (2001) Traveling on parallel tracks: Chinese parents and English teachers. *Educational Research* 43 (3), 311–328.

Rossabi, M. (1975) *China and Inner Asia*. London: Thames & Hudson.

Rousseau, J.J. (1762) *Emile*. Paris: Garnier Frères, c. 1964.

Shanghai Primary and Secondary Curriculum and Materials Reform Commission (1999) *Facing the 21st Century: Research Report on Principles for Action in Shanghai Primary and Secondary Foreign Language Education Reform*. Shanghai Education Commission Office of Pedagogical Research, Shanghai: Shanghai Education Press. [上海中小学课程教材改革委员会办公室、上海市教育委员会教学研究室 1999《面向21世纪上海市中小学外语学科教育改革行动纲领 (研究报告)》, 上海：上海教育出版社。].

Shanghai Education Commission Office of Pedagogical Research (2000) *Shanghai Education Commission Office of Pedagogical Research Work Report*. Shanghai: Shanghai Education Commission. [上海教育委员会教学研究室 (2000)《上海教育委员会教学研究室工作报告 2000》, 上海：上海教育委员会。]

Shanghai Education Commission (2002–2003) 上海教育委员会 2002–2003 http://www.shmec.gov.cn如, http://www.shmec.gov.cn/web/news/show_article.php?article_id=6732, http://www.shmec.gov.cn/web/news/show_article.php?article_id=1778, http://www.shmec.gov.cn/web/news/show_article.php?article_id=19186.

Shen, X. (1985/1997) Bright hope for the future (G. Zhong, English trans.). In Y. Gao (ed.) 1997, *Collected Essays of Shen Xiaolong on Chinese Cultural Linguistics* (pp. 35–43). Changchun: Northeast Normal University Press. [Original Chinese version, Xiwang zhi Lu: Zhongguo Wenhua Yuyanxue. *Yuyan Xuexi* 1985 (5), 40–42).]

Spence, J. (1982) *The Gate of Heavenly Peace*. Harmondsworth: Penguin.

Teng, S.Y. and Fairbank, J.K. (1954) *China's Response to the West – A Documentary Survey 1839–1923*. Cambridge, MA: Harvard University Press.

Wilson, R.W., Greenblatt, S.L. and Wilson, A.A. (eds) (1981) *Moral Behaviour in Chinese Society*. New York: Praeger.

Yang, L.W.L. (1994) *Crosstalk and Culture in Sino-American Communication*. Cambridge: Cambridge University Press.

Yu, K.C. (2004) Writers: Protecting Chinese imperative. In report by Zou Huilin on the Literature and Humanistic Care Forum, Shanghai Tongji University. *China Daily* (newspaper), 27 May, p. 5.

Yue, D.Y. (1991) Welcoming the new period of cultural reorientation. Paper presented at the *Chinese Studies Association of Australia Conference*, The University of Sydney, June 1991.

Zhang, Z. (1898) 劝学篇, Quàn Xué Piān (Exhortation to Study), Changsha, Hunan: *Xiang Xuebao*. Samuel I. Woodbridge (trans) (1901) *China's Only Hope: an appeal by her greatest viceroy*. Edinburgh; London: Oliphant, Anderson & Ferrier

Zhao, Z. (2002) *The Australian Financial Review*, 10 May, p. 26.

Part 2

Learners, Identities and Purposes

Chapter 4

Language and Identity: State of the Art and a Debate of Legitimacy

GAO YIHONG

Introduction

Since the revival of academic research in the early 1980s, research in the People's Republic of China pertaining to social psychological aspects of the learning of English as a foreign language (EFL) has largely followed the classical paradigm of Gardner (1985) and its expansions (e.g. Dornyei, 1994). Its focus has been on 'individual factors' influencing target language proficiency, such as motivation, personality and cognitive styles, with implications for pedagogical solutions (e.g. Gui, 1986; Li & Wu, 2007; Shi, 2000; Wang & Liu, 2002; Wen & Wang, 1996; Wu *et al.*, 1996; Zhou, 1996; Zhu, 2006). For example, in their quantitative study on the influence of individual factors on English proficiency, Wu *et al.* included 18 learner variables and 13 demographic features. Results showed that 63.4% of the variance in language achievement was accounted for by six variables, the first two being language attitude and motivation. Some later studies employed more complex statistical instruments to investigate relationships among multiple learner variables, such as learning motivation, beliefs and strategies (e.g. Wen, 2001; for a detailed review on Second Language Acquisition research in China, see Guo, 2004).

From the late 1980s and increasingly into the mid-1990s, cultural issues have engaged the attention of language teachers, especially those of EFL. There has emerged a considerable body of literature concerning the comparison between Chinese and English linguistic and cultural charac-teristics, including pragmatic conventions, behavioural patterns and value orientations, although mostly at a general level (e.g. Chen & Tan, 1993; Hu, 1988, 1994, 1999). It is commonly acknowledged that the learning/teaching of a language is bound also to involve the teaching and learning of the target culture. However, little attention was paid to the learner as a whole person, other than to classical 'individual factors' influencing language proficiency. Learner identity studies began to appear in the 1990s, led by a group of which the present author and associates are engaged advocates (e.g. Gao *et al.*, 2004). Recently, the legitimacy of such studies in a foreign language context has been challenged (e.g. Qu, 2005). While the particular critique came from a single source, it exemplifies trends of thinking in China's EFL circles that make it important for EFL learning and identity studies beyond the particular to accept and respond to.

In this chapter an overview of the studies on identity and EFL learning in mainland China will be provided and the related criticism will be responded to. In doing so, the epistemological distinction between structuralism and constructivism will be clarified and a structuralism–constructivism continuum that can accommodate stances stated or implied in existing empirical studies and criticism will be presented. It is argued that while the criticism was launched from a structuralist perspective, the studies critiqued demonstrate a constructivist orientation. The implications for identity studies in EFL contexts in general are further discussed.

An Overview of Research on EFL Learning and Identity Development

Productive bilingualism among 'the best foreign language learners'

Gao (2001, 2002) proposed the concept of 'productive bilingualism', in contrast with Lambert's (1974) widely adopted 'subtractive bilingualism' and 'additive bilingualism', long a beacon in language learning and identity studies. When subtractive bilingualism occurs, the learner's native language and cultural identity (expressed in lifestyle, values, etc.) are replaced by target language and target cultural identity; when additive bilingualism occurs, the learner's native language and cultural identity are maintained, while the target language and cultural identity are additionally acquired, and the two co-exist, being used in different communicative situations. When productive bilingualism occurs, competence in native and target languages/cultures are enhanced by knowledge of each other, and the learner benefits from general cognitive and affective growth and increased creativity.

Gao's 'productive bilingualism' was theoretically derived from Erich Fromm's (1948) general social psychological concept of 'productive orientation' or 'productive character'. According to Fromm, productiveness is the ability to realize one's own potentials; those with a productive orientation are independent, and at the same time able to integrate with others and the world. The empirical grounding of Gao's study came from open interviews with 52 students nationally recognized as among the 'best foreign language learners' in China.

In speaking of their learning experiences, the students revealed shared qualities of openness to both native culture (C1) and target culture (C2), critical awareness of C1 and C2 and an integration of the two. Such qualities were associated with cognitive and affective gains and creative achievements. Although 'cultural identity' had not been an explicit concept adopted in that study, the importance of the issue became evident as some interviewees expressed views such as, for example, 'I believe I'm more Chinese than many Chinese, and more Western than many Westerners'. As the participants in the study were limited to a small group of high-achieving language learners, the findings prompted the question of whether the same productive model could be expected to apply among ordinary language learners.

Attitudes, motivation and identity development of ordinary language learners

Funded by a national grant, research on language learning and identity changes was extended in the new millennium to university students, as ordinary learners of English. A series of empirical studies were conducted by the researcher and colleagues in 2004 that attempted to examine the social psychology of EFL learning in general, and of students' learning motivation and identity development in particular. While not designed as a replication of the earlier study of the 'best foreign language learners', identity changes nevertheless were found which were similar, albeit with more diversified directions and dimensions. Table 4.1 presents a summary of these studies and is followed by some examples illustrating some of the quantitative and qualitative studies.

Quantitative study example

The study by Gao *et al.* (2004) (Row 1, Table 4.1) investigated Chinese undergraduates' English learning motivation types, motivational intensity and self-identity changes associated with English learning. The stratified sample consisted of 2278 undergraduates from 30 universities in 29 Provinces, Autonomous Regions and Municipalities and the instrument was a Likert-scale questionnaire.

Findings show that out of the six pre-defined categories of identity change (self-confidence, additive, subtractive, productive, split and nil

Table 4.1 Summary of EFL learning and identity studies on university students in China (Gao and project Team, 2004)

Author(s)	Topic	Participants	Method	Major findings
1. Gao, Y.H., Cheng, Y., Zhao, Y. and Zhou, Y.	Motivation types and self-identity changes among undergraduates	2278 undergraduates from 30 universities, selected through stratified sampling	Questionnaire	Seven motivation types were found through factor analysis. Level of self-confidence is the most prominent change; productive and additive changes are above critical level
2. Li, S.J., Gao, Y.H. and Qian, M.	Motivation types and self-identity changes among graduates	1017 graduate students from 16 universities, selected through stratified sampling	Questionnaire	As above
3. Li, L.C.	Case studies of non-English majors	15 non-English major undergraduates at a key university	Case study by interviews	Four bases of learning motivation: English as certificate, fun, instrument and quality, respectively
4. Gao, Y.H., Li, Y.X. and Li, W.N.	Case studies of English majors	Three English major undergraduates at a key university	Case study by interviews	Consistency was maintained in multiple identity construction. Individuals exercise different degrees of agency in their construction of identities and learning environment
5. Wang, Z.X. and Wang, J.	Attitudes toward four spoken linguistic varieties	634 undergraduates from eight universities	Matched guise test	Three major influencing factors on language attitude: status, modern personality and solidarity. British English received the highest rating, China English the lowest

6. Zou, M.Y.	Perception of in-class relationship and voluntary responses	Teachers and students in six College English classes at a university in Beijing	Class observation and interviews	Students observed were classified as hand-raisers, answer-yellers and turn-waiters. Willingness to give voluntary responses in class was related to perceptions of interpersonal relationships in the classroom
7. Tian, G.S. and Zheng, Y.L.	Use of English names	1350 students from eight universities in seven cities	Questionnaire and interviews	95.75% of English majors and 32.26% of non-English majors had English names. 69.68% of the students acquired English names themselves and used these names with teachers, and among classmates and good friends
8. Shen, L.X. and Gao, Y.H.	What 'Crazy English' means to learners	Twenty students in a 'Crazy English' class	Class observation and interviews	'Crazy English' for learners was associated with the expression of suppressed emotions, expression of individuality and success through hard effort. It symbolizes a self who is centred on esteem needs, unlike the traditional Chinese self who is centred on belonging needs
9. Li, Y.X.	A study of college 'English Corners'	1832 students from 20 universities in seven regions	Questionnaire and interviews	English learners in China develop multi-dimensional, dynamic and fragmented self-identities. English Corners provide an environment accommodating and facilitating such identity changes
10. Li, Z.Z., Gao, Y.H. and Li, F.F.	Self-identity construction in personal statement	Nine student personal statements to be used in applying to graduate programs in US universities	Discourse analysis and interviews	While trying to meet the conflicting expectations of the target culture and native culture, the applicants struggled to negotiate a new academic identity. Their stances varied from self-effacement, boasting and justified self-praise

change), a change in level of 'self-confidence' ranked the highest. The next highest was 'nil change' (there is no change in the person except for development in language skills), a category that contrasted with identity changes; its ranking did suggest particular characteristics of the foreign language environment. Nevertheless, ratings of productive and additive changes[1] were above the critical level, showing self-perceived cultural identity changes. It was also found that productive changes, on the one hand, and identity split, on the other, both correlated with a native-culture-oriented 'social responsibility' motivation,[2] a motivational force not present in the social psychological paradigm of Gardner and associates. Replications of this study with 1017 graduate students (Li, Gao & Qian [2004], Row 2, Table 4.1) and with about 200 students from the commercial language school New Oriental School (Huang *et al.*, 2004) showed results similar to those of this large-scale study on undergraduates (English report: Gao *et al.*, 2005).

Qualitative study example

Whereas quantitative studies gave an overall picture of learners' perceptions of changes in their sense of self, qualitative studies provided some detailed accounts of the internal processes of these. In a case study on English majors (Gao *et al.*, 2002, Row 4, Table 4.1), for instance, an informant beginning her MA study experienced what she felt was an identity conflict, particularly in association with the learning of English writing style. Before entering college, this female student had been fond of reading Chinese literature and writing Chinese prose. After several years of strict training in the 'linear' style of English essay writing, she was shocked to find that her discursive Chinese writing style had shifted toward a linear style: 'My god, how could that have been written by me?!' she exclaimed. At first she felt fearful of losing her original Chinese writing identity: 'I feel a bit sorry .... I enjoyed the leisurely loose and roundabout style. Now I am afraid I can never find that look of mine anymore ... the style of a free man of letters'. Yet rather than rejecting her emerging writer identity, she decided to 'let it be', and 'look at the baby after it's born'. As time went on, she developed a productive orientation that enabled her to explain her appreciation of the beauty of literary Chinese as sheer enjoyment, and to perceive Shakespeare beyond being just a representative 'English writer' or 'foreign writer'. She said,

> I have a 'blind worship' for literature since I was a child. I am a 'victim' of literature. Yet I used to judge other cultures from the standpoint of Chinese culture, imposing labels on them. In the past I viewed Shakespeare as 'the best English writer' and read him to get a taste of

what 'foreign literature' was like, from a Chinese reader's perspective. I'm no longer like that. Now I take Shakespeare as MY writer. I'm keenly interested in this person writing from a rich, genuine, and enthusiastic heart. It's direct communication between two persons.

Other qualitative studies produced similar findings. The study on 'personal statements' regarding application for admission in English-speaking countries (Li *et al.*, 2004, Row 10, Table 4.1) showed that while going through revisions of the statements, the applicants negotiated their self-presentation strategies and academic identities among various alternatives, including a competent and confident identity oriented to the target culture, and a self-deprecating ('modest') identity oriented to the native culture. In the study on communication styles and identities in the English Corner (Li, 2004, Row 9, Table 4.1) some participants said that it was a place where they became more open and aggressive, very different from the traditional Chinese communication conventions usually expected. In a study of attendants of 'Crazy English' (Shen & Gao, 2004, Row 8, Table 4.1), an unconventional commercial English learning program, it was found that many students were attracted by, discovered or later constructed an outspoken, individualistic, emotion discharging, or 'crazy', identity that is a part neither of traditional Chinese culture nor of the ordinary communication conventions in English-speaking cultures. On the whole, the results from the qualitative studies tended to show identity change or development characterized by a dynamic process, across multiple dimensions, and the presence of unintended change, best conceptualized within a framework of social constructivism (Gao, 2006). This will be addressed in more detail later in this chapter.

Longitudinal expansion

More recently, identity research on ordinary language learners has been extended vertically, in a four-year longitudinal study on some 1300 university students in five universities of various types in Beijing. The study employs both quantitative and qualitative methods, comprising questionnaires, English learning journals, interviews and classroom observation. Preliminary results from the first two years show the following concerning identity development: (1) change in the level of self-confidence was the most prominent kind of identity development associated with English learning; (2) subtractive changes were prominent; (3) productive and additive changes were above critical levels, but limited in depth; (4) with more and deeper cultural learning, English majors had higher cultural identity changes than non-English majors (Gao *et al.*, 2007). Partial results of this longitudinal study have been reported by Bian (in this volume), Gao *et al.*

(2007), Liu and Gao (2008), Gao and Liu (2009) and Wang (2009), Zang (2009). These preliminary findings are largely congruent with the group of studies in 2004 summarized earlier, but provide a more microscopic, dynamic view of the identity development in progress.

Apart from Gao and her associates, during this time, also other researches on the identity development of Chinese learners of English have obtained evidence of productive changes (e.g. Liu, 2007; Ma & Cao, 2004). Some suggested that productive bilingualism had become the objective of foreign language teaching in China (Liu & Peng, 2006). From a similar yet perhaps more psychologically oriented perspective, Wang (2004) studied English pronunciation acquisition and learners' self-concept. A 'hypothesis of foreign language pronunciation learning' was proposed, supported by empirical data, according to which, learners' self-concept regarding second language (L2) pronunciation will influence their self-concept as a whole, and this, in turn, will promote or inhibit learning.

Theoretical Challenges

The studies on EFL learners' identity change, on the whole, have not attracted a great deal of attention in China, and do not fit well into the mainstream of research concerns on language proficiency and individual learner factors as in the social psychological paradigm. Among limited direct response, criticism was dominant. Responding to the work of Gao and her associates (2004) on cultural identity change, Qu Weiguo (2005) made the following arguments:

(1) The definitions of 'identity' and 'cultural identities' are not clear, and lack operational definition. Similarly, 'when identity change involves a second language, it signifies confrontations between two cultures, or two set of values derived from the two cultures' (Qu Weiguo, 2005: 113). 'Before we have set up unequivocally a set of traits that can be considered as characteristically Chinese in the identity set, research on identity change is impossible' (Qu Weiguo, 2005: 110).

(2) A linear cause–effect relationship between language learning and identity changes is not established. 'Language-related change in identity should be attributable to the language in question' (Qu Weiguo, 2005: 113). It is unclear whether identity changes among the students can be exclusively attributed to English language learning, as other sources are not ruled out.

(3) Cultural identity change associated with language learning presupposes a second language environment in its narrow sense, which is

absent in China. 'The discussion of a second language's contribution to identity change presupposes at least a bilingual community, and a speaker's proficiency of that language. In a context where English is a foreign language, and it is mainly learnt and used in educational contexts, we need to exercise caution with regards the role of English in such process' (Qu Weiguo, 2005: 93).

In the author's experience, these views on the legitimacy of language learning and identity research, especially the second and third points, seem representative of the views of a large number of Chinese EFL teachers. Thus the author has been questioned on various occasions about the instrumental nature of English learning in China, EFL learners' limited exposure to the target culture, and related to this, the relevance of learner identity research.

There is still another level of potential challenge to EFL learning and identity research in China, although no explicit criticism in this respect has been directed to the studies mentioned above. That is, when the status of EFL or second language has increasingly changed into that of an international auxiliary language, when its cultural attachment to any country of origin is challenged, English may have become a 'post-identity language' (Lo Bianco, 2005), and hence the issue of identity in its learning may be irrelevant.

Reflections on the Issue of Relevance and Legitimacy

While the first issue listed above appears to be about definitions, the language in which it is couched – 'operational' definitions, 'unequivocally' – are evidence of difference at the deeper level of epistemology, between structuralist and constructivist perspectives. This difference will lead to differences in definitions of key concepts such as 'culture' and 'identity', in assumptions about the relationship among various factors involved, and in preferred research methodologies. A discussion of the difference between these two perspectives, and acknowledgment of the prevailing dominance of the structuralist view, as set out below, serve to reveal much about the state of language learning research in China today.

Structuralist and constructivist perspectives

Qu's challenge brings up the epistemological distinction between structuralist and constructivist perspectives of culture and identity. Such a distinction will lead to differences in definitions of key concepts,

assumptions about the relations among various factors involved and preference of research methodologies. Defined by following the sociological
and social psychological tradition, 'structuralism' perceives a target
concept, here 'culture', 'identity' or 'language', as an entity with a definite,
stable and inherent structure. The structural elements, often in a hierarchical framework, are objective or real, and can be unpacked and singled out
for discrete measurement. Moreover, there are direct links between these
structural entities, one influencing the other. A number of terms are often
used for such an orientation, with varied emphasis. Thus 'structuralism' is
related to several other terms. To the extent that emphasis is on structural
elements as objective facts or a reality independent of human subjectivity,
structuralism is associated with 'objectivism' or 'realism'. To the extent
that emphasis is on the existence of essential nature shared by all members
in the conceptual category, it is associated with 'essentialism'. To the extent
that emphasis is on the requirement of observable, especially quantifiable,
evidence to access structural elements and their relations, it is associated
with 'positivism'. Yet here, for the purpose of our discussion, the direct
correspondence between structural entities is particularly highlighted.

In the post-structuralist era, the objectivity and fixity of structures are
challenged. 'Constructivism' is a school of thought of this kind, with
different branches. Radical constructivism highlights the importance of
human agency, whereas social constructivism stresses interaction between
objective, external factors and subjective, internal factors. From this
perspective, identity is a process as well as a product of interaction between
external social structures and language use with human agency. To capture
the complicated interaction between the 'internal' and 'external', qualitative methods are often preferred in research. In this chapter, 'constructivism' means the latter stance.

The above structuralism–constructivism distinction is a theoretical one.
In actual practice, structuralism and constructivism orientations form a
continuum, where the positions of researchers or particular studies are
located. In the past half a century, there has been a theoretical shift from
structuralist to constructivist in Western social sciences (e.g. Checkel,
1998), including the social psychological study of language learning and
language use. Structuralist theories perceive one-to-one correspondence
between linguistic varieties and large social categories, where social factors
are deterministic. The binary distinctions between 'in-group' and 'out-
group' (Tajfel, 1981), between 'restricted code' of working class and 'elaborated code' of middle class (Bernstein, 1971–1975), and between different
linguistic varieties as with Labov (1972), constituted models of this sort.
Such an orientation gradually gave way to a constructivist one, beginning

with Gumperz's *Language and Social Identity* (1982), and La Page and Tabouret-Keller's acts of identity theory (1985). The one-to-one correspondence between language use and social identities and the deterministic orientations were weakened; more attention was given to interactions and individual acts. Insights of sociological theories, such as Bourdieu's (1977) concept of language as a *cultural capital*, and Giddens' concepts of 'duality of structure' (1984) and 'self-identity', provided some room for individuals' negotiation of identities in the society, and inspired studies on second language learning and identities (e.g. De Fina *et al.*, 2006; Leander, 2002; Norton, 1997, 2000; Norton Peirce, 1995; Thesen, 1997; for more details, see Gao *et al.*, 2008; Joseph, 2004).

The structuralist–constructivist continuum provides a frame where the debate of EFL learners' identity research can be perceived and explained. Whereas the critique is launched from a structuralist–essentialist position, empirical studies carried out in China on the whole are oriented toward the constructive end.

Issues of Debate Viewed from Structuralist and Constructivist Perspectives

Definitions of identities and cultures

From a structuralist–essentialist perspective, identity refers to clear-cut external social categories such as nationality and socioeconomic class, or subjective classifications based on such social categories – when 'subjective' classifications are taken as objective entities, rarely changing. From a constructivist perspective, identity is self-defined, pluralistic and dynamic, constantly negotiated between the individual agent and the social environment. According to Giddens (1991: 244), self-identity is 'the self as reflexively understood by the individual in terms of his or her biography'. The epistemological distinction having been clarified, the fact that 'identity' is an ambiguous concept without a unified definition among different researchers should then be natural.

Likewise, from a structuralist point of view, a cultural identity – such as 'Chinese identity' and 'American identity' – is based on a clear 'set' of cultural characteristics. Before the list of traits of the set is clearly and exhaustively delineated, there is no talk of 'culture' or 'cultural identity'. Yet from a constructivist perspective, cultures may have clear cores but the boundaries are fuzzy. Each linguistic act is a situated 'act of identity' (Le Page & Tabouret-Keller, 1985), and might involve multiple dimensions of identity.

Relationship between language learning and identity change

The structuralist–positivist approach assumes a linear cause–effect relationship among language learning, its influencing factors and results. It is essential to have 'operational definitions' of each variable, and keep out the influence from sources other than the selected independent variable(s). In contrast, a constructivist view would perceive the relationships as complex, interactive or reciprocal. The absence or impossibility of showing an exclusive cause–effect relationship does not rule out the necessity to examine the phenomena.

Bilingual speech communities and language proficiency

A structuralist–essentialist approach would assume a clear-cut distinction between 'bilingual' versus 'monolingual' speech communities, 'genuine' (ESL) versus 'fake' (EFL) intercultural communication situations and 'high' versus 'low' target language proficiencies pertaining to the possibilities of cultural identity change. From a constructivist perspective, such clear-cut distinctions may not offer meaningful help in understanding the phenomena under consideration. While it is commonly assumed that the ESL–EFL distinction determines the dose of target language and culture input to learners, it should not be forgotten that in an ESL situation, learners' 'affective filter' may prevent them from changing the input to intake, whereas in an EFL situation, learners' high motivation or 'investment' (Norton Peirce, 1995) may prompt them to construct micro-level learning environments characterized by high doses of the (perceived) target culture. Much of the empirical studies mentioned above have shown this point. In the information age, high technology available to the public has facilitated the learners' construction of their own language environment, so the dose of input has become increasingly dependent on the learning agents.

Structuralist and constructivist perspectives are driven by different human needs for knowledge, and the paradigm shift can partly be accounted for by a time frame. Structuralist frames will reduce complex phenomena into a handful of categories comfortable for the limited capacity of human cognition; therefore they are very handy when a new pattern is emerging and awaits verification. Constructivist perspectives, in contrast, will feed our thirst for the more complex, dynamic and subtle aspects of knowledge, and are more appropriate when a new territory is explored or a breakthrough is expected. Looking retrospectively at the identity research the author and her associates have carried out, it can be said that the early work on productive bilingualism had a structuralist tint, whereas later studies on ordinary learners were more constructive.

The *ti-yong* Dilemma and Fear of Identity Loss

Apart from a cognitive account, the common concern over the relevance or legitimacy of language learners' identity research in China should also be understood in its own social historical context. As already described in Chapter 1, there has long existed a tradition of distinguishing *ti* from *yong* in language and cultural learning in China. *Ti* refers to the essence or substance of a culture, whereas *yong* refers to its utility. From the late 19th century up to now, the predominant principle of education in general and language education in particular has been 'Chinese learning as *ti*; Western learning as *yong*'. Thus Chinese and Western cultures have been taken for granted by many as totally different 'sets', without a common denominator; hence the boundaries between them cannot be crossed or permeated. The perception of English as, and merely as, a 'foreign language' is functionally handy and ideologically safe, for its influence is then justifiably restricted to the 'educational contexts' as a pure instrument. While this commonly held view concerning the external 'EFL' environment seems to embody objective truth, it also has embedded in it a profound fear of cultural or national identity loss, which has haunted the Chinese since the traumatic Opium Wars in the second half of the 19th century and has become part of the collective unconscious. It is much less disturbing and more positive to talk about improving technical skills in the language. The relatively limited yet acutely critical attention that learner identity research has encountered in China is, therefore, no surprise.

Conclusion

Research on English learning and learners' identity development in the Chinese context started in the 1990s with some 'best foreign language learners', from which emerged the concept of 'productive bilingualism'. While based on empirical data, this concept was used to tackle the identity dilemma associated with two conflicting systems of *ti*: that of the native culture and that of the target culture. The research was expanded to ordinary learners in the new millennium, where a large variety of identity changes were found including, but not confined to, those related to the target culture. While learners' identity studies have not attracted mainstream attention in the circle of English education in China, recently challenges have been made concerning the legitimacy of such research. A major argument is that China's EFL environment does not provide enough experience of target culture to cause identity changes. The discussion in this chapter proposes that the debate over legitimacy stems from the researcher's structuralist or constructive stance, and that the structuralist–essentialist stance among Chinese scholars is deeply rooted in a social historical tradition where a rigid *ti–yong* distinction has been made so as to guard against threat to national identity loss.

The social constructivist perspective on identity research has several implications for China's English education. First of all, as identity is not simply given but built up through symbolic interaction, language cannot be dispensed with in the process of identity construction, and the learning of a new language is bound to have an impact on the person as a whole. At an individual level, identity development may be part of the unexpressed 'practical consciousness' and 'unintended consequences of action' of the agent, which is to be transformed into 'discursive consciousness' (Giddens, 1984). At a sociocultural level, English learning in China is not merely a 'barometer of modernization' external to that process, but a part of that very process. This process is characterized by a 'duality of structure' (Giddens, 1984).

The constructivist view also opens up new possibilities that go beyond the dichotomy between target culture and native culture. In an era when the binary distinction between ESL and EFL is replaced by EIL (English as an International Language) or World Englishes, the function of English learning in identity development is broadened. Even as a 'basic skill', the learning of English helps to construct learner identities of various kinds – competitive job hunters on the international market, competent professionals, successful ambassadors of the native culture, among others. English is not, in fact, a 'post-identity' language, one that is 'no longer a foreign language', as Lo Bianco (2005) has suggested. By being associated with a wide range of 'imagined communities' (Norton, 2001), EIL is acquiring an ever more pervasive role in learners' identity construction.

Along this line of thinking, it seems that the concept of 'productive bilingualism' can be expanded to refer to not only mutual enhancement of 'native culture' and 'target culture' identities, but also in a broad sense, mutual enhancement of the original identity (e.g. being a 'Chinese businessperson') and a newly adopted one (e.g. being an 'international businessperson'). For 'EFL' or EIL learners in the context of globalization and glocalization, the productive relationship may typically occur between perceived membership of the native/local culture, on the one hand, and membership in a world community on the other hand. When Fromm (1948) proposed 'productiveness', he meant a general 'orientation', which might be realized in various relationships. The move toward a broader type of productive bilingualism, however, has led to an expanded meaning of the term 'bilingualism' beyond the original 'capacity in two languages', so that now it also encompasses multilinguistic competence and multicultural awareness. This expanded productive bilingualism is a direction that future empirical research might fruitfully explore.

Notes

1. Example of productive change: 'As my ability of appreciating English literature and art increases, I have become more interested in Chinese literature and art.' Example of additive change: 'I have an English name in addition to my Chinese name. They are used in different situations'.
2. Example of social responsibility motivation: 'Only when I have a good command of the English language can I contribute to China's prosperity'.

References

Bernstein, B. (1971–1975) *Class, Codes and Control* (Vols 1–3). London: Routledge and Kegan Paul.

Bourdieu, P. (1977) The economics of linguistic exchanges. *Social Science Information* 16 (6), 645–668.

Checkel, J.T. (1998) The constructivist turn in international relations theory. *World Politics* 50 (2), 324–348.

Chen, J.M. and Tan, Z.M. (eds) (1993) 语言与文化多学科研究 *Yuyan yu Wenhua Duoxueke Yanjiu* [*Multidisciplinary Studies of Language and Culture*]. Beijing: Beijing Language Institute Press.

De Fina, A., Schiffrin, D. and Bamberg, M. (2006) *Discourse and Identity.* Cambridge: Cambridge University Press.

Dörnyei, Z. (1994) Motivation and motivating in the foreign language classroom. *Modern Language Journal* 78, 273–284.

Fromm, E. (1948) *Man for Himself.* London: Routledge and Kegan Paul.

Gao, Y.H. (2001) *Foreign Language Learning: "1 + 1 > 2".* Beijing: Peking University Press.

Gao, Y.H. (2002) Productive bilingualism: 1 + 1 > 2. In D.W.C. So and G.M. Jones (eds) *Education and Society in Plurilingual Contexts* (pp. 143–162). Brussels: VUB Brussels University Press.

Gao, Y.H. (2006) 外语学习社会心理的结构化理论视角 Waiyu xuexi shehui xinli de jiegouhua lilun shijiao [A structuration theory perspective of social psychology factors in foreign language learning]. 中国外语 *Zhongguo Waiyu* [*Foreign Languages in China*] 2006 (4), 43–49.

Gao, Y.H. and Project Team (eds) (2004) 中国大学生英语学习社会心理-学习动机与自我认同研究 *Zhongguo Daxuesheng Yingyu Xuexi Shehui Xinli – xuexi dongji yu ziwo rentong yanjiu* [*The Social Psychology of English Learning by Chinese College*

Students – Motivation and Learners' Self-Identities]. Beijing: Foreign Language Teaching and Research Press.

Gao, Y.H., and Project Team (2007) 大学生英语学习社会心理：基础阶段跟踪研究 *Daxuesheng Yingyu Xuexi Shehui Xinli: Jichu jieduan genzong yanjiu* [*The Social Psychology of English Learning by Chinese College Students: A Longitudinal Study of the First Two Years*]. Unpublished project completion report. China's National Grant of Social Sciences, 2005–2007.

Gao, Y.H. and Liu, L. (2009) English learning motivation and self-identity development – the first two years of English majors in a Chinese comprehensive university. In P.K. Cheng and J.X. Yan (eds) *Culture Identity and Language Anxiety* (pp. 113–144). Guilin: Guangxi Normal University Press.

Gao, Y.H., Li, Y.X. and Li, W.N. (2002) EFL learning and self-identity construction: Three cases of Chinese college English majors. *Asian Journal of English Language Teaching* 12, 95–120.

Gao, Y.H., Cheng, Y., Zhao, Y. and Zhou, Y. (2004) 英语学习动机与自我认同变化-对本科生的定量考察 Yingyu xuexi dongji yu ziwo rentong bianhua – Dui benke-sheng de dingliang kaocha [Motivation types and self-identity changes among Chinese college undergraduates]. In Y.H. Gao and project Team Zhongguo Daxuesheng Yingyu Xuexi Shehui Xinli: Xuexi Dongji Yu Ziwo Rentong Yanjiu (*The Social Psychology of English Learning by Chinese College Students: Motivation and Learners' Self-Identities*) (pp. 25–62). Beijing: Foreign Language Teaching and Research Press.

Gao, Y.H., Cheng, Y., Zhao, Y. and Zhou, Y. (2005) Self-identity changes and English learning among Chinese undergraduates. *World Englishes* 24 (1), 39–51.

Gao, Y.H., Xiu, L.M. and Ding, L.P. (2007) 英语学习动机与自我认同变化-综合大学英专一年级跟踪 Yingyu xuexi dongji yu ziwo rentong bianhua – Zonghe daxue yingzhuan yi nianji genzong [English learning motivation and self-identity changes – a longitudinal study on first-year English majors in a comprehensive university]. *The Journal of Chinese Sociolinguistics* 2007 (1), 95–106.

Gao, Y.H., Li, Y.X. and Bian, Y.W. (2008) 从结构观到建构观-语言与认同研究纵观 Cong jiegouguan dao jiangouguan – Yuyan yu rentong yanjiu zongguan [From structuralist to constructive perspectives – a review of language and identity research]. 语言教学与研究 *Yuyan Jiaoxue yu Yanjiu* [*Language Teaching and Research*] 2008 (2), 19–26.

Gardner, R.C. (1985) *Social Psychology and Second Language Learning: The Role of Attitudes and Motivation*. London: Edward Arnold.

Giddens, A. (1984) *The Constitution of Society*. Berkeley, CA: University of California Press.

Giddens, A. (1991) *Modernization and Self-Identities: Self and Society in Late Modern Age*. Stanford, CA: Stanford University Press.

Gui, S.C. (1986) 我国英语专业学生社会心理分析 Woguo yingyu zhuanye xuesh-eng shehui xinli fenxi [An analysis of the social psychology of English majors in China]. 现代外语 *Xiandai Waiyu* [*Modern Foreign Languages*] 1986 (1), 1–67.

Gumperz, J. (ed.) (1982) *Language and Social Identity*. Cambridge: Cambridge University Press.

Guo, J.G. (2004) 二十年中国的第二语言习得研究 Ershi nian zhongguo de dier yuyan xide yanjiu [SLA research in China in the recent two decades]. 国外外语教学 *Guowai Waiyu Jiaoxue* [*Foreign Language Teaching Abroad*] 2004 (4), 1–6.

Holliday, A., Hyde, M. and Kullman, J. (2004) *Intercultural Communication: An Advanced Resource Book*. London: Routledge.

Hu, W.Z. (ed.) (1988) *International Communication: What it Means to Chinese Learners of English*. Shanghai: Shanghai Translation Publishing House.

Hu, W.Z. (ed.) (1994) 文化与交际 *Wenhua yu Jiaoji* [*Culture and Communication*]. Beijing: Foreign Language Teaching and Research Press.

Hu, W.Z. (ed.) (1999) *Aspects of Intercultural Communication – Proceedings of China's 2nd Conference on Intercultural Communication*. Beijing: Foreign Language Teaching and Research Press.

Huang, Q.H., Zhou, L. and Gao, Y.H. (2004) "新东方"学员英语学习动机与自我认同变化 'Xindongfang' xueyuan yingyu xuexi dongji yu ziwo rentong bianhua [English learning motivation and self-identity changes among New Oriental School trainees]. 中国社会语言学 *Zhongguo Shehui Yuyanxue* [*The Journal of Chinese Sociolinguistics*] 2004 (2), 51–63.

Joseph, J. (2004) *Language and Identity: National, Ethnic, Religious*. New York: Palgrave Macmillan.

Labov, W. (1972) *Sociolinguistic Patterns*. Philadelphia: University of Pennsylvania Press.

Lambert, W.E. (1974) Culture and language as factors in learning and education. In F.E. Aboud and R.D. Meade (eds) *Language and Social Psychology* (pp. 186–192). Oxford: Basil Blackwell.

Le Page, R.B. and Tabouret-Keller, A. (1985) *Acts of Identity: Creole-Based Approaches to Language and Ethnicity*. Cambridge: Cambridge University Press.

Leander, K. (2002) Locating Latanya: The situated production of identity artifacts in classroom interaction. *Research in the Teaching of English* 37, 198–250.

Li, N. and Wu, Y.A. (2007) 任务特征与学习动机研究 Renwu tezheng yu xuexi dongji yanjiu [A study on task characteristics and learning motivation]. 外语教学 *Waiyu Jiaoxue* [*Foreign Language Teaching*] 2007 (2), 43–47.

Li, S.J., Gao, Y.H. and Qian, M. (2004) 英语学习动机与自我认同变化-对研究生的定量考察 Yingyu xuexi dongji yu ziwo rentong bianhua – Dui yanjiusheng de dingliang kaocha [Motivation types and self-identity changes among Chinese graduate students]. In Y.H. Gao and project Team Zhongguo Daxuesheng Yingyu Xuexi Shehui Xinli: Xuexi Dongji Yu Ziwo Rentong Yanjiu (*The Social Psychology of English Learning by Chinese College Students: Motivation and Learners' Self-Identities*) (pp. 63–86). Beijing: Foreign Language Teaching and Research Press.

Li, Y.X. (2004) 高校英语角考察：交际模式与自我认同建构 Gaoxiao yingyujiao kaocha: Jiaoji moshi yu ziwo rentong jiangou [Language learning and self-identity construction – a study of college 'English corners' in China]. In Y.H. Gao and project Team Zhongguo Daxuesheng Yingyu Xuexi Shehui Xinli: Xuexi Dongji Yu Ziwo Rentong Yanjiu (*The Social Psychology of English Learning by Chinese College Students: Motivation and Learners' Self-Identities*) (pp. 202–226). Beijing: Foreign Language Teaching and Research Press.

Li, Z.Z., Gao, Y.H. and Li, F.F. (2004) 留美"自述"中的评价资源，谦虚策略与学术身份建构 Liumei 'zishu' zhong de pingjia ziyuan, qianxu celue yu xueshu shenfen jiangou [Appraisal and modesty – self-identity construction in personal statements]. In Y.H. Gao and project Team Zhongguo Daxuesheng Yingyu Xuexi Shehui Xinli: Xuexi Dongji Yu Ziwo Rentong Yanjiu (*The Social Psychology of*

English Learning by Chinese College Students: Motivation and Learners' Self-Identities) (pp. 227–248). Beijing: Foreign Language Teaching and Research Press.

Liu, L. and Gao, Y.H. (2008) 英语学习动机与自我认同变化-综合大学英专二年级跟踪 Yingyu xuexi dongji yu ziwo rentong bianhua – Zonghe daxue yingzhuan er nianji genzong [English learning motivation and self-identity changes – a longitudinal study on second-year English majors in a comprehensive university]. 中国外语 *Zhongguo Waiyu* [*Foreign Languages in China*] 2008 (2), 124–125.

Liu, Q. and Peng, Y. (2006) 全球化背景下中国英语教学文化双赢目标的实现 Quanqiuhua Beijing xia zhongguo yingyu jiaoxue wenhua shuangying mubiao de shixian [The realization of a double-win cultural objective for China's English language teaching in the context of globalization]. *Sino-US English Teaching* 25, 1–5.

Liu, S.M. (2007) "准"英语情境下的生产性双语现象-高职英语专业学生自我认同的建构 'Zhun' yingyu qingjing xia de shengchanxing shuangyu xianxiang – gaozhi yingyu zhuanye xuesheng ziwo rentong de jiangou [Productive bilingualism in 'para-genuine' English environment – self-identity construction of English majors in professional colleges]. 当代教育论坛 *Dangdai Jiaoyu Luntan* (*Xueke Jiaoyu Yanjiu*) [*Forum of Contemporary Education – Studies on Education in Various Subjects*] 8, 124–125.

Lo Bianco, J. (2005) No longer a (foreign) language: The rhetoric of English as a post-identity language. *The Journal of Chinese Sociolinguistics* 2005 (2), 17–40.

Ma, C.Y. and Cao, T.J. (2004) 大学本科生英语学习中自我认同变化探究 Daxue benkesheng yingyu xuexi zhong ziwo rentong bianhua tanjiu [A study on English learning and self-identity changes of college undergraduates]. 黑龙江教育学院学报 *Heilongjiang jiaoyu xueyuan xuebao* [*Journal of Heilongjiang College of Education*] 2004 (3), 51–55.

Norton Peirce, B. (1995) Social identity, investment, and language learning. *TESOL Quarterly* 29, 9–31.

Norton, B. (1997) Language, identity, and the ownership of English. *TESOL Quarterly* 35, 307–22.

Norton, B. (2000) *Identity and Language Learning: Gender, Ethnicity and Educational Change*. Harlow: Pearson Education.

Norton, B. (2001) Non-participation, imagined communities, and the language classroom. In M. Breen (ed.) *Learner Contributions to Language Learning: New Directions in Research* (pp. 159–171). Harlow: Pearson Education.

Qu, W.G. (2005) On issues concerning English and identity research in China. *The Journal of Chinese Sociolinguistics* 2005 (2), 93–116.

Shen, L.X. and Gao, Y.H. (2004) "疯狂英语"对于学习者的意义 'Fengkuang Yingyu' duiyu xuexizhe de yiyi [What 'Crazy English' means to Chinese students]. In Y.H. Gao and project Team Zhongguo Daxuesheng Yingyu Xuexi Shehui Xinli: Xuexi Dongji Yu Ziwo Rentong Yanjiu (*The Social Psychology of English Learning by Chinese College Students: Motivation and Learners' Self-Identities*) (pp. 190–201). Beijing: Foreign Language Teaching and Research Press.

Shi, Y.Z. (2000) 大学生英语学习动机调查 Daxuesheng yingyu xuexi dongji diaocha [A survey of university students' English learning motivation]. 国外外语教学 *Guowai Waiyu Jiaoxue* [*Foreign Language Teaching Abroad*] 2000 (4), 8–11.

Tajfel, H. (1981) Social stereotypes and social groups. In J.C. Turner and H. Glies (eds) *Intergroup Behavior* (pp. 144–167). Oxford: Basil Blackwell.

Thesen, L. (1997) Voices, discourse, and transition: In search of new categories in EAP. *TESOL Quarterly* 31, 487–511.

Wang, C.M. (2004) 自我概念与外语语音学习假设 Ziwo gainian yu waiyu yuyin xuexi jiashe [Self concept and foreign language pronunciation learning hypothesis]. 外语教学与研究 *Waiyu Jiaoxue yu Yanjiu* [*Foreign Language Teaching and Research*] 2004 (1), 56–63.

Wang, X.L. and Liu, X.L. (2002) 影响理工科学生英语阅读效率的学生因素调查 Yingxiang ligongke xuesheng yingyu yuedu xiaolu de xuesheng yinsu diaocha [A survey of learner factors affecting English reading efficiency of science majors]. 外语教学 *Waiyu Jiaoxue* [*Foreign Language Teaching*] 2002 (1), 49–54.

Wang, X.Y. (2009) 基础阶段英语专业大学生英语学习动机的特点和变化–对一所外语类大学英语专业本科生的跟踪调查 Jichu jieduan yingyu zhuanye daxuesheng yingyu xuexi dongji de tedian he bianhua – Dui yisuo waiyu lei daxue yingyu zhuanye benkesheng de genzong diaocha [On Chinese English-major students' motivation change during their first-two-year university life. A longitudinal study on the English-major students from a foreign language university]. 语言学研究 *Yuyanxue Yanjiu* [*Linguistic Research*] 7, 201–210.

Wen, Q.F. (2001) 英语学习动机，观念，策略的变化规律与特点 Yingyu xuexi dongji, guannian, celue de bianhua guilu yu tedian [English learning motivation, beliefs, and strategies: Patterns and characteristics of change]. 外语教学与研究 *Waiyu Jiaoxue yu Yanjiu* [*Foreign Language Teaching and Research*] 2001 (2), 105–115.

Wen, Q.F. and Wang, H.X. (1996) 学习者因素与大学英语四级考试成绩的关系 Xuexizhe yinsu yu daxue yingyu siji kaoshi chengji de guanxi [Relations between learner factors and College English Test Band 4 scores]. 外语教学与研究 *Waiyu Jiaoxue yu Yanjiu* [*Foreign Language Teaching and Research*] 1996 (4), 33–43.

Wu, Y.A., Liu, R.Q. and Jeffrey, P. (1996) Learner factors and learning achievement – a study of the effect of factors affecting English language learning. In G.Z. Xu (ed.) *ELT in China 1992* (pp. 1–38). Beijing: Foreign Language Teaching and Research Press.

Zang, Q. (2009) 理工科大学生英语学习与自我认同变化的跟踪研究 Ligongke daxuesheng yingyu xuexi yu ziwo rentong bianhua de genzong yanjiu [Non-English Majors' Self-identity Changes and English Leaning—A longitude Study of the First Two Years in a University of Science and Engineering]. 语言学研究 *Yuyanxue Yanjiu* [*Linguistic Research*] 7, 232–240.

Zhou, Y. (1996) Social psychological factors and language learning. In G.Z. Xu (ed.) *ELT in China 1992* (pp. 49–83). Beijing: Foreign Language Teaching and Research Press.

Zhu, Z.Y. (2006) 普通高师大学英语学习策略研究报告 Putong gaoshi daxue yingyu xuexi celue yanjiu baogao [A study of learning strategies employed by non-English majors in normal colleges]. 中国外语 *Zhongguo Waiyu* [*Foreign Languages in China*] 2006 (4), 12–15.

Chapter 5

Beautiful English *versus* The Multilingual Self[1]

LI ZHANZI

Introduction

In this chapter we compare Zhang Haidi's *Beautiful English* (translations by the present author) (2004) with Natasha Lvovich's *The Multilingual Self* (1997). By focusing on the former, I will refer to identity construction in the English learning experiences of Chinese youth during the 1980s. The analysis is informed by the use of critical pedagogy theory and especially its ideas of ownership and appropriation.

Zhang Haidi was a youth model in China during the 1980s, known for her tenacious willpower and desire to make herself useful to society. Natasha Lvovich is a professional language teacher who migrated from Russia to the United States. Their autobiographical works on language learning form an interesting contrast but there are also points of comparison. Physical disability and never having travelled abroad confined Haidi to her own world. She took up writing and publishing in Chinese, and taught herself English and Japanese, in addition to the social work she was doing as a youth model. Lvovich, by contrast, lived in many places before migrating to the United States via Italy. She is a multilingual person well versed in French and English, and she also taught herself Italian and now teaches Russian in America. At a first glance, the rationale for comparison is not strong. However, if we examine the struggle of identity construction and their respective evaluations of their language-learning experiences, a comparison arises which in turn sheds light on English teaching in contemporary China.

Beautiful English is acclaimed as a book of methodology and inspiration for English learners throughout China. It is both a self-help manual

120

and an autobiography. As a self-help manual, it is clearly oriented toward meeting market needs, containing many quotes and illustrations. As an autobiography, it relates the author's personal life story, but also serves as a cross-cultural document with rich material on language learning. Below I analyze its evaluations and reflections on the construction of identity and cross-cultural encounters to reveal its many implications for English teaching in today's China. By contrast, *The Multilingual Self* is Natasha Lvovich's doctoral thesis but it also serves as a language-learning autobiography. As Pavlenko (2007) notes, language-learning autobiographic narratives 'offer insights into people's private worlds, inaccessible to experimental methodologies, and thus provide the insider's view of the process of language, attrition and use' (Pavlenko, 2007: 164–165).

Structurally, the works under discussion each weaves around a series of interrelated topics. Zhang's book comprises 20 chapters and centres around her experience and method of English learning. The chapters are given suggestive titles, for example 'My first English letter', 'I'm Mariana', 'From Chinese to English', 'On the streets of Tokyo', to mention just a few. Similar organization can be found in *The Multilingual Self*, which contains chapter titles like 'My French self', 'Confession of a Synesthete', 'My Italian self', 'American diary' and 'Russian as a second language', etc. Ethnographers find that narration of feminist life is neither chronological nor gradual, but discontinuous, fragmentary and autonomous in itself, rather than containing continuous, logically related sections. The organization of these two works typically displays this kind of fragmentary structure.

I am Mariana versus French Self

Recent development in critical pedagogy has contributed some highly relevant concepts for our analysis of the two works. Among them, the concept 'imagined community' transcends the boundary of the possibility of self. As Norton points out, the imagined community of a learner embeds an imaginative identity and the investment of the learner in the target language must be understood in this context (Norton, 2001: 166).

Human beings are capable of connecting with the community that transcends the given time and space, and their investment in this kind of imagined community significantly affects their effort of identity construction and language learning. This concept can enhance our understanding of the impact of time and space on learning. On the temporal scale, by understanding the imagined community, we can connect the learner's expectation of the future with their present action and identity; and things that have not happened can become the motivation underlying the learner's present behaviour. On the spatial scale, we can examine the interaction between the ideology of the nation and the identity of individual learners, and the impact of globalization on identity construction.

As Kanno and Norton (2003) note, the imagined community concept provides a theoretical framework for exploring creativity, hope and desire in identity construction. By this reasoning our identity is not only to be understood as our investment in the 'real' world, but also as our investment in 'possible' worlds, which provide attractive possibilities for educational reform.

What particularly attracts me as a discourse analyst here is the second chapter of *Beautiful English* entitled 'I am Mariana'. Here the author tells the story of how she gives herself an imagined identity in order to learn English. This is in addition to recommending to the reader the method of 'imagined identity'. The implication is that to learn a foreign language one acquires an imagined identity and consequently that an imagined community is itself enacted by this imagining of an identity. Apparently the author has given some thought to the question of language and identity and has undertaken an endeavour of her own. We will try to illustrate just what kind of endeavour this is.

At the beginning, it is a rather arbitrary and vacant identity, as the name may have appealed to the author by the pleasantness of its rhythm, and/or her contact with some literary figure. The chapter itself poses this question when it asks:

> Why Mariana and not other names? ... This is because the name Mariana is purely the result of my inspiration. When the name crosses my mind, I know it is my choice. (Zhang, 2004: 16)

The author also explains how she enriches this beautiful new identity of her own choosing:

> As I explore further in English learning, I make more and more description of Mariana. Her life keeps changing. ... I enjoy this way of writing novels and am passionate with expectations of the role I play. (Zhang, 2004: 21)

> Yes, at this moment I am Mariana. I am she. This virtual experience is fantastic beyond words. (Zhang, 2004: 21)

In *The Multilingual Self*, we also read about the hypothetical identity, in this case a French self:

> By using its language I could penetrate into its depth, step onto its land, and become part of it. A French personality, after all, was much

less confusing and safer than being a Jew in Soviet Russia. It was a beautiful Me, the Me that I liked: I spoke French without an accent. (Lvovich, 1997: 9)

Lvovich chose French out of her dislike for her identity of a Russian Jew, that is, through taking an ideological stance, while for Haidi, Mariana seems to be an aesthetic invention. This possibly bizarre identity brings Haidi a personal vision and a heightened motivation:

Ever since I named myself Mariana, I start to write my diary in English, and write my friends in English too. *It is very important to create a virtual English context for self-taught English learners* (emphasis added). (Zhang, 2004: 16)

Note the emphasized component; this is the self-help ingredient of the book. This suggestion about 'virtualizing an identity' is sometimes simplified as 'using your imagination' in some language-learning how-to books. We cannot tell without research whether this method is effective and whether every English learner in China is willing to give him or herself an English name as a preliminary phase of imagining an identity. But in Haidi's case, through naming herself Mariana and expanding the imagination, she seems to claim some imaginary ownership of the language. Given the special circumstances of her relatively confined life, this could work well as a source of motivation. A more recent work 'Unruly Bodies', published in 2007 by Susannah Mintz, suggests an intriguing line of thought, about how women autobiographers portray their lives by resisting the cultural stereotypes of triumph-over-adversity. Zhang's work suits with this kind of autobiography in that she implicitly insists on her disabilities as a core but not diminishing aspect of identity. Our analysis of her 'imagined identity' in teaching herself English is a case in point. What supplies continuity for such imagination is precisely her relative confinement caused by her disability.

However, things differ considerably for the youth today, as the explosion of stimulations brought about by the information age can make it extremely difficult for English learners to have a sustained imagined identity. We are coming to a discussion of language ownership below.

Also worth noting here are the simplified feelings or happiness brought about by this imagined identity. It was the hallowed or revered English Mariana immersed herself in, namely, the literary heritage like classic novels and lyrical poetry, not the living language that functions in daily life and engages itself with such activities as complaining, quarrelling and perhaps musing.

As evidence of this immersion, the following is what she jotted down in her notebook when she let herself play the role of Mariana:

> Perhaps you have read Jane Eyre. My home village is near the place the story occurred. Here it was winter. The sky was gray and the weather was cold. All tree leaves fell early before the fields seemed vast and solitary under the cover of white snow. Occasionally several sounds came from the distant bell tower, which reminded people the existence of time. If you look in the distance, you will find there are no trails of life, even the wild rabbits had also disappeared. Only before a dozen days or more I saw a carriage driving across the solitary fields. I did not know where it was going, but it surely took messages there, no matter if they were good news or bad ... (Zhang, 2004: 20)

In another development, in proposing the hypothesis 'new language= new identity', Zhang encounters difficulty reconciling this with the implied equation 'nation=language':

> I know I am not the persona that speaks English. I am Haidi and I'm learning to use another language. I am even refusing to use that way of using another language and sometimes only treat these English sentences as semiosis of another language. I cannot get rid of the instinct of life itself. I was born on the Chinese-speaking land and born to be a Chinese-speaker. So speak and write in Chinese I must. I cannot speak and write in English. (Zhang, 2004: 17)

Zhang actually raises two questions in this reflection. First, is a foreign language merely semiosis, without actual meaning? Second, must one mainly speak Chinese just because he or she is Chinese by birth? To answer the first question – there is no foreign language or 'another's language'. The language that is others' language can be the native language of the others themselves. So no language is just semiosis of language expression; every language has its semiosis and corresponding functions. For foreign language learners, if they are kept away from the functions of language use, or put it another way, if they cannot function in that language community, they may fall into the fantasy of semiosis.

The second question calls for more tentative treatment. Kramsch notes in her *Language and Culture* (Kramsch, 2000: 65) that although people tend to equate a culture with a language, the identity of a nation is not monolithic. However, in Haidi's book we notice:

> But my mind is not lonely. As I live in another world. There I read aloud English text, like a film conductor. I direct the characters and

> plots and settings and use my imagination to the full. In this way I
> learn texts and words by heart. (Zhang, 2004: 29)

Later she intensifies the identification of nation and language or
personal characteristics that Kramsch was problematizing.

> I am moved to tears by many English songs and without knowing I
> lose myself in another world, enjoy and indulge, seek and explore in a
> world of different culture, race and history ... as I truly love pop
> music, blues etc. The rhythmic enthusiastic modern music adds
> passion to life and fills one up with imagination and vitality. ... Ah, I
> also truly love the songs of my mother's time, such as ... But these are
> all Chinese, so also Asian. Why do I miss these songs? I think maybe
> it is because of my black hair and black eyes. (Zhang, 2004: 58)

Haidi loves English songs for two reasons. First, their difference; as to
her they seem to come from another world. The other is their rhythm and
enthusiasm. She is aware enough of dilemmas of identity to mention her
inclination toward the Chinese songs, which to her seem to be a natural
outgrowth of nationality traits – 'black hair and dark eyes'. After her expression of admiration for a different culture perhaps Haidi feels vulnerable, or
exposed, or nostalgic, and feels it is prudent to return to the original.

In order to further explore the relationship between Zhang's imagined
identity and her emotional experiences, we leave these two big questions
for a while and return to the book itself to focus on the affective expressions
it contains. In common with all self-help books, positive feelings reign:

> Maybe some people think learning is like plowing and is therefore a
> painstaking job. But I have found the seed of joy in the soil. And as
> time goes on, the seed sprouts in the bottom of my heart and blos-
> soms. I feel the joy of harvest. (Zhang, 2004: 22)

Joy becomes the predominant feeling throughout the whole book. It is
of course highly likely that when positive feelings predominate, the motivation to study will grow. But we ask are beauty and joy the result of the
author's new identity? Are they brought about by Zhang's involvement
with the imagined community animated by her imagined identity, and
her detached state of mind, or is English itself 'beautiful English'. Or does
the author recommend to anxious English learners a recipe – be beautiful
and joyful.

This actually is an important feature of self-help books. Self-help books
often propose active new approaches, and an activist disposition, in the
belief that social forces will give way to the will of independent, energetic

individuals. It is a characteristic of all self-help books to propose a series of steps and systematic information that centre on self-belief and self-change. One particular feature of such books for females is that they always contain encouragement to readers, by saying that so long as the readers are self-confident, they will be free of any inner problems, and that there are no limits to personal achievement with confident and active approaches. Transparently this ethos often ignores the constraints of social or economic conditions. Instead, characters are often very independent agents capable of personal transformation through will power and positive thinking. Moreover, these books suggest that readers should seek power, success and happiness for themselves as individuals, and not for the community or social groups to which they belong. They also elevate such social values as compassion and emotional sensitivity (Gauntlett, 2000).

Lvovich's book has the subtlety of an autobiography, but it also takes on the features of a self-helper at places in suggesting that individuals can always take an upper hand in transcending social–cultural constraints they encounter. As argued in early work on diary studies by Kathleen Graves, taken up more recently by Pavlenko (2007), this raises issues of clear relevance to English as an international language at a time when it is clear that no one 'owns' this language and no one can predict its future. In the following sections we are going to make further analysis of the views in the two books about language learning.

English Learning = Moral Virtue versus English Learning = Learning to Drive = Exercising Control of the Self

In research about learners, a large variety of metaphors are established, for example, the learner as a sufferer, as a problem solver, as a traveller, as a struggler and as a worker (Ellis, 2001: 65–85).

We find two more in these two books, namely, the learner as a climber and the learner as a driver, one focusing on perseverance and moral virtue, similar to the sufferer, struggler and traveller images and the other focusing on skills, similar to the problem-solver image.

In this part we will compare the different conceptions of English learning in these two books.

First let us look at the two learner metaphors in Zhang's books:

> For instance, some people want to learn a foreign language and they make up their minds many times. Maybe many a time they dream about themselves speaking a fluent foreign language ... no matter what that language is ... But months go by and more time elapses and

they find their progress slow, at least not as fast as they have imagined. ... (Zhang, 2004: 162)

People may be temporarily satisfied with their material pursuit, but there is no stopping their spiritual pursuit. *This is just like climbing high mountains* – people always aspire higher peaks. For someone who seriously love learning, the road of seeking knowledge always tempts him to explore and create, though the road is long and strenuous and calls for our utmost patience ... Actually English learning is just like that. You have to keep review what you have learned and lay a solid foundation before you can apply your abilities of listening, speaking, reading, writing and translating. (emphasis added) (Zhang, 2004: 163)

In these metaphors about mountaineering and walking, Haidi connects the strenuous efforts of English learning with moral requirements such as 'spiritual pursuits' and 'patience', and her utmost goal is to speak as fluently as a native speaker. If we refrain from discussing whether this goal is appropriate in terms of second language learning, and concentrate instead on the moral and personal injunctions in her work, we can deduce the following equation: English learning = knowledge pursuit = moral perfection.

This is indeed an over-loaded equation. It might be acceptable when proposed by a youth model like Haidi; for most young Chinese today, the ambition for English is less high flying; instead they hope to acquire a sufficient dose of English to pass the exams their society requires of English learners, and to apply English to other practical purposes. Relating English learning to such lofty goals as Haidi proposes converts the routine practice of compulsory language study into a sacred and therefore daunting personal mission.

In *The Multilingual Self*, English learning is more often than not connected with mastering skills and achieving proficiency. This is apparent in the following sequence.

As a language learner, I have experienced only short periods of discomfort and frustration with my language acquisition; as a driver, this period of learning was horrendous. It was a revealing process, therefore, about the individual variables in human learning and an insight into the problems, struggle, and suffering of a less successful or slower language learner.

My experience of learning how to drive shows, however, that there are no insurmountable barriers in human learning, that what seems impossible in the beginning finally becoming possible, and that there are no standard ways, styles, or time frames for human learning: Individual variables are endless. (Lvovich, 1997: 77)

The contrast between the previous high moral purpose and the mundane act of driving suggests two radically different modes of reasoning. When English learning is connected with moral injunctions, the extra motivation that is imposed is the burden of self-perfection. But will our learning under such conditions become over-stressed? In comparison, when we parallel English learning with learning to drive, are we ignoring the social–cultural implications of learning a language and its impact on identity construction? And does this, in its turn, neglect to address the rich implications of mass English learning in China as a social activity with implications for identity? If we relate the aspect of moral injunction to the narratives of an older-generation English educationalists in China (Li, 2005a, 2005b, 2005c: 35), we can venture a generalization that high moral purpose has been a pervasive understanding of English learning in China for some time, as it is not confined to those born during or following the 1980s.

Storing for Future Use versus For Real Communication

An additional quality to foreign language learning in Zhang's book is its storage for future use, and this lends the activity itself a future-oriented dimension. As she recalls her success she almost preaches this quality of a reserve skill stored up for subsequent application, an investment in a future life.

> Many years ago when I started learning Japanese, I did not expect that I would be able to go to Japan. Then one day I was on board Boeing 747 to Tokyo, I realized as time went by, my dream of applying another language came true in my persistent efforts. (Zhang, 2004: 166).

> Walking along the streets of Tokyo, I realized not everyone has the chance to go abroad and not every one can have an ideal language context. The important thing is to learn to create chances and to keep up the passion for learning. Also important is to give up the eagerness to achieve, but to wait patiently for the day to come when one can actually use the language. (Zhang, 2004: 165).

Similarly, Lvovich's story treats contact with native speakers as a turning point in her language learning

> Frank's visit was perhaps the first encounter I had with the American culture, language, and reality. Frank was a nice, pleasant, and grateful guest, and I felt quite comfortable with him, despite my poor, unpracticed English. I discovered, talking to him, that my language represents only sets of rules I had learned in class, and that it had no spirit

and no soul. It was a distant shapeless cloud suspended in the sky quite artificially, and therefore it did not produce real communication, which is in its major part emotional – there was no rain coming from that cloud. (Lvovich, 1997: 84)

We can predict from present circumstances that few will have the chance to communicate with native speakers. But for the majority of English learners, English is becoming useful in the here and now in diverse ways, such as writing resumes for going abroad, making out the bilingual public signs as China uses more English in public spaces, listening to the radio, watching CCTV 9, watching imported Hollywood movies in the original and chatting on the internet, to mention just a few. So there is no need to store English for future use, although a learner may have to wait in order to communicate directly with native speakers, such as when they do travel abroad or engage with English speakers. However, it is worth asking why among the many uses of English is direct interaction with native English speakers the one that is most valued? The explanation can be simple: Language use requires feedback which is exactly what self-taught learners lack. The feedback is not limited to the binary between true or false forms of language, which can after all be supplied by the computer, the textbook or the teacher in the classroom. Instead, there is another kind of feedback, a more subtle cultural- and identity-based kind, which perhaps lies behind this privileging of the encounter with native speakers. This kind of feedback relates to the information and interaction that constructs meaning in two lives, which Bakhtin (1981) calls the current that lights the bulb.

However, if we look at the situation from the other end, according to many predictions, a large amount of all future communication in English will take place between non-native speakers of English. Strong evidence can be found already on the internet. Rather than waiting for the chance to communicate with a native speaker at some future time, for many Chinese it is now possible at this time, or at any time. Successful English communication does not necessarily imply the participation of native speakers. For learners, an attitude or disposition of being ready to use English in the here and now, as internet-mediated communication makes possible, may prove more helpful in strengthening the motivation to learn than the mentality of storing the language for future use.

Aesthetic Longing versus the Gaining of Ownership

Another dimension of similarity and difference between the two works relates to the axis of aesthetic longing versus the admission to a community of ownership of a learned language. In exploring this, let us first look at three excerpts from Haidi's book about her aesthetic longings:

> Actually, at that time, I was not clear to what end I was learning Japanese. You know I was living in a tiny county, from where it was very difficult to reach outside by transportation. I can even say it was a very isolated little town. One had no idea learning a foreign language there could ever lead anywhere. But learning foreign languages is my dream and desire. I believe foreign languages are like windows to the outside world. Through them I was bound to see the most beautiful scenery. (Zhang, 2004: 168)

> At that time I knew not the limit of the ken, and was burning with unquenchable passion for learning all day. My learning process was like a zigzagging slippery path and I was my own guide, stumbling ahead all the time. (Zhang, 2004: 221)

> I was moved by the original, as if hearing the echo from the nine-teenth century – the call of a British woman which was not strange to me. I could understand the call from the bottom of her soul. (Zhang, 2004: 226)

We can summarize the creation of self image in Haidi's book as 'passion + painstaking process = an aesthetic self'. Similar to Haidi's self-satisfaction in being able to understand Jane Eyre's crying of the soul, Lvovich also reports her huge self-satisfaction in entering the world of literary imagination, in this case French literature.

> The factual material of his class was challenging and reached beyond the frames set by the Soviet ideology: we were passionately initiated in the best of French writers and poets whose work was inaccessible to the average reader. Our intellectual journal included the profound analysis of the French symbolist poets, the challenge of the surrealists, and the depth of the classical literary heritage of Hugo, De Vigny, Musset, Balzac, Maupassant, Flaubert. (Lvovich, 1997: 21)

A key difference is escape; Lvovich describes the source of her passion in learning French as the running away from the political ideology of her homeland. The result is that she entered a new community, a club of privilege.

> French literature, with its intellectual and democratizing power was especially meaningful in a totalitarian country, and I was eager to identify with it. It also created one of the most significant and effective

inputs in my learning of French, in becoming fully functional in French, in acquiring a French identity. (Lvovich, 1997: 33)

With the acquisition of privilege, Lvovich declared her ownership of the French language.

The huge literary heritage of the French culture formed my thinking and feeling, and along with it – my use of the language. I could not think of French as a 'foreign language'; it was not foreign, it was mine. (Lvovich, 1997: 33)

Here we need to say a few more things about the concept of ownership. The concept is suitable in describing the proficiency level of English speakers, as it avoids the static binary division between native and non-native speakers. Ownership is a constructed notion, and has two broad dimensions, localization and legalization.

In his 1994 article 'The Ownership of English', Henry Widdowson points out that ownership refers to the way speakers appropriate English for their own use. In this discussion he notes that native speakers are no longer the sole authority of which forms of usage and which norms of expression are grammatical. This is because when a language becomes as widely used as English is, the norms and standards can no longer be determined only by native speakers. In Widdowson's analysis:

You are proficient with a language to the extent that you possess it, make it your own, bend it to your will, assert yourself through it rather than simply submit to the dictates of its form. (Widdowson, 1994: 394)

This sentiment suggests flexibility for or with English and in this context the issue of plural centricity of norms becomes a critical focus of research.

However, whether varieties of international English should be given equally legitimate status as native speakers' English is not an idea shared by all, or at least seems to call for more theorization (Higgins, 2003: 620).

We can also understand ownership as *legitimacy*. Norton (1997) conceptualizes ownership within a broader framework than the foregoing, an approach that is useful for examining the complex linguistic identity of speakers of international varieties of English such as Chinese. She argues that the categorization of speakers in native and non-native speakers sets up a rigid dichotomy that prevents learners from owning English because they are prevented from becoming legitimate speakers of it.

Drawing on Bourdieu's notion of language as a form of cultural capital, Norton writes, 'If learners invest in a second language, they do so with the understanding that they will acquire a wider range of symbolic and material resources' (Norton, 1995: 17).

Norton is referring here to immigrants mainly, and she comments that these speakers' investment in English yields legitimacy for them because it allows them to participate more fully in their new host societies, equipped with all the necessary resources. In later work she (Norton, 1997: 422) reveals how speakers' investment in the language which they are acquiring ultimately leads to ownership via a sense of the right to speak (i.e. legitimacy as a speaker): 'If learners of English cannot claim ownership of a language, they might not consider themselves legitimate speakers of that language'.

Applying this notion to Lvovich's later experience of learning Italian, we can further perceive what acknowledgement of ownership can do to encourage a language learner.

> I was surprised myself to be able to do it in Italian, but I enjoyed it so much that I was willing to take the risks of the ridiculous mistakes by acting out being Italian. I guess you can do it only when you really like your role, and I was truly in love with Italy. (Lvovich, 1997: 48)

> It was not only a pleasure, but an emotional need to speak to them in their language to repay their hospitableness, to understand them and their life to the roots, to feel adequately and at home. My 'home' was the language. (Lvovich, 1997: 48)

After experiencing the hardships of immigrating and job hunting, and confronting the situation of having to make a living now that she has emigrated to the United States, she made an attempt to deny her ownership of French, and declared that she would acquire ownership of English. And here we can see how she struggles with her 'imagined community' and tries to come in touch with reality:

> Can I try to love New York, love America, love people? Not just the fantasy about people and about the country, as I did before ... While learning French, I traveled into the depth of the language because I was in love with its culture and the cream of its people, but had I ever faced the real culture, real life, real people, in all their diversity and not just mirrored in literature and movies? ... The only thing I loved was the fantasy, and I hated the real world around me. I have to learn how to love it. Then my English will touch base with real meaning. (Lvovich, 1997: 64)

The author eventually makes a negative evaluation of her French – at a time when she has finally gained ownership of English.

> And then it started to make sense to me. I did not have to continue being French in America. I did not have to expose my French self as a defensive shield against the society. I did not have to exhibit my French identity in order not to be Russian, Jewish, Soviet. I did not have to create a fantasy of the noble, old, and beautiful French culture, ... My role is not seeking refuge in language learning; it is seeking a normal, healthy, and better life. I could build an American Self and a real life with it, ... However, this time I would do it for a healthy purpose – for taking the responsibility of the real life, with a real career, with real benefits for my family. (Lvovich, 1997: 72)

Lvovich here contrasts a pragmatic need to her fantasy need, to 'create a fantasy of the noble, old, and beautiful French culture', which is exactly what Haidi does with English, namely, create the legend of 'beautiful English'. Since Haidi's book is a self-help autobiography, and not a doctoral thesis, we cannot expect it to explore this further. But to some extent each involves identity change as reported in autobiographical narrative. We can say that Lvovich was fortunate to acquire some degree of unity of identity. This is how she expresses it:

> The transformation that had occurred in me and made sense of my different selves, nourished and expressed by different languages, led me to the understanding of the multilingual personality as an enriched and harmonic social identity, the whole. (Lvovich, 1997: 105)

She eventually becomes a foreign language teacher in America, teaching Russian. Her native language now becomes her second language. Interestingly, when she heard her students' exclamation of the grandeur of Russian culture and Russian history, she remarks:

> By the end of this emotional experience, I knew that something positive, peaceful, and enriching was coming to me – not instead, but beyond – and that this truly teaching/learning experience profoundly touched my new self. This complex process of healing, taking place in me, was taking place in me, was receiving along with giving out. It marked the birth of a balanced social and language ego, without which functioning in a new language and culture is impossible. (Lvovich, 1997: 68)

In view of the choice Lvovich made when confronted with the tension of ideology change and immigrant life, she seems to have gained a balance among competing identities and minds she has inhabited. But Haidi's two personas are not so well integrated and are far from united. This made her conscious of the fact that she should not indulge herself in enjoying the English songs, but should think of Chinese folk songs from time to time. She was enchanted by 'beautiful English' and immersed herself in the imagination of 'I am Mariana'. She achieved considerable English proficiency as a result of her perseverance, extensive reading, translation exercises and communication with English-speaking friends. But she does not reveal adequately how all this changed her identity and self-conception. Perhaps the explanation is simply that expressed by the book designer who called Haidi's work 'a book of methodology and inspiration for English learners'.

Coda

In China, English learning used to be a symbol of spiritual pursuit for some people, and our analysis of Haidi's account is a case in point. Now English has become the 'Open Sesame' for job hunting, career building and even identity construction. How can the gap between the two situations be overcome? Perhaps it is not possible. Perhaps English should be demoted a little in China; perhaps it should go down the shrine to become a more ordinary foreign or second language? But if we just treat English as a foreign language, we are actually ignoring its unique social–cultural context and the unique context of its place in Chinese society. The aspiration for mastering English is a reflection of the mentality of contemporary Chinese youth and, in this way, can be seen as an indication of our pursuit of multiple identities and our endeavour to break away from constraints of identity (Kramsch, 2002; Norton & Kelleen, 2004).

The rest of the question is: for the millions of Chinese who will not live in the United States, how can they integrate what will be their English identity, their imagined community, like 'Mariana' or 'Peter' into their lives in China? How will the ways that they do affect their learning of English? Is this new self superficial, like a mere veneer to a secure Chinese identity, or is it a barrier that will inhibit them in some ways, or will it be a means for facilitating enhanced proficiency in English? If it is the latter, how can an imagined new identity, belonging to an imagined new community, acquire a realistic footing (Breen, 2001)?

The situations of young Chinese people will differ considerably in the many diverse conditions and circumstances of mass learning of English in China, but pursuing these questions and supplying some general descriptions should be illuminating to the project of English learning in contemporary Chinese society. As Pennycook (2001: 102) points out, it is time to start ESL classes 'with a critical exploration of student contexts rather than a priori concepts of what they need to know'.

Note

1. A previous version of this chapter in Chinese has been published online at 李战子 2004a 美丽的英语 多语的自我 – 两部英语学习自传的比较[J] http: // www. cc. org.cn. It is a part of the 2003 National Social Science Project (03BYY015) 'Cross-culture Autobiographies and English Teaching and Learning'.

References

Bakhtin, M.M. (1981) *The Dialogic Imagination* (M.C. Emerson and M. Holquist, eds and trans.). Texas: University of Texas Press.

Breen, M.P. (ed.) (2001) *Learner Contributions to Language Learning*. Glenview, IL: Pearson Education.

Ellis, R. (2001) The metaphorical constructions of second language learners. In M. Breen (ed.) *Learner Contributions to Language Learning* (pp. 65–85). Glenview, IL: Pearson Education.

Gauntlett, D. (2000) *Self-Help Books and the Pursuit of a Happy Identity*. On WWW at http://www.theoryhead.com/gender.

Higgins, C. (2003) Ownership of English in the outer circle: An alternative to the NS-NNS dichotomy. *TESOL Quarterly* 37, 615–644.

Kanno, Y. and Norton, B. (2003) Imagined communities and educational possibilities: Introduction. *Journal of Language, Identity, and Education* 2 (4), 241–249.

Kramsch, C. (2000) *Language and Culture*. Shanghai: Shanghai Foreign Language Education Press.

Kramsch, C. (ed.) (2002) *Language Acquisition and Language Socialization – Ecological Perspectives*. London and New York: Continuum.

Li, Z. (2004) The paradoxical situation of identity politics. *Wai Guo Yu* [*Foreign Languages*] 5, 56–63.

Li, Z. (2005a) English and its relationship to their academic lives – a comparison of three types of English-learning narratives. *Zhong Guo Wai Yu* [*Foreign Languages in China*] 4, 35–42.

Li, Z. (2005b) French lessons – language acquisition, cultural identity and autobiography. *Si Chuan Wai Yu Xue Yuan Xue Bao* [*Journal of Sichuan International Studies University*] 4, 70–75.

Li, Z. (2005c) An appraisal-analysis approach to Zhao Yuanren's *My Linguistic Autobiography*. *Yu Yan Xue Yan Jiu* [*Linguistic Studies, PKU*], 32–42.

Lvovich, N. (1997) *The Multilingual Self*. New Jersey: Lawrence Erlbaum.

Mintz, S. (2007) *Unruly Bodies*. Chapel Hill: University of North Carolina Press.

Norton, B. (1995) Social identity, investment, and language learning. *TESOL Quarterly* 29, 9–31.

Norton, B. (1997) Language, identity, and the ownership of English. *TESOL Quarterly* 31, 409–429.

Norton, B. (2000) *Identity and Language Learning – Gender, Ethnicity and Educational Change*. Harlow, England: Longman/Pearson Education.

Norton, B. (2001) Non-participation, imagined communities and the language classroom. In M. Breen (ed.) *Learner Contributions to Language Learning* (pp. 159–171). Glenview, IL: Pearson Education.

Norton, B. and Kelleen, T. (eds) (2004) *Critical Pedagogies and Language Learning*. Cambridge: Cambridge University Press.

Pavlenko, A. (2007) Autobiographical narratives as data in applied linguistics. *Applied Linguistics* 28/2, 163–188.

Pennycook, A. (2001) *Critical Linguistics: A Critical Introduction*. Mahwah, NJ: Erlbaum.

Widdowson, H.G. (1994) The ownership of English. *TESOL Quarterly* 31, 377–389.

Zhang, H. (2004) *Mei Li De Ying Yu* [*Beautiful English*]. Beijing: Writers Press.

Chapter 6

'Just a Tool': The Role of English in the Curriculum

JANE ORTON

Introduction

Educational systems are official bodies with tasks to carry out on behalf of the local, often national, society, one of which is to establish school curricula that fit and serve society's goals. Principal among these goals is the passing on of the best from the past and, at the same time, education of the current generation to improve on that past. For all societies there is an inherent tension involved in managing these two objectives. Similarly, subjects offered on the curriculum reflect community regard for those fields of study, and members expect this to be made clear to their children. On the other hand, within the formal education system, at least, there will be strong community expectation that the curriculum designed by the educational system will not present matters that unduly challenge community norms. Yet introduction to certain areas – a new language and society, for example – inevitably offers the risk of introducing considerable variations to local moral, cultural and economic values and practices.

In China, handling the ever-present tension in messages from the community to its school children about the value of foreign languages and their societies has been dealt with almost exclusively by staff at the People's Education Press (PEP). As Adamson (2002) has documented extensively, for decades these educators have been employed by the Chinese government to develop curriculum and write the textbooks used by Chinese school children and, more recently, also to vet and decide the acceptability of resources produced by other publishers. In carrying out their tasks, not only must the PEP curriculum teams keep within the bounds of current ideological demands, but also, as everywhere, they

137

must do so within the practical constraints of time and setting, teacher knowledge and examination system. As everywhere, too, these conditions mean there are formidable constraints on what any textbook, or even a series of textbooks, can present to learners. The outcome, as Freebody has pointed out, is that

> the visual, graphic and electronic representations of language and objects in textbooks are 'crafted communications' ... they embody a number of purposeful choices about what is to be presented and about how reality is to be displayed. (Freebody, 2003: 174–175)

In like vein, referring specifically to language textbooks, Brown says,

> Nothing in the textbook would be gratuitous. Every grammar rule, every picture, graph, chart, document or whatever would be figured as part of a signifying act which will have been pre-established by the author(s) with specific aims in mind. (Brown, 1991: 115)

Once made, these forced choices mean that only certain parts of certain target-language-use worlds, and certain ways of communicating in the target language in those selected worlds, can be presented. What is in their language textbook thus powerfully shapes learners' perceptions of target-language-use communities and their capacity to participate in them (Kelly Hall, 2002). Furthermore, unless specifically said to be otherwise, from the learners' perspective, 'it is assumed that what is presented in the textbook is to be considered as 'normal', 'acceptable', 'right', 'good', 'the way things ought to be', 'what people [we/they] do, or not' (Gee, 1999: 2).

Textbooks for Chinese school learners have been crafted by the PEP to provide students with the knowledge and skills it is deemed by the government that they need, in line with National Policy on linguistic, moral and sociopolitical matters, and on pedagogy. As a subject now taught in all Chinese high schools, the choices made in English textbooks are a rich source of information on that thinking. The views of effective and appropriate pedagogy in the PEP textbooks have been very thoroughly documented and analysed by Adamson (2002), and will not be further examined here. Instead, the enquiry focuses on the role it is intended that English should play in 21st century China, and the handling of dilemmas of identity that such a role presents. These are examined in the English textbooks used in China's main cities in two modern periods, a quarter of a century apart. What is sought is the construction of Chinese and other users of English, and of the language itself, in terms of the nature and scope of content and the purposes for which it is to be used, and the moral values attributed to various phenomena and behaviour. The objective is to perceive in the role of English presented the options afforded the learners in the sociocultural, political and moral domains.

China's English Language Textbooks

Selection

Two time periods have been selected and examination is made of two sets of English language textbooks in use during each of them. The first period is 1981–1983, when the books being used were the first published after the start of the Open Door period, which marked the break from the Maoist era. These books represent the beginning of modern English teaching in China and thus make an appropriate starting point. The second period is the early years of the 21st century. Comparing the sets synchronically and diachronically reveals choices that needed to be made at the time they were published, and shows those perspectives that have remained constant and those that have changed over the intervening 25 years.

The two 1981 sets both comprise six small books to be used over the three years of junior high school. These 12 books plus the two compact senior high school textbooks in use then, published by the PEP, have been examined in their entirety. The first of the two sets, *Series Six*, was published by the PEP in 1978–1979. The author taught English Teaching Methodology at Beijing Teachers College from 1981 to 1983, and these were the books her students were preparing to use in their teaching, as they were used pervasively in high schools in Beijing and elsewhere at that time. Although Adamson (2002: 149) claims that they were put together in some haste, a great deal of their content was still carried over to the more carefully designed *Series Seven*, published in 1982. They can, therefore, be taken as representing the major thinking at the time on how English was to be constructed in the minds of the coming generation and their teachers. The first books in the second set from that time (Li & Ding, 1981) were published by the Education Science Press. A couple of years later, the whole set was published by Beijing Normal University Press (Ding, 1984). Labelled 'experimental', they were intended to be radically new in content and method. In 1981 they could be found in some of the most prestigious Key Schools in Beijing. The author was one of the native speaker editors of this series.

The two sets of 2007 textbooks selected are recent publications, both series coming out gradually since 2001, the one published by Shanghai Foreign Language Education Press and the other by the PEP in conjunction with Longman. Some 340 pages of both sets have been examined, comprising *Senior High School Books 2 and 3* of the Shanghai set and *Senior*

Students' Book 3 of the latter. Books for the later years in high school in this period have been chosen because, due to the students' comparative maturity and higher proficiency in English, authors are less constrained in the content and complexity of what the texts can present at this level. They thus reflect well the role for English it is intended to craft. The particular sets were selected because they are now in use in many high schools, especially Key Schools, in Shanghai and Beijing. Both these recent sets are claimed to address contemporary English education requirements in China as set out in the National Policy, and endeavour to be improvements on what else is available. Their use in the prestigious high schools of China's main cities is recognition of their quality.

In order to avoid the considerable repetition that presenting each of the sets in turn would cause, only the analysis of the first set is presented here in detail. This information is then used as the reference point in relation to which description and discussion of the other sets are presented.

Procedure

The focus of analysis was the sociocultural and sociolinguistic elements of the books. Drawing on the work of Ramirez and Kelly Hall (1990), Gee (1999) and Freebody (2003), the topics, participants' roles and actions and the attitudes found in the contents of the texts, exercises and notes were first recorded. The content was considered with respect to the number and kind of references to English-speaking countries/groups made through both visual and written modalities. Sociocultural elements of identity were sought, firstly, in the quality and quantity of social information and cultural themes concerning beliefs and values, social organisation and relationships of the English-speaking world that were introduced, as well as the routines, practices and artefacts of daily life that were presented. The situations, objects, people and actions noted were also analysed to discover where, when, by whom, what for and how English was shown as being used. The overt and covert implications of the role English was to play in Chinese people's lives, and when and how it could properly be used by them, emerged from the roles, relationships, activities and objects included and those omitted.

These outcomes were then considered in terms of Norton's (2000) notion of *imagined community*, and the following questions were raised: What positions are being offered to learners by the particular factors in the textbook? What range of voices is afforded learners in the community projected in the textbooks? What groups is it suggested they could aspire to join by learning English? Finally, on the basis of these findings, it was possible to address the issues of role and identity being presented: What is English to be used for, and how does knowing it relate to being Chinese?

Results

1981 – Set 1

Design

As the illustrations on their covers show, the contents of Books 1–6 of the 1979 *Series Six* set are about:

- Chinese children at school – work and play.
- Chinese life – medical care, the arts, manufacturing and agriculture.
- International facts – folk stories and natural science.
- Human achievements – science and the built environment.
- Politics – social oppression, literature and famous people.

The six small books for the three junior high school years comprise an average of 150 pages each, divided into chapters that present a dialogue for oral practice, an expository report or narrative account as a reading text, grammar notes and exercises, and some rhymes and songs. Dialogue speakers are designated A and B and, as the accompanying pen and ink illustrations show, are almost always Chinese children and their teacher, or Chinese workers. Like school books everywhere, the textbook writers have taken seriously their role as moral guides on behalf of the community, and the children represented in the dialogues are diligent and obedient and the adults in their life are wise and patient. While there are some chapters in the latter books devoted to the wider world and beyond, it is language relating to the basic social structures and daily life of China that predominate. The development over each book is based on the gradual presentation of grammatical structures and vocabulary relating to the life of a typical teenage Chinese learner: the people, objects and activities of the home, school, street and country.

Year 1 content

In the two books for the first year of junior high school, in addition to language for the universal objects and activities of the home, street and schoolroom, terms for communist party roles – Youth League, Young Pioneer, Party Member – and topics such as Army Day, soldiers, jeeps and tanks, workers and tractors, commune and factory visits appear, as do the major geographical features of China and the many Chinese public holidays. Beyond China, there is a chapter on the Planets. The fable of *The Hare and the Tortoise*, the rhyme *Good Better Best*, the proverb *If at first you don't succeed* and the song *Twinkle Twinkle Little Star* are introduced. In the first two books, there is one line among the exercises stating that 'English is spoken in England', and another advises that 'The US is bigger than Europe'. The name *Norman Bethune* is mentioned without further information. One text consists of a three-sentence letter from Alice Brown, a 12-year-old American girl. She writes to 'Dear Friends', and states that her parents 'are friends of New China' and that 'they tell their students about your country'. There is no mention of the content or significance of this decontextualised and rather wooden little text in any other part of the chapter or, indeed, of the book.

Year 2 content

Books 3 and 4, to be used in the second year, introduce tenses and expand vocabulary for life in China. There are a great many moral exhortations to cleanliness, diligence and perseverance. In Book 3, three texts introduce native English speakers. Neither is contextualised, so it is unclear in which country they are living. One concerns Jack, who helps a blind man cross a busy street; another is about Tom, a white boy, who befriends Mustapha from southeast Asia, who is being bullied for being foreign by other white boys at school. With the aid of Tom's older brother, they confront and physically fight the bullies to victory; a third is a wryly amusing story of a schoolboy who does not do his homework on time. The *Arabian Nights* is introduced through one of what will be several stories from it presented in the next three books. In Book 4, a slew of English girls' names is introduced as the speakers in what are otherwise ethnically neutral dialogues about such things as going to the cinema. The illustrations of these dialogues are equally neutral, showing surroundings that might be anywhere in the world. Lenin and Lizst appear, the latter in a story reporting his benevolence to a poor young pianist. The name of the book *Tom Sawyer* is mentioned and three native English speakers appear in the text. The first is a black woman, who tells of life in Harlem living on welfare, cotton picking in the South and the racism of whites. The second is Jenny, a schoolgirl who is treated unfairly by her teacher. The third is Jack, a boy from Australia who is living in Beijing with his parents, who have come to China to teach. In a very realistic text, written as a letter to 'Frank' in Sydney, Jack tells of the challenges of mastering Chinese and the joys of learning to skate on natural ice. He mentions 'my Chinese friends' and sends Frank a stamp, saying 'Are you surprised to see Einstein on a

Chinese stamp?' In one set of exercises in this book there is also mention of a group of Chinese-speaking Canadians visiting a school. These last two texts allude, for the first time in the set, to contact between Chinese people and native speakers of English, albeit only indirectly and not commented on further. In both cases, the foreigners speak Chinese.

Year 3 content

In the two books for the final year of junior high school, there is considerable development in linguistic complexity, both in texts and in the notes containing metalinguistic information. There is also an expansion of topics about the world. The natural world concerns biology and physics, the rest presents facts about other countries and the built environment, in both of which a certain amount of quite specialist vocabulary is included – for example, baleen, mammal, genie and Egyptian mummy. Major among these texts are accounts of ancient Egypt and Greece, stories of the discoveries of Galileo and Edison and the story of Nathan Hale's martyrdom for his country at the hands of the British. There is also an extract from *Gulliver's Travels*. Texts concerning contemporary native English speakers include the history of Negro [*sic*] oppression in America; garbage collectors on strike in a major English city; a mechanic who foils a car thief; a man who steals money from his friend; a former thief who is attacked by his workmates for his past wrongdoing; an attack on the conservative power of newspaper owners in the West; and two texts set in the future centring on the use of a *visionphone*, a machine not far removed from today's computers. The only socially specific information in these books is the description and visual of a mechanic eating a sandwich and drinking milk, and in one exercise, there is the line 'American football is quite different from the ordinary football'.

Senior high school content

As there was no oral examination at the end of senior high school, in the two books called *Senior English I* and *II*, respectively, which were used to follow the above set, there are almost no dialogues. By far the greater number of texts in Book I is focused on topics of natural science: the seasons, wood, pollution, penicillin, ants, eyes and more. There are a few Chinese stories of loyal workers, and one admiring account of the patriotic death of an Italian boy during war with the Austrians. There are introductions to Lincoln and Washington, the story of William Tell, and an episode involving Napoleon; on the literary side, there are extracts from

Robinson Crusoe, a Maupassant short story, and the fable of *The Blind Men and the Elephant*. Only a couple of neutral dialogues present living native speakers, one of which concerns a couple who leave London for the peace of living in the country – socially significant information, as this was not a move likely to be made voluntarily by city Chinese at the time. Four supplementary readings introduce the basic geography of Great Britain and Ireland, describe the aristocratic sport of horse jumping, discuss the language knowledge of the native speaker and tell a story about some community-minded young English-speaking boys.

Book II involves quite long texts, some of which are narratives with dialogue embedded in them. Most are historical accounts: events in Chinese history, including an account of Edgar Snow's time in China during the war; the Trojan Horse; Washington's battle at Trenton and an abridged biography of Albert Einstein. On the literary side, there are extracts from *Tom Sawyer* and the tale of *The Emperor's New Clothes*; and from science, chapters on coal and the physics of water. One chapter tells of the first moon landing, ending with an account of Deng Xiaoping's visit to the Houston Aerospace Centre. These factual pieces involving native English speakers are accompanied by contemporary fictional texts recounting the fear of street gangs of a white boy in a big city in the United States; the oppressed life of a black man born in a poor part of Brooklyn and the story of two Chinese children taken to Europe by their parents, where they see homeless people on the street who are beaten by the police. They are greatly relieved to return to China. The final chapter of the book, and of the whole series, discusses the importance of English in the modern world and concludes:

> English has in fact become the language of international co-operation in science and technology ... A scientist who speaks and writes English is in closer touch with the scientists in other countries than one who doesn't. (*Renmin Jiaoyu Chubanshe*, 1980: 286)

Summary of sociocultural elements

In all six years of high school English presented in these books, there are only three mentions of contact between living Chinese and people from English-speaking countries: Jack living in Beijing, the Canadians who visit a school one morning and Deng Xiaoping's visit to Houston. None of these texts record the contact directly. There has been an introduction to the basic geography of English speaking and other Western countries and some seemingly random extracts from important pieces of their history and literature. The only socially specific information provided at all is the mention of someone having a sandwich and milk for lunch, and the existence of a public petrol station. Other references to native speaker life and society concern only neutral, humdrum activities of no cultural import, used for the practice of grammatical structures. These appear against a social background of oppression and difficulty, among which latter theft is a major component.

1981 – Set 2

Design

As is made explicit on the title page by their being called 'experimental', the books in the second 1981 set represent an intentional shift in textbook design. They relate the doings of a class of Beijing school children like the learners themselves, who are followed over their three years of junior high school. The characters have real names and express realistic personalities comprising strengths and weaknesses – one is kind, but a bit lazy about school work; another a very keen athlete, but not so quick at his studies; another an excellent student and leader, and so on. As the drawings on the cover, congruently, show, these children are modern and appealing: they wear smart clothes, the girls with hair in swinging pony tail or winged bob, the boys tall and in jeans and a baseball cap. Each chapter recounts their various exploits at home and school and in the community. Their lives follow the rhythms of the learners' own lives, but are packed with action and initiative. Most noticeably, the language they use is plausibly the language of young people (e.g. *Wow! Hey, that's great!*) and, radically, follows the American norm (e.g. *Mom, you guys*). The participants have also adopted certain American customs, such as celebrating birthdays with presents and a party, which was rare in China at that time, parents more usually providing at most just something special to eat. However, there is nothing frivolous about the presents and other treats; all are linked to scholastic success.

Content

A sample dialogue from each of the two 1981 sets shows clearly the differences between them.

Set 1 dialogue (PEP, 1979–1981, Book 2: 94)

A: What does he do?
B: He makes steel.

A:	Does he make tractors, too?
B:	No, he doesn't.
A:	Is he making steel now?
B:	Yes he is.

Set 2 dialogue (Li & Ding, 1981, Book 3: 109)

Mother:	Happy birthday from us both.
Bai Di:	Oh, thanks. Hey, look! A new English-Chinese dictionary. That's great! Oh, thanks, Mom, thanks, Dad. It's just what I wanted.

There is an account of Edison in Book 4 and, like Newton, he is referred to as 'one of the men they [the students] admire most' (136). This admiration is due to the scientists' enquiring minds, albeit in Edison's case it is also for aiming 'to bring out the secrets of nature and use them for the benefit of people'.

The above innovations aside, and with some exceptions in Book 6 detailed below, these books present very much the same content as the PEP *Series Six* set. Texts and dialogues centre on daily life in China and the Chinese protagonists all speak English to one another. There are narrative accounts of real and fictional people similar to those found in the other set, and also some traditional stories. For example, texts include *Solomon's Judgement, The Hare and Tortoise, The Little Boy who Cried Wolf*, an anecdote about Mark Twain and the story of Joe Hill, and a few children's rhymes also appear; mention by name is made of Anderson's story of *The Little Match Girl* and of an imaginary story called *Little Tom – A Poor Black Boy*. The names of foreign countries, cities, personal names and some famous people are also introduced in these books, and these also often appear only in the decontextualised single sentences that make up the grammar drills: What time is it in New York now? What colour are Tom's shoes? Winston Churchill's famous V for victory was sign language. In these experimental books, there are no native speakers until very late, when in Book 4 'an American' visits the school. But this is just a one-off.

Book 6 in this set is distinctive among all the junior high school books in the two sets in its relatively full presentations of information about some aspects of the English-speaking world that are more typical of some texts found in the *Senior English* books outlined above. Thus in Book 6 there is factual information about the American Civil War and the setting up of the Union; an introduction to the notion that 'an Englishman's home is his castle' and to 'do it yourself' work around the house; the life story of Charles Dickens (and of Picasso), and an account of the origin of English surnames. Nonetheless, actual contact with native English speakers is only alluded to, in the form of a letter from the Chinese American cousin of one of the students, saying he is coming to China. Unique in all the books from 1981, however, one Book 6 drill introduces a tolerant, intercultural perspective on Sino-American difference:

A:	I've heard Americans are always on the move. Don't you think that's strange?
B:	If Americans seem strange to you, remember that they feel the same way then they visit your country.
A:	Oh, yes, I know people living in different cultures do many daily things differently from one another.
B:	What a dull world it would be if they didn't. (Book 6, p. 101).

The Role of English in 1981

In both sets of books from this period, as a language English is constantly portrayed as an available alternative mode of expression among Chinese to go about their daily life. This is most unusual in a foreign language textbook. And when they use this English, although they maintain standard Anglo/American linguistic forms, the Chinese speakers do so to discuss topics of interest to Chinese, using Chinese ways of interaction and, not least, expressing Chinese viewpoints and values. Perseverance and benevolence from the great towards the poor, for example, are also Western virtues, but in a Western textbook even of that era one might expect to see more emphasis on the values of intellectual curiosity and individual initiative rather than these.

Beyond this use of English in China, throughout the books the language is, indeed, shown to be just a tool to know the world (Yu, 2004) – the natural world and world discoveries, world events, world people. Nowhere is it projected as a means of Chinese interaction with native speakers – or even other speakers of English – although it can be used to access some very limited information about both. Not that the learner might feel inclined to have contact with the contemporary native speakers in the texts, who are almost uniformly constructed negatively, essentially as oppressors or oppressed. Only Jack from Australia is presented both as a good, living person and one who is in regular face-to-face contact with

Chinese people. This actual contact is not shown, and like the few other mentions of contact, it will, anyway, take place in Chinese.

Taken together, the factors listed above construct the English of all these early books as a language crafted in many ways with a curiously contemporary identity, as an *Asian* language: *Chinese English* (a term not to be confused with the quaint or incorrect forms of so-called *Chinglish*). In the imagined community proposed in these books, this English is to be used by Chinese people to go about their Chinese lives and to access basic information about the outside world, but not to interact with it in any other form.

2006 Set 1

Design

Looking first at what has stayed constant, the 'New Century English' senior books currently in use in Shanghai schools can be seen to have some aspects in common with the 1979 books. Although the texts are all prose, they combine narrative and expository styles and in content include information about the natural environment, the discoveries of science and the valour of good human beings and famous people. Indeed, a number of stories from the earlier senior books have survived as they were (Marie Curie, Helen Keller), or in kind (Poor Black John). Being addressed to older students, the texts are naturally longer than the earlier junior high school texts, and the range of topics within each category is wider than in the earlier senior books. For example there is more and deeper information about non-Anglo countries such as France, and when presented, this is likely to be contemporary fact rather than traditional tale.

There has also been considerable development in these books from the senior books of 25 years ago. Visually, they are attractively produced, with colour photos and illustrations throughout and they make liberal use of comic strips and cartoon-like drawings. The covers present major monuments from all the native English-speaking countries and the content inside is globally focused. The linguistic base for progression is now functional rather than grammatical.

Content

While as in the past, the quite long chapters are largely devoted to natural science topics (Book 1) and social studies topics (Book 2), almost all refer to modern life. There are two noticeable developments from a sociocultural perspective. The first is the new positioning of China as part of the international community, linked to world problems and successes as a participant and stakeholder. Thus global problems such as pollution are discussed from the perspective of *we* (human beings); and a section that introduces the Louvre and the British Museum also introduces the Shanghai Museum. The second development is the amount of information presented on modern life outside China, including in English-speaking countries. Discussion of these topics centres around a general theme – sport, food, animals and so on – and provides a certain amount of factual information about, for example, the place of sport in Australian life or the diet of the typical American. However, apart from mention of particularly famous individuals (the Brazilian soccer player Pele, for example) this information is entirely impersonal. Attitudinally there is a much more positive view of English speakers, with Americans in particular being admired for the natural wonders of their land and praised for their ingenuity.

It is all the more salient, then, that while the Chinese in these books do not speak English to one another, they are not afforded any other voice in English: in some 340 pages there are only two instances of them using spoken English at all. Even in these two cases, the direct Chinese–Anglo interaction shown is limited to people acting in formal roles: a student in one cartoon speaks to Mr Green, his Australian teacher, and in another text a librarian explains procedures to a Chinese student as she gets her library card at an American university. In addition, there is a text in which a Chinese who has visited Australia talks about the Opera House, another concerning Mr and Mrs Green living in China for ten years and one exercise which asks how the learner would help a foreign friend at dinner who had never eaten Chinese food before, all of which tacitly imply contact.

2006 Set 2

Design

The second contemporary set of textbooks, *Senior English for China*, which is used today in many Key Schools in Beijing, has a lot in common both with the older senior books and the contemporary Shanghai books. Thus there are reading texts expounding biological, social and technical aspects of today's world, such as bees, hibernation, food production, office equipment and advertising; stories about famous people, such as Madame Curie, Helen Keller and Mahatma Gandhi, and some anecdotes concerning the benevolent rich or the wronged worker. As well, there are long, seriously informative, non-pejorative texts about the land, history, original inhabitants and contemporary society of the USA, the United Kingdom, Australia and

New Zealand, as well as texts on the European Union and France. A couple of detective stories and an extract from *The Merchant of Venice* provide a more literary note. The books are attractively designed, with colour photographs of Chinese and international sights, including a cover showing a collage of New York City and Sydney landmarks. The linguistic framework is grammatical and the dialogues and reading texts are all presented in very natural, native-like language and discourse structures.

Content

Like the modern Shanghai texts, these books present some general information about living in the United States, with one short text on going for a picnic and another on the owning of guns; a third provides information on the common practice of taking a part-time job while studying and a fourth tells of the importance of understanding the command 'Freeze', so as not to be shot by police. One of the writing tasks requires the learner to write a letter in English to his/her parents asking for money, and a few other writing tasks also involve Chinese people using English to communicate with other Chinese.

Most strikingly new in the 342 pages of the final book (*Senior Book 3*), however, are four dialogues, the first three of which are headed, respectively,

(1) Mr Zhu is taking a school party to the seaside [in which 'Jane' is one of the students].
(2) Tang Ling and Bob are building an out-door platform for plays and concerts at the university.
(3) Wang Bing and Carl are having lunch in a café in Los Angeles.

The new features of particular note in these texts are that, firstly, these are dialogues that involve direct and sustained Chinese–native English speaker contact, which is managed in English. It is not made clear in the text where Mr Zhu and Jane, or Tang Lin and Bob, are – they could be in China or not. But quite evidently, Wang Bing and Carl are in the United States. And while the first two relationships are formal (teacher–student; co-workers), it seems Wang Bing and Carl have chosen to eat together and, indeed, reading the dialogue makes it clear that they are friends. The second interesting point about these conversations is that they are all totally *ordinary* in content – there is no major action occurring, no moral imperative being illustrated. While from a linguistic perspective they may have been included simply to provide social information and vocabulary, uniquely in all the books examined, they also enact natural

Chinese–English speaker engagement which is cordial, or actually for pleasure. This presents a new role for English used by a Chinese speaker. In this vein, the most interesting of these dialogues is the fourth text, the opening of which is presented below.

> *Yang Pei and Jackie are going camping in the Australian bush with some other friends.*

Yang Pei:	I'm enjoying this. Where exactly are we going?
Jackie:	We're going to a really nice place down by the river ...
Yang Pei:	Be careful! Don't throw your cigarette out of the window. If you do that, you might start a fire. ....
Burt:	Sorry, I wasn't thinking. Bonny, take the next dirt track on the left. (*Renmin Jiaoyu Chubanshe*, 2001: 13).

This text shows a Chinese–native English speaker contact of clear choice on both sides and the objective of the contact is a purely leisure activity. Yang Pei is presented as totally at home: he knows what to do in a country a long way from China, even in the special environment of the Australian wilderness; and he is obviously among close friends, people with whom he can speak his mind and tell what to do. As with the other three dialogues involving direct contact, we do not know who the people in the text are beyond the little reported. We do not even know here, for example, if Jackie is male or female. As in the other three dialogues also, in this text ethnicity has been transcended: while his name denotes Yang Pei as Chinese, there is nothing saliently Chinese about him, nor anything especially Australian about the others. All are simply presented as people from one background who mix with people from their own or other backgrounds, taking part by choice in an activity together, and using English as a common language.

The Role of English in 2006

The two sets of recent textbooks suggest that a Chinese senior school student should be well informed about the basics of world geography and understand the historical roots of contemporary conditions in the world, including tensions, especially in countries neighbouring China and English-speaking countries. Demonstrably in these books, English is a means of learning about such matters. The student should also recognise that China is part of the same world, sharing the common benefits of modern science and technology and subject to the same difficulties. Chinese people may move in and out of China, using English in the course of professional development in service to China. Insofar as they need to have contact with people abroad, it is suggested that Chinese will generally find them pleasant, and things to do in their country interesting. However, within these limited frames of engagement, there is no need for knowledge of native speaker belief systems and values, or for details about what they think about how they live their lives. Thus, as in the earlier PEP series (Adamson, 2002: 156), the construct of English in these contemporary sets remains almost entirely that of the 19th century reformers: just a tool to know the world – albeit showing a greatly expanded notion of 'the world', and a considerable narrowing of the separation between Chinese and other speakers of English, when compared to 25 year ago. With the exception of a few clearly artificial writing tasks, in neither of these sets of books do Chinese use English among themselves. Thus the identity of the language projected in the 2006 textbooks can be seen to have shifted from *Chinese English* to *International English*.

In one dialogue in one book, however, the separation between Chinese and other speakers of English has completely disappeared. The characters are no longer 'Chinese' and 'non-Chinese', but modern hybrids. What the basis of the relationship between these people is, we simply do not know: it may be work or study, or they may be neighbours. But as the text proposes, whatever the base, it is a relationship that may include voluntary joint leisure activities undertaken purely for fun. The text projects a new group the Chinese learners might imagine themselves eventually being part of, one in which their voices will not be that of the non-native speaker in among those of the native speakers, but just one among several voices speaking the international language they have in common.

Conclusion

In their government-approved English textbooks, today's young Chinese are afforded the opportunity to imagine themselves having an engaged role in a global community, interacting in English with a set of native and other speakers who are considerably more complex, interesting and likable people than those in the books of earlier years. It seems reasonable to assume that this broadening in scope over the past 25 years is intended.

Given the thrust of what was presented in the textbooks of 1981, most Chinese school learners of English at that time could have had little reason to suppose that the one maverick text projecting friendly Chinese–non-Chinese cooperation (Jack's letter) was proposing a target-language-user world that they might dare to imagine themselves a part of. Yet just such a world is the norm now projected in contemporary textbooks. It is interesting to speculate, therefore, that the maverick text of 2006 (Yang Pei's Bush trip) might also be the harbinger of a socially broadening trend that will become the norm in future textbooks. For the moment, however, all that can be said is that it remains uniquely different in its imagined possibilities from the role of English and possibilities for Chinese identity portrayed in all the other texts. In 1981, English was clearly constructed as just a tool to know the world. While the target-language-user world has grown considerably, in the Chinese high school textbooks in use in 2006, the projected identity of English is still very much that of 'a tool to know the world'. But the evidence provided by Yang Pei justifies hesitation over also including the word *'just'* in this designation.

References

Adamson, B. (2002) Barbarian as a foreign language: English in China's schools. *World Englishes* 21 (2), 257–267.

Brown, J.W. (1991) *Semiotics and Second-Language Pedagogy*. New York: P. Lang.

Ding, J. (1984) English Books 1–6, *Chuzhong Shiyan Keben* [Junior High School Trial Textbooks]. Beijing: Beijing Shifan Daxue Chubanshe [Beijing Normal University Press].

Freebody, P. (2003) *Qualitative Research in Education – Interaction and Practice*. Thousand Oaks: Sage.

Gee, J.P. (1999) *An Introduction to Discourse Analysis: Theory and Method*. London and New York: Routledge.

Kelly Hall, J. (2002) *Teaching and Researching Language and Culture*. Harlow and London: Pearson Education Limited.

Li, Q. and Ding, J. (1981) English Books 1 and 2, *Chuzhong Shiyan Keben* [Junior High School Trial Textbooks]. Beijing: Jiaoyu Kexue Chubanshe [Education Science Press].

Morgan, C. (1995) Cultural awareness and the national curriculum. *Language Learning Journal* 12, 9–13.

Norton, B. (2000) *Identity and Language Learning: Gender, Ethnicity and Educational Change*. Harlow: Pearson Education.

Ramirez, A. and Hall, J.K. (1990) Language and culture in secondary level Spanish textbooks. *The Modern Language Journal* 74 (1), 48–65.

Renmin Jiaoyu Chubanshe English [People's Education Press] (1979–1981) *Yingyu* [English]. Quanrizhi shinianzhi xuexiao chuzhong keben 1–6 [fulltime ten-year system schools junior high textbooks 1–6]. Beijing.

Renmin Jiaoyu Chubanshe [People's Education Press] (1980). Gaozhong daiyong keben. *Yingyu* I, II [Substitute senior high school English textbooks I and II]. Beijing.

Renmin Jiaoyu Chubanshe [People's Education Press] and Longman (2001) Quanrizhi putong gaoji zhongxue jiaoke ben xiuding – bixiu – *Yingyu di san ben* [full time regular senior high school textbook, revised trial material – compulsory courses. – Senior English for China, Students' Book 3]. Beijing.

Shanghai Waiyu Jiaoyu Chubanshe [Shanghai Foreign Language Education Press] (2002–2006) Yingyu (Xin shijie ban). New Century English *Gaozhong Ernianji Di Yi Xueqi; Sannianji di Yi Xueqi (shiyan ben)* [Semester 1, Year 2 and Semester 1, Year 3, Senior High School (trial material)]. Shanghai.

Yu, K.C. (2004) Writers: Protecting Chinese imperative. Report by Zou Huilin on the Literature and Humanistic Care Forum, Shanghai Tongji University. *China Daily*, 27 May.

Chapter 7

The More I Learned, The Less I Found My Self

BIAN YONGWEI

Background

Learning a foreign language, such as English in China, has become an integral part of the educational process, for students at all levels of education, from the primary grades to college. At all these levels, subtle and complex issues of identity are found in relation to English learning in the Chinese context. Identity questions can and often include issues affecting students' self-confidence. The level of English competence which is gained in formal education can also lead to a broader evaluation of the learner. While, as Goldberg and Noels (2006) argue, students may have their perception of themselves or of people speaking that language influenced after learning it, they will also come to identify with that language community by way of acquiring some salient, distinctive characteristics of the people in that group (Genesee, 1987).

In the tradition of Chinese academic appraisal, the attainments students achieve are a crucial means to evaluate their abilities and determine their potential for the development of a good, secure future career. The social expectations for competence in English, together with the traditional appraisal system, are deeply rooted in the minds of the students, either consciously or unconsciously. To obtain good marks and to reach a high competence level in English are therefore rewarded by social and economic conditions, and influence learner decisions about English study. Inevitably the success or failure to achieve such goals has consequences for their self-confidence.

English, however, is not a subject like mathematics or physics. English also carries culture(s). Learning English in China, which opens for the learner greater access to various media, and cultural information and forms via digital and electronic devices, brings with it more intimate contact with cultural values and life views that can differ very strongly, or be completely brand new, from the original cognitive, affective and social implications conveyed in Chinese with which the students were born and socialized. In the process of acquiring English beyond the routines of memorization of grammar and vocabulary, there can be personal challenges for learners that push them to the boundary where they might feel that 'the interior part' of their identity, encircled by Chinese language and culture, is exposed to influence from the exterior, by the different values and practices made possible by English. In this way acquiring English can involve membership identification challenges, such as claims on which cultural group, English or Chinese, is to exert the stronger influence on the learner. Even if this is not generally true, membership identification challenges and conflicts can occur at certain points or on certain issues, and in certain circumstances.

In the following, there will be some reviews on self-confidence, learners' belief in their ability to learn/use an L2 and theories on bilingualism related with culture identity, in which learners are dealing with the differences between the L2 and their native language. This issue will be discussed below drawing on thinking about linguistic self-confidence.

Self-Confidence

Linguistic self-confidence was first introduced as a concept by Clément *et al.* (1977) to examine learners' beliefs in their ability to produce results, accomplish goals or perform tasks competently in their English learning. The term is defined operationally as 'a low anxious affect and high self-perceptions of L2 competence' (Clément *et al.*, 1994: 422), with the former the affective factor and the latter cognitive. The notion of linguistic self-confidence was mostly considered as a determinant of attitude and effort expended towards second language (L2) learning, both in a multi-cultural setting with possible interethnic contacts (Clément, 1980; Clément & Kruidenier, 1985) and in a foreign language classroom, when the students are exposed to poor learning situations, for example course difficulty, or negative evaluations by the teacher or by peers (see also Clément *et al.*, 1994; Foss & Reitzel, 1988; Horwitz, 1986; Horwitz & Young, 1991).

However, linguistic self-confidence has also been examined as the consequence of L2 learning (e.g. Gao *et al.*, 2005; Yashima *et al.*, 2004). In Gao (2004), self-confidence was designed as a dependent variable, a state that resulted from English language learning. In this research Gao found that change in students' self-confidence was prominent, which 'might reflect characteristics of Chinese English as a Foreign Language (EFL) context, distinguished from English as a Second Language ESL contexts: limited exposure to the target culture, yet very high value attached to the target language' (Gao, 2004: 44).

Cultural Identity

Over the course of many writings Lambert (1963a, 1963b, 1967, 1975) has proposed a social psychological model for L2 learning, and pioneered the study of bilingual development and identity changes (Gardner, 1985). From this work he proposed two kinds of bilingualism: additive and subtractive. Under conditions of additive bilingualism the learner's target language and cultural identity are acquired while his/her native language and cultural identity are maintained. By contrast, in subtractive bilingualism the native language and cultural identity are eroded or even replaced by the target language and cultural identity, which may bring to the learner the sense of loss of his/her native cultural identity or isolation from the native cultural community (Gardner, 1985). In a similar vein, Schumann's Acculturation Modal (1975, 1978a, 1978b, 1986) of L2 learning stressed the importance of subtractive bilingualism 'in the form of complete "acculturation"'(Gao *et al.*, 2005). In this approach subtractive bilingualism might motivate the learner, directly or indirectly, to reach a higher level of L2 proficiency. Although the Intergroup Model developed by Giles and Byrne (1982) also supported Schumann's argument that subtractive identity changes enhanced L2 learning, additive bilingualism has still been regarded by many as an ideal type of bilingualism (Gardner, 1985; Kim, 2001; Lo Bianco, 2000; see also Gao *et al.*, 2005).

The encounters of learners with the L2 in foreign language contexts, however, may be different from those of second language learners in fundamental ways that impact on these models and what they say about a learner's identity and bilingualism. ESL learners are usually located in settings where the L2 is dominant and this contextual reality has a bearing on the kind of experience the learner has with the target language as well as on their learning goals. As an alternative to additive and subtractive bilingualism, Gao (1996, 2001, 2002) has put forward the notion of 'productive bilingualism'. This term was defined as 'the command of the target language and that of the native language positively reinforce each other; deeper understanding and appreciation of the target culture goes hand in hand with deeper understanding and appreciation of the native culture. In the process of learning another language and related culture, the learner's personality becomes more open and integrated at the same time'. (Gao, 2002: 143). While this might not be a stable state of learning, with the learner's constant exploration and reflection, the ideal status of productive bilingualism might be reached more frequently (Bian & Gao, 2006). The original empirical basis of productive bilingualism consisted of interviews with some recognized 'best foreign language learners', mostly professors, researchers and translators (Gao, 2001). There have also been some questionnaire quantitative studies with both undergraduate and graduate students, and qualitative analyses of discourses written by undergraduate students about their English study. In these examples and also among ordinary college students a state of productive bilingualism was found (Bian & Gao, 2006; Gao, 2004).

Research Method

The present study, commencing in 2005, is part of a four-year, five-site longitudinal research project on Chinese college students' English learning motivation and self-identity changes, a continuation of a major 2002 nation-wide horizontal survey (Gao, 2004) of these issues among English learners at college level in diverse parts of China. The whole project adopted a range of investigating instruments, such as questionnaire survey, journals, interviews and observations, but the present chapter only reports the questionnaire results on self-identity changes in the first two years in one of the five universities. The self-identity changes included the changes in positive self-confidence, negative self-confidence, additive identity, subtractive identity, split identity and productive identity. The latter four followed the categorization of identity changes used in the 2002 survey (Gao, 2004), but some items have been rephrased to make them less confusing and more easily understood:

> Additive change – the co-existence of two sets of languages, behavioral patterns and values, each specified for particular contexts. An example: 'I can easily switch between Chinese and English according to situational needs';
>
> Subtractive change – the native language and native cultural identity are replaced by the target language and target cultural identity. An example: 'With the improvement of my English proficiency, I feel my Chinese is becoming less idiomatic';
>
> Split change – the struggle between the languages and cultures gives rise to identity conflict. An example: 'I feel weird when my speech in Chinese is subconsciously mixed with English words';

Productive change – the command of the target language and that of the native language positively reinforce each other. An example: 'With the improvement of my English proficiency, I can better appreciate the subtleties in Chinese'. (Gao *et al.*, 2005: 42)

The four categories can be considered cultural identity changes, while 'split change' might have the additional quality of describing a state of learning in which the learner feels cognitive dissonance between two sets of social and cultural values. The research also makes use of an additional category for comparison: zero change – absence of self-identity changes; an example is 'No matter which language is used for expression, I remain to be myself' (Gao *et al.*, 2005: 42).

For the present research the category of 'self-confidence change' from the 2002 study was split into 'positive self-confidence' and 'negative self-confidence'.

Positive self-confidence change – positive change in the perception of one's own competence. 'With the increase of my English proficiency, I become more and more confident about myself'.

Negative self-confidence change – negative change in the perception of one's own competence. 'When I have difficulties in English learning, I begin to doubt my own ability'.

The questionnaire was designed in Chinese, and comprised 35 statements on self-identity changes, measured by a five-point Likert scale (1 = strongly disagree; 5 = strongly agree).

Two pilot studies were carried out in two universities in Beijing, from which some items were adjusted. The resulting version of the questionnaire has been administered to students in the five universities three times in the first two college years, the first two at the beginning and end of the first year, and the third at the end of the second year. The university whose data are reported in this chapter has placed strong emphasis on English teaching and learning since its establishment in the 1950s. Even non-English majors received intensive basic English skills training in their first two college years. Specifically, there are two more hours of English reading classes each week for non-English majors in this university than in other universities, and two-hour oral English classes instructed by English native speakers, which non-English majors in other universities do not have.

There were 359 non-English majors who were admitted to this university. In all, 38 Japanese majors did not have English classes in their first college year, so they were not included in the questionnaire survey. A total of 321 questionnaires were sent out to non-English majors, of which 319 were returned during the first administration, a valid return rate of 99.38%; for the second administration 261 questionnaires were returned, representing a valid return rate of 81.31%. On the third administration 275 of the 321 questionnaires were returned, a valid return rate of 85.67%. The number of students who participated varied, according to the attendance of students in class.

The specific research question posed in this study was: Do the students' self-identities change in the process of English learning in their first two-year college career?

Results and Discussion

Data analysis was performed with SPSS 14.0. The Cronbach α was first calculated. The reliability for the entire questionnaire was 0.51 for the first administration, 0.52 for the second and 0.71 for the third. For the identity change section, it was 0.32 for the first administration, 0.39 for the second and 0.61 for the third.

Generally speaking, positive self-confidence, additive identity, productive identity and zero identity reached a comparatively higher level, among which positive self-confidence ranked the most prominent one, while other categories remained low.

In order to examine the effects of time factor on self-identity changes, ANOVA was conducted with the six types of identity changes as dependent variables and testing time as the sole independent variable, and post hoc examined to see at what stage, or more specifically, the first year or the second, the students experienced changes in their self-confidence or cultural identities (Figure 7.1).

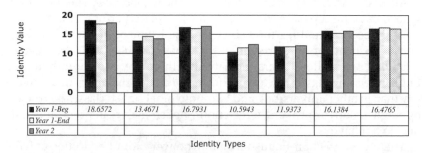

	Year 1-Beg	Year 1-End	Year 2
Year 1-Beg	18.6572	13.4671	16.7931	10.5943	11.9373	16.1384	16.4765
Year 1-End							
Year 2							

Identity Types

Figure 7.1 Identity changes in the first two college years

Self-confidence decreased

In between the three test administrations, ANOVA test results indicated that positive confidence ($F = 7.4$, $p = 0.001$) and negative confidence ($F = 4.63$, $p = 0.01$) reached a significant level 0.05. As for positive confidence, the mean values in test 2 (17.66) and test 3 (18.01) were lower than that in test 1 (18.66), and both reached their significance level ($p_{12} < 0.000$, $p_{13} = 0.013$), while for negative confidence, the mean values in test 2 (14.52) and test 3 (14.05) were higher than that in test 1 (13.47), but only the difference between the values in tests 1 and 2 reached the significance level ($p_{12} = 0.003$). The values between tests 2 and 3 in positive self-confidence increased a little, and those in negative self-confidence declined a little, but neither reached the significance level. Thus, the general tendency of this development indicated that the students' self-confidence decreased in the first two years of college English study. The more students learned English in the university, the less confident they felt about their English learning or even about themselves. Though at a later stage their confidence resumed a little, it never regained the level it had been at when they had entered the university.

The confidence of these students was at its peak when they entered the university, with years of effort to prepare for the English test in the college entrance examination. However, when they came to the specific context of English learning in the university, they encountered difficulties such as non-standard pronunciation, or that their oral English was not as fluent as was expected, or that their listening ability was not as sharp as their peers. The result of these comparisons with others in various indicators of spoken and used English was to break the confidence they had reached based on achievement in the written examination on vocabulary memory and grammar mastery. Lack of systematic guidance as to the content and nature of the college English proficiency tests, unlike the preparation provided for the college entrance examination, combined with blind fear eroded students' confidence. Despite some performance improvements over time, such as when they became more used to the pressure from their peers and the college learning environment during their second year, and even if they passed one proficiency test after another, suggesting to them an improvement of their English level, their confidence still did not equal the peak point it had reached when they entered the university. They had lost their self-confidence; they had lost themselves.

Findings such as these on self-confidence were prominent in some previous relevant studies too (e.g. Bian & Gao, 2006; Gao *et al.*, 2005). Also, the pattern of change during the first year in students' self-confidence is also reported at another site, a science university with non-English majors as subjects (Zang, 2007). Perhaps due to the limited contact with English culture in the foreign language learning context, the attention of students was drawn towards to evaluation of their English proficiency. As a result, language competence played a crucial role; the more competent they felt about their English level, the more confident they were about themselves; and the less competent, the less confident.

Identification with native language and culture decreased

A pattern of eroded identification with native language and culture also was found. ANOVA tests indicated that subtractive change ($F = 17.08$, $p < 0.000$) reached the significance level 0.05. The mean value in test 3 (12.44) was higher than that in test 2 (11.65), and that in test 2 was in turn higher than that in test 1 (10.59). Furthermore, the differences between the three tests, respectively, reached the significance level ($p_{12} = 0.001$, $p_{13} < 0.000$, $p_{23} = 0.019$). These results seem to suggest that the more the students learned English, the more they felt attached to English language, its culture and customs, and the more this appears to distance them from the Chinese language, its culture and customs. This result is consistent with the findings in some previous studies (e.g. Bian & Gao, 2006) that English majors in the foreign language context might experience subtractive identity changes when they advanced further in their language learning.

This university attached great importance to English learning, and the English teaching for non-English majors even emphasized training on listening and speaking, the requirement for which was much higher than in other universities for non-English majors. There were large numbers of listening–transcribing assignments, and students were encouraged to listen to CRI (China Radio International), and watch CNN and originals of English language films and TV programs. Having native Chinese speakers as their oral English teachers meant that this was not accessible to most non-English majors in other universities. In this highly focused, highly concentrated English skills training, students got closer to different dimensions of English culture(s), which they started to imitate, some with exaggerated manners and expressions that appeared 'funny' and 'fashionable', and others by emulating the directness and candidness, and a focus on oneself, which they believed were part of English culture(s). In this way, the students who were more sensitive to differences between the Chinese and English cultures began to move beyond the border of the native and target languages and cultures. They approached closer with curiosity to the foreign alienness and edged hesitantly away from their native familiarity. This was a partial loss of their previous cultural identity and cultural practices, which might denote a loss of part of the self that had existed prior to their language and culture learning of English.

Conclusion and Study Limitations

This study aimed to explore the first two-year self-identity changes related to English learning among Chinese non-English majors in an English-oriented arts university. The findings might indicate that the more the students learned, the more they could not find themselves, in the sense that they lost self-confidence as English learners, and that they lost part of their cultural self as a Chinese.

The general tendency during the two-year period for students' self-confidence was a decline in confidence. After the fierce national college entrance examination, the students who might proudly top others in written exam scores in their high schools ended up being average in college among other equally good if not better students. What made the situation even worse for these students was that this negative comparison made some suffer doubts as to their English competence in general and even their quality as a person on the whole, due to their 'non-standard' pronunciation, 'poor' oral English, 'weak' listening ability, etc. The students' self-confidence, related mostly to doing exercises, passing exams, obtaining the certificate/s associated with future job opportunities and enhancing the skills of listening and speaking, improved a little after passing the College English Test 4 or 6 (proficiency test for non-English majors), or Test for English Majors 4.

General improvement in their basic language skills in the second school year also helped. However, the strength of this finding suggests that efforts should be made to assist students understand the essence of L2 learning: to use the language, explore better ways of communication, pursue personal growth, rather than to focus only on the mastery of grammar and vocabulary. Left unsolved this problem of declining personal confidence tied to declining performance in English is difficult for students, who need to maintain their self-confidence while they face new and unfamiliar learning tasks. They need support to expand the scaffolding of their self-confidence in the fulfillment of those tasks. On a more positive tone though, the temporary loss and confusion due to new challenges might lead to the exploration of students' personal potential, which could be considered as an opportunity for personal or guided reflection on both language learning and self-growth.

The research has also found a general tendency during the two-year period for students' subtractive identity change to increase. This appeared to provoke a distancing from the native language and culture, as students were exposed more to English-language TV programs, films, pop music, etc., unfamiliar circumstances and customs. These offered many outlets for the younger generation to express rebellious independence from parents, native culture and traditions. This might of course be temporary and not lead them astray from their attachment to their native language and culture. Once it came to the identification with language and culture, the students claimed that they 'adored what they were born with', a claim that was explicitly voiced but also implied very often. Subtractive identity change in the EFL context should be different from what occurs in the ESL context, in that the loss of or the isolation from native language and culture for second language learners can be permanent and unchangeable as they assimilate into the new society but this might not be experienced bitterly and cruelly by foreign language learners. It might in any case be part of the mutually influenced view of life and the world under globalization, an ongoing process leading towards a never-ending identity integration and productive identity change (Bian & Gao, 2006). This change might be viewed as an opportunity for learners to detach from aspects of native language and culture that have been blindly adopted. If educators are able to put educational interventions into effect that strengthen the learner, the experience of challenge might make it possible to observe the native language and culture from a new angle, that of the L2 world, and then the L2 language and culture can become a perspective to explore the native language and culture as well.

It would be wise not to speculate too much about these findings. The study is limited to the extent that the research reported above comes from a longitudinal project of research in one university. The representativeness of the subjects was sacrificed for the feasibility of conducting the study. To compare the results of the questionnaire over the administration period, the questionnaire itself had to remain the same and was unable to be adjusted according to what was being discovered through other methods of data collection. Moreover, the reliability for the identity changes in the first and second administration was rather low, but for the third administration reliability was acceptable. One reason for this might be that the students understood better the items in the questionnaire, since each time the reliability of the questionnaire increased. Lastly, self-confidence and cultural identity are not stable states of mind, about which interviews, journals, etc., can reveal more life-like, changeable and multiple features in the development of such complex and subtle phenomena as identity.

Nevertheless, the study does throw light on the actual subjective experience of students who are part of the mass learning and compulsory teaching of English in China today.

References

Bian, Y.W. and Gao, Y.H. (2006) Yingyu Xuexi Zizhuanxing Wenben Zhong De Ziwo Rentong Jiangou [EFL students' identities in their autobiographical narrative]. *Foreign Language and Literature* 1, 34–39.

Clément, R. (1980) Ethnicity, contact and communicative competence in a second language. In H. Giles, W.P. Robinson and P.M. Smith (eds) *Language: Social Psychological Perspectives* (pp. 147–154). Oxford: Pergamon.

Clément, R. and Kruidenier, B.G. (1985) Aptitude, attitude and motivation in second language proficiency: A test of Clément's model. *Journal of Language and Social Psychology* 4, 21–37.

Clément, R., Gardner, R.C. and Smythe, P.C. (1977) Motivational variables in second language acquisition: A study of francophones learning English. *Canadian Journal of Behavioural Science* 9, 123–133.

Clément, R., Dörnyei, Z. and Noels, K.A. (1994) Motivation, self-confidence, and group cohesion in the foreign language classroom. *Language Learning* 44, 417–448.

Foss, K. and Reitzel, A. (1988) A relational model for managing second language anxiety. *TESOL Quarterly* 22, 437–454.

Gao, Y.H. (1996) "1 + 1 > 2" model of foreign language learning. In G.Z. Xu (ed.) *ELT in China 1992* (pp. 417–432). Beijing: Foreign Language Teaching and Research Press.

Gao, Y.H. (2001) *Foreign Language Learning*: 1 + 1 > 2. Beijing: Beijing University Press.

Gao, Y.H. (2002) Productive bilingualism: 1 + 1 > 2. In D.W.C. So and G.M. Jones (eds) *Education and Society in Plurilingual Contexts* (pp. 143–162). Brussels: VUB Brussels University Press.

Gao, Y.H. (ed.) (2004) Zhongguo Daxuesheng Yingyu Xuexi Shehui Xinli: Xuexi Dongji Yu Ziwo Rentong Yanjiu [*The Social Psychology of English Learning by Chinese College Students: Motivation and Learners' Self-Identities*]. Beijing: Foreign Language Teaching and Research Press.

Gao, Y.H., Cheng, Y., Zhao, Y. and Zhou, Y. (2005) Self-identity changes and English learning among Chinese undergraduates. *World Englishes* 24 (1), 39–51.

Gardner, R.C. (1985) *Social Psychology and Second Language Learning: The Role of Attitudes and Motivation*. London: Edward Arnold.

Genesee, F. (1987) French immersion in Canada. In F. Genesee (ed.) *Learning through Two Languages* (pp. 305–324). Cambridge: Newbury House.

Giles, H. and Byrne, J.L. (1982) An intergroup approach to second language acquisition. *Journal of Multilingual and Multicultural Development* 1, 17–40.

Goldberg, E. and Noels, K.A. (2006) Motivation, ethnic identity and post-secondary education language choices of graduates of intensive French language programs. *Canadian Modern Language Review* 62 (3), 423–447.

Horwitz, E. (1986) Preliminary evidence for the reliability and validity of a foreign language anxiety scale. *TESOL Quarterly* 20, 559–564.

Horwitz, E.K. and Young D.J. (1991) *Language Anxiety: From Theory and Research to Classroom Implications*. Englewood, NJ: Prentice-Hall.

Kim, Y.Y. (2001) *Becoming Interculture: An Integrative Theory of Communication and Cross-Cultural Adaptation*. Thousand Oaks, CA: Sage.

Lambert, W.E. (1963a) Psychological approaches to the study of language. Part I: On learning, thinking and human abilities. *Modern Language Journal* 14, 51–62.

Lambert, W.E. (1963b) Psychological approaches to the study of language. Part II: On second language learning and bilingualism. *Modern Language Journal* 14, 114–121.

Lambert, W.E. (1967) A social psychology of bilingualism. *Journal of Social Issues* 23, 91–109.

Lambert, W.E. (1975) Culture and language as factors in learning and education. In A. Wolfgang (ed.) *Education of Immigrant Students* (pp. 55–83). Toronto: Ontario Institute for Studies in Education.

Lo Bianco, J. (2000) Multiliteracies and multilingualism. In B. Cope and M. Kalantzis (eds) *Multiliteracies: Literacy Learning and the Design of Social Futures* (pp. 92–106). New York: Routledge.

Schumann, J.H. (1975) Affective factors and the problem of age in second language acquisition. *Language Learning* 25, 209–235.

Schumann, J.H. (1978a) *The Pidginization Process: A Model for Second-Language Acquisition*. Rowley, MA: Newbury House.

Schumann, J.H. (1978b) The acculturation model for second language acquisition. In R.C. Gingras (ed.) *Second Language Acquisition and Foreign Language Teaching* (pp. 27–50). Washington, DC: Center for Applied Linguistics.

Schumann, J.H. (1986) Research on the acculturation model for second language acquisition. *Journal of Multilingual and Multicultural Development* 7, 379–392.

Yashima, T., Zenuk-Nishide L. and Shimizu K. (2004) The influence of attitudes and affect on willingness to communicate and second language communication. *Language Learning* 54 (1), 119–152.

Zang, Q. (2007) The relationship between English learners' motivations and self-confidence change: A year-long study of non-English majors' motivations and self-confidence change in English learning. MA thesis, Beijing University.

Part 3

Landscapes and Mindscapes

Chapter 8
Language, Ethnicity and Identity in China

ZHOU QINGSHENG

Introduction

China is a unitary multi-ethnic state of 56 ethnic groups. Among them, the ethnic group Han forms the large majority, comprising about 91.59% of the population. The other 55 are ethnic minorities accounting for 8.4%. While previous Chinese governments traditionally acknowledged the Han, Man, Mongol, Turkish and Tibetan ethnic groups, the current Chinese government officially recognizes 56 ethnic groups, including the Han. The Han majority as well as the Hui and Man minorities speaks Chinese, but most of the minority ethnicities speak other languages, which fall into five main language families.

The ethnic group autonomous areas constitute 64.5% of Chinese territory, mostly in the border regions. China exercises a policy of regional autonomy for various ethnic minorities, allowing the diverse ethnic groups living in compact communities to establish self-government and direct their own affairs. This chapter discusses the relations between language, ethnicity and identity through an examination of ethnic identifications as recorded in the 1950s and 1960s.

The chapter is divided into three sections: first, there is a discussion of the criteria and practices of ethnic identification; second, there is a discussion of the correspondence of language to ethnic group and language functions; third, there is a discussion of the non-conformity of language, ethnicity and ethnic identity.

Criteria and Practices of Ethnic Identifications

China is not a homogeneous country, and does not aspire to a *one-nation, one-language and one-culture* model of development. In common with some other large states, China is a multi-ethnic polity whose constitutional arrangements provide for self-government in ethnic group autonomous areas. As a result of this national aspiration after the founding of the People's Republic of China, ethnic identification practices of the various ethnic groups became an important question for government policy.

Implementing the plans for development and education in ethnic regions requires that a certain number of ethnic groups be acknowledged. Certain rights also have to be acknowledged to these groups in order to ensure effective administration of entitlements and governance.

Table 8.1 lists the names of the ethnic groups that comprise the Chinese population, the number of people present in each group and the main geographic areas of concentration of these populations. The data are for the year 2000, drawn from the fifth census issued in 2003 by the National Statistical Bureau of China.

In the early 1950s, the Chinese government initiated a large-scale ethnic identification process. The criteria for ethnic identification were the 'four characteristics', namely, common language, common area, common economic life and culture and common psychology, as proposed by Joseph Stalin: '*A nation would not be a nation without any one of the four characteristics*' (Stalin, 1953: 295). Applying these criteria meant that if a particular ethnic group lacked a common language, then it could not be regarded as an ethnic group.

However, in specific practice, the experts involved in ethnic identification found that Stalin's criteria were not entirely applicable to the actual situation in China. The category of 'ethnic group' as defined by Stalin in 1953 indicated one that was formed when Western Bourgeoisie was on the rise. Most of the ethnic groups to be identified in China were in the stage of pre-capitalism, and did not necessarily possess the four characteristics that Stalin proposed. Therefore, the experts (Huang, 1989; Yang, 1986) reformulated the basis of identification according to the social and demographic circumstances pertaining in China, and combined Chinese history with Stalinist theories, as well as with scientific identification processes, and with the desires and aspirations of the ethnic groups (ethnic identity). In this way, a new approach to ethnic identification was formulated, based on the method of etic categorizing. Although departing from the Stalin criteria the new approach still carried the influence of the former Soviet Union.

Table 8.1 Ethnic minorities in China

Ethnic group	Number	Main concentration
Zhuang	16,178,811	Guangxi, Yunnan
Man	10,682,262	Liaoning, Jilin, Heilongjiang
Hui	9,816,805	Ningxia, Gansu
Miao	8,940,116	Guizhou, Hunan, Yunnan
Uygur	8,399,393	Xinjiang
Tujia	8,028,133	Hunan, Hubei
Yi	7,762,272	Sichuan, Yunnan
Mongol	5,813,947	Inner Mongolia, Liaoning
Tibetan	5,416,021	Tibet, Sichuan, Qinghai
Bouyei	2,971,460	Guizhou
Dong	2,960,293	Guizhou
Yao	2,637,421	Guangxi, Guangdong
Korean	1,923,842	Jilin, Liaoning, Heilongjiang
Bai	1,858,063	Yunnan
Hani	1,439,673	Yunnan
Kazak	1,250,458	Xinjiang, Qinghai
Li	1,247,814	Hainan
Dai	1,158,989	Yunnan
She	709,592	Fujian
Lisu	634,912	Yunnan
Gelao	579,357	Guizhou
Dongxiang	513,805	Gansu
Lahu	453,705	Yunnan
Shui	406,902	Guizhou
Wa	396,610	Yunnan
Naxi	308,839	Yunnan
Qiang	306,072	Sichuan

(Continued)

Table 8.1 _Continued_

Ethnic group	Number	Main concentration
Tu	241,198	Qinghai, Gansu
Mulam	207,352	Guangxi
Xibe	188,824	Xinjiang
Kirgiz	160,823	Xinjiang
Daur	132,394	Inner Mongolia, Heilongjiang
Jingpo	132,143	Yunnan
Maonan	107,166	Guangxi
Salar	104,503	Qinghai, Gansu
Blang	91,882	Yunnan
Tagik	41,028	Xinjiang
Achang	33,936	Yunnan
Primi	33,600	Yunnan
Ewenki	30,505	Inner Mongolia
Nu	28,759	Yunnan
Gin	22,517	Guangdong
Jino	20,899	Yunnan
Deang	17,935	Yunnan
Bonan	16,505	Gansu
Russ	15,609	Xinjiang
Yugur	13,719	Gansu
Uzbek	12,370	Xinjiang
Monba	8923	Tibet
Oroqen	8196	Inner Mongolia
Derung	7426	Yunnan
Tatar	4890	Xinjiang
Hezhen	4640	Heilongjiang
Gaoshen	4461	Fujian, Zhejiang
Lhoba	2965	Tibet

Table 8.2 Ethnic identifications in China

Period	*Number of registered groups*	*Number of identified ethnic groups*	*Total*
1949–1954	Over 400	38	38
1954–1964	183	15	53
1965–1982	–	2	55

The large-scale ethnic identification process started in 1953. According to the registration records from the first census of that year, there were more than 400 registered names of ethnic groups throughout the country. After ten years of ethnic identification, these were further categorized into just over 50 ethnic groups.

In 1979, an important development occurred in Chinese ethnic identification practices. The identification of the ethnic Jino marked the formation of the final pattern of the Chinese nation: 1 (ethnic Han as majority) + 55 (ethnic minorities) (Table 8.2).

Since this pattern was formulated, the Chinese government has not identified or distinguished any further new ethnicities except for restoring, altering or combining some ethnicities which have not altered the total number. The fact that there are 56 ethnicities/ethnic groups in China has come to assume the status of a 'solid truth'.

Correspondence of Language to Ethnic Group and Language Functions

A central issue in the relationship between language and ethnicity revolves around the question of whether the majority of the members of an ethnic group are able to use their native language or not. The dimensions of this issue can be seen by the disparity between ethnic group and language functions. At present there are over 80 languages, and by some estimates 130 languages, used by the 56 ethnic groups. This means that the number of ethnic groups falls to the level of two-fifths of the number of languages.

There are three major types of relationships of correspondence between language and ethnicity in China. The first correspondence is 'one-to-one', which means one ethnicity equates to one language. The second is 'one-to-plural', which means one ethnicity equates to plural languages. The third is 'plural-to-one', which refers to the existence of plural ethnicities equating to one language. These correspondences between language and ethnicity are discussed below.

One ethnicity, one language

One relationship of ethnicity to language is that an ethnic group has its own independent language, and the majority uses it as their native language. The language is the most important tool for social communication among members of the ethnic group and the most distinctive mark of ethnic identity. Outside the ethnic group, language is a barrier for communication between them and other ethnic groups and becomes a criterion to distinguish one ethnicity from another due to lack of mutual intelligibility. The language is a major characteristic used for ethnic identifications and one that can evoke the feeling of ethnic identity within the ethnic group and therefore it can be used as a criterion for delimitation of the ethnic group.

There are 38 ethnic groups among the 56 that share the 'one ethnicity, one language' characteristic. They are the Han, Mongol, Tibetan, Uygur, Miao, Yi, Zhuang, Bouyei, Korean, Dong, Bai, Hani, Kazak, Dai, Li, Lisu, Wa, Lahu, Shui, Dongxiang, Naxi, Tu, Daur, Mulam, Qiang, Blang, Salar, Maonan, Achang, Primi, Tagik, Ewenki, Deang, Bonan, Gin, Derung, Lhoba and Jino.

One ethnicity, plural languages

The relationship of one ethnicity and plural languages can be divided into 'one-to-plural without a common language' and 'one-to-plural with a common language'.

The former occurs in five ethnic groups. The Yao in the South has more than five languages, the Nu in Yunnan has seven, the Yugur in Gansu has three, while the Jingpo in Yunnan and Monba in Tibet have two languages, respectively. The latter pattern, that is, 'one-to-plural with a common language', mainly occurs in three ethnic groups in the North. The Uzbek in Xinjiang use four languages, the Tartar in Xinjiang use three, while the Oroqen in Major and Minor Xing'anling Mountains use two.

Ethnic split and ethnic cohesion are two completely different functions of languages in the model of 'one ethnicity, plural languages'. The split function of language means that those languages in the model of 'one ethnicity, plural languages' can maintain a split inside the ethnic group, but they can also promote the assimilation between one sub-ethnic group and another. This function operates mainly through members of an ethnic group shifting to another ethnic language as their native tongue.

The cohesive function of language means that those languages can maintain ethnic unity within the native community where the common language is spoken.

In the process of evolving ethnic identity, no language, including a native language in the 'one ethnicity, plural languages' model, is available as a symbol or mark of an ethnic group. Although a native language could have been a common language during a historical period for the group, the split inside the group and assimilation into other ethnic groups continue. If the native language, when the population of native language speakers has decreased to 50% or less, was used as a criterion of ethnic identity, half or more than half of the population who have shifted to another language would be excluded from identification with the ethnic group. These members would be unable to accept this kind of identity for the future.

Plural ethnicities, one language

The term 'plural ethnicities, one language' refers to situations in which most members of two or more ethnic groups stop using their original or native language and shift to the use of a different language as their mother tongue. In this pattern 'most' means more than two-thirds of the ethnic population.

Such a phenomenon mainly occurs in eight ethnic groups – Hui, Man, She, Tujia, Gelo, Hezhen, Xibe and Gaoshan (Ouyang *et al.*, 1994). Most or all of their members use Chinese as their native language.

Summary

Among the three models of the language-ethnicity correspondence, the model of 'one ethnicity, one language' reflects coherence between language and ethnicity. It is a basic, stable and major model. A total of 70% of all ethnic groups are classified as belonging to this model. The two other models of 'one ethnicity, plural languages' and 'plural ethnicities, one language' reflect the variability and differences between language and ethnicity. Those correspondences are secondary, changing and non-mainstream. Ethnic groups belonging to the latter two models make up about 30% of all ethnic groups in China.

Table 8.3 shows the list of ethnic groups, and their percentage of the total, that correspond to one or other of the three language-ethnicity models used in China (Zhou, 2000: 98–102). The data here refer to only 54 ethnic groups since the Russ and Kirgiz groups are not included.

Non-Conformity of Language, Ethnicity and Ethnic Identity

In the case of China, language in the 'one ethnicity, one language' correspondence is a very important basis for ethnic identity (Smith, 1986).

Table 8.3 Corresponding relationship between language and ethnicity in China

Language–ethnicity relation	Number of ethnic groups	% of total ethnic groups	The ethnic identity/label functions of languages
One ethnicity, one language	38	70	+
One ethnicity, plural languages	8	15	–
Plural ethnicities, one language	8	15	–
Total	54	100	

The relationships between language and ethnicity, in the 'one ethnicity, plural languages' correspondence and the 'plural ethnicities, one language' correspondence, however, are very complicated.

In order to give a clear description of these relationships, I consider four aspects: ethnic origin, ethnic group, language and ethnic identity. The relationships that emerge by applying these four aspects to the ethnic groups can roughly be divided into four categories: (1) different origins, same ethnicity, different languages; (2) same origin, same ethnicity, different languages; (3) different origins, different ethnicities, same language; and (4) same origin, same ethnicity, different languages.

Different origins, same ethnicity, different languages

When different groups move into a common area, it is possible for them to still maintain linguistic differences, but develop the same ethnic identity. This has occurred in the case of the Yao in Dayao Mountain in Guangxi who were from five different ethnic groups outside of the mountains.

After moving to a common geographic area and living in contact with each other for about 500 years, the ethnic characteristics are converging and becoming quite similar. However, due to the high mountains keeping them apart, they still use five different languages, being Mian, Bunu, Lajia, Baheng and Jiongnai. This linguistic diversity does not stop them from identifying collectively as having a shared ethnicity. During the ethnic identifications research in the 1950s, all of these groups regarded the other groups living on the mountain as being of their own kind and considered outsiders as strangers (Fei Xiaotong, 1988: 6). The mountain people do not want to be separated from each other, and reported themselves as belonging to the same ethnic group.

An ethnic group, who were conquered for hundreds of years and who have merged to share the characteristics of the conquering ethnicity, would lose many of its ethnic characteristics, but probably maintain its native language. For example, after the fall of the Tang Dynasty (618–907), some of the Qiang living in the six river valleys in Southwest China were conquered by the Tibetan forces, *Tubo/Tufan* Court. These groups lived under the *Tubo/Tufan* Court for a long time and were deeply influenced by Lamaism. Currently their customs, religions and dress are the same as the other Tibetans' and they have become ethnic Tibetans, although their mother tongue, the Qiang language, is still used in the village and at home (Sun, 1988).

Same origin, same ethnicity, different languages

Although moving to another community because of the displacement caused by war and shifting to another's language, an ethnic group may still retain its ethnic identity hundreds of years later. An example of this phenomenon is the Mongolian ethnic group.

Historically the Mongolians were nomadic and warlike, and Mongolian forces used to be very powerful. They had conquered many parts of Eurasia from Moscow in the north to Yunnan in the south of China and in fact the Mongolians established the Yuan Dynasty (1271–1368) in China.

Some Mongolians who followed the Mongolian army into the present Yunnan province settled there. Several hundred years later, they have lost many Mongolian characteristics, but still maintain their Mongolian identity and call themselves Mongolians. Some Mongolians in Tonghai near Kunming, the capital of Yunnan Province, are descendants of a Mongolian force remaining there from the time of the Yuan Dynasty. They are unable to use the Mongolian language but have shifted to use the Kazhuo language, a relatively recent mixed form of language based on the Yi and Naxi languages. Kazhuo is closer to the Yi languages of the Sino-Tibetan family.

Different branches of an ethnic group may disperse to several places of residence. After hundreds of years, the different dialects used by the subgroups may change and eventually become different languages. The ethnic Nu in Biluoxue Mountain in Yunnan province fits this pattern. Those residing on the western side of Biluoxue Mountain speak the Nusu language, while those on the eastern side use the Rouruo language. According to historical records, both branches originate from the same ethnic group, and the differentiation of language occurred at least 1200 or 1300 years ago.

Different origins, different ethnicities, same language

The ancestors of the ethnic Hui were Arabic- and Persian-speaking merchants who came to mainland China by sea in the seventh century. They gradually stopped using their native languages and shifted to Chinese during long-term contact and communication with the ethnic Han. Over 500 years later, the Mongolians conquered the Middle Asian countries, and another large number of Muslim merchants and craftsmen moved into China with the Mongolian army. These are the main components today of Hui ancestry. Most Hui used Arabic and Persian languages, and a few spoke Uygur. The Chinese language came to be used by the ethnic Hui as the native language in the late 14th and 15th centuries, due to their residential environment of 'small groups in large-scale dispersion', Hui–Han exogamy, commerce and social contacts and so on, for some 2–300 years.

The direct ancestors of the ethnic Man were the Nüzhen people from Northeast China in the Ming Dynasty (1368–1644), during which time the Man had their own language but lacked a writing system. Based on the Mongolian script, a writing system of Man, called 'old Man script', was created in 1597 and improved in 1632. Before the script could be promoted in the Man community, however, the Man majority had occupied Shanhaiguan Fortress in 1644 and established the Qing Dynasty (1644–1911). About one million Man came to inhabit Chinese communities. During the 260 years from then till 1911 when the Qing Dynasty fell, the Man language had basically become extinct.

Same origin, different ethnicities, same language

Xibe and Man are two different ethnic groups. Several historians have proved that they have the same ethnic origin, though in early times they used different languages. From the late 16th to the early 17th centuries, the ancestors of the Xibe were conquered by the Man. The former began to learn and use the language of the latter.

After the Man established the Qing Dynasty in 1644, the government sent a large number of Xibe to the border regions in northwest and southwest China on four occasions to prevent them from causing trouble if they lived in compact communities. In 1764, the Qing government moved approximately 3000 Xibe soldiers, officers and their relatives to the Yili River valley in Xinjiang in order to open up wasteland and guard the border. Since then, there are two major places of residence for the Xibe: in the northeast and the northwest. Until the late 1950s, due mainly to geographic, natural, economic and language influences, the Chinese and Mongolian languages were the main means of communication used by the Xibe in northeastern China, while the Man language was used by the Xibe in Xinjiang. There are now few Man who can speak the Man language anywhere in China.

The differences between the Man language used by the Xibe in Xinjiang and the Man language used by the Man in the northeast might be even slighter than those between British English and American English. The Xibe in Xinjiang have been speaking Man for approximately 200 years. During the ethnic identification process in the 1950s, however, the Xibe did not identify their language, script and ethnicity as Man but as Xibe.

Nevertheless, as far as many linguists are concerned, due to the small differences between Xibe and Man, the Xibe language is considered a development and continuation of the Man language in the Qing Dynasty. The Xibe script was developed from a Man base in 1947, and can be regarded as a branch of the Man language. At present, most of the researchers of the documents in Man at the Forbidden City are Xibe. This tells us that claimed identity is much more important than language alone in identifying ethnic groups.

Conclusion

The non-conformity relationship between language, ethnicity and ethnic identity is complex and varies across China according to historical circumstances. The abstractions that this non-conformity involves are given in Table 8.4 as a conclusion to this description of official identification processes in contemporary China.

Table 8.4 Non-conformity of language, ethnicity and ethnic identity

Ethnic speaker	Origin	Language	Ethnicity	Identity
Yaos speaking Mian, Bunu, Lajia, Baheng or Jiongnai	−	−	+	+
Tibetans speaking Tibetan or Qiang	−	−	+	±
Mongols speaking Mongolian or Kazhuo	+	−	+	+
Nus speaking Nusu or Rouruo	+	−	+	+
Huis speaking Chinese; Hans speaking Chinese; Xibes speaking Xibe	−	+	−	−

Acknowledgments

I wish to acknowledge Professor Björn Jernudd for reading a draft version of this chapter and making some linguistic suggestions, which have been adopted.

References

Fei, X. (1988) Diaocha Yaoshan wushi nian [A survey of the Yaos for 50 years]. In J. Qiao (ed.) *Proceedings of Yao Studies*. Beijing: Ethnic Press.

Heberer, T. (1989) *China and its Minority Nationalities: Autonomy or Assimilation?* Armonk, NY: M. E. Sharpe.

Huang, S. (1989) Minzu shibie: kunnan he tupo [Ethnic identification and its theoretical significance] *Chinese Social Sciences* 1, 107–116.

Ouyang, J., Zhou, Y., Dob and Tan, K. (eds) (1994) *Zhongguo Shaoshu Minzu Yuyan Shiyong Qingkuang* [The Situation of Ethnic Minority Languages in China]. Beijing: China Tibetan Studies Press.

Smith, A. D. (1986) *The Ethnic Origins of Nations*. Oxford: Basil Blackwell.

Sun, H. (1988) Yuyan shibie yu minzu [Language identification and ethnicity]. *Ethnic Linguistics* 2, 9–17.

Stalin, J. (1953) *Complete Works of Stalin* (Vol. 1). Beijing: People's Press.

Yang, K. (1986) Guanyu minzu he minzu wenti de jidian yijian [Several opinions on ethnicity and ethnic problems]. *Ethnic Studies* 4, 11–2.

Zhou, Q. (2000) *Yuyan yu Renlei: Zhonghua Shehui Yuyan Toushi* [Language and Man: A Sociolinguistic Perspective on the Chinese Nation]. Beijing: Central University for Ethnicities Press.

Chapter 9
Ethnic Minorities, Bilingual Education and Glocalization

XU HONGCHEN

Introduction

Globalization is primarily an economic process on which there has been a great deal of current research into its effects from both socio-economic and political angles. According to Giddens (1991), globalization not only influences existing economic processes, but also alters our perceptions of time and space. Traditional social life, which is closely related to space, tends to be undermined by globalization because the latter reduces the influence of distance on social activities, including the use of language. In light of this effect the present author argues that globalization implies a re-evaluation of some basic human attitudes towards language, and further that English, the lingua franca of today's world, alters our sense of ownership of the language since the distinctions between learner and user become blurred. In turn, this already profound change tends to obscure the boundaries between the learner of a language and any target language community.

Glocalization seems to operate in a similar way to how globalization manifests itself. According to Robertson (1995), glocalization is a mixture of the global and the local. It signifies a certain 'homogeneity' in a specific geographic and socio-political locality rather than across the whole world (or globe). Taking this definition and applying it to the specific setting of Chinese ethnic minorities, we can see that China's constituent minority populations are experiencing glocalization within the geo-political entity of China. Within China the national minorities are more and more engaged in the economic and technological modernization of the country, and *Putonghua*, like English in the world, functions as the internal national lingua franca among all the components of the Chinese citizenry. Ethnic minorities therefore learn the Chinese lingua franca as they use it to participate in national life. *Putonghua* is therefore not only a tool for communication but also a way for ethnic minorities to identify as members of the People's Republic of China while at the same time maintaining their distinctive ethnic identities as members of their respective ethnic groups.

In the present chapter the situation of *Putonghua*-ethnic language bilingual education in China will first be introduced (see also Zhou, this volume), and then, utilizing the notions of 'imagined community' and 'Ideal L2 Self' proposed by Norton (2001) and Dornyei (2005), respectively, I will discuss the relationship between the languages and identities, the particular ethnic language and *Putonghua* and the corresponding ethnic identities (both ethnic and national) in China.

Prior to this discussion, it is necessary to clarify some terms and notions, made all the more necessary because of the interlingual (English–Chinese) context within which this globalization–glocalization phenomenon is occurring. While both 'ethnic minority' and 'nation' are translated as *minzu* in Chinese, they are truly different in reference. The former refers to groups which share similar culture, kinship and geography and which sometimes also share a unique language. The latter term, 'nation', typically refers to the group that not only shares these features but also, and most importantly, has a shared statehood. In this way the political nation (cf. Jin, 2000: 152; Ma, 2005: 15–26) can be distinguished from the cultural nation. This is a crucial distinction and should be rendered in Chinese as *shaoshuminzu*, 'ethnic minority', while the term for the Chinese nation would most appropriately be *zhonghuaminzu*.

It is also critical to clarify the meaning and use of such a common term as 'identity', which in the present discussion means 'membership' (cf. Fei & Zhang, 1988: 45). 'Ethnic identity' means the feeling a member of a certain ethnic group might have for their membership of that group. Thus, the identity of 'Chinese nation' refers to the feeling of a person who identifies as a member of the category of Chinese people. In the writings of Norton and Dornyei, identity (either ethnic or national) is understood as an imagined membership or an ideal self in an imagined community (i.e. the people living in China).

Finally, the term 'bilingual education', which has a range of meanings, is here used to describe learning in and through *Putonghua* and a given ethnic language of a national minority group of the Chinese nation. Although China is itself a bilingual country, lacking public regulations and official national status for languages other than *Putonghua*, bilingualism is a very common phenomenon in some ethnic municipalities, which commonly use two or more languages, one of which is usually *Putonghua*.

A Brief Survey of *Putonghua*-Ethnic Language Bilingual Education

Systematic research documenting bilingualism in China began in 1979, when the Academy of Teaching *Putonghua* to Ethnic Minorities was founded in ethnic universities. In 1985, the organization was renamed the China Academy of Bilingual Education for Ethnic Minorities (Ma, 1999). At that time, the focus of research was on the teaching of *Putonghua* rather than an examination of the processes or outcomes from bilingual teaching. However, by the 1980s, the task assigned to the Academy changed to include descriptions of the bilingual situation in certain ethnic municipalities so that further research on language comparison could be conducted. In the course of this new role the Academy was able to devise a research method appropriate to documenting bilingualism and in doing so bilingual education research was transformed from experiential description to empirical investigation (Chen, 1997).

The overall goal of bilingual education in China is to equip ethnic minorities with two languages and their related cultures. In order to achieve this goal, two types of bilingual education are applied: one is ethnic language-oriented teaching in which Chinese functions as an auxiliary language, the other is *Putonghua*-oriented teaching in which the ethnic language serves as the auxiliary tongue (Hu, 1996). In the course of this research and categorization of Chinese, the types of bilingual education researchers have identified new kinds of teaching, known as Paradigms. Setting out with a conventional classification drawn from European and North American documentation of bilingual education, especially in the work of M.F. Mackey and M. Siguan, a range of types, or paradigms, such as the 'Six Geographical-Distributional Paradigm' by Yan Xuejiong, the 'Seven-type Paradigm' by Zhou Yaowen, the 'Three-plan Paradigm' by Zhang Wei and the 'Three-type Paradigm' by Zhou Qingsheng have emerged (Wang, 1999). While it is beyond the scope of the present chapter to describe these, they are included to indicate the great complexity that exists at the level of locality across China where significant variation in the conditions of language, culture and constitutional arrangements make for a very complex reality.

The achievements and outcomes from *Putonghua* teaching to ethnic minorities during the 1980s were reported in *The Collections of Papers on Ethnic Minorities Bilingual Education in China* of 1990 by *Zhongguo Shaoshu Minzu Shuangyu Jiaoxue Yanjiuhui* (China Academy of Bilingual Education for Ethnic Minorities). Since then, much attention has been focused on cognitive outcomes of *Putonghua* learning (such as the level of proficiency attained in *Putonghua*, the influence of ethnic languages on *Putonghua* knowledge and use, and comparisons between the ethnic languages and *Putonghua*); bilingual education policy (e.g. Su, 2005), bilingual textbooks, teaching methodology and teacher training (e.g. Deng, 2000; Zhang & Cai, 2005; Zhou, 2004) and bilingual education theories (e.g. Dai, 1997; He, 1998; Zhou, 2000).

There has also been documentation of socio-psychological outcomes from *Putonghua* learning, important among which is the work of Wu (2003), who argues that bilingual education is helpful in developing ethnic students' concept of self. In Wu Qiyun's research the development of self-concept tends to follow a three-step process. First, the learner comes to develop a sense of self-identity so that they can realize 'who I am'. On the basis of such an accomplishment the second step involves the learner developing his or her ethnic self-identity so that they can identify their own ethnic cultures. Finally, in the third step, the learner is able to forge a sense of national self-identity so that they can extend their ethnic identities to encompass the identification with the nation. This three-step process therefore involves moving from, but still retaining, personal, ethnic group and national identifications.

Norton's Imagined Community and Dornyei's L2 Motivational Self System

In this section I shall draw on Norton's (2001) concept of an 'imagined language community' and Dornyei's (2005) 'Ideal L2 Self' to review the ethnic identity of Chinese minorities.

According to Dornyei (2005: 106), the L2 Motivation Self System consists of three components: Ideal L2 Self (the L2-specific facet of one's ideal self), Ought-to L2 Self (the attributes that one believes one *ought to* possess ... in order to *avoid* possible negative outcomes) and L2 Learning Experience (the situation-specific motives related to the immediate learning environment and experience). Although the system as proposed by Dornyei (2005) focuses on the motivation that a learner has in acquiring language skill, in the following analysis an attempt is made to apply this construct to the discussion of identity in the context of glocalized Chinese-ethnic minority settings. Essentially I adapt Dornyei's notion to argue that ethnic learners create images of themselves as users of *Putonghua* and these images serve to represent an ideal state that they want to realize.

These images are an outcome of social interactions that the individual conducts with members of a given community. This process of social interaction also occurs in the imagination of learners, such as when they picture themselves engaged in communication with target language speakers and visualize themselves conducting their part of the conversation and representing themselves and all their identities in such interactions. Therefore even in the case where there is no immediate contact with the target language community and where no such contact would be available, it is possible for learners to be influenced by their membership and participation in imagined communities. What impact this has on their own ethnic identities would be interesting and important to research and speculate about.

Ethnic Language Learning and Ought-to L2 Self

According to the researcher Yu, the people of Dehang have a deep love for their ethnic language, which is called the *Miao* language, and regard it as symbolic of their very ethnicity. This is so important to the people of Dehang that they would 'prefer to sell their lands rather than change their ethnic language' (Yu, 2003: 62). Similarly, recent research on the *Korean* ethnic group by Wang (2004) and the investigation on the *Yi* ethnic group by Teng (2000a) both support Yu Jinzhi's finding. In all of these cases we see strongly held attachments towards native languages, which in turn reflects a particular and strongly held type of ethnic identity.

However, some ethnic minorities in China have adopted *Putonghua* as their mother tongue because their own ethnic languages have already died out or are fading from use and are today seldom used in everyday communication. Despite the loss of practical daily communicative use of the ethnic language, many of these communities will still nominate that language as their own mother tongue, despite most of them knowing little about the language and not using it for most communication.

One clear example of this is *Man*. The people known as Manchu claim Man as their mother tongue although the whole group has already shifted to using *Putonghua*. Influenced by such phenomena Dai Qingxia and He (1997) propose two criteria for 'native language'. They believe that the concept of 'native language' should not only mean a concrete language (or a dialect), that is, a language that is the practical medium of communication for a given population, but that the term also implies an attitude and an orientation of value. These scholars therefore distinguish 'native language' in a linguistic or psychological sense from the notion of 'second native language'.

According to this approach, *Putonghua*, to those who do not have their own ethnic languages, is 'a second native language', rather than simply a 'second language'. The *Manchu* ethnic identity mirrors such a linguistic categorization, in that _Manchu_ people report to researchers that they regard themselves as a group different from _Han_ or any other ethnic group despite having adopted _Putonghua_ as their native language. For them, _Putonghua_ is nothing but a tool for communication and using this linguistic tool does not alter their ethnic identity.

According to Dornyei (2005: 106), Ought-to L2 Self _'refers to the attributes that one believes one ought to possess (i.e. various duties, obligations, or responsibilities) in order to avoid possible negative outcomes'_. I argue that this definition of the Ought-to L2 Self can be usefully applied to explain the above-mentioned phenomenon, in which ethnic minority students believe they still belong to their own ethnic group despite having shifted to practical daily use of _Putonghua_. The Ought-to L2 Self of such groups reminds them to maintain their own ethnic identity as distinctive and separate. In this way the ethnic language (including the second native language, _Putonghua_) acts as a basic tool for them to get involved in social practices and requirements of their wider national identities while maintaining their own ethnic identities.

Putonghua Learning and Ideal L2 Self

Research has shown that a positive attitude towards _Putonghua_ learning is beneficial to ethnic identity maintenance and its extension, while a negative attitude will block _the ethnic identity_ from being extended and as a result consolidate a negative ethnic identity.

Research conducted by Wang and Wan (2003) on Tibetan students shows this phenomenon in action. This research has found that the students' acceptance of _Han_ ethnic group and the duration of _Putonghua_ study tend to enhance these students' Tibetan ethnic identity. The longer the time of _Putonghua_ study is, the more the Tibetan students can maintain their own ethnic identity and at the same time accept _Han_ culture. Similarly, Cai and Liu's investigation (2000) also shows that in interpersonal communication, students of _Yi_ ethnic group, whose language of instruction is mainly _Putonghua_ with _Yi_ language as the assisting language, perform much better than those whose language of instruction is mainly _Yi_ language with _Putonghua_ in the assisting role.

Extended involvement in _Putonghua_ study has tended to concern some ethnic groups. For example, researches by Dai and He (1997) and Zhong (2002) have discovered that in programmes aiming to teach _Putonghua_ as a second language, some ethnic minorities express concern that their ethnic languages will be replaced as native languages through the adoption of _Putonghua_, which they identify as the language of another ethnic group.

Li (2000) reports the same worries in research in the Xinjiang region of western China. In all these cases the groups have a close identification with the native language and this identification is the basis of their concern for its potential loss or erosion through *Putonghua* teaching.

In official Chinese policy, however, it is not the intention that the study of *Putonghua* should eradicate ethnic languages or respective ethnic identities. *Putonghua* is promoted instead as a means of communication among ethnic groups, and therefore as a Chinese lingua franca (Teng, 2000b; Qi, 2003; Yang, 2006) in the context of glocalization in China today. In this way, *Putonghua* functions like a mirror of how the wider Chinese state aims to include English for international lingua franca communication. The declared intention of the Academy and other official Chinese policies is that the ethnic identity will not be replaced but extended. The research has shown that those communities that have a more active and positive notion about *Putonghua* and see it as extending their linguistic range, are more likely to extend Chinese identity while also maintaining it.

The present author argues that ethnic learners of *Putonghua* are developing their Ideal L2 Selves as fluent *Putonghua* users in the communication with the *Han* ethnic group or other ethnic groups in China. In this way the process of glocalization demands that they learn *Putonghua* well, otherwise they will be marginalized, the opposite state to what they might aspire to reach in their Ideal L2 Selves.

From Ethnic Identities to Nation Identity in the Imagined Community

Despite the existing ethnic identities that pertain to ethnic minorities, these identities are extended further with acquisition of *Putonghua*. This claim is based on the idea that identity is a multiple notion, people are capable of many interlocking identities, with one group in one situation and another in another situation. Because much of our identity is imagined, different identities can exist together; in relation to the present issue a person can be first a member of a certain ethnic group, and second a member of the nation of China. By transferring ethnic identities across layers and points of view, these can be marked by the context in which they occur and who the interlocutor in different situations is.

The socio-cultural situation in China today, as expressed in linguistic behaviour, can be seen as having a plural-integrative configuration, and this complex configuration is the foundation for the extension of identity (Liu, 2003). The *guoyu* (national language), that is, *Putonghua* in the present chapter, serves as the link among the diverse identities of the people in

China, the various ethnic minorities and the majority *Han* ethnic group. This implies that there is something in common among them, the same political nation (Zhou, 1995), although the cultural nations might vary. The shared national identity requires that shared experiences of international life, when the Chinese nation is identified as a single entity, in the globalized world and experiences (Hu, 2004) change collectivity.

The creation or the emergence of a lingua franca is a difficult historical process that can take extremely long periods of time to develop. A lingua franca succeeds because it is efficient, and the convenience of communication that it offers explains the importance of *Putonghua* as a lingua franca among the ethnic groups in China (Ding, 2004) for glocalization, in just the same way that English as a lingua franca for globalization develops from the efficiency it offers.

Conclusion

From the above analysis, it is apparent that the development of the ethnic minority students' identity is closely related with the learning of *Putonghua* and their own ethnic languages. Chinese ethnic minority students' learning of *Putonghua* as a second language is an approach to realize their Ideal L2 Selves (a national identity as a Chinese), in the present case a fluent user of *Putonghua* in interaction with other members from the same imagined community – all the people from different ethnic groups in China, while the learning of their own ethnic languages is a means to maintain their Ought-to L2 Selves (an ethnic identity as a member of their own ethnic groups).

This happens in the context of glocalization of China and it is safe to say in the context of globalization ethnic minority students will continue this process of identity extension to include English, the lingua franca in the world imagined community.

References

Cai, H. and Liu, C.F. (2000) Yizu shuangyjiaoyu lianglei moshi daxuesheng shehui shiying nengli diaocha baogao [A report on the adjustment ability of Yi ethnic group in two bilingual teaching paradigms]. *Xinan Minzu Xueyuan Xuebao (Zhe She Ban)* [*Southwest Ethnic Institute Transaction*] (*Social Section*) (3), 115–118.

Chen, Y.H. (1997) Zhongguo shaoshuminzu shuangyujiaoyu yanjiu xianzhuang yu quxiang [Present situation and tendency of ethnic minority bilingual education in China]. *Guizhou Minzu Yanjiu* [*Guizhou Ethnic Research*] (1), 99–105.

Dai, Q.X. (1997) *Zhonguo Shaoshu Minzu Shuangyu Jiaoyu Gailun* [*Ethnic Bilingual Education in China: An Introduction*]. Shenyang: Liaoning Ethnic Press.

Dai, Q.X. and He, J.F. (1997) Lun muyu [On native language]. *Minzu Yanjiu* [*Ethnic Research*] (2), 59–64.

Deng, Y.L. (2000) Di'er yuyan 'Hanyu' jiaoxue zhong de hanwenhua jiaoxue [Teaching Chinese culture in teaching Chinese as a second language]. *Minzu Jiaoyu Yanjiu* [*Ethnic Education Research*] (1), 26–32.

Ding, S.Q. (2004) He'erbutong Qiutongcunyi: lun shuangyu xianxiang fasheng de wenhua dongyin [Dissimilarities in similarities: On the cultural reasons of bilingualism]. *Xinan Minzu Xueyuan Xuebao* (*Zhe She Ban*) [*Southwest Ethnic Institute Transaction*] (*Social Section*) (1), 57–61.

Dornyei, Z. (2005) *The Psychology of the Language Learner: Individual Differences in Second Language Acquisition*. Mahwah, NJ: Lawrence Erlbaum Associates.

Fei, H.Y. and Zhang, P.S. (1988) *Shehui Xinlixue Cidian* [*A Dictionary of Socio-psychology*]. Shijiazhuang: Hebei People's Press.

Giddens, A. (1991) *Modernity and Self-Identity: Self and Society in the Late Modern Age*. Stanford, CA: Stanford University Press.

He, J.F. (1998) *Zhongguo Shaoshu Minzu Shuangyu Yanjiu: Lishi yu Xianshi* [*Research on Ethnic Minority Bilingualism in China: History and Status Quo*]. Beijing: China Ethnic University Press.

Hu, Q.Y. (2004) Quanqiuhua yujing zhong de xiandai wenhua rentong jiangou [The construction of modern cultural identity in globalization]. *Guizhou Minzu Xueyuan Xuebao* (*Zhe She Ban*) [*Guizhou Ethnic Institute Transaction*] (*Social Science Section*) (4), 41–44.

Hu, S.J. (1996) Shilun woguo minzu jiaoyu yu minzu yuyan de guanxi [On the relationship of ethnic education and ethnic languages in China]. *Xinan Minzu Xueyuan Xuebao* (*Zhe She Ban*) [*Southwest Ethnic Institute Transaction*] (*Social Section*) (3), 112–115.

Jin, B.H. (2000) *Zhongguo Minzu Lilun Yanjiu Ershi Nian (1978–1998)* [*Research on Ethnic Theories of China (1978–1998)*]. Beijing: China Ethnic University Press.

Li, X.X. (2000) Liangnan de xuanze: dui shaoshuminzu xuesheng jinru hanyu shouke xuexiao de diaocha yu fenxi [A report on ethnic minority students studying Chinese: A dilemma]. *Xinjiang Shifan Daxue Xuebao* (*Zhe She Ban*) [*Xingjiang Normal University Transaction*] (*Social Section*) (4), 94–101.

Liu, J.C. (2003) Minzu rentong yu zhonghua minzu de fazhan [Ethnic identity and the development of Chinese nation]. *Guizhou Minzu Xueyuan Xuebao* (*Zhe She Ban*) [*Guizhou Ethnic Institute Transaction*] (*Social Section*) (4), 33–38.

Ma, R. (2005) *Minzu Shehuixue Daolun* [*An Introduction to Ethno-sociology*]. Beijing: Peking University Press.

Ma, X.L. (1999) Lun shuangyu xianxiang he shuangyu jiaoxue zhong de jige wenti [Some aspects of bilingualism and bilingual education]. *Ma Xueliang Minzu Yuyan Yanjiu Wenji* [*Collections of Papers on Ethnic Languages by Ma Xueliang*]. Beijing: China Ethnic University Press.

Norton, B. (2001) Non-participation, imagined communities and the language classroom. In M.P. Breen (ed.) *Learner Contributions to Language Learning* (pp. 159–171). Harlow: Longman.

Qi, D.C. (2003) Shi tan Yunnan min han shuangyuwen jiaoxue leixing ji xingshi [On the bilingual education types in Yunnan province]. *Minzu Jiaoyu Yanjiu* [*Ethnic Education Research*] (5), 54–60.

Robertson, R. (1995) Glocalization: Time-space and homogeneity–heterogeneity. In M. Featherstone, S. Lash and R. Robertson (eds) *Global Modernities* (pp. 25–34). London; Thousand Oaks, CA: Sage.

Su, D. (2005) Shaoshu minzu shuangyu jiaoyu yanjiu gaishu [A survey of bilingual education to ethnic minorities]. *Minzu Wenti Yanjiu [baokan fuyin ziliao] [Ethnic Issues Research]* [Photocopies]. China Renmin University (2), 56–61.

Teng, X. (2000a) Liangshan Yizu diqu xuexiao shishi Yi-Han shuangyu jiaoyu de biyaoxing [On the necessity of Yi-Han bilingual education in Liangshan Yi schools]. *Minzu Jiaoyu Yanjiu [Ethnic Education Research]* (1), 5–25.

Teng, X. (2000b) Yingxiang yu zhiyue Liangshan Yizu shequ xuexiao Yi-Han lianglei moshi shuangyu jiaoyu de yinsu yu tiaojian [Factors influencing the two types of Yi-Han bilingual education in Liangshan Yi schools]. *Minzu Jiaoyu Yanjiu [Ethnic Education Research]* (2), 45–52.

Wang, Q. (1999) Lun woguo shaoshu minzu shuangyu jiaoxue de moshi [On the mode of China ethnic bilingual education]. *Guizhou Minzu Yanjiu [Guizhou Ethnic Research]* (1), 157–163.

Wang, Y.X. (2004) Hebeisheng Funingxian Chaoxianzucun de yuyan shiyong zhuangkuang he shuangyu jiaoxue [Research on the language use and bilingual education of the Korean village in Funing County Hebei Province]. *Minzu Jiaoyu Yanjiu [Ethnic Education Research]* (4), 47–54.

Wang, Y.P. and Wan, M.G. (2003) Zangzu daxuesheng de minzu rentong jiqi yingxiang yinsu yanjiu [Research on the ethnic identity of Tibetan college students and the influencing factors]. *Minzu Jiaoyu Yanjiu [Ethnic Education Research]* (4), 65–70.

Wu, Q.Y. (2003) Duoyuan wenhua shiye zhong de shuangyu jiaoxue [Bilingual education in multi-cultural perspective]. *Minzu Jiaoyu Yanjiu [Ethnic Education Research]* (1), 55–59.

Yang, D.F. (2006) Minzu diqu zhongxiaoxue hanyu jiaoyu de xingzhi ji hanyu jiaoyu yu minzuyu jiaoyu zhijian de guanxi [The nature of Chinese education in elementary level in ethnic districts and the relationship between Chinese education and ethnic language instruction]. *Minzu Jiaoyu Yanjiu [Ethnic Education Research]* (1), 88–93.

Yu, J.Z. (2003) Jingji zhuanxing yu shuangyu bianqian – Dehangcun shuangyu bianqian gefan fenxi [Economic change and bilingual process – a case study in Dehang Village]. *Minzu Jiaoyu Yanjiu [Ethnic Education Research]* (5), 61–64.

Zhang, Q. and Cai, Q.J. (2005) Qianlun shuangyu shizi de xianzhuang yu peiyang [On the status quo and nurture of bilingual teacher training]. *Minzu Jiaoyu Yanjiu [Ethnic Education Research]* (2), 89–92.

Zhongguo Shaoshu Minzu Shuangyu Jiaoxue Yanjiuhui [China Academy of Bilingual Education for Ethnic Minorities] (1990) *Zhongguo Shaohu Minzu Shuangyu Jiaoyu Yanjiu Lunji [The Collections of Papers on Ethnic Minorities Bilingual Education in China]*. Beijing: Ethnic Press.

Zhong, R.X. (2002) Makesizhuyi yu yuyan he minzu de guanxi [Marxism and the relationship between language and ethnicity]. *Xinan Minzu Xueyuan Xuebao (Zhe She Ban) [Southwest Ethnic Institute Transaction] (Social Section)* (8), 168–172.

Zhou, Q.S. (2000) *Yuyan yu Renlei – Zhonghua Minzu Shehui Yuyan Toushi [Language and Human Beijings – A Panorama of Ethnic, Society and Language in China]*. Beijing: China Ethnic University.

Zhou, S. (2004) Xinjiang Mengguzu xuexiao shuangyu jiaoyu moshi de goujian [The construction of bilingual education modes in Mongolian schools in Xinjiang]. *Minzu Jiaoyu Yanjiu* [*Ethnic Education Research*] (2), 81–86.

Zhou, Y.W. (1995) Lun yuyan shehui gongneng daxiao yu jiaoxue yuyan shiyong cengci gaodi [On the relationship between language social functions and language instructions in classroom teaching]. *Zhongguo Shaoshu Minzu Yuwen Shiyong Yanjiu* [*China Ethnic Languages Usage Research*]. Beijing: China Social Sciences Press.

Chapter 10

English at Home in China: How Far does the Bond Extend?

JOSEPH LO BIANCO

Introduction

On 20 January 2001 China issued a decree making English compulsory in primary schools from grade 3 onwards, although in several large cities and in the private and non-formal sectors English study begins earlier. A new English language curriculum for senior secondary schools was published in the People's Education Press in April 2003, notable for including both a 'humanistic' and an 'instrumental' aim in English education (Wang, 2006). The 1999 curriculum that it replaces had stressed receptive skills like reading, but the new emphasis is on productive skills for interpersonal communication, perhaps responding to criticism that learners were 'dumb and deaf' (Wen & Hu, 2007).

By 2005 approximately 176.7 million Chinese were engaged in some kind of English learning (Graddol, 2006). Compulsory and 'humanistic' English learning, and what increasingly language educators know about the intimate connection, the necessary tie, between learning and use suggest some deep and as yet largely unasked questions about this immense enterprise of making English Chinese.

Most commentators cite Beijing's hosting of the 2008 Olympic Games and Shanghai's preparation for the 2010 World Expo, each accompanied by ambitious English learning schemes, as responsible for accelerating policies and schemes of English education. Perhaps even more decisive has been China's admission into the World Trade Organisation on 11 December 2001 (Pang *et al.*, 2002).

Substantial investment in English is justified by utilitarian reasoning about material benefits flowing to China by having more of its population proficient in English. But alongside these claims, and their documentable gains, what are the repercussions of making English compulsory for ordinary Chinese people, such as the various ethnic groups, and Han in both rural and urban areas, who might not have much cause to interact with English speakers? The mass investments in English have been interpreted as showing a 'bond' between English and China's national needs (Wen & Hu, 2007). How far does this bond between English, China and the Chinese extend?

English as the World's First Foreign Language

Recent documentation by Yun Kyung Cha and Seung Hwan Ham (2008) compares the choice of first foreign language (FFL) in the curricula of primary and secondary schools across the world over the past 155 years. Their data make possible an analysis that ties language curriculum to social and political change on a global scale, and hence the trends represent a barometer testing the atmospheric temperature of the world as revealed by the acquisition of the languages of dominant powers. The study reveals a dramatic and rapid redistribution of the languages learned for communicating beyond national frontiers.

The period 1850–2005 is divided into seven phases contrasting the presence of five languages, English, French, German, Russian and Spanish, as FFL in education systems. The number of countries included grows from 15 and 12 for primary and secondary levels, respectively, in the first phase 1850–1874, to 151 and 154 for primary and secondary levels, respectively, in the latest phase 1990–2005.

In the first two phases, foreign language (FL) teaching was confined to secondary schools with German being dominant, French prominent and English marginal. Spanish and Russian were missing altogether.

During the 1850–1874 phase, German represented 50% and French 33.3% of FFL while English accounted for only 8.3%. The place of German as the world's main foreign language, sustained by a national reputation for advanced science and technology, was destroyed by the tumultuous geo-politics of the first half of the 20th century. German declined to 44.4% in 1875–1899, and then more sharply to 24.3% during 1900–1919, and was overtaken by both French and English for the first time, English achieving 27.0% and French 45.9% of the sampled world curricula.

As the number of countries included in the research increased, this trend intensified. German dropped to 14.8% in the 1920–1944 period but erosion set in for French too, which declined to 35.2%, almost equalled by English at 33.3%.

The post-World War II period is divided into three phases: 1945–1969, 1970–1989 and 1990–2005. In the first phase, of the 128 countries sampled, 59.4% include English as FFL in secondary schools, 28.1% French and 7.8% Russian, with zero preferences for German and Spanish. The appearance of Russian reflects Soviet hegemony in Eastern Europe and the communist countries of Asia, especially China (Wen & Hu, 2007) but also Cambodia, Laos, North Korea and Vietnam. This is also the first period during which a significant FL presence is recorded in primary schools, distributed between a dominant English, a substantial presence of French and a minor presence of Russian. During the 1970–1989 phase, English climbs to 45.7% of primary curricula (140 countries) and 67.4% of secondary curricula (135 countries), French declines slightly to 16.4% and 17%, respectively, and Russian achieves 5.7% and 5.9%, while German and Spanish are entirely absent.

In the final phase 1990–2005, English reaches 67.5% in primary schools in 151 countries and 81.2% at the secondary level in 154 countries. French declines to 13.2% and 13.6%, respectively. German makes a modest re-emergence with 0.7% and 0.6%, respectively. Russian declines to a meagre 3.3% and 3.2%, respectively. Spanish remains absent. Regional concentrations highlight the overall pattern, so that 100% of secondary school curricula in Asian countries nominate English as FFL, a status shared with French in Africa.

The early part of the 20th century saw a large transfer of secondary curriculum FL effort from German to French and a small transfer from German to English; the middle part of the century transferred the remaining German presence to English and initiated a transfer from French to English. The overall pattern was of consolidation of English via leakage from French and obliteration of German. The Cold War division of the world into ideological spheres of allegiance temporarily disrupted the overall trend with the admission of Russian, but this was relatively short-lived. The 1990–2005 phase commences with the fall of the Berlin Wall and is underscored by the rapid globalisation of financial markets and the lowering of trade protectionism. These events have led to the transfer of approximately half the Russian numbers into English as Eastern European countries and China replaced Russian with English. There was also a loss of French numbers in Asia and to a smaller extent in Africa, also in favour of English. Although there was a modest subject-specific re-emergence of German and some presence for Spanish, in no country was either accorded status as FFL.

This struggle between the West's dominant national languages reveals their status as geo-politically dispersed but also their association with the world's traffic in goods, services, science and communication, and marks the post-1945 transfer of economic dominion to the United States from imperial Europe. It is likely that in future documentation of preferred foreign languages, Asian languages, in particular Chinese and possibly Japanese, and Spanish will feature. Japanese experienced rapid growth as an FL during precisely the same period that marked the phenomenal expansion of English. Today that energy has been transferred to Chinese (Lo Bianco, 2007a), but in many countries Japanese and Chinese are designated optional or second foreign languages.

Post-1949 in China, both ideology and pragmatism characterised the choices and purposes of foreign language teaching (Lam, 2005), but curriculum was characterised by '... increasing depoliticisation' (Adamson, 2007: 37). Several writers deploy the Maoist metaphor of a politico-ideological pendulum oscillating between 'redness' and 'expertise'. While broadly true, Adamson's review of the post-1949 junior secondary school English curriculum finds more support for oscillation between academic and linguistic ideals, rather than political ideology. Major political or economic orientations might influence or determine selection of languages and claimed purposes for their teaching but do not always transfer ideology to education practice.

Today, education policy is for the most part devoted to instructional concerns, pedagogical effectiveness, programme design, textbooks (Lam, 2005; Wen & Hu, 2007) and assessment. Epitomising this is the conversation Coulmas reports between F and C about scientific publishing in English (Coulmas, 2007). F laments the extra burden he faces in having to submit research papers for publication in an English acceptable to publishers and the academic research community, and C expresses unsentimental pragmatism about language choice; while acknowledging the extra burdens of preparation imposed on non-native users of English, C finds much that is commendable about the situation. They part, with F convinced of the value of translation and interlanguage experimentation while rushing off to meet a deadline and C announcing that 'I registered for an intensive Chinese course yesterday' (Coulmas, 2007: 13).

Consequences for Chinese Education

To assess what consequences mass and obligatory teaching of English might have on Chinese education, it is necessary to look at the overall pattern of learning an additional language in the context of China's broad communication resources. This overall pattern involves the effects of language education planning for China's minority communities and for the majority Han, who comprise 90% of the population.

Language education for these two groups is linked in two ways: Chinese learning for minorities and English learning for both. The intended effects of these policies would be bilingualism for the majority community but trilingualism, or first language shift, for minority communities. The far greater demands on minorities are a reflection of their communicative subordination, speaking circumscribed languages in contexts in which national communication is predicated on mastery of a second language, and international communication predicated on mastery of a third language. Communication contexts everywhere are characterised by linguistic dominance of this kind. In a survey of international models compared with Chinese ones, Lam (2007) suggests that the Chinese case is implicitly trilingual + biliterate (occasionally triliterate): 'overtly bilingual but covertly trilingual' (Lam, 2007: 19).

China's linguistic diversity includes two broad categories of language, both of which are internally highly varied, which will be called here the non-Chinese languages of China and the Chinese languages of China. The non-Chinese languages comprise 55 officially recognised sub-national communities (see Zhou, this volume), which are accorded formal recognition, representing 80–120 languages and more than 106 million people. The Chinese languages of China show wide variation as well. The term 'Chinese' referring to languages has varying meanings. Mostly it is taken to refer to *Putonghua*, or common speech, and more technically modern standard Chinese; however, in Hong Kong, 'Chinese' refers to Cantonese. A sweep of north to south-west 'dialects' is included under the term Chinese, but the various forms of Cantonese dominant in the south of the mainland and also Macao, Hong Kong and in diaspora Chinese communities across the world are also often called Chinese. However, the prevailing practice is that 'Chinese', Mandarin and *Putonghua* are broadly interchangeable. This complexity does not address status diversities within Chinese languages, which on their own constitute a challenge to the categories with which language planners typically operate (Lo Bianco, 2007a).

Obligatory learning of English by speakers of all these forms of interacting speech has variegated ripple effects. A series of longitudinal assessments of the identity consequences of mass English learning for the majority community, Han speakers of Chinese, is the subject of examination by Gao (see Gao, Chapters 2 and 4, this volume) and her collaborators.

English, Chinese and Local Language at School

In this context of linguistic diversity, the demand for English is buoyant and even frenetic. In Hu's estimation, English is already tied to vested interests within Chinese society, so that the 'English juggernaut' crashes through any who try to resist, especially in a 'scramble' (Hu, 2007: 98) for bilingual education facilitated by administrative changes by the Shanghai Education Commission exploiting central government autonomy granted during the 1980s.

This led to moves to diversify and increase English provision by lowering starting ages, extending subject coverage and renovating textbooks. This expansion of English is justified by recourse to discourses of modernisation and academic improvements, but it crucially depends on local commitment to English competence. This has reached the point where it operates with local reward systems that interact with and intensify or extend central government prescriptions. Among these changes are various forms of bilingual education, such as content-based language teaching, in which English is 'an instructional language' (Hu, 2007: 95) delivering Information and Communications Technology or Geography.

If compulsory English teaching impacts in these ways in Han communities, it is likely that it will have distinctive effects and perhaps more pronounced ones in communities where non-Han languages are spoken. Several scholars attribute to the English juggernaut complicating effects and even a loss of enthusiasm for minority language maintenance. It would not be surprising to find linguistic assimilative pressures in China like those we find in most multi-lingual polities. In a global survey of the effects of linguistic assimilation and the prospects of minority language survival, Fishman argues that many societies impose an ideology of 'incorporative modernity' (Fishman, 2001: 21) in which minority language speakers are required to demonstrate their attachment to the national community, leading to pressure for language shift.

Minorities are required to learn two additional languages, one for national citizenship and cultural interaction within the polity, and the other for internationalism as interpreted in public policy. It is rare in any national setting to find educational design or resourcing equal to the required task, and it is not surprising that in the Chinese case Dai and Cheng note a 'decline in native language enthusiasm' (Dai & Cheng, 2007: 91) alongside declining competence. These writers show how public expectations of the lingual capabilities of minority Chinese populations elevate *Putonghua* and increasingly English and illustrate the multi-dimensional and complex nature of bilingual education research that studies the resultant challenge. The picture these writers paint is one in which society, ideology and education interact with history and the aspirations and relations among various communities.

Although the general tendency is one of attrition and assimilation, there is no single unvarying response to the additional language requirements on minorities, and the long-term outcomes are diverse. Wan and Zhang

(2007), for example, discuss the doubly nested minority of Tibetans of Zang nationality distributed across five regions of the Chinese mainland. In an elaborate account of the specific impact on this distinctive ethnic group of dispersed geography but compact community and culture, the writers provide an intriguing account of Tibetan–Chinese bilingual education convinced that it is beneficial for Tibetan education, educational equity and national unity (Wan & Zhang, 2007: 142). Rather than fearing, or finding, loss of native language enthusiasm or competence, or failure in English, they report educational equity in test scores in Tibetan, mathematics and Chinese. On the basis of these data, they call for the expansion of bilingual education and in turn validate the policy aim of *Min-Han jiantong* (minority language, Min + standard Chinese) or in this specific case *Zang-Han jiantong* (Tibetan + standard Chinese).

This policy aim has given rise to diverse kinds of implementation, such as 'Integrated English' (IE). IE is a form of content-based instruction that researchers Feng and Wang defend as a legitimate approach of bilingual education to 'reinforce instruction in the student's native language' (Feng & Wang, 2007: 150), in which the responsibility for content learning lies with other content subject teachers as IE focuses on theme-based courses that are language driven. The history of IE is traced to 'failure' of Hong Kong immersion programmes and the subsequent adaptation of international bilingual education to Chinese contexts. IE methods, like other Chinese innovations in teaching English, Chinese and native languages, are numerous and are perhaps not as well known as they might be because these are modes of teaching rather than models. Models of educational practice are designed with a sense that they might be portable across contexts, whereas a mode of teaching is more likely to be conceived as a localised response to a particular need or unique context of languages, scripts and policies. In either case such innovations can respond to children's cognitive development, language competence and effective pedagogy as much as they respond to central policy prescriptions.

Trilingualism as the 'covert' policy multiplies teaching responses and programme models greatly. In this respect China is similar to other linguistically complex nations where at least three levels of language education policy interact: the *extra-national* (expressed in English), the *national* (expressed in the national standard variety) and the *sub-national* (expressed in any one or more of locally circumscribed languages). The choice of medium for imparting mainstream subject matter is shaped by what is prescribed centrally, what has texts and materials readily and cheaply available, and also by local literacy levels and language status. Cobbey (2007) makes reference to Malawi and Zambia claiming that English medium education in those two African countries constitutes a barrier rather than a bridge 'to knowledge' and contrasts this to the Chinese setting, which is marked by the distinctiveness of its writing system. Surveying four markedly different Chinese settings she finds that the main determinants of how central policy gets translated into action at local levels are the relative strength of the *Min-Han jiantong* policy, local community values, issues of script and orthography, and differing levels of community involvement. All these produce a highly differentiated set of practices responding to the common policy.

English, Chinese and Local Language at University

In 2001 the Chinese Ministry of Education issued a stipulation that universities should provide 5–10% of undergraduate instruction in English or other foreign languages (Pan, 2007). In the seven years since the declaration, there has been considerable growth of bilingual education in universities, usually the inclusion of disciplinary content within language programmes, for the most part in English, often accompanied by quality assurance standards.

Although the percentage of undergraduate instruction in English might seem low, any such change would represent a major implementation challenge for an institution, a teaching challenge for academic staff and a learning challenge for students, particularly language minority students. An evaluation of the experience of one institution, East China University of Science and Technology in Shanghai, found problems of implementation and uneven readiness. However, by 2006 the English stipulation was 'flourishing' and producing results superior to traditional English teaching approaches (Pan, 2007: 212).

Teachers are critical to success in such an endeavour, but research on teacher 'attitudes toward and perceptions of this new phenomenon hardly exists' (Huang, 2007: 219). A study undertaken with senior undergraduate students at five tertiary institutions in Guangxi investigated aspects of university bilingual education and the effects on the Zhuang language 'in this push for E–C bilingual teaching' (Huang, 2007: 235). The research uncovers positive attitudes, high awareness and a willingness to innovate, alongside concerns about too rigid and too rapid implementation. Students are expected to achieve *guojixing rencai* (international capabilities), usually seen as a specifiable cognition but sometimes referring to personal dispositions as well. While quantitative targets are achievable, quality was found to be lacking. The academics report little concern for effects on Zhuang students' competency in Zhuang, a view the researcher contests, concluding that Zhuang speakers 'are perhaps further marginalised in this bilingual teaching movement' (Huang, 2007: 237) because of their Zhuang accent. The upshot is a call for more attention to the consequences for minority ethnicities in the pursuit of English–Chinese bilingualism.

In all these cases, the essential challenge involves a pre-existing sub-national sociolinguistically complex reality, compounded by status differentials between the national and extra-national languages involved. Highlighting precisely this conjunction of sociolinguistic hierarchies is recent research in Gansu Province, where a study in four minority areas compared minority and majority learners and their learning of English and *Putonghua*.

Reported by Jiang *et al.* (2007), the research was conducted with 896 English as a Foreign Language (EFL) learners, 567 of whom were of non-Han background. The researchers found lower motivation and 'negative L2 transference' and concluded that non-Han learners are disadvantaged by E–C bilingual education because both English and Chinese prevail in status. A major part of the problem is that the professional workforce lacks trilingual competence and so forces many learners to operate in their second, rather than first, language when learning the foreign language, that is, to learn English through *Putonghua*. Unless 'trilingual cognitive processes, trilingual classroom code-switching, and trilingualism ...' (Jiang *et al.*, 2007: 253) can be better accommodated in such programmes, such problems will persist.

Fear of Influences

As observed earlier, the overt policy for Han and non-Han Chinese citizens is bilingualism, but sociolinguistic realities convert this into a trilingual goal for minorities. The different linguistic starting point in relation to the extra-national language, English, makes 'the two differ greatly in political and cultural terms' (Feng, 2007: 259). In Feng's account, the effective policy aim for minorities is for 'perfect bilinguals' with bicultural identities (minority + cultural identification with the Han majority) and 'more importantly political allegiance to the nation state' (Feng, 2007: 259), whereas for the majority, bilingual education does not involve addition or change to identity or political allegiance.

However, we should, like Feng, ask whether it is ever possible to learn languages and remain unaffected by their associated cultures? More pragmatically, we should ask whether one part of China's language education enterprise that proclaims English as an unproblematic instrumental skill for use in the world is not contradicted by other parts of the same enterprise that desire and promote knowledge of native English speakers, Anglophone countries and their national and cultural histories and values. Are, as Feng puts it, culture and language as 'manoeuvrable as politicians and educationists wish them to be' (Feng, 2007: 260)? Wierzbicka (2006) supplies some compelling counter-argument to the dominant stream of writing within contemporary TESOL (Teaching English to Speakers of Other Languages) that proclaims a virtually unimpeded internationalism for English. In Wierzbicka's analysis, an Anglo epistemic paradigm holds strong in grammatical, lexical and expressive practices within English even in its far-flung dispersion from its British or American homes. What are the implications, and limits, of such inherited grammatical characteristics of a language for its everyday teaching and use in distant places and different times?

Foreign language education is always and everywhere an interested and motivated activity. Teachers 'represent' the language they teach and its associated culture(s) for learners in the course of even quite routine procedures of teaching, but especially clearly when they engage in three kinds of activity. The first is *rhetoric*, or speaking 'on behalf' of the language and its speakers (this occurs when teachers construct and enact the culture for learners, how they say it exists); the second is *interpretation* (when teachers mediate cultural products, items or processes for learners); and the third, and most directly, is when teachers engage in *advocacy* (in which teachers serve interests associated with the language and its speaker communities) (Freadman, 2001).

From this it seems that what Feng (2007) calls the 'fear of influences' underlying official views about mass English teaching undermines the unattainability of *Min-Han jiantong* (or rather makes unattainable its maximal ambition of equi-bilingualism), especially when for minorities the policy carries implicit cultural assimilationist assumptions. In Feng's analysis the key ideologies contained in *Min-Han jiantong* are 'concealed assimilation', utilitarianism and binary conceptions of Han/non-Han and Chinese/non-Chinese. He calls for an alternative interpretation of *Min-Han jiantong* in conjunction with the allied general education goal of *zhuanye waiyu fuhexing rencai* (expertise combining professional skills and foreign language skills). Any revised interpretation of the broad *Min-Han jiantong* meta-policy, or any specification of more precise subsidiary goals, would raise issues about the 'influences' on learners of language study, the direction and impact of those influences, and their duration and significance. Such reconsideration would also encourage public discussion around asymmetrical challenge, for minorities, of mass English education.

Desire for Influence

If the pursuit of English skills for extra-national involvement aims to keep influences at bay, the teaching of Chinese abroad, on the other hand, appears to make influence central: not fear of influence, but desire to influence. This shift is hinted at in the very name of the international agency the Chinese state has created to encourage Chinese learning abroad, the classic civilisational figure of Confucius. National cultural agencies of many countries aim to institutionally embody cultural influence, often personified in key literary or philosophical figures, for example, Goethe Institute, Dante Alighieri Society and Cervantes Institute.

China's interest in propagating language and culture abroad is institutionally organised today, but was not shapeless in the past. Like most large states encompassing internal diversity, the spread of standardised norms, in either speech or writing, and their central cultural messages form part of a linked process of linguistic consolidation. Linguistic consolidation is clear intranationally, as well as internationally, and is longstanding and inevitable for a great civilisation. 'The Han civilization ... saw its mission as one of civilizing the entire rest of the world in time, but more immediately as one of civilizing the peoples within its political, and potentially within its cultural, sway' (Harrell, 1993: 98).

The promotion of Chinese abroad is no longer accompanied by overt domestic assimilationist agendas; in fact, China has constitutionally formalised the idea of a multi-ethnic state more extensively than many other nations (Lo Bianco, 2007a). However, as Harrell notes and as Feng shows, the 'old project' is still implemented in interethnic interactions, and where policy conflicts, or when policy and practice collide, these can be attributable to contradictions between old and new projects (Harrell, 1993: 98). We have noted in the present chapter, too, that English, and its massive presence in Chinese society, has its own, probably incidental, effect on the linguistic accommodation between Han and non-Han languages within China.

The dissonance between the expectations and treatment of minority and majority population bilingualism is not unique to China. It is found everywhere. We see it in how majority children receive more praise for their foreign language accomplishments than minority children for language maintenance. We see it in how many policies treat minority languages as problems rather than resources. It is seen in how political discourse often depicts foreign language knowledge as serving the national interest, by supplying needed skills, whereas maintaining minority languages is often represented as a threat to the stability of the polity or to the vitality of the national culture.

The Sub-National Domain

Everywhere defending the teaching of minority languages requires the deployment of arguments to ease majority concerns. Minorities are often expected to engage in continuing displays of patriotic loyalty precisely because they perceive that majorities are concerned about cultural fragmentation or political disloyalty. Writing about immigrants mainly, and the United States in particular, Kloss (1971) described the ideology that underlies this as the 'price' of language sacrifice that immigrants are expected to pay to belong to a new nation. For indigenous minorities there are similarities and differences. While indigenous minorities are not typically challenged about belonging to a given geographic space, the ways in which this space is constituted as a polity, and the language forms this polity takes, impose on indigenous minorities forms of bilingualism marked by symbolic domination.

This dominance is realised in education by privileging the national standard over the local minority language in multiple ways. It is also a message conveyed symbolically. Minority status often implicates issues of citizenship and deeper questions of loyalty and so reassuring displays of attachment to the secure single sovereign state are expected, continually reproducing a symbolic order of statuses (Bourdieu, 1991).

The disparity between esteem for foreign-located languages and local languages is evident in how the foreign is construed discursively as academically rigorous skill acquisition that extends needed national competences. By contrast, intergenerational language maintenance for minorities requires institutional supports, partial social separation and intact social networks (Fishman, 2001) and can too readily be associated with fragmentation, or tolerated only as circumscribed life chances or colourful embellishment.

These modes of organising the national communication load are widespread in developing and developed states, in the Americas and in Asia, and in Europe and in Africa; they are more strongly felt when the majority is itself constituted on sociolinguistic grounds, or its own achievement of political unity was recent or remains fragile. China is neither fragile nor recently constituted, but has a historically acute sense of concern for territorial integrity due to turmoil and instability from the fall of the Qing Dynasty, the rise of the Republic, the invasions of the early 20th century, civil war and the establishment of the People's Republic. In this tumultuous and relatively recent period, the cohesion of the state was a central concern, exacerbated because territorial concessions were demanded by imperial powers, both Western and Asian.

The massive boom and high status that English is accorded in Chinese education is due largely to the opposite force, not national cohesion but international participation (Wen & Hu, 2007). English-knowing bilingualism is more secure than *Putonghua*-knowing minority language bilingualism and involves only one additional language. English does not imply language shift for ethnic Han *Putonghua* speakers, but the *Putonghua*–English combination appears to provoke deterioration and even loss for some, perhaps many, minority languages. Obligatory English in the absence of appropriate trilingual education resourcing seems to impose considerable demands on learners, teachers and institutions.

Domestic Language Arrangements

Sociolinguistics and bilingual education merge because learning and the use of languages combine in social interaction. The commonsense assumption about languages is that they are tied inextricably to nations, whether these nations have autonomous states or not, and efficiency and equity are predicated on universal access to high literacy in single standardised languages. Further, widely held commonsense holds that minority bilingualism is unstable or undesirable. The adoption of language skills by majorities for encountering foreign others and managing relations with them carries a surface-level reassurance of positive contribution to general welfare, while the maintenance of domestic minority language bilinguals is associated with locally controlled institutions and potential loss of social cohesion and, in extreme cases, with national sedition (Fishman, 2001; Lo Bianco, 2008).

An unspoken aim therefore, often the ultimate ambition, of education concessions to minority language groups is that they should transit rapidly to mainstream instruction in mainstream institutions delivered in mainstream languages and inculcating mainstream culture. The contrast with majority children has already been noted, in which language education policies typically envisage an extension to their linguistic repertoire with competence in a nationally approved 'foreign' language, by definition external to the nation and desirable (even 'a basic skill') and posing considerably less challenge to national cohesion and citizen loyalty.

The radically different sociologies of the sub-national and national types of bilingualism suggest that convergence at the sociocultural, policy and pedagogical levels may mask underlying political and ideological differences. These differences correlate with different outcomes, so that perhaps in a real-politic way, in the end, the outcome must be a kind of intention, too.

A Single Global Society?

Cha and Ham (2008) suggest that a 'single global society' is emerging in the wake of privileged mass education in English: a shared linguistic identity, qualifications that are standardised, portable and traded in an interlinked marketplace of skills. They conclude their survey of English as the FFL in world curricula, claiming that this universal status of English means that the language cannot strictly be considered 'foreign'. Unstated but implied is the idea that since English occupies a unique status as 'basic skill' or 'foundational knowledge' in diverse education systems, its acquisition produces a horizontally common domestic social status for English.

It is significant that the growth of English they document is independent of whether countries were part of the British Empire or directly under American influence. In several Asian cases the prominence of English represents restoration of the language into teaching, examination and certification systems from which it had been ejected in the immediate post-colonial context.

For example, in 2001, the year in which China made English compulsory in primary schools from grade 3 onwards, English was the partial medium of instruction in Sri Lanka and Malaysia and fully in Singapore: three countries which in 1956 had independently removed English from public life in their societies (Lo Bianco, 2007b).

Given the interconnection between language use and language learning, we can re-model Cha and Ham's claim of an emergent 'single global society'. These writers propose the emergence of this 'single global society' from evidence of widespread study of English. The scholar C engaged in discussion with F (Coulmas, 2007) about the dominance of English in academic publishing is convinced that a community of academic communication of such a kind, dependent on English and realised through English, is a reality. One of the things societies contain is taxes, and if this linguistically founded 'single global society' exists, it will no doubt have taxes. In a separate domain, Van Parijs (2007), also a proponent of unsentimental acceptance of English's domination, proposes a linguistic tax, which he argues should be levied on native speakers to defray the costs of acquisition of the international lingua franca by all others. Particularly relevant to the current discussion is his extra claim that such subsidies should be directed 'disproportionately' to the Chinese. In his calculation, Chinese people would receive a €32.20 subsidy per capita from 'the Anglo population', whereas the French would be granted a €24.24 subsidy and Danes would each receive €23.76 from 'Anglophones' (Van Parijs, 2007: 85).

Beyond study and scholarly publishing, however, retention of learned language skills requires formal maintenance activities and mobility, and generates domestic contexts of English use. Enacted in a range of societies, these social communicative processes in effect result in a shared English-knowing component of domestic social life in most, or even all, societies, operating as a horizontal network across national boundaries. Since active English competence is limited to elite strata and privileged institutional domains, Anglophone social niches are generated that function as extra-national cosmopolitan elements within overwhelmingly non-English dominant nations.

It is clear that English learning is unlike the teaching and learning of other FLs in ways beyond issues of scale or size. Global English learning is not at all comparable to the teaching of Asian languages for commercial advantage in Australia, nor the teaching of Spanish in the United States or French in Canada. What distinguishes mass English education in China from these other kinds of FL education is more than its greater scale or scope or purposes. This difference can be perceived in the domestic administrative roles it is accorded within Chinese education. China is regarded as an EFL country (Wen & Hu, 2007), but the depth of penetration and the variegated roles assigned to English, the 'local reward systems' available through English, point to levels of domestication more typical of English as a Second Language (ESL) settings. This implies that English is imagined to have, and Chinese society has taken steps to bring about, *domestic social functions* for English: English for Chinese purposes in Chinese settings. In a key, if limited, sense, this aims to make English a Chinese language.

English in China does resemble Spanish in the United States in that the taught language is construed as having potential domestic social roles. However, this resemblance can be misleading because Spanish teaching in American settings arises mostly through large-scale immigration and geographical proximity of Spanish-speaking countries. While there is a symbolic concession to the historic presence of Spanish in the 48 contiguous states, in several cases preceding that of English, it is immigration, both recent and longstanding, and the geographic proximity of Spanish-speaking nations, that has brought about the vast enterprise of Spanish language education in the United States. As a result, Spanish serves multiple roles in American society: an indigenous, proximal, recent immigrant and long-standing heritage language. Nowhere in mainland China does English qualify as an immigrant or heritage language, nor, apart from a minor presence in Hong Kong, can it be classified as a proximal language.

French in Canada is even less like English in China, deriving its official national status and widespread presence in education largely from political moves to stem the domestic language-centred secessionism of the province of Quebec.

The sociology of English in China far exceeds its EFL-ness. Its presence in schools, colleges and universities, as a language of learning and use and as a hurdle test for various administrative and higher education entry procedures, arises overwhelmingly for reasons of transnational utility. However, the depth of its penetration suggests anticipated domestic functions (Coulmas, 2005) beyond what would normally be predicted by external utility. The term 'single global society' appears excessive perhaps, but accounting for 100% of the secondary school curricula across Asia in which English is designated FFL, and the many Asian countries creating domestic social environments where English is expected to be used naturalistically to enhance its acquisition, requires a search for descriptive categories more satisfactory than the classical binary of EFL and ESL society.

Conclusion

Between 1850 and 2005, there were radical and rapid shifts in the favoured foreign language in the curricula of virtually all countries. German started strongest but over time ceded first to French and then to English. In turn French assumed prominence but then ceded to English; Russian started late, gained a secure presence but was practically obliterated, benefiting English. The global conditions that dictated these shifts are active today in an unprecedented transfer of economic, though not yet political, power to a China-centred Asia.

There is no guarantee that English will retain its current pre-eminence as FFL indefinitely. For a considerable time most non-Chinese will conduct their communication with China through translations and directly through English. As larger numbers of non-Chinese acquire Chinese language competence, it is inevitable that Chinese will feature as FFL in some, possibly many, societies (Lo Bianco, 2007a; Lo Bianco & Liu, 2007). Perhaps through such developments the scale and depth of penetration of English within Chinese educational institutions will lessen, though at present there is only evidence of its further consolidation.

China's large investment in English, the compulsory imposition of English learning even in minority areas where it constitutes an additional administrative and learning burden, the growing functions English plays institutionally and its unrivalled status as the language of international scientific publication, demonstrated not so much by the large number of students but by the utilisation of English as a hurdle requirement for access even to Chinese national education institutions, suggest path-dependence. This involves a self-reinforcing pattern of local interests and contexts for English, attracting and consolidating other local interests and contexts and constraining moves away from English. Once taken, English-favouring decisions make more likely subsequent decisions that in turn strengthen English.

More intangible than how local communication activity is expanded and changed to include English are the issues of identity that arise in this process. In what ways will this presence of English impact on self-image, communication style and identity of Chinese people? How will English, legitimised as a foundational national skill but expanding beyond instrumental compartmentalisation within Chinese society, come to influence what Chinese users of English will feel themselves able to do in and with English? What identity consequences will be generated by such domestication of English in Chinese cultural and social arenas? What lasting effects will there be from mass English acquisition on China's minority languages? What are the longer-term consequences of asymmetrical learning of English by Han compared to non-Han Chinese? Conversely, what will be the effects on English learning in China of increased learning of Chinese in the rest of the world?

These questions pose problems of internal linguistic consolidation and communication efficiency with problems of privileged external relationships. They require close monitoring of communication patterns and identity indicators. The questions interrogate issues of a large national scope that only studies of individuals and communication events, networks and interactions can answer.

In an overview of the history of policy of English education, Wen and Hu point out that, despite discrepancies of implementation and changes in different historical periods, 'the bond between English education and the political and economic needs of China is very close, and each is intricately and intimately intertwined with one another' (Wen & Hu, 2007: 28).

The questions raised here are directed at an adjacent but interlinked problem: how far and in what ways does the 'political and economic' bond between English education and the Chinese state extend?

References

Adamson, B. (2007) Depoliticisation in the English curriculum. In A. Feng (ed.) *Bilingual Education in China: Practices, Policies and Concepts* (pp. 34–49). Clevedon: Multilingual Matters.

Bourdieu, P. (1991) *Language and Symbolic Power*. Cambridge, MA: Harvard University Press.

Cha, Y-K. and Ham, S-H. (2008) The impact of English on the school curriculum. In B. Spolsky and F. Hult (eds) *The Handbook of Educational Linguistics* (pp. 313–328). London: Blackwell.

Cobbey, H. (2007) Challenges and prospects of minority bilingual education in China. In A. Feng (ed.) *Bilingual Education in China: Practices, Policies and Concepts* (pp. 182–199). Clevedon: Multilingual Matters.

Coulmas, F. (2005) *Sociolinguistics; The Study of Speakers' Choices.* Cambridge: Cambridge University Press.

Coulmas, F. (2007) English monolingualism in scientific communication and progress in science, good or bad? In A. Carli and U. Ammon (eds) *Linguistic Inequality in Scientific Communication Today* (pp. 5–14) (*AILA Review*). Amsterdam: Benjamins.

Dai, Q. and Cheng, Y. (2007) Typology of bilingualism and bilingual education in Chinese minority nationality regions. In A. Feng (ed.) *Bilingual Education in China: Practices, Policies and Concepts* (pp. 75–93). Clevedon: Multilingual Matters.

Feng, A. (2007) Intercultural space for bilingual education. In A. Feng (ed.) *Bilingual Education in China: Practices, Policies and Concepts* (pp. 259–286). Clevedon: Multilingual Matters.

Feng, Z and Wang, J. (2007) Integrated English. In A. Feng (ed.) *Bilingual Education in China: Practices, Policies and Concepts* (pp. 147–165). Clevedon: Multilingual Matters.

Fishman, J.A. (ed.) (2001) *Can Threatened Languages be Saved? Reversing Language Shift, Revisited.* Clevedon: Multilingual Matters.

Freadman, A. (2001) The culture peddlers. *Postcolonial Studies* 4 (3), 275–295.

Graddol, D. (2006) *English Next.* London: The British Council.

Harrell, S. (1993) Linguistic hegemony in China. *International Journal of the Sociology of Language* 103, 97–114.

Hu, G. (2007) The juggernaut of Chinese–English bilingual education. In A. Feng (ed.) *Bilingual Education in China: Practices, Policies and Concepts* (pp. 94–127). Clevedon: Multilingual Matters.

Huang, B. (2007) Teacher's perceptions of Chinese – English bilingual education. In A. Feng (ed.) *Bilingual Education in China: Practices, Policies and Concepts* (pp. 219–240). Clevedon: Multilingual Matters.

Jiang, Q., Liu, Q., Quan, X. and Ma, C. (2007) EFL education in ethnic minority areas in Northwest China. In A. Feng (ed.) *Bilingual Education in China: Practices, Policies and Concepts* (pp. 240–258). Clevedon: Multilingual Matters.

Kloss, H. (1971), Language rights of immigrant groups. *International Migration Review* 5, 250–268.

Lam, A. (2005) *Language Education in China: Policy and Experience Since 1949.* Hong Kong: Hong Kong University Press.

Lam, A. (2007) Bilingual or multilingual education in China: Policy and learner experience. In A. Feng (ed.) *Bilingual Education in China: Practices, Policies and Concepts* (pp. 13–34). Clevedon: Multilingual Matters.

Lo Bianco, J. (2007a) Chinese teaching: Language planning categories. In J. Lo Bianco (ed.) *The Emergence of Chinese, Special Issue, Language Policy* (Vol. 6, Issue 1, pp. 3–26). Dordrecht: Springer.

Lo Bianco, J. (2007b) Advantage plus identity: Singapore's medium of instruction policy. In V. Vaish, S. Gopinathan and Y. Liu (eds) *Language, Capital, Culture* (pp. 5–22). Amsterdam: Sense Publishers.

Lo Bianco, J. (2008) Policy activity for heritage languages. In D. Brinton, O. Kagan and S. Bauckus (eds) *Heritage Language* (pp. 53–71). New York: Laurence Erlbaum.

Lo Bianco, J. and Liu, G. (2007) Australia's language policy and ecology of Chinese language education. In *Chinese Teaching in the World* (Issue 3, pp. 120–131), Shijie Anhyu Jiaxue.

Pan, J. (2007) Facts and considerations about bilingual education in Chinese universities. In A. Feng (ed.) *Bilingual Education in China: Practices, Policies and Concepts* (pp. 200–218). Clevedon: Multilingual Matters.

Pang, J., Zhou X. and Fu Z. (2002) English for international trade: China enters the WTO. *World Englishes* 21 (2), 201–216.

Van Parijs, P. (2007) Tackling the Anglophones' free ride: Fair linguistic cooperation with a global lingua franca. In A. Carli and U. Ammon (eds) *Linguistic Inequality in Scientific Communication Today* (pp. 72–87) (*AILA Review*). Amsterdam: Benjamins.

Wan, M. and Zhang, S. (2007) Research and practice of Tibetan–Chinese bilingual education. In A. Feng (ed.) *Bilingual Education in China: Practices, Policies and Concepts* (pp. 127–147). Clevedon: Multilingual Matters.

Wang, W. (2006) Teacher beliefs and practice in the implementation of a new English language curriculum in China. In J. Huang, M. Gu and P.K.E. Cheung (eds) *Research Studies in Education* (Vol. 4, pp. 198–208). Education, Hong Kong: University of Hong Kong.

Wen, Q. and Hu, W. (2007) History and policy of English education in mainland China. In Y.H. Choi and B. Spolsky (eds) *English Education in Asia, History and Policies* (pp. 1–32). eduKL, Seoul: AsiaTEFL.

Wierzbicka, A. (2006) *English: Meaning and Culture*. Oxford: Oxford University Press.

Chapter 11
Motivational Force and Imagined Community in 'Crazy English'

LI JINGYAN

Introduction

With China's increasingly active involvement in globalization and international cooperation, English learning in the country has exploded. In the past two decades, especially since winning the right to host the 2008 Olympic Games, an unprecedented English fever has swept the whole country. To meet the huge demand for English learning, various private training centres have mushroomed, many seeking to provide more options in the structure and content of programmes than have been available in universities. Among these new programmes, 'Crazy English' (CE) is one of the most radical and most popular.

CE was founded by Li Yang in response to what he claims is 'the tragedy of traditional teaching' in China (Li, 2000–2001). Li's learning method employs various techniques to overcome learners' reticence in speaking English. The most famous of these is having students shout out phrases in English, a practice aimed not only at meeting the physiological demands of fluency, but also at the characteristic self-censuring of Chinese learners from fear of public failure, the key constraint on Chinese success in speaking English identified by Li Yang. Two other innovative practices fundamental to the CE approach are the so-called 3-ly method, by which learners are encouraged to speak English 'as *clear*ly as possible', 'as *loud*ly as possible' and 'as *quick*ly as possible', and the teaching of pronunciation using hand modelling of mouth and tongue positions and hand movements, which model pitch level, breath intensity and sound contour.

As a method, CE has been controversial since its inception. Learners declare that the method heightens their motivation and generates positive learning (Wang, 2002). Academics, on the other hand, have been critical of CE's unorthodox teaching practices, extravagant claims of learning outcomes and unabashed pursuit of commercial success. They question 'whether one can learn the theory of relativity by repeatedly screaming $E = MC^2$' (Meijdam, 1999). Yet a decade on and still growing, CE is clearly more than just a passing phenomenon. Indeed, it seems that CE has become a 'subculture' in China (Shen & Gao, 2003: 201). The Academy can no longer continue to criticize CE without having made a systematic examination of its concepts and practice.

The author has been involved in a qualitative study of CE through document analysis, interviews with the creator, administrators, teachers and students, and 10 weeks of classroom observation. The aim has been to document and examine pedagogical practices and motivational force. In this chapter, the findings from data gathered on the motivational force of CE are presented. They show a complex and sophisticated approach to gaining and maintaining learner interest and effort, much of which has been explicitly orchestrated in the design and running of the programme. Drawn mostly from intuitive sense and concrete experience, when analysed according to academic learning theories, in large part they are, nonetheless, found to be sound and sustainable. As is shown in this chapter, this is particularly so with respect to motivational force.

Theoretical Framework

Dörnyei (2001: 7) defines motivation as involving both the choice of a particular action and the effort expended on it and the persistence with it. His process-oriented approach (Dörnyei, 2003; Dörnyei & Ottó, 1998) is used in the study to understand the dynamic character and temporal variation of learning motivation. The essence of this model is an analysis of the overall motivational process into several discrete temporal segments. These are organized along a progression that describes how initial wishes and desires are first transformed into goals and then into operationalized intentions, and how these intentions are enacted, leading to the accomplishment of the goal, followed by an evaluation of the process. Accordingly, in line with Dörnyei's model, analysis of the learning process here has been divided into three phases, *preactional*, *actional* and *postactional*, each of which is subject to different motivational influences.

Dörnyei's model helps capture the conscious dynamics of motivation in the course of the learning process. Norton's (2000, 2006) notions of investment, identity and imagined community add the less often articulated, perhaps only tacitly held, desire to join an 'imagined community' that underlies the learner's investment, which the teaching procedures and resources can be seen to create or foster. This places imagination rather than integration at the core and views the learner as a social being, and learning as both a social and a psychological process. Norton's theory is used in the present study as a means of reflecting on the learner's experience as a whole.

Data Presentation and Discussion

The cases presented here are drawn from a short survey and face-to-face interviews with three CE learners, Xu, Ao and Zhang, about their motivation to choose CE, their learning experiences in the course of the 10-week programme and the outcomes from it. They were chosen from a group of 27 students observed, because their experience with CE includes a number of representative features common to members of the whole group: the range of their responses to survey questions, their regular attendance at the CE class and their willingness to cooperate in the study. Their stories are similar yet different, individually interesting and yet not untypical.

Analysis according to Dörnyei's three phases, showing the progression of development in the CE learner's motivation before, during and after their programme, is presented first and then the case is reflected on as a whole in light of the motivational force of Norton's notion of imagined community.

Preactional Phase

Case 1

Xu is a 26-year-old man from the rural area of Hubei Province, who has been through vocational school, majoring in the Chinese language. He used to work in a bookstore in Shenzhen (not far from Hong Kong) and now works as an administrative assistant in a technology company in Beijing. Speaking of his English proficiency before beginning the CE programme, he said that he had only been able to *recite the alphabet, label simple objects* and *form very simple sentences like* 'I love you', 'How are you?'. Xu was interviewed for approximately one hour each time: at the beginning, middle and end of the programme.

Xu's initial contact with CE started with seeing the advertising video-tapes of the programme played at the bookstore where he worked and then he had attended a lecture given by Li Yang in Shenzhen. Xu gave six reasons for choosing CE. First, he was attracted by CE's integration of the concept of English learning with the pursuit of success. Second, he admired Li Yang and took him as a role model. Third, he had a strong desire for social mobility. Xu stated that he was learning English to be 'promoted to an upper level of the society' as he believed that 'those with a good command of English usually have more choices and chances', and 'to change his destiny as well, no longer like his parents bending over to the soil with the back to the sky all their lives'. Then, he hoped to get better pay. Filial piety was another driving force, by which he meant the socially approved obligation to respect, care for and love one's parents, especially when they are ageing. Finally, he hoped to learn good English for patriotic reasons, in order to do something for the country.

Case 2

Ao is a 22-year-old woman; she has a Bachelor of Science with a CET-6 certificate, which is an advanced level national English test for non-English-major college students in China and a requirement for graduating with a bachelor's degree in many universities and colleges. She is from a small town in Zhejiang Province and graduated from a university in Beijing. She now works as a software engineer in a foreign enterprise in Beijing. Ao was interviewed for approximately one hour at both the beginning and end of the programme.

Ao's initial contact with CE started with a CE brochure that offered her a free trial lesson. She gave four reasons for choosing CE. First, she wanted to continue to develop her potential by learning sufficiently good spoken English so as to enter a bigger international company, which, second, would also mean better pay. The key to this, she felt, was to learn authentic pronunciation and, thirdly, because developing good pronunciation is a key focus of CE, she had signed up.

Case 3

Zhang is a 32-year-old man; he has a Master of Medicine with a CET-6 certificate. He is from Liaoning Province in China's northeast and graduated from a university in Beijing. He now works as a physician in a prestigious hospital in Beijing. Zhang was interviewed for approximately one hour at both the beginning and end of the programme.

Zhang was initially introduced to the CE classroom by a colleague. He was impressed, and shortly afterwards joined a two-month programme. Zhang gave three reasons for doing the course. First, he was attracted by CE's promise of developing good spoken English with an authentic

American pronunciation. He wanted to achieve this in order to be able to go abroad as a research fellow, which would enable him to get promoted to a higher position. Second, he liked Li Yang's advocacy of positive thinking, as he holds that 'one takes on the colour of his company'. Finally, he identified with some CE values and beliefs. He stated candidly that he wanted to 'make more money internationally', as CE's promotions suggested. By going abroad, he could earn more money while 'accumulating advanced clinical experience'. He also admired Li Yang's 'courageous, realistic and honest' concept of patriotism combined with personal development. 'If one could learn good spoken English while accepting some cutting-edge ideas, why not [choose it]?'

Despite their different educational backgrounds, social status and English proficiency levels, what the three case learners share in their motivation to choose CE is the desire to improve their spoken English in order to achieve social mobility, develop their personal potential and get better pay. Thus Xu stated that he was learning English 'to be promoted to the upper level of society', and Ao aimed to further improve her situation by entering a bigger international company, although she already had a very good job. Better spoken English was the next 'stepping stone' on her path upwards. As a physician from one of the best hospitals in China, Zhang hoped to go abroad as a research fellow to advance his career. Improving his spoken English could enable him to 'gain in both wealth and fame'.

Long-term goals, however, are not sufficient to directly determine specific action. In addition to aligning with these longer-term goals, the three learners found that participating in a CE programme also served to help them launch into action in the short term.

Some influences energizing the learners to choose CE, however, do not fit easily into the categories proposed by Dörnyei. For example, Xu is moved by filial piety, believing his parents 'had experienced too many hardships in their lives' and he hoped to help them improve their lives. Beyond personal benefits, Xu hoped to learn good English so as to 'help make China more widely known'. Zhang is moved by CE's combined objectives of patriotism, self-improvement and making money. He admired Li Yang's courage to proclaim publicly that making money is a legitimate goal, as this goes against Chinese convention.

Actional Phase

Case 1

Xu reported that two of the central pedagogical practices of CE that had kept him highly involved were 'repeating and shouting'. He quoted, with approval, Li Yang's saying 'Even the pig by the temple is able to chant scriptures', agreeing that the only way to successful learning was to repeat, repeat and repeat. 'Practice makes perfect ... the most primitive method is often the most effective'. Xu also said that he loved shouting English because, on the one hand, it could help him remember things better and longer and, on the other, it made him feel good. Evidence of this came one day when class was over. With both hands raised, Xu shouted to no one in particular: 'It's terrific to shout English!' And then he continued shouting English while he went to the toilet.

Xu asserted that, in addition to English, CE had had an important affective influence on him, helping him to develop self-confidence and persistence. He recalled that when he first came to Beijing, he had felt a sense of inferiority: 'Beijing is so big and has an abundance of talented people. I suddenly feel that I am nothing and even depressed'. He said that quite often, at such moments, he would draw inspiration from the CE class and from the posters of Li Yang and CE slogans on the walls, and this helped him to no longer feel insignificant.

At the same time, however, Xu claimed that his CE learning experienced ups and downs as a result of being tired from work or encountering difficulties in learning. And, indeed, he sometimes did look quiet and inactive in class, although normally not. At these times, he said, he could often get 'pumped up' by the value of persistence proposed by Li Yang, and this sustained his study. 'Li Yang's poem *No Matter How* often worked on me in this way', he said, and began reciting it then and there.

> No matter how bad my pronunciation is, I will keep on improving!
> No matter how terrible my memory is, I will keep on repeating!
> No matter how many people give up, I will keep on working hard!
> No matter how many people laugh at me, I will keep on practicing!
> No matter how many mistakes I make, I will keep on speaking!
> No matter how many obstacles I meet along the way, I will keep on striving until I reach my goal! (Li, 2006: iii)

'Some people may take it as just big slogans', he said, 'but I think those are [the] moments I have experienced in my English learning'.

Case 2

Ao said that she enjoyed her CE experience in four ways. First, she believed that she had benefited from CE's emphasis on pronunciation.

> Here the teacher can identify where my problem is ... demonstrates and corrects me. Then I practise and get it. That's all I'm after.

She also approved of the use of gestures and believed that they were really effective and motivating.

> I enjoy gesticulating, really fun. My tongue didn't touch the upper gingival when producing words with [the sound] /l/. Now I can remember to lift it when making this gesture [gesticulating].

During observations of classes, Ao was noted to often move around gesticulating when practising reading or reciting.

Ao spoke highly of the friendly and relaxed classroom atmosphere, which left her 'looking forward to going to class' rather than feeling she 'had to go', as before.

> I like the class, no competition, no test, no anxiety ... and I can feel the improvement.

Finally, she attributed part of her progress to the quality of the teacher.

> I am often unconsciously influenced by her enthusiasm and involvement. I appreciate her positive feedback and encouragement. I used to lose confidence in speaking English because my former [English] teacher said that my tongue was short. But she [CE teacher] told me that I could improve it by practising more and I think it true.

Case 3

Zhang's greatest achievement in CE learning was that he could now really speak some English in public, something he had never been able to before. He jokingly described his previous incompetence using the title of a song, *English, I Love You More Than I Can Say*. He attributed his improvement to three CE pedagogical practices. First, he thought he had benefited from shouting English. He said that 'shouting together is really effective in breaking through some psychological barriers and helping me to concentrate [on the task]'.

Second, his pronunciation had greatly improved. As a non-English major, he had had no instruction in phonology, such as what the shape of the mouth should be, the position of the tongue and so on. 'Now', he said, 'this gap is filled'.

Finally, practising speaking in front of the class was an effective method for him:

> The teacher always asks us to come to the front to show off our English. Like cures like. I think it most effective to train our courage. So I am now getting used to speaking English in public ... But I don't think gestures are necessary, sometimes even distracting.

It was noted during observation that Zhang did not gesticulate as much as the other learners did, but he often volunteered to recite or role-play in front of the class.

Two by-products of his CE learning, Zhang mentioned, were changes in his personality: he was becoming more positive and 'making fewer complaints'; he was also now 'less silent than before'. Zhang had accepted that he was too introverted to speak much, even in Chinese, let alone in English. So he had not realized these changes until the day his wife teased him saying that she would invite Li Yang to dinner so that he could see what a talker his method was producing.

Zhang felt that, in particular, it was the dynamics of the classroom environment that were pivotal to these improvements.

> Here, nobody knows who I am. So I can put my face aside and shout with them. High involvement will result in gain.

He saw the class as a 'training field for athletes', with the teacher as 'coach'. The other learners were his 'training partners' and the exaggerated training methods were 'the stimulant'. It was exactly the environment he had been seeking in order to be able to 'reproduce orally the input accumulated at university'. His improvement had been successfully tested on a trip to Japan, where he interpreted all the way for his group and won praise from his boss.

Despite his enthusiasm, Zhang's motivation could be weakened at times. When a new teacher took over the class in the middle of the programme, he stopped coming, explaining that he was not used to her style. But he came back when he discovered that 'without the class atmosphere', he 'lost his interest and the feel for the language'.

All three learners were able to articulate how their executive motivation was actively maintained and protected by activities in their CE class, and thus positive learning resulted. For his part, Xu deemed that what motivated him lay in the quality of his CE experience on two levels. Pedagogically, he was stimulated by constant repeating and shouting in English. Affectively, he believed that his self-image had changed as his self-confidence increased. He was also stimulated by Li Yang's emphasis on the quality of persistence. Like Xu, Ao was inspired by certain practices in the CE classroom. She enjoyed practising pronunciation and gesticulating, and she had made progress in this area of central importance to her. In addition, she loved the atmosphere in the class and the teacher. Zhang shared some common executive motives with Xu and some with Ao. Like Xu, he enjoyed shouting English; like Ao, he benefited from the crazy classroom atmosphere. Together these had helped him improve in speaking English in public. Unlike Ao, however, he did not like gesticulating and considered it 'unnecessary' and 'distracting'. As his success on the Japan trip proved, he was no longer unable to say how much he loved English. In the affective domain, like Xu, he had experienced some change in his personality. He was also inspired by some CE values; he demonstrated a depth of understanding them.

The three accounts above show that CE practices and setting affect the actual learning process within the classroom and exert motivational influences on the learners' overall disposition (Dörnyei, 2003). As the process unfolded, the learners' technical ability improved and there were also qualitative changes in them, affecting aspects of themselves that extended beyond the classroom setting. Progress, however, was not uniform. As Dörnyei (2001) points out, when executive motivation cannot be maintained, ongoing learning will fluctuate. Thus Xu was noted to have periods of low enthusiasm and Zhang even had a brief period of withdrawal.

Postactional Phase

A 'learning contract' is a motivational strategy that Dörnyei (2001) recommends. It is a formal agreement negotiated between teacher and student to formalize students' goals. A similar agreement is adopted in the CE programme during the first class, which turned out to produce very positive results. In the Agreement, learners are asked to set out both their short-term sub-goals in terms of English learning and their long-term goals. In the following weeks, learners are asked from time to time to check their Agreement and see to what extent they had achieved their goals. Reflecting on their CE experience at the end of the programme, all three case study learners said that the Agreement had played a significant role in their successful learning.

Case 1

Looking back on his experience of the 10-week programme, Xu said that one of the most valuable things he had encountered through CE was its belief that 'we are what and where we are because we have first imagined it' (Li, 2004: 28).

> ... [It's] just like a saying in our countryside. People are much more productive boldly. How can you achieve anything if you don't have the courage to first imagine it?

Looking ahead, he said that he longed to join what he called Li Yang's army of International Chinese in the age of globalization. He went on:

> ... I admire Li Yang's view of the 21st century as one for China and for Chinese people ... so we have to shape and reshape ourselves to fit into the new century ... I feel a kind of pressure that I can't sit back, but [should] take immediate action to join the world.

Xu visualized that he would implement his plan to take part in China's internationalization by making use of his bilingual expertise in Chinese and English:

> I am interested in cultural exchange, teaching foreigners Chinese and transmitting our Chinese culture and history, making China widely known.

As well, he would honour his filial debt: '... I will bring my parents here [Beijing]'.

He said that these aspirations developed out of his CE experience. And his motivation continued to be nurtured by his participation in the CE programme. He affirmed that he was going to join another CE programme after this one.

Case 2

In retrospect, Ao believed that she gained more than she had expected from the 10-week CE programme. In particular, she referred to the Agreement, which had prompted her to see herself in the distant future. What she had put down in the Agreement was to be a bookshop owner:

> I dream of owning a small bookshop where coffee is also sold. I love books and I love the smell of coffee ... A small one, not crowded, and in good taste, with a few tables and sofa ... At a good location in Hangzhou ... Locals and tourists from different countries and nationalities come. I speak fluent English. ...

She asserted that her CE learning had clarified her dream and helped bring her closer to its realization. From her CE experience, Ao said that her pronunciation and fluency, and so was more confident about obtaining a position in a bigger international company than where she currently worked. The salary she would earn there would allow her to save enough money to set up the bookshop, and then she would start 'to live [my] ideal life'.

Case 3

Reflecting on his CE experience, Zhang admitted that what he called 'the game-like piece of paper' (i.e. the Agreement), in fact, did work as 'a sort of psychological suggestion', because 'what is said cannot be retracted. After all, I did sign my name to it ...'.

What he had put down in the Agreement was a desire already in his mind, that he wanted to become 'a famous, first-class, scholarly physician with rich clinical experience and highly-developed research ability who could communicate academically and naturally in English without an interpreter'.

Zhang said that his goal had 'broadened' after his CE experience, inspired by Li Yang's concept of International Chinese. He now had further knowledge about Norman Bethune, a Canadian physician, who came to China to help during the anti-Japanese war in the 1930s.

> My dream is to be a Chinese Bethune, to offer my expertise abroad, to developed countries, as China will be more powerful then. Meanwhile, millions of Bethunes will come to China to learn Chinese medicine. At that time, they will have to learn Mandarin as I am now learning English.

He believed that after taking up the CE programme, he was on the right path and making good headway in fulfilling both his Agreement and the beginnings of his own aspirations. The learners' postactional reflections show that the CE practice of written Agreements and reflection on goals during the programme can lead learners to create and sustain an imagined community for themselves to aim to join.

Conclusion

In sum, Dörnyei's process-oriented framework allows one to understand the development of CE learners' motivation over the whole programme, and thus the dynamic nature of learning motivation. All three learners experienced motivational flux during the programme. Also, the three different motivational phases are fuelled by different motives, some of which fit well into the categories proposed by Dörnyei, while some others translate distinctively traditional Chinese values as well as his modern concepts. What is important to note during the process is that when they look back at what they have achieved from the 10-week CE programme and evaluate it, once again a new set of motivational components become relevant to the learners, which is a kind of idealized view of themselves envisaged in their imagination. Although Dörnyei's framework is not mentioned in CE literature, or by those in charge, it can be seen that CE practices intentionally and systematically provide for the stages and content it presents as reliably likely to create, maintain and develop language learner motivation over the duration of a course such as CE's 10-week programme.

Norton (1995) suggests that it may be more relevant to ask what the learner's investment in the target language is, rather than asking what motivates the learner. While Dörnyei's framework is evidently useful for mapping the cases over time, Norton's perspective has been found to provide further insight into what prompts CE learners to begin and to continue their crazy learning. While investing time, money and energy in CE, Xu, Ao and Zhang also invest in the intangible communities of practice, which in their imagination they are becoming part of. Aspects of identity generally change across time and space, and the identities of the three learners have undergone and are still undergoing significant changes from when they left home and first came to Beijing, in particular, since their CE experience. When they entered the CE classroom, their idealized views of their English-speaking bilingual selves in the future had extended beyond the four walls. Xu, Ao and Zhang project themselves in their imagined communities, which again enhances their confidence and their English learning.

They created their own imagined communities with encouragement from CE and these visions were also projected by CE in the case of Xu, clarified in the case of Ao and broadened in the case of Zhang. All three participants have dreams they think can be achieved through learning English. As Norton (2000, 2006) claims, although not yet real, private visions may provide a strong impetus for language learning. Analysis of the data presented suggests that this may be the case for these three CE learners, who, as noted, are not untypical of their whole class.

Although it has not been the image of 'Crazy English' portrayed by the Chinese press or the Academy, analyses presented here show that, very much in accord with accepted motivational theories, as they work at their English, CE practices can nurture learners' imagination, offer them a receptive community of practice and introduce 'new images of possibility and new ways of understanding one's relation to the world' (Norton, 2001: 163).

References

Dörnyei, Z. (2001) *Motivational Strategies in the Language Classroom*. Cambridge: Cambridge University Press.

Dörnyei, Z. (2003) *Attitudes, Orientations, and Motivations in Language Learning.* Michigan: Blackwell Publishing.

Dörnyei, Z. and Ottó, I. (1998) Motivation in action: A process model of L2 motivation. *Working Papers in Applied Linguistics* 4, 43–69.

Li, Y. (2000–2001) From 2000–2001, Li Yang will lead 20 million Asian English learners to launch a final year-long war against English! *CE Brochure.* Guangzhou: Stone-Cliz International English Promotion Workshop.

Li, Y. (ed.) (2004) *The Secret of Failure for Chinese English Learners.* Beijing: China Record Company.

Li, Y. (ed.) (2006) *Li Yang Standard American English Pronunciation & Spoken English Crash Course.* Guangzhou: Li Yang Culture & Education Development Co., Ltd.

Meijdam, A. (1999) Pumping up the volume! *Asiaweek*, 30 July.

Norton, B. (1995) Social identity, investment and language learning. *TESOL Quarterly* 29 (1), 9–31.

Norton, B. (2000) *Identity and Language Learning: Gender, Ethnicity and Educational Change.* Harlow: Longman.

Norton, B. (2001) Non-participation, imagined communities and language classroom. In M. Breen (ed.) *Learner Contributions to Language Learning: New Directions in Research* (pp. 159–171). London: Pearson Education.

Norton, B. (2006) Second language identity. In K. Brown (ed.) *Encyclopaedia of Language and Linguistics* (2nd edn, Vol. 5, pp. 502–507). Oxford: Elsevier.

Shen, L.X. and Gao, Y.H. (2003) What 'Crazy English' means to Chinese students. In Y.H. Gao (ed.) *The Social Psychology of English Learning by Chinese College Students: Motivation and Learners' Self-Identities.* Beijing: Foreign Language Teaching and Research Press.

Wang, Y. (2002) Analysing Li Yang. Newspaper article. *China Education Resources*, 2 January 2002, p. A2.

Part 4

Narratives

Chapter 12

Understanding Ourselves through Teacher Man

LI ZHANZI

Narrative and Identity

Since identity is continuously and constantly produced and reproduced, sketched and designed, and often co-constructed by 'self' and
'other' interactively, we should strive to demonstrate how identities are
(re)produced through language (and other media) and how they come
into existence through social interaction (De Fina *et al.*, 2006: 22) and what
these contemporary ways to depict identity can reveal about the teaching
of English in contemporary China.

Scholars in the field of discourse and identity have come to realize that
identities are not only shaped within social practice, but the process of
identity construction itself is also interactional. These interactions may take
various forms, and the analyses of them also vary. 'Yet practices as varied
as narrative, life story, interviews, letter writing, and conversation all
provide systematic (yet emergent) means of "doing" things through talk
that simultaneously provide means of "being"' (De Fina *et al.*, 2006: 22).

In this chapter I analyze the interaction between narrative and identity
in Frank McCourt's novel *Teacher Man*, and explore its implications for the
identifications we develop as teachers of English in China.

Increasingly self-conception is rendered intelligible within ongoing
relationships, and the more static view of self as an individual's personal
and private cognitive structure is cast away in these changing perspectives. Insofar as self as narration is concerned, self is more appropriately
viewed as discourse about the self – the performance of languages available in the public sphere (Gergen, 2001: 247).

As we live by stories, both in the telling and the realizing of the self,
'Self-narratives function much like oral histories or morality tales within a

society. They are cultural resources that serve such social purposes as self-identification, self-justification, self-criticism, and social solidification' (Gergen, 2001: 249). A growing number of scholars suggest that the 'form of stories (their textual structure), the content of our stories (what we tell about) and our storytelling behavior (how we tell our stories) are all sensitive indices' of our personal, social and cultural identities (Schiffrin, 1996: 170). Mishler (1999: 20) argues that narratives are performances in which individuals 'speak' their identities. This way of connecting narrative and identity challenges prevailing assumptions about the self (Bell, 2006: 235). Narrative analysts who focus on time order have a preference for grand narration, which gives our life a unified, coherent meaning, and which is of a higher order (MacIntyre, 1984; Taylor, 1991). But, in fact, 'neither the trajectories of our lives nor the stories we construct to understand ourselves and others are smooth, continuous and progressive. Each is marked by fits and starts, detours and hiatuses' (Mishler, 2006: 43).

That is why we find the author of the selected text retelling his childhood story, his story of his mother, etc. These form part of the teacher man and are something he cannot do without.

Teacher Man and His Narrative

Before I proceed to explore the relationship between the author and his narrative, it will be useful to include some brief biographical information on the author Frank McCourt and his work.

Born in 1930 in Brooklyn, New York, to Irish immigrant parents, McCourt grew up in Limerick, Ireland, but at the age of 19 he returned to America. Surviving initially through a string of casual jobs, spending every spare minute reading books from the public library, McCourt began a process of self-education that led to a professional career as a high school teacher. *Teacher Man* is the final memoir in a trilogy that started with *Angela's Ashes* and continued in *Tis*. The novel focuses on McCourt's 30-year teaching career in New York's public high schools, beginning at McKee Vocational and Technical School in 1958.

McCourt acquired authority in the classroom through the narration of his childhood story, which implies a close connection between self-narrative and identity. In his attempt to reach self-understanding, he repeats and revises his childhood stories. In the classroom, he makes an attempt to construct his teacher identity:

> I'm a teacher in an American school telling stories of my school days in Ireland. It's a routine that softens them up in the unlikely event I might teach something solid from the curriculum. (McCourt, 2005: 31)

A traditional understanding of teachers appears to deny them self-narration, since they are more often than not stereotyped. If this is so, a teacher with a self-story overturns the narrating emptiness of the traditional teacher image and conjures up a new teacher image, one in which the personal resources – life stories – are available as teaching resource. This would produce a new, multidimensional teacher image for Chinese teachers of English; their trajectories of learning English can also serve as examples for students to draw inspiration. While making his childhood stories resources for teaching, McCourt strives to construct a new teacher identity – the personal becomes resourceful. The flat teacher image becomes more substantial.

The following excerpt from the book showcases how he engages, reproduces and resists the traditional discourse of teaching:

> My life saved my life. On my second day at McKee a boy asks a question that sends me into the past and colors the way I teach for the next thirty years. I am nudged into the past, the materials of my life. (McCourt, 2005: 24)

A review from *Publishers Weekly* comments, 'He tried to present a consistent image of composure and self-confidence, yet he regularly felt insecure, inadequate, and unfocused. After much trial and error, he eventually discovered what was in front of him (or rather, behind him) all along – his own experience'.[1] He also deals with the relationship between writing and storytelling:

> In the world of books I am a late bloomer, a johnny-come-lately, new kid on the block. My first book, 'Angela's Ashes', was published in 1996 when I was sixty-six, the second, 'Tis', in 1999 when I was sixty-nine. At that age it's a wonder I was able to lift the pen at all. ... (McCourt, 2005: 3)
>
> I never expected Angela's Ashes to attract any attention, but when it hit the best-seller lists I became a media darling. ... (McCourt, 2005: 4)

'Personal narratives ... are of interest precisely because narrators interpret the past in stories rather than reproduce the past as it was' (Riessman, 2002: 705). In McCourt's narrative, he keeps reinterpreting the past to acquire his teacher man identity. In practice, he was teaching how one reads and interprets one's life experiences. He has his own unique ways to persuade his students to write:

> Dreaming, wishing, planning: it's all writing, but the difference between you and the man on the street is that you are looking at it,

friends, getting it set in your head, realizing the significance of the insignificant, getting it on paper. You might be in the throes of love or grief but you are ruthless in observation. You are your material. You are writers and one thing is certain: no matter what happens on Saturday night, or any other night, you'll never be bored again. Never. Nothing human is alien to you. Hold your applause and pass up your homework. (McCourt, 2005: 291–292)

The difference between McCourt and the rest of the world is that he is a teacher with a life story (which has become a best seller). He owns it and the latter shapes his teaching style, that is, using his life stories in the classroom whenever the students ask for it. He used his life to teach, and his job and life became one. How many teachers are willing to do this, or how many of us are courageous and candid enough to think our life experiences are worthy of classroom exposure? It seems McCourt was saying this to the Chinese teachers of English: write out your stories and they are bound to have something fresh for your students. Students need a behavior model who is right there in daily contact with them in the classroom. And as you write and rewrite your trajectory of learning a foreign language, you will come to see the connection between teaching and being. That also explains why most teachers have the split identification of themselves as teachers and as ordinary human beings. McCourt sets a good example of how to be able to integrate the two dimensions of his identity.

Here we would like to make a distinction between being a teacher versus just teaching, and also the difference between veteran teachers and new teachers. The latter insist on the difference between teaching as a job and living a life outside the classroom. A crucial question is: How are we to engage in the ongoing construction of our identities? If one tries harder, one can become a 'teacher man'; otherwise, one is just teaching.

The review of McCourt's reflection on teaching from AudioFile proves that he has become a 'teacher man' instead of just teaching. The evidence is in the feedback from his students, scattered throughout the book: 'McCourt recounts his experiences in New York's urban classrooms with perspective and the indomitable flair of a story teller. ... His thirty-year teaching career is punctuated with small triumphs, pitfalls, and the difficult choices, but always candor and respect for his students'.[2] In the Chinese context of English teaching, we need more teacher-man narratives, although not necessarily best sellers, as our students need to have an all-round picture of their English teachers and to perceive directly what might be involved in the struggle to approach bilingual flexibility.

Construction of Teachers' Group Identity

This process of relating unique experience and connecting it to the actual lives and learning of students made McCourt a charismatic teacher, with his life story becoming a source of personal charm. In this section I analyze the construction of teacher identity according to the following dimensions: American scenario, teachers' group image, observation of the classroom, reflections on teacher–student relationship, showcase of the successful teaching methodology, thoughts on educational ethics and a description of the dilemmas.

If we reflect on the stereotypical understanding of teachers, it will not be difficult for us to acknowledge the re-cognizing and re-identification of teachers through McCourt's writing. As Shawn Carkonen puts it, McCourt is 'a dazzling writer with a unique and compelling voice, McCourt describes the dignity and difficulties of a largely thankless profession with incisive, self-deprecating wit and uncommon perception'.[3]

American scenario

Everywhere in the book, we read about American scenarios. The following is a typical script:

> Mr. McCourt, you're lucky. You had that miserable childhood so you have something to write about. What are we gonna write about? All we do is get born, go to school, go on vacation, go to college, fall in love or something, graduate and go into some kind of profession, get married, have the two point three kids you're always talking about, send the kids to school, get divorced like fifty percent of the population, get fat, get the first heart attack, retire, die. (McCourt, 2005: 292)

When McCourt summaries the American scenario in such plain and humorous language, he is implying that teaching is not such a noble-minded profession (as is the case in China) and that teachers are just ordinary human beings who share the ordinary American scenarios.

Philosophy of education

In spite of the helpless rambling here and there, McCourt slipped in his educational ideals:

> This is where teacher turns serious and asks the Big Question: What is education, anyway? ... from Fear to Freedom ... what I am trying to do with you is drive fear into a corner. (McCourt, 2005: 300–301)

Such an idealistic understanding of education helps to portray the image of a noble teacher.

Capturing the elements in teaching: Students, classroom, teacher's voice

In many places in the book there is a generous sharing of love–hate sentiments toward students:

> ... I don't want to be bothered by them. I don't want to see or hear them. ... I wish the kids would disappear. I'm not in the mood. (McCourt, 2005: 302–303)

> Other days I'm desperate to get into the classroom. I wait, impatient, in the hallway. I paw the ground. Come on, Mr. Ritterman. Hurry up. Finish your damn math lesson. There are things I want to say to this class. (McCourt, 2005: 303)

As *The Globe and Mail* (Toronto) commented, McCourt's observations may be a little repetitive but his depictions of daily classroom trials are extremely sharp and form the core of the teacher man.[4] Also worth noting is McCourt's unique description of the classroom experience, which is likely to be representative of the teacher group:

> The classroom is a place of high drama. You'll never know what you've done to, or for, the hundreds coming and going. You see them leaving the classroom: dreamy, flat, sneering, admiring, smiling, puzzled. After a few years you develop antennae. You can tell when you've reached them or alienated them. It's chemistry. It's psychology. It's animal instinct. ... (McCourt, 2005: 303–304)

McCourt evokes the myth of the teacher image in the mind of those outside the teaching circle:

> Maids downstairs, side doors, talk about them with mercy, congratulate them on 'all the time off'.

All the time he is conscious that teachers are only supposed to have a practitioner's local voice:

> Newspapers will ask you, mere teacher, for your opinion on education. This will be big news: A teacher asked for his opinion on education. Wow. You'll be on television. (McCourt, 2005: 6–7)

In other words, people care little about teachers' views on education, although they are in the best position to make comments. As Gee (2000: 77) notes, researchers and teachers alike always assume that teachers have only a 'local' voice on such issues. Rarely are teachers invited into – or do they have access to – a 'national voice'. Even when invited to speak at national conferences, teachers usually speak as representatives of their local areas and their own experiences, while researchers speak as transcending locality and their own experiences.

You have the makings of a fine teacher: Innovative teaching

The fact that McCourt makes an excellent teacher can well be explained by some basic facts, one of them being his love of Shakespeare. And by quoting others' evaluation, he mentioned several times in the book:

> You have the makings of a fine teacher.... (McCourt, 2005: 66–7) A grammar lesson in full – how he tried all out to teach grammar. (McCourt, 2005: 92)

> English teachers say if you can teach grammar in a vocational high school you can teach anything anywhere. My class listened. They participated.... (McCourt, 2005: 98)

At the end of the book, he describes the new world he enters when teaching becomes inspirational:

> I was finding my voice and my own style of teaching. I was learning to be comfortable in the classroom. Like Roger Goodman, my new chairman, Bill Ince, gave me free rein to try out ideas about writing and literature, to create my own classroom atmosphere, to do whatever I liked without bureaucratic interference, and my students were mature and tolerant enough to let me find my own way without the help of the mask or the red pen. (McCourt, 2005: 242)

The revelation appears at the end of the work. The health struggles recounted in the story of one of his former students, Guy, made them realize the grace of being able to live and work with health:

> This is their last high school class, and mine. There are tears and expressions of wonder that Guy is sending us on our way with a story that reminds us to count our blessings. (McCourt, 2005: 306)

Situational and innovative teaching forms the real source of his excellence as a teacher. By 'Innovative', we mean not only using life stories, but also combining sociocultural situations, for example, inquiry about dinner the previous day, lunch investigation, review of school canteen and neighborhood restaurants (McCourt, 2005: 266). Direct, lively, inspirational teaching means being in tune with middle school starting-from-life ethics, although somewhat inconsistent with stick-to-the-curriculum requirements. It is a good reconciliation of both aspects of his teaching practice. In a similar vein, teaching English in China also calls for innovative ideas. This not only concerns teaching materials and methodologies, but also our understanding of what changes we can bring to students through teaching them a foreign/international language. When teaching English as an international language in China to Chinese students, we have to pay much attention to linguistic form, and the daunting task of teaching the whole grammatical system of a new language often prevents us from being truly innovative.

McCourt always combines situational teaching and innovative teaching in his class. For example, he gives students imaginative assignments, such as writing excuses for historical figures, suicidal notes, sing alongs (featuring recipe ingredients as lyrics), field trips (taking 29 rowdy girls to a movie in Times Square). Take writing excuse notes for example. He asks students to write not only an excuse note from Adam to God, but also an excuse note from Eve to God, and then asks them to think about anyone in the world at present or in history who could use a good excuse note (McCourt, 2005: 106).

And he is very insistent on innovation:

> (when he was teaching in a college) That was something I should have known all along: the people in my classes, adults from eighteen to sixty-two, thought their opinions did not matter. Whatever ideas they had came from the avalanche of media in our world. No one had ever told them they had a right to think for themselves. I told them, You have a right to think for yourselves. (McCourt, 2005: 142)

Identity of middle school teachers

McCourt reasoned about the identity of middle school teachers and in doing this, he is acting as a spokesperson for the group. As he puts it, 'I didn't call myself anything. I was more than a teacher.' And here is the exaggerated list of hybrid middle-school-teacher roles he listed:

> I didn't call myself anything. I was more than a teacher. And less. In the high school classroom you are a drill sergeant, a rabbi, a shoulder to cry on, a disciplinarian, a singer, a low-level scholar, a clerk, a referee, a clown, a counselor, a dress-code enforcer, a conductor, an apologist, a philosopher, a collaborator, a tap dancer, a politician, a therapist, a fool, a traffic cop, a priest, a mother-father-brother-sister-uncle-aunt, a book keeper, a critic, a psychologist, the last straw. (McCourt, 2005: 23)

[These roles may sound too much for college teachers, but for college English teachers, some roles fit quite well, as teaching English as a second/foreign language is so very different from teaching other subjects in college that the job can be demanding on teachers to the extent that they sometimes must learn to be as versatile as middle school teachers.]

And he went to extremes to exaggerate on the differences between middle school and college teachers:

> I have read novels about the lives of university professors where they seemed to be so busy with adultery and academic infighting you wonder where they found time to squeeze in a little teaching. When you teach five high school classes a day, five days a week, you're not inclined to go home to clear your head and fashion deathless prose. After a day of five classes your head is filled with the clamor of the classroom. (McCourt, 2005: 3–4)

> ... In college there were courses on literature and composition. There were courses on how to teach by professors who did not know how to teach. (McCourt, 2005: 31)

About differences between universities and middle schools, he emphasized the necessity of updating teaching notes:

> In universities you can lecture from your old crumbling notes. In public high schools you'd never get away with it. American teenagers are experts in the tricks of teachers, and if you try to hoodwink them they'll bring you down. (McCourt, 2005: 80)

And as mentioned above, he emphasized the practice orientation in middle school teaching:

> Professors of education at New York University never lectured on how to handle flying-sandwich situations. They talked about theories and philosophies of education, about moral and ethical imperatives, about the necessity of dealing with the whole child, the gestalt, if you don't mind, the child's felt needs, but never about critical moments in the classroom. (McCourt, 2005: 19)

Dilemmas of teaching

McCourt's efforts at constructing teachers' group identity are most manifest in his presentation and sharing of the dilemmas of teaching. We summarize below the dilemmas in the following few aspects.

The first dilemma that is closely related to the success of the book is whether teachers should tell life stories in class. Although his students like his stories, parents are against his telling them in class. The different expectations from students and parents made it hard for teachers to adjust. He chose to give students' need the priority and uses his life stories as bait to arouse their interest in learning.

> ... They know when they have you on the run. They have instincts that detect your frustrations. There were days I wanted to sit behind my desk and let them do whatever they damn well pleased. I just could not reach them. ... You entertain them with stories of your miserable childhood. They make all those phony sounds. ... (McCourt, 2005: 94)

Coming to a more subtle dilemma that is also a fact of life in a teacher's work, here in an English teacher's writing assignment, educational ethics is what bothers teachers very often. In other words, to what extent does a teacher hold himself responsible for a student's well-being. This is how he recounts it in the composition assignment:

> I could give this paper to a guidance counselor. Here, Sam, you take care of this. If I didn't, and it came out later that the stepfather abused the girl and the world knew I'd let it slip by, important people in the school system would summon me to their offices: ... they would want explanations. How could you, experienced teacher, let this happen? My name might even blaze across page three of the tabloids. (McCourt, 2005: 224)

He also faces the common dilemma of career advancement, as he puts it, 'aging teacher ... still a student ...'.

> I was twenty-two then and now, at thirty-eight, I was applying to Trinity College. Yes, they would consider my application if I sat for the American Graduate Record Examination. ... (McCourt, 2005: 193)

> Thirty-eight was on my mind. Aging teacher sailing to Dublin, still a student. Is that any way for a man to live? (McCourt, 2005: 199)

Of keen interest to our present purposes are the specific identity dilemmas for English teachers. McCourt has to settle this 'where are you from', which is a bit too complicated to explain to people, and which boils down to the question of how much nativeness one expects of an English teacher.

> I was confused. I was born in America. I grew up in Ireland. I returned to America. I'm wearing the American uniform. I feel Irish. They should know I'm Irish. They should not be mocking me. (McCourt, 2005: 189)

As non-native teachers of English, Chinese teaching English to other Chinese, having ourselves learned it, we own a rich terrain for sharing stories and experience, but in some ways the identity gap may be bigger. Our students sometimes look at us with suspicion when we try to teach how it is that Americans do this and that. Some learners expect an evident authenticity from their English teachers, ignoring or forgetting that English is no longer attached to the archetypal image of a language reflecting a single national culture.

Another dilemma of teaching is whether to teach through reading recipes to make students enjoy their time in class or to strictly abide by the curriculum to make students extract more knowledge from books. For English teachers, teaching language and teaching analysis has long been a dilemma. Chinese English teachers experience their own unique version of this dilemma. McCourt was satirical about the helplessness of the situation and ironical about the teachers' efforts at digging deeper meaning:

> The other thing I like about the recipes is you can read them the way they are without pain-in-the-ass English teachers digging for the deeper meaning. (McCourt, 2005: 247)

> Sometimes, but this is a poem and you know what English teachers do to poems. Analyze, analyze, analyze. Dig for deeper meaning. That's what turned me against poetry. Someone should dig a grave and bury the deeper meaning. (McCourt, 2005: 265)

He describes his uneasiness about reading aloud recipes in the classroom:

> You bear a heavy responsibility as you go forth and it would be criminal of me, the teacher, to waste your young lives with the reading of recipes no matter how much you enjoy the activity. (McCourt, 2005: 255)

> I know we're all having a good time reading recipes with background music but that is not why we were put on earth. We have to move on. That is the American way. (McCourt, 2005: 255)

> On the A train to Brooklyn I feel uneasy over the direction this class is taking, especially since my other classes are asking why can't they go to the park with all kinds of food and why can't they have recipe readings with music? How can all this be justified to the authorities who keep an eye on the curriculum? (McCourt, 2005: 248–249)

As substitute for analysis, he asked students to respond, as they would after seeing a movie (McCourt, 2005: 265). After the self-irony of digging for deeper meaning, he mentions people, especially students' high expectations of English teachers for their encyclopedic knowledge. Obviously, this is a demanding expectation for teachers with a heavy workload:

> ... Also, I ought to scan a newspaper in order to keep up with the world. An English teacher should know what's going on. You never knew when one of your students might bring up something about foreign policy or a new Off-Broadway play. You wouldn't want to be caught up there in front of the room with your mouth going and nothing coming out. (McCourt, 2005: 223)

This rings true for Chinese teachers of English. Their great workload combines with the expectation of students that teachers have encyclopaedic knowledge makes their job a demanding one.

Concluding Remarks

McCourt speaks for himself when he is speaking for teachers as a whole, and vice versa. The teacher man he constructs is complementary to the protagonist in his previous two works – unique and yet ordinary. His understanding/identification of himself is achieved through his efforts to speak for the teachers.

In Johnson's study of 'the discursive construction of teacher identities in a research interview', the finding is that: As the interview proceeds, the teacher's identity construction becomes increasingly agentive. She shifts from a dilemmatic (how she and others at the school are affected by parental expectations for good student results when students are not academically able) discourse to a more positive construction of how her teaching practices help students to fulfill parental expectations, therefore positioning herself as a good practitioner (Johnson, 2006: 214). We also see that at the end of the book, McCourt presents us with a life-like devoted teacher man who reflects about driving fear into a corner and achieving freedom (McCourt, 2005: 301).

When it comes to a perspective on reading, we should make a distinction, hard as it is, between the following constructions: the identity construction of Chinese teachers of English; English teachers in China; teachers of English in China; and China's English teachers. With more non-natives teaching English as a second or foreign language, researchers are noticing the unique contributions these people make to the field and their advantages (Llurda, 2005).

In his study of professional identity among English teachers in the United Arab Emirates, Clarke (2008: 82) notes that 'for some student teachers, choosing teaching was linked to the prestige and practicality of English as an increasingly global language'. This also rings true for Chinese English teachers. On the one hand, they are aware of the increasing importance of English in a student's career development; on the other hand, they also enjoy the opportunity of making the subject of study complicated and challenging.

Reading *Teacher Man*, especially exploring the connection between his narrative discourse and his identity construction gives us revelations about how to understand ourselves as English teachers in China. Among the dilemmas we face in the field of English teaching, how to identify ourselves may come first. And we also need to reflect on the resources we have as non-native teachers of English. Life stories prove to have transforming power in McCourt's case, whereas for us, trajectories of language learning can also be revealing for students. As to how to transcend the authenticity complex, one way could be to deconstruct it and to bring our own understanding into the curriculum. Talking about student teachers, Clarke emphasizes that 'their professional identities are constrained in terms of pre-existing, "global" and "local" discursive configurations' (Clarke, 2008: 92).

We need to take this into consideration too when discussing Chinese teachers of English. For them several layers of teaching identity are current: they incorporate the traditional Chinese sense and meaning of being a teacher, as they adjust to the changing demands and expectations of being an English teacher in the global context pertaining to English, and of being a professional person, as part of the community of English teachers worldwide.

Notes

1. See http://www.amazon.com/Teacher-Man-Memoir-Frank-McCourt/dp/0743 243773.
2. See http://www.amazon.ca/Teacher-Man-Memoir-Frank-McCourt/dp/0743 294173.
3. See http://www.amazon.com/Teacher-Man-Memoir-Frank-McCourt/dp/0743 243773.
4. See http://www.metacritic.com/books/authors/mccourtfrank/teacherman.

References

Bell, S.E. (2006) Becoming a mother after DES: intensive mothering in spite of it all. In A. De Fina, D. Schiffrin and M. Bamberg (eds) *Discourse and Identity* (pp. 233–252). Cambridge: Cambridge University Press.
Clarke, M. (2008) *Language Teacher Identities: Co-constructing Discourse and Community*. Clevedon: Multilingual Matters.

De Fina, A., Schiffrin, D. and Bamberg, M. (eds) (2006) *Discourse and Identity*. Cambridge: Cambridge University Press.

Gee, J.P. (2000) *An Introduction to Discourse Analysis: Theory and Method*. Beijing: Foreign Language Teaching and Research Press.

Gergen, K. (2001) Self-narration in social life. In M. Wetherell, S. Taylor and S.J. Yates (eds) *Discourse Theory and Practice* (pp. 247–260). London, Thousand Oaks, New Delhi: Sage.

Johnson, G.C. (2006) The discursive construction of teacher identities in a research interview. In A. De Fina, D. Schiffrin and M. Bamberg (eds) *Discourse and Identity* (pp. 213–232). Cambridge: Cambridge University Press.

Llurda, E. (ed.) (2005) *Non-Native Language Teachers: Perceptions, Challenges and Contributions to the Profession*. New York: Springer.

MacIntyre, A. (1984) *After Virtue: A Study in Moral Theory* (2nd edn). Notre Dame: University of Notre Dame.

McCourt, F. (2005) *Teacher Man*. New York: Green Peril Corp.

Mishler, E.G. (1999) *Storylines: Craft Artists' Narratives of Identity*. Cambridge: Harvard University Press.

Mishler, E. (2006) Narrative and identity: The double arrow of time. In A. De Fina, D. Schiffrin and M. Bamberg (eds) *Discourse and Identity* (pp. 30–47). Cambridge: Cambridge University Press.

Riessman, C.K. (2002) Analysis of personal narratives. In J.F. Gubrium and J.A. Holstein (eds) *Handbook of Interview Research* (pp. 695–710). Thousand Oaks: Sage.

Schiffrin, D. (1996) Narrative as self-portrait: Sociolinguistic constructions of identity. *Language in Society* 25 (2), 167–203.

Taylor, C. (1991) *The Malaise of Modernity*. Concord, Canada: Anansi. On WWW at http://www.amazon.com/Teacher-Man-Memoir-Frank-McCourt/dp/0743243773. On WWW at http://www.amazon.ca/Teacher-Man-Memoir-Frank-McCourt/dp/0743294173. On WWW at http://www.metacritic.com/books/authors/mccourtfrank/teacherman.

Chapter 13
Negotiated (Non-) Participation of 'Unsuccessful' Learners

LI YUXIA

Introduction

Conceptualizing second language learning (SLL) as a site of conflict or negotiation between a variety of different discourses, identities and powers, some recent researchers have adopted a social constructivist approach to challenge the very notion of 'unsuccessful language learners', understanding this category as an institutionally imposed construction exposing a mismatch between learners' preferred identities in classrooms and the surrounding social context. One outcome of such an approach would be to encourage a focus on SLL as a situated process rather than a product (Duff, 2002; Harklau, 2000; McKay & Wong, 1996; Norton, 2001; Siegal, 1996; Thesen, 1997) and thereby shift attention away from a rigid classification of a group of learners.

However, most of these studies were conducted in an SLL context. This is quite different from settings such as China, where the bulk of English learning and teaching resembles the foreign language learning (FLL) context in which the learner's encounter with English will be infrequent and usually mediated through, or located in a context of, Chinese language and culture.

Drawing on Lave and Wenger's (1991) and Wenger's (1998) ideas about situated learning and communities, and Giddens' reflexively organized self-identity (1984, 1991), this chapter analyzes the biographical narratives of three 'unsuccessful' college English learners. The English learning experiences of Xun, Yang and Tan shed new light on our understanding of what it means to be 'unsuccessful' foreign language learners in the modern world and whether and how these categories of learner apply to the vast enterprise of English teaching and learning in contemporary China.

Community of Practice, Participation and Non-Participation

The terms 'participation' and 'non-participation' are drawn from the work of Wenger (1998) who understood learning as a process within a 'situated learning' framework in which a person moves toward full understanding and participation in a community of practice. In this journey, a person experiences a series of identity modifications (Lave & Wenger, 1991). In accounting for this complex process and ideas, Wenger deploys the concept of *participation* and argues that a person's identity is not only produced through participation but that it is also defined by that person's *non-participation* in certain practices (Wenger, 1998: 164).

Another theoretical resource of the current research is Giddens' (1984, 1991) concept of reflexive self-identity. This is defined as a series of reflexively organized narratives about the life experience of the self. Giddens argues that reflexive self-identity is influenced by three kinds of consciousness, including *discursive consciousness*, which is a person's ability to provide reasons for their actions, *practical consciousness*, which is a person's understanding of implicit knowledge of the conditions of actions, and *non-consciousness*, which comes from the sense of ontological security.

The Study Methods, Context and Participants

This study was undertaken at University Anon,[1] a large national university in China. The participants were three male second-year college students aged 21 and 22 years, enrolled in an international education program. They are Xun, from a small northeastern town close to the Russian border; Tan, from the capital city of Beijing; and Yang, from a city in central China with thousands of years of history and characterized as having 'Yellow River culture'. Xun, Tan and Yang were placed in English Class F according to their performance in the previous year's English exam. This ranking indicates that the three were located in the bottom 1/6th of the grade. Additionally, Xun, Tan and Yang were classified as typical 'unsuccessful' English learners by their English teacher.

The international program curriculum provides for two years study in China plus two years in the Netherlands leading to the award of a bachelor's degree. Since it is not state-supported, the international program is much more expensive than a regular program at University Anon, with fees about 5 times more expensive than those of a common national university, while fees abroad approximately 15 times more expensive.

Admission to the program requires a relatively low examination grade, but students are required to have an International English Language Testing System (IELTS) score of 6.0 before they can continue their more specialized study in a vocational university in the Netherlands. To help students meet this language requirement, the domestic part of the program is heavily focused on English courses.

Data Collection and Analysis

A qualitative approach was adopted to gain an in-depth and holistic understanding of the participants' English as a Foreign Language (EFL) learning experiences and perspectives. Data were mainly collected over a 10-month period from September 2004 to July 2005 through interviews with the focal participants and their teacher, supplemented by participant observation. Follow-up data collected over a longer period from the participants' personal blogs, emails, QQ messages, informal conversations with the teacher and other EFL students in the same program and the web pages of the international program also provided useful information.

Below, each of the three students' English learning is discussed in terms of how it can be understood as a practice of self-identity reflexively monitored and constructed through participation or non-participation in English learning.

Xun

Xun is the only son of a well-off family in a northeastern border town near Russia. His father, a former military officer and hero of a period during which China and the USSR were in conflict, was head of the municipal police. Xun's mother worked as a tax official. The busy lives his parents led meant that Xun's upbringing had been entrusted to the care of his grandfather, a retired commander of a regiment and a hero of anti-American struggles at other times in Chinese history. The grandfather lived in the family home. Xun's parents took great care to satisfy their son's material needs, including purchasing an expensive computer and hand-held video games and supplying him with a substantial monthly financial allowance. Neither the parents nor the grandfather speaks English.

Junior high school: (Non-)participation as a way to intimacy
Xun started learning English in junior high school at the age of 13 coinciding with the time that English was made a required course in the

school curriculum. He regarded English as not so important a subject, noticing that nobody spoke English in his hometown because 'Russian used to be dominant'[2] and commenting that 'all English teachers were newly recruited and under-qualified, unable to speak English well'.

However, Xun did participate in the English class and reviewed the lessons diligently, largely to please his grandfather. In the course of the pleasant daily routine of doing homework and lesson review with his bespectacled grandfather, while playing hand-held games on the side, Xun constructed identities of himself as a good learner and an adored, filial grandson. 'My grandpa never urged me to learn English, but if I did he would be very pleased' was the reason he gave for studying English hard at that time. However, when Xun, at age 14, witnessed his grandfather's sudden death, it provoked a crisis in his life. His identities had been constructed in intimate interaction with the now deceased grandfather, but thereafter he was often left alone and could not easily get support from his parents who were preoccupied with bureaucratic and social formalities.

To ease his sorrow, Xun had to adjust his former identity construction by changing his learning and life routines. He did this by making use of the most easily accessible resource at home, his computer, but soon became a 'wild' and 'degenerated' boy 'who did not care about learning but only thought of video games'.

Parental involvement with him evidently increased during Xun's third year in junior high school. His mother arranged intensive individual tutorial classes for four hours per weekday after school, and six hours on Sunday so as to force him to study various subjects including English. However, this newly forged routine only destroyed the earlier meaning of participation in learning as a way to intimacy, and had the effect of making Xun resist study, declaring that 'it was hell'.

Senior high school: Non-participation as resistance and negotiation of participation

Xun's attainments in the Senior High Entrance Exams were low, but his parents were able to ensure his enrollment in a top-level school in the city by drawing on the influence of family relations and paying for extra tuition. Xun responded initially by attempting to improve his English study upon entering senior high school but discovered that the teacher cared only about how to 'force English knowledge into your head'. He began to express dissatisfaction through non-participation in the English class or attending it in an unengaged way, and his exam scores declined. Xun's parents continued their carrot-and-stick interactions, scolding him seriously when he did badly in exams but at other times rewarding him with money or expensive gifts. But neither approach prevented Xun from embracing a loser identity in formal English learning.

> I have gotten used to failures ever since my childhood. Things were always not in my hand and I did not have confidence. (Xun, 19 October, 2004)

Other aspects of life, however, gave Xun opportunities to position himself more favorably. His abundant monthly allowance made it possible for him to become a 'big brother' among his male classmates, who often would go on a spree with him, and to become a 'hero' in the virtual world of war and adventurous video games, a behavior not only befitting the gender expectations of Chinese northeastern schoolboy subculture, but also expressing his wish to identify with a courageous and successful leader like his late grandfather and his father.

Unlike his resistance and non-participation in the English class at school, Xun was very keen on learning English vocabulary from newly imported video games. This served an important purpose for him because understanding words and expressions like those gave him status as a very 'in' and 'cultured' boy among his peers.

On the other hand, mastery of those English words and expressions, which mostly consisted of militant terms and names of animation creatures and strange deities, gave him a sense of superiority over the 'uninformed' English teachers. In this way, Xun constructed a cool, cultured game player identity and an identity as a free English user, and this outside class identity allowed him also to resist the identity of a loser and failure ascribed to him by the formal practices of teachers and by his parents.

Because of this alternative means of defining a positive social identity, Xun gradually came to enjoy his marginal participation in the formal English learning practices, which gave him a sense of detached sophistication. 'We only learned useless nonsense in the English class', he quoted Han Han, a writer and car racer born in the 1980s who quit high school and became a youth icon, to challenge the dominant Chinese discourse about English education. Outside of school, Xun was able to negotiate what counted more for him, a successful identity resisting formal education, just like Han Han.

College: Ambivalent participation in search of new identities

Although Xun's results in the National College Entrance Exams would have allowed him to enter a vocational college, this would have disappointed the higher expectation of his parents, who then decided to pay the extra-high fees to get him admitted to the international program at Anon University in Beijing. This was despite Anon University not offering Xun's favorite specialty computer science course. In this new context, Xun's rationalization of his English learning became very sophisticated.

In the interview excerpt below, Xun defines himself as an economically and spiritually indebted son, having a filial obligation to repay his parents with academic and career success.

> I lied to my aunties about the university fees, I said it was like any other university. I am too old to feel easy about depending on my family. ... I don't want to be any burden for them (parents). I hope I can win credit for the whole family. ... My mum has always been saying, 'Your road is paved with our money'. ... If I can't pass IELTS and go abroad to get my degree, if I can't even walk through the money-paved road to success, how can I have the face to face my mum?' (Xun, 19 October, 2004)

The compulsory language requirement of the international program and the highly competitive and degree-oriented society that became familiar to him in Beijing combined to provoke a reflexive adjustment of the importance of English learning in Xun's mind.

> Is there anyone who doesn't speak English today? Even the street cleaner has to be a college graduate nowadays. (Xun, 19 October, 2004)

Xun showed more commitment to his academic English learning than before. He bought large quantities of learning materials for IELTS and updated his portable electric learning machine. Several months before the IELTS Test, Xun sold his computer so that he would stop playing electronic games, and he canceled his mobile service to avoid his disturbing friends. Both the teacher's comments and my observations proved that Xun was now attentive in class, and he had initiated interactions with the teacher several times, and even with the researcher once, to relate his anxiety about learning English, requesting advice on language learning.

However, the increasing parental support and rising significance of English in the community also pushed Xun into a more powerless position to negotiate an ideal future identity. As a result, Xun became more critical of some aspects of the teaching of English in China and the way of life that his parents had assigned to him. He showed defiance toward IELTS and was aware of the uncertainty English learning could bring:

> IELTS is just a form that we need to conform to. Now I hate the IELTS freaking questions cranked out by those foreigners. ... I came to Anon because I had no choice. ... The foreign university? It is easy to get

enrolled but hard to get graduated. Sometimes I thought, why hadn't I been born abroad? Then I could have picked up my favorite specialty. (Xun, 19 October, 2004)

Apart from that, ambivalence in participation was also reflected in Xun's efforts to keep himself popular among former and new peers and his constant shift between learning hard and giving up. In this way, Xun seized agency in order to search for an identity balanced between parental force, social force and his own wish. As Xun remarked in his personal blog in 2006, his future seemed 'not wanna-be but ought-to-be', and he was searching for 'a road of my own that I will not complain about'.

Yang

Yang was from an extended family in a central farming region of China. He was an only son, and although neither of his parents spoke any English, both had decent salaries and social status, working in a state-owned basic energy resource company. Yang's father was an engineer and his mother a worker. It was his father who mainly took care of Yang's education, but some members of the extended family also played an active role. *Si Shu*, the fourth paternal uncle, who owned a pharmaceutical company in Beijing, was Yang's role model and adviser on education and career planning. *Er Jiu*, the second younger maternal uncle, who worked in the local Bureau of Education, often gave Yang books as gifts.

Junior high school: Non-participation as a result of the
peripheral stance in a changing community

Yang started English learning at age 13 in junior high school and ranked among the best in his class for the first year. However, in the second year, he experienced a considerable setback after missing English classes for a month due to illness. Yang attributed the setback to his failure to get individual support from the English teacher and lack of support and resources from other parts of the society, and so he 'did not care to listen to the teacher's lecturing any more'.

The English teacher was not worried (about my falling behind) ... She had no sense of responsibility ... Our head teacher cared only about major subjects ... English is not so valued in my hometown, so it seems like a minor subject ... From the local people's point of view, English does not go along with our local language. And the parents do not care, either ... My father would scold me if my achievements in major subjects, like Chinese, math, physics and chemistry, were low, but not so for English ...

Yang's rationalization of his non-participation in English learning defines himself as an incapable and inexperienced English learner, a learner who needs to be taken care of by thoughtful parents, responsible teachers, compelling school curriculum and supportive social atmosphere so that he could become a more sophisticated participant in English learning. Since none of these factors had played any active role in helping or urging him to catch up with the English class, his setback was not surprising.

This learner identity was obtained in a community of practice that has a thousand-year tradition of positioning adolescent learners in such a way. Adhering to such a tradition, Yang's learning was rigorously structured and taken care of by his school and adult family members. At school, the 6 am to 9:30 pm learning schedule ensured teacher supervision of nearly every minute of the students' learning activities on weekdays. And classes, especially English classes, were in the form of 'the teacher lecturing above and students taking in passively below', encouraging more obedience than agency from students. At home, not only was his father very concerned with Yang's academic achievement, but also other adults in the extended family such as *Si Shu* and *Er Jiu* also took great care in guiding his education.

According to Lave and Wenger (1991), such a 'peripheral' position may facilitate new members of a community of practice being open to change and moving toward fuller participation. However, in a community of practice that is yet to form, where new factors and values are competing with and in juxtaposition with older ones, a peripheral identity may hinder learning.

Yang's English learning was situated in a context where the local economic development and educational practice was out of step with a significant rise in the value of English in education and job market nationwide. In such a radically changing community of practice, older members need to cope with the new uncertainties together with the younger members. Depending too much on older members, Yang had not been given enough agency to cope with the situation. In this sense, Yang's non-participation in English learning was the result of his uncritical acceptance of a peripheral position and his acceptance of the negative attitude of some of the older members or local institutions toward English learning.

Senior high school and college: Fuller participation as a result of accepting peripheral position

Yang's non-participation went on until his third year of senior high school, when he had to face the fierce competition of National College

Entrance Exams, with English as a subject at least partly determining whether a student could enter higher education. There was consequently a great change within Yang's school curriculum, in which the English class hours almost tripled. In addition, family support for Yang's English learning also became stronger. *Er Jiu* provided Yang's father with information related to high school English education and sometimes gave Yang brand new English learning materials as gifts.

With all these factors changing, Yang's acceptance of a peripheral position meant that he was now motivated to more actively participate in English learning than before. He made good use of the class hours to learn English grammar from the teacher and spent one-third of his private study hours doing English reading comprehension exercises 'like crazy'. In the end, his national exam English scores were 20 points higher than usual on a total of 150.

At Anon University, Yang continued to embrace a peripheral participant identity, learning English with the help of older people, especially *Si Shu*, who owned a Beijing-based pharmaceutical company with international trade relations. Having been a role model and adviser to Yang ever since his childhood, *Si Shu* provided advice and even promised a job offer so that Yang could make education and career plans. As a result, Yang applied for the biology specialization of the international program and planned to become a researcher or manager in *Si Shu*'s company. All these decisions helped to foster the significance of English learning in Yang's mind. *Si Shu* also intentionally provided many opportunities for Yang to have personal interactions with English-speaking people.

> As long as there were foreigners, Si Shu would invite me along. That was to offer me opportunity to practice English. Once, Si Shu invited me and his foreign friends to visit the Great Wall. ... I felt frustrated because I couldn't catch them. ... I think from then on I began to feel that English is so important. (Yang, Interview, November 19, 2004)

This experience helped Yang to seize agency in English learning by initiating interactions with English-speaking people. According to his college English teacher Ms Ho, the two foreign teachers of the international program were amazed by Yang's enthusiasm in making appointments with them to practice speaking English. Unlike other 'inactive', 'unsuccessful' students, Yang would meet each of the two foreign teachers once a week for an hour. This raised Ms Ho's expectations of progress from Yang, and in this way Yang was able to negotiate fuller participation in the college English learning context.

Yang's case indicates that 'legitimate peripheral participation' is not constantly positive for learning in a community of practice that undergoes great change. Yang's acceptance of an immature and inexperienced identity prevented him from coping with the rapid change of the value of English language in China. Although, at University, the same peripheral identity helped him to obtain fuller participation, in a result- and achievement-oriented system, Yang's path to success in English learning is still a very long road.

Tan

Tan is the only son of a nuclear family in the capital city of Beijing. His father was a non-combatant army officer and his mother a bookkeeper. Because his mother had not been in good health for a long time, Tan's father took the primary responsibility for his education. Neither of Tan's parents speaks English.

Private English lessons in primary school: Participation as a compromise

Born in Beijing, Tan's exposure to English was the earliest among the three participants. Understanding the advantage of having high English proficiency in the opening up of China, Tan's father had sent nine-year-old Tan to private English lessons given by a primary school English teacher in their neighborhood. Tan recalled that he was delighted to have another little boy for company and felt 'relaxed', 'stress-free' and 'interested' in the sessions given by the 'friend-like' tutor.

The fact that Tan did not mention anything about the subject he was learning indicates that in general Tan did not perceive English learning as purely a knowledge acquiring activity, or a practice that promised him full participation in the future in a community of practice where English is valued. Tan's active participation in the English private lessons was more directed toward more skillful and sophisticated interactions with people. If we take the following excerpt from his interview into consideration, it seems that it was more a temporary escape from his father's jurisdiction.

> (6-second pause) I was a very, very introverted person, very introverted when I was a little boy, not even daring to talk to familiar people, maybe because my father was too strict with me. He was a militant, and got a really hot temper ... hard on me literally. And I was seldom allowed to go out and play. (Sigh and 4-second pause) How I wish he could have let go a little bit more. (Tan, December 12, 2004)

Tan's participation was not, principally, the outcome of his recognizing the significance of English learning as valued by his father, but the result of a negotiation in which Tan had a desire (practical consciousness) to become a boy with reasonable independence and social skills while remaining an obedient son, and his father wished to extend his supervision over all of Tan's life. Indeed, the private English lesson was one of the very few reasons for which Tan's father would allow him to go out after school.

Junior high school: Covered-up non-participation as expression of agency

When Tan was in junior high school, English became a compulsory part of the municipal senior high school entrance exams as well as the school curriculum. During school hours, the head teacher of his class was 'extremely strict' and 'kept close watch every minute' over students' English learning. And after regular school hours, Tan's parents forced him into an English enhancement class despite his own wish to go to a computer class. All these conditions helped Tan to reflexively adjust his identity as an English learner, building up into his discursive consciousness the importance of academic English performance for his future success in important exams and his future career.

However, Tan did not embrace this new identity wholeheartedly. He felt the teacher and his parents had been 'whipping' him into study, as if they were imposing the learner identity on him, making him someone he would not like to be, or driving him into a place he did not wish to go. So in his mind being in the English enhancement class was 'chaos'. The computer class, by contrast, seemed ideal, with many of his boyhood friends taking it and the male computer teacher being easygoing and encouraging his students to be self-directed and an asset for their family. In other words, it could be a community where Tan could participate not only to become more knowledgeable in computer science, but also to become more responsible for himself and grown up, both attributes valued in his peer community.

In any case, Tan attended English classes as his teacher and parents wished. Unlike Xun, Tan never expressed overt resistance to English learning. Obedience, at least in form, seemed to come out of his 'practical consciousness', that as a son and student he should comply with his parents' and teachers' wish. But interestingly, this seeming participation was just a cover-up for non-participation:

> I was not concentrated in English learning, making use of every opportunity to do all things but study. (Laughs) ... Like listening to music in learning hours, or reading extracurricular books in each class. And I copied my classmates' homework every morning. (Tan, 12 December, 2004)

Tan's fooling around in the study periods was a habitual yet concealed reaction to the teacher's and parents' prohibition of his outdoor social activities, an expression of his agency to secretly turn the time-space regulated by powerful others into a comfort zone of his own, thus negotiating a more self-controlled identity.

As Tan had put it, 'The more he (father) didn't allow me to play, the more I would make use of learning hours to fool around with things at hand'. As a result, Tan's initial interest in English learning faded away, English became 'like a class' for him and 'kind of a burden', and his academic achievement was 'mediocre'.

Senior high school and college: Non-participation as
withdrawal from individual agency

In senior high school and college, when English became even more closely related to entrance to the next level of education and career planning, and out of a similar strong filial desire to repay the aging parents by successful academic achievement and good job, Tan also had a stronger discursive consciousness about the significance of English learning.

> Just for my own interest. Thinking of the fact that in the future I need to live by myself, that my parents cannot take care of me all my life, and that almost every job has an English proficiency requirement, English is quite useful. (Tan, December 12, 2004)

However, this has not made Tan participate in English learning more actively. Tan had by then got used to his parents' monitoring of his life and withdrew from his responsibility of reflexively understanding himself and planning for his own future.

> My families have arranged everything too perfectly for me. And I feel that I have no concern for the overall direction of my life ... Well, the current direction is of course going abroad ... Ever since I was young, I haven't been bothered to worry about anything. I have done whatever they asked me to. What I need to do has been to follow the track they set up for me. (Tan, December 12, 2004)

In general, Tan's failure in English learning can be understood as his failure to develop a sophisticated individual agency. His forced seeming participation in English learning was actually a cover-up non-participation that helped him to avoid parental manipulation and created a comfortable and secure zone for him to maintain some self-control.

Discussion and Conclusion

Several salient points emerge from this study of three college EFL learners in China. The findings on the whole confirm findings in the field of SLL that language learning should be understood as related to the language learners' situated identity construction and negotiation, but some of their ideas have been also extended or refined as follows.

First, the 'unsuccessful' EFL learners in this study are socially situated in a setting of ever-changing multi-communities of practice, in which new values, rules and standards are yet to be negotiated into being. The mass nationwide EFL movement in China is not heading toward the creation of another English-speaking nation. Therefore, we need to avoid the tendency in some previous SLL studies to regard learning and participation as a linear process toward full participation and directed toward native speakerism. Instead it is necessary to regard language learners as peripheral participants striving for higher language competence with the help of the more experienced in the community of practice. In this light, the non-participation as well as the participation of the 'unsuccessful' EFL learners is not simple acceptance or resistance of some existing practices or positioning or merely negotiation of a new identity. Instead it makes more sense to see this as a multi-faceted effort to express agency and attempt to negotiate and reconstruct the communities of practice itself.

As a result, the 'unsuccessfulness' of EFL learners may just be a temporary less favorable identity situated in the still reforming communities of practice. The multiple forms of participation and non-participation of EFL learners are better understood as their ambivalent participation in forming communities of practice, through which the learners could more critically and deeply understand the older and newer values and standards.

Second, the EFL learners' identities are reflexively organized, in the sense that they can develop discursive and practical understanding of the conditions of their participation or non-participation. Despite this, in the emergent multi-communities of practice, reflexively developed individual agency is crucial if learners are to cope with an ever-changing situation.

Last but not the least, interactions with family members play a very important role in Chinese EFL learners' identity reconstruction. More research needs to be carried out in this area, which, in its breadth and depth, possibly reflects a distinctively Chinese reality for FLL research and understanding of some key concepts in applied linguistics.

Notes

1. All the names of teachers, students and the universities are pseudonyms.
2. All quotations are from interview transcripts.

References

Duff, P. (2002) The discursive co-construction of knowledge, identity, and difference: An ethnography of communication in the high school mainstream. *Applied Linguistics* 23, 289.

Harklau, L. (2000) From the 'good kids' to the 'worst': Representations of English language learners across educational settings. *TESOL Quarterly* 34, 35–67.

Giddens, A. (1984) *The Constitution of Society: Outline of the Theory of Structuration.* Cambridge: Polity Press.

Giddens, A. (1991) *Modernity and Self-Identity.* Cambridge: Polity Press.

Lave, J. and Wenger E. (1991) *Situated Learning: Legitimate Peripheral Participation.* Cambridge: Cambridge University Press.

McKay, S. and Wong, S. (1996) Multiple discourses, multiple identities: Investment and agency in second language learning among Chinese adolescent immigrant students. *Harvard Educational Review* 3, 577–608.

Norton, B. (2001) Non-participation, imagined communities and the language classroom. In M. Breen (ed.) *Learner Contributions to Language Learning: New Directions in Research* (pp. 159–171). Harlow: Pearson Education.

Siegal, M. (1996) The role of learner subjectivity in second language sociolinguistic competency: Western women learning Japanese. *Applied Linguistics* 17, 356–382.

Thesen, L. (1997) Voices, discourse, and transition: In search of new categories in EAP. *TESOL Quarterly* 31, 487–511.

Wenger, E. (1998) *Communities of Practice: Learning, Meaning, and Identity.* Cambridge: Cambridge University Press.

Chapter 14

Teachers' Identities in Personal Narratives

LIU YI

Background

For a couple of decades, second language (SL) research has been learner-focused while research on SL teacher development has been in a secondary position. Since the 1980s, western applied linguists have started some theoretical discussion on language teachers, and the 1990s witnessed more empirical studies (e.g. Velez-Rendon, 2002). As the concern over SL learners' identity increased in recent years (e.g. Gao *et al.*, 2002; Mckay & Wang, 1996; Norton, 1997), SL teachers' identity has also been attracting more attention from researchers (e.g. Case, 2004; Duff & Uchida, 1997). Among the various perspectives, a newly emerged perspective is SL teachers' personal narratives and identities, which is compatible with the shifting concern to teachers' development in SL education, caring more about teachers' inner self as a person, as against teachers' training, and caring more about teachers' observable teaching practice. Born out of personal experiences and telling a person's life story within the boundaries of specific situations and contexts, narrative study has become quite widely accepted within educational research and professional development since the 1980s. Through narratives, teachers can reflect on their career development, have a holistic understanding of their past and present and formulate an orientation for future development.

In the context of foreign language education, culture, power, voices and multiplicity of identity from the perspective of post-structuralism have recently been heatedly discussed (e.g. Armour, 2004; Simon-Maeda, 2004). The native/non-native dichotomy has also caused a lively debate in the past decade (Braine, 1999), especially in the narrower sense of an SL education context (e.g. Lin *et al.*, 2002; Pavlenko, 2003). However, the dichotomous categorization of native/non-native speaker has been criticized by Varghese *et al.* (2005), who claim that teacher identity lies in the reliance on oppositional and static social categories and does not allow us to look at the evolution of teacher identity, the moment-by-moment production of that identity, the impact of the interaction between different networks and memberships on teacher identity and the individual variation. Instead they advocate a more constructivist perspective.

This chapter adopts a constructivist perspective, perceiving identities as multiple, dynamic, continuous, interactive and multidimensional, and focuses on the issue of how the professional identities of college English teachers (those teaching non-English major students in Chinese universities) are constructed in interviews involving their personal narratives of their professional development.

The Study

Research questions

The research questions are: (1) how are the professional identities of college English teachers constructed in the narratives regarding their professional development, and (2) what factors are involved in the construction of a teacher's professional identities.

Definition of teachers' professional identity in a constructivist perspective

Among the identity theories from a constructivist perspective, Giddens' theories on self-identity have lately drawn the attention of SL researchers (e.g. Gao, 2005; Holliday *et al.*, 2004; Orton, 2005). Giddens defines self-identity as 'the self as reflexively understood by the individual in terms of his or her biography' (Giddens, 1991: 244). Although Giddens' 'biography' is an abstract and metaphorical term for elaborating a person's identity development, personal narrative is regarded as one of its embodied, specific and discursive representations. Here this meaning has been integrated with the notion that identity is 'the conscious and unconscious thoughts and emotions of the individual, her sense of herself and her ways of understanding her relation to the world' (Norton, 1995: 32), and the term defined as 'professional identity':

> reflexively understood thoughts and emotions of an EFL teacher on his/her profession, his/her sense of him/herself as a teacher and his/her ways of understanding his/her relation to the world as a teacher, in terms of his/her personal narratives regarding his/her professional development.

The informants

The profiles of the two college English teachers, Ms Ying and Mr Lee, are set out in Table 14.1.

Both informants could be conveniently accessed and, in addition, Ms Ying had been my colleague and Mr Lee my fellow student at university. However, the major reason for choosing them was that they were willing to participate in the research project because doing so offered them a chance of self-reflection, conducive to their professional development. Tsui (2003) argues that one of the key factors leading to the success of a research project on teacher development is the willingness of cooperation of the participant teachers. In addition, their relatively richer professional experiences and their experiences of living abroad are also believed to make the exploration of their professional identity construction more interesting and fruitful.

Research methods

The research adopted a case study methodology and interviewing as the specific method for data collection. The interviews produced personal

Table 14.1 Informant profiles

	Ms Ying	*Mr Lee*
Year of birth	1950s	1960s
Education background	Bachelor of Arts	Master of Education
Overseas experience	10 months in the US on a government exchange program in the 1980s	Two years in the US for a Master's degree on a program supported by the government in the 1980s
Years of teaching	14 years	20+ years
Other professional experiences	Interpreter in Tibet and in a university	Part-time and contract teachers for other universities and language schools; owner of a private language school
Current employer	A comprehensive university in a capital city in the northeast	A comprehensive university in a capital city in the north
Academic position	Associate professor	Associate professor

stories of their professional development and these rested largely in the hands of the informants. The interviewer's main task was to encourage them to talk as fully as possible about their world. The researcher did not have a fixed interview schedule. Each informant was interviewed for more than three hours and the sessions were audio-recorded. Afterwards, the interviews were transcribed and the transcription with the interviewer's comments was sent to the informants for reflection and feedback.

Findings and discussion

Critical incidents in the trajectory of their professional identity development

Giddens defines the trajectory of self-identity as 'the formation of a specific lifespan in conditions of modernity, by means of which self-development, as reflexively organized, tends to become internally referential' (1991: 244). The personal narratives of the two informants demonstrate how the critical incidents (Tripp, 1993) shaped the trajectory of their professional identity construction and how they revised and constructed their life plans according to alterations of circumstances and reflection. The constructed continuous identities have been like a thread pulling throughout their narratives and integrate their repertoire of self-identities as a coherent whole.

Ms Ying: I am a product of the times

Ms Ying regards herself as 'a product of the times'. Her professional trajectory has mainly been shaped by three critical incidents.

Incident 1: Choosing English as her major in spite of disliking English

Unlike those who were older than her, she began learning English as a foreign language in her primary school instead of Russian when the three-year Natural Disaster broke the relationship between China and the former Soviet Union. She recalled the reason why she chose English as her major:

> In the early 1970s, I watched the news on TV or some documentaries and I saw Chairman Mao met the foreign guests. His interpreters were Tang Wensheng and Wang Hairong. Their elegance and politeness impressed me and I admired them. I thought that being an interpreter would be a decent job. So I applied for English major when I filled in the application form for universities.

The motivation for being an elegant person and having a decent job had led Ms Ying to decide to choose English as her major, although she mentioned several times in the narratives that she did not like English, which she had regarded as the language of imperialism since a child. She explained that what was important was not to choose a major that one liked, but to choose one that would offer her a decent job and a living in those tough times.

Incident 2: Going to Tibet after graduation

In the interview, Ms Ying said that choosing to work as an interpreter in Tibet after graduation was due to her belief that working in a remote area would challenge and develop her, a view then held by a lot of ambitious young people. This period of experience played a decisive role in her life and she has clung rigidly to the beliefs developed during that time throughout her professional life. As she put it in the interview: 'the time of working in Tibet is a period when I grew the fastest in my life and it was also a period when my life pattern got shaped'. She also reiterated that the excellent interpreters in Tibet influenced her: their commitment to the nation, to the people and to their career; their strong sense of responsibility; their skills in interpreting; and their strict self-discipline, she admitted, had a pervasive influence on her identities of being a teacher. Some mottos marked with the traces of the historical era repeatedly appeared in her narratives: 'to serve the people whole heartedly', 'to be dedicated to the nation without asking for returns', 'never to put a black mark against the name of a teacher of people'.

Incident 3: Starting teaching in her 40s as a late entrant

The third critical incident in Ms Ying's career occurred in 1993 when she quit her job as an interpreter and took teaching as her career:

> In 1993, the economic reform brought many English teachers into business and there were insufficient resources of English teachers in universities. At that time, I also suffered from the conflicts between my own value and the modern ideologies, and I sometimes had to do something against my own beliefs. I decided to quit my job of interpreter and took teaching as my new career .... teaching is more influential.

It is interesting that in the interview, Ms Ying not only shared stories of influencing her students' morality, but also her experiences of influencing her students' behaviors, even their dressing habits and sense of beauty. She regards herself as a model of charm and integrity for the students to follow. It can be seen that what Ms Ying means by 'influential' is to influence her students not only in terms of English knowledge, but also how to be a refined person. She recalled that in her youth she herself has been influenced by her outstanding teachers in similar ways. This late entrant to teaching has extended the skills and talents realized in her early career and life experience.

Mr Lee: My lifespan is shaped by English

Mr Lee owes all his success and achievements to English study and the confidence gained through English learning and teaching. He said that it was English that constructed him from a shy boy from a working class family to a confident teacher of a university. In the course of this transformation he has been through two critical incidents:

Incident 1: Being admitted into a teacher's university as an
English major student

Mr Lee's choosing English as his major was totally thanks to his English teacher in high school, who suggested that he choose English as his major since he had beautiful pronunciation, while he himself had no idea at all of what even a foreign languages university was. In addition, he had never thought of being a teacher: 'I hated the idea of working as a teacher because, in my time, teaching was a profession with no bright expectations'. His application to a military foreign language university, however, was rejected because of his poor eyesight and he was admitted to the English Department of a teachers university. After graduation, he was assigned to teach in a university. Although he did not like teaching, he stated that 'different from the college graduates, we were not picky on what jobs we would have, and in those days, we were assigned by the authorities to where we were needed'.

Incident 2: Being sent to the United States on a Master's program

Mr Lee's unwillingness to work as an English teacher and his frustration at his lack of knowledge of effective teaching in his first year motivated him to seek other professional choices. In 1987, he applied for the selection examination of a Master's program in the United States sponsored by the Chinese government, which turned out to be an intensifier for his teacher identity, keeping him clinging to the profession with enthusiasm and confidence till the present. With fluent spoken English as his advantage, he was successfully selected as a candidate in one of the earliest groups of teachers sent to the United States by the Chinese government. It was also due to the appreciation of his 'beautiful English' in the United States that he gained the encouragement to resume his career of English teaching:

> The Americans who first talked with me would say, 'You know our language. You speak good English. You were born to be a language teacher'.... At that time, only a few teachers returned from the overseas. You spoke American English beautifully and your telling American stories were welcomed by the students. Gradually, I fell in love with the teaching profession and I can not live without it now.

In addition, he also states that living abroad made him more open-minded and flexible and he said he is now more tolerant of differences.

Although played out in different ways, the narratives of both informants indicate the pervasive impact of the different historical stages of Chinese social development on them as individuals and how they negotiated with the social objects as active agents. What should be noted is that all the discussed incidents along each informant's professional trajectory are interactive and dynamic. From a constructivist perspective, 'trajectory' is not a foreseeable and chartable single linear path, but an ongoing, continuous and interactive process of multiple convergent and divergent paths in the social context (Wenger, 1999: 154). In addition, there is a referential incident in each informant's trajectory which is of significant influence on the informant's professional identities: Ms Ying's experience in Tibet and Mr Lee's experience in the United States. All the incidents along their professional trajectory shaped their professional identities: Ms Ying as a teacher of influence on students and a teacher of commitment, responsibility and integrity; and Mr Lee as a teacher of beautiful pronunciation and rich paralanguage, someone with more power than his students, and confident in himself.

The professional identities reflected in the metaphors in the teachers' narratives

Lakoff and Johnson (1980) argue that by examining the metaphors embedded in the language of individuals, we can obtain a clearer understanding of how people conceive and experience the reality that they try to represent in words and sentences. The formulation of metaphors about teaching and the constructing effect of the metaphors on teaching at present and in the future have significant impact on, and indicators of, the teachers' professional identities.

Ms Ying: A craftsperson and a pump of an oil well

In the interview, Ms Ying shared a couple of stories on how she changed from being a teacher who hated the students who did not work hard in English into one who could appreciate each student:

> ... as a piece of artwork which needs a bit refinement. Each student has his own characteristics. In the past, I was not like this. This kind of feeling came to me only during the latest two or three years.

Ms Ying regrets that she did not take up teaching earlier because she has only come to know how to appreciate students just before she is about to retire. Her metaphor suggests that Ms Ying unconsciously identifies herself as an artist who will refine each piece of art with care and love. It also implies that she believes that a teacher has the dominant power and influence to carve students into what she expects them to be like.

Another metaphor she used is that of a pump. She stated, 'An oil well will not produce oil without a pump giving pressure. Students need some pressure to learn English well'. She recalled that in her childhood, she was seldom praised by parents, which made her always attempt to be better so as to please them. She reflected that this experience may be one of the major reasons why she also gives her students pressure. While talking about the pressure she puts on her students, she said:

> I ask them to come to classes ten minutes earlier and play part of an English speaking competition. I ask them to answer questions after watching. At first, they trembled, but now they volunteer to answer questions. ... I asked if these kinds of exercises would be beneficial for them in the future. They said yes and I asked them if this kind of pressure was necessary and they all said yes.

She regards herself as a pump, giving students a certain pressure so that they will make progress. On the other hand, the positive response of her students to her enforcing pressure encouraged her to keep this metaphor as part of her professional identities. This metaphor reveals the influence of the ideologies of the 1950s and 1960s when the motto of a model oil worker, Wang Jinxi, was very popular: 'A person without pressure will make no progress; a well without pressure will not produce oil'.

Mr Lee: A respected master and responsible guide

Mr Lee repeatedly stated that as a teacher, he regarded himself as a respected master in the eyes of his students, and among all the qualities of being a respected English teacher, beautiful pronunciation is the most important:

> Just as what Confucius advocates, students must regard me as their master with respect and admiration. To make students admire you, the benchmark is that you should have beautiful pronunciation. Only when they admire you, they would respect you ... This is related to my childhood tradition, my own experiences as a teacher and my experiences in the U.S. Even in the U.S., students respected me as their master.

Mr Lee's identity of being a respected master was also displayed in the stories he shared about how he was annoyed by disrespectful students and his disappointment with the students nowadays who were ignorant of the custom of helping teachers erase the blackboard and who regarded their teaching work as a kind of commodity.

Another metaphor Mr Lee used in his narratives was that of the teacher as a guide: 'Teachers should be like a responsible guide to take students to the destination. You cannot just dump them halfway'. Similarly to Ms Ying, Mr Lee maintained that teachers should not only guide students academically, but should also give them advice about their personal life. His story of guiding a student in a love affair was an indicator of this identity. He said that his students liked to get suggestions from him regarding their daily life because they admired him for his beautiful spoken English. By the same token, this image in students' eyes, and their trust and admiration, acted as a catalyst on him to make more efforts in self-improvement.

Comparing Ms Ying and Mr Lee, I find that both of them emphasize the authoritative position of being a teacher and are in the pursuit of personal power to influence their students (although they have both developed from a new teacher of less tolerance to students' misbehaviors to an experienced teacher with mastery of the art of managing classes). Both of them repeatedly mentioned 'respect' in their narratives. What is different is that Ms Ying's identity of being a pump and a craftsperson implies an image of putting students in a powerless position of following teachers' words strictly, while Mr Lee's identity of being an admired and respectful master and guide implies an image of imparting relatively more power to students themselves with teachers giving guidance. The metaphor differences of the two teachers also indicate the differences of the two informants' personal experiences in their identity development, which is worth another article to explore in depth.

Dilemmas and uncertainties in professional identity construction

In the age of high modernity, globalization, hi-technology, commercialization, depersonalization and other social and cultural changes have put human beings in a position of facing both opportunities and risks simultaneously (Giddens, 1991). English teachers are no exception, especially in the age of curriculum reforms in Chinese universities. Throughout the teachers' narratives, there are embedded dilemmas and uncertainties regarding professional identity construction and their attempts to negotiate with them.

Dilemmas of being a researcher and a teaching practitioner

Gao *et al.* (2000: 89) categorize English teachers into four groups according to their attitudes to academic research in English as a Foreign Language (EFL) education in Chinese universities: (1) 'the researcher', engaged in research for its pure joy of discovery; (2) 'the teacher researcher', enthusiastic about research for pedagogical purposes; (3) 'the researching teacher', primarily involved in teaching but trying to gain access to research; and (4) 'the teacher', devoted to teaching but distanced from research. While interviewing Ms Ying and Mr Lee, it is difficult to put them into one definite category as both experience being a researcher and a teaching practitioner as a dilemma, and find themselves struggling between the two.

Ms Ying: I think academic research can bear only abstract theories, but no benefit to practice. ... Some just want to get promotion. When I was in college, my professors did not conduct any research, but they were responsible and capable .... I had thought of doing some research on teachers' influence on students' learning, but I need to do a large-scale survey by questionnaires. I cannot do it now. My health is not well enough .... And I have 12 hours' teaching per week and have to grade students' assignment. I need to be responsible for my students. So I would rather give up the promotion .... Most of published papers don't have any empirical data and they just copy words here and there.

Mr Lee: To be a professor or not is not important for me anymore .... My leader once claimed the reason that I did not get promotion to lecturer was due to my not asking for it. ... I think I am more a teaching practitioner .... I would like to do some research, but it must be an area that I am interested in and it would be better if I cooperate with someone instead of work lonely .... I think research should be meaningful, of social value .... A lot of teachers do research only for promotion and they copied here and there and paid money and got published. It is meaningless .... My vision of my future is that I turn to be a well-known teacher in the area where I work.

The narratives of the two informants indicate that their experience in the academic field and with professional promotion has left them feeling that a lot of research papers are just a piece of patchwork and of no academic or practical value. With this stereotype for the word 'research' in mind, they would prefer to be a teaching practitioner instead of a so-called researcher. Although they are interested in conducting some research, their powerlessness in the promotion process and their heavy teaching load have forced them to withdraw from becoming a 'researcher'. In addition, the institutional constraints on them have left them in a state of depression and hopelessness concerning promotion to the position of professor. However, they still maintain their own objectives for life: to be a good teacher, responsible for their students.

Dilemmas of CET 4 and communicative competence development

The nationwide English test for all Chinese tertiary students, College English Test (CET 4), puts both teachers and students under a lot of pressure. This proficiency test has turned out to be the gatekeeper for many professional positions. Although both of the teachers interviewed regard spoken English as the most important aspect of English learning, the curriculum reform has given priority to communicative competence; they have had to subordinate themselves to the social constraints and cover some CET 4 training in classroom practice.

For Ms Ying, the tension between following her preference for spoken English practice and the requirements of CET 4 have tortured her since she took up teaching:

> After I worked as an interpreter, I found the problem with Chinese EFL education. For example, some students are good at reading, but can't express themselves in English .... However, I have to follow the way of teaching ... Students have to pass CET 4. If I did not follow the way, the students of other teachers would have a higher pass rate .... I am tortured with this conflict, but what I can do? I can only tell my students to practice more speaking and it will help them in their future career.

For Mr Lee, there are conflicts between his previous teaching beliefs and his learning experiences, and between the ways he taught in the past and at present.

> In the late 1980s and 1990s, CET 4 was a guiding baton for non-English major English teaching in Chinese universities. At that stage, I also regarded the test as the sole criterion to assess students' English proficiency. Like other teachers, I also adopted the methods of bombarding students with CET practice. However, the feedback for the students in job-seeking changed my belief: their CET 4 certificate does not guarantee their success of job seeking because their listening and speaking was not good enough. ... I am determined to reform my teaching. Though it has certain conflicts with what I used to believe on teaching, it is compatible to my own experiences of learning English.

The informants' narratives on CET 4 show the teachers' struggle between following their own beliefs in terms of their professional identities and social constraints: a teacher who should develop the learners' communicative competence and a teacher who should submit to the power of CET 4 in China. By actively negotiating between themselves and the social constraints, these college teachers have constructed their professional identities amid the dilemma and uncertainties.

Conclusion

According to Giddens' structuration theory (1984), human beings are active and knowledgeable agents, reflexively monitoring the flow of interaction with one another, in which subjects and social objects construct each other in an ongoing flow of social life. Personal narratives are not purely individual productions, but are powerfully influenced by social, cultural and historical events.

The data analysis presented here shows how society, school, colleagues, students, family and even interaction between the researcher and the informants construct EFL teachers' professional identities. In an age of high modernity, college English teachers in China, under the impact of fragmentation, deskilling, authority loss, commoditization, marginalization and continuous curriculum reforms, have been through an endless stream of struggles, uncertainties, chances, risks and identity crises. Offering opportunities for these teachers to make their voices heard by themselves as well as the public as they tell their narratives should bring emancipating power for their future professional development.

SL teachers' professional identity study in China is still in its preliminary stage, and analysis of narratives is a very complex matter that requires many more than two cases to explore even just the issues raised here. As well, other aspects of professional identity such as gender, and the teacher's social/cultural identities, remain to be analyzed even in these two cases. Nonetheless, it is hoped that this exploratory study will shed some light on the significance of English teachers' professional identity study and so contribute to the better development and education of SL teachers in China.

References

Armour, W. (2004) Becoming a Japanese language learner, user, and teacher: Revelation from life history. *Journal of Language, Identity and Education* 3 (2), 101–125.

Braine, G. (1999) *Non-Native Educators in English Language Teaching*. Mahwah, NJ: Lawrence Erlbaum Associates.

Case, R.E. (2004) Forging ahead into new social networks and looking back to past social identities: A case study of a foreign-born English as a second language teacher in the United States. *Urban Education* 39 (2), 125–148.

Duff, P.A. and Uchida, Y. (1997) The negotiation of teachers' social cultural identities and practices in postsecondary EFL classrooms. *TESOL Quarterly* 31 (3), 451–479.

Gao, Y.H. (2005) A structuration theory perspective of the social psychology of foreign language learning. *Research in Foreign Language and Literature* 5 (2), 25–36.

Gao, Y.H., Li, L.C.H. and Wu, H.L. (2000) What "research" and "research methods" mean to EFL teachers: Four cases. *Modern Foreign Languages* 23 (1), 89–98.

Gao, Y.H., Li, Y.X. and Li, W.N. (2002) EFL learning and self-identity construction: Three cases of Chinese college English majors. *Asian Journal of English Language Teaching* 12, 95–120.

Giddens, A. (1984) *The Constitution of Society: Outline of the Theory of Structuration.* Cambridge: Polity Press.

Giddens, A. (1991) *Modernity and Self-Identity.* Cambridge: Polity Press.

Holliday, A., Hyde, M. and Kullman, J. (2004) *Intercultural Communication – An Advanced Resource Book.* London: Routledge.

Lakoff, G. and Johnson, M. (1980) *Metaphors We Live By.* Chicago: University of Chicago Press.

Lin, A., Wang, W., Akamatsu, N. and Riazi, A.M. (2002) Appropriating English, expanding identities, and revisioning the field: From TESOL to teaching English for globalized communication (TEGCOM). *Journal of Language, Identity, and Education* 1 (4), 295–316.

McKay, S.L. and Wang, S.C. (1996) Multiple discourses, multiple identities: Investment and agency in second language learning among Chinese adolescent immigrant students. *Harvard Educational Review* 3, 577–608.

Norton, B. (1997) Language, identity, and the ownership of English. *TESOL Quarterly* 35, 307–322.

Norton Peirce, B. (1995) Social identity, investment, and language learning. *TESOL Quarterly* 29, 9–31.

Orton, J. (2005) English and identity in China: A native speaker's perception. Paper presented at the Roundtable Conference on Language and Identity, Peking University, October 25–27, 2005.

Pavlenko, A. (2003) 'I never knew I was a bilingual': Reimaging teacher identities in TESOL. *Journal of Language, Identity, and Education* 2 (4), 251–268.

Simon-Maeda, A. (2004) The complex construction of professional identities: Female EFL educators in Japan speak out. *TESOL Quarterly* 38, 405–436.

Tripp, D. (1993) *Critical Incidents in Teaching: Developing Professional Judgment.* London: Routledge.

Tsui, B.M. (2003) *Understanding Expertise in Teaching: Case Studies of Second Language Teachers.* Cambridge: University of Cambridge.

Varghese, M., Morgan, B., Johnston, B. and Johnson, K.A. (2005) Theorizing language teacher identity: Three perspectives and beyond. *Journal of Language, Identity, and Education* 4 (1), 21–44.

Velez-Rendon, G. (2002) Second language teacher education: A review of the literature. *Foreign Language Annals* 35, 457–467.

Wenger, E. (1999) *Communities of Practice – Learning Meaning and Identities.* Cambridge: Cambridge University Press.

Part 5

English for China in the World

Chapter 15
East Goes West

JANE ORTON

Introduction

In the first decades of the 20th century, the Chinese imperial examination system gave way to a curriculum based on the American education system, traditional clothing gave way to Western apparel and intellectuals began advocating vernacular literature and championing 'Mr Science and Mr Democracy'. In the face of so much new and foreign, the central task for Chinese remained the construction and maintenance of a coherent narrative of Chinese self-identity (e.g. Feng, 2000). At heart, the constant question was: How foreign did they need to become in order to achieve their goal – did becoming modernised need to mean becoming Westernised? One hundred years after they set out 'to learn the superior skills of the barbarians in order to control them' (Wei Yuan, 1842; in Teng & Fairbank, 1954: 30), the desire to expand and adopt new ways and yet not be overwhelmed by what was brought in was still the central dilemma confronting Chinese leaders.

> To nourish her own culture China needs to assimilate a good deal of foreign progressive culture ... whatever is useful to us ... However, we should not gulp any of this foreign material down uncritically. ...
> (Mao, 1942, trans., 1965: 667)

At times, tension has arisen internally, between the competing pull of Chinese tradition and the draw of modern practices, with arguments raging among idealistic scholars and pragmatic realists; at other times the question has been agonised over in relation to the external foreign behaviours being introduced with Western knowledge. A key campaign of the Cultural Revolution in the 1960s, 'Destroy the "Four Olds"'(破四旧 *po si jiu*) – old ideas, cultures, customs and habits – was one of the many public examples of the former, while both sources of tension occurred in (and about) the controversial TV series 'River Elegy' (河殇 *He Shang*) of the 1980s. Decrying China's relationship to the weight of its tradition and fear of identity loss, the narrator of the Elegy plaintively says at one point, 'The French are modern but still French, the Italians are modern but still Italian. Why can the Chinese not also be modern and still Chinese?'

In all of the debates since the 19th century, modernising while maintaining the Chinese sense of self was framed as a one-way process of bringing foreign knowledge in from outside: 'Western things to serve China' (洋为中用 *Yang wei Zhong yong*), as a 20th century Maoist slogan put it. At each stage of development, the uncertainty of the endeavour produced those who lamented the deskilling that inevitably accompanied the re-skilling, fearing that losses in traditional ways amounted to a weakening of Chinese essence. Some were fiercely conservative, others disagreed and yet others felt torn between the two views. In a survey conducted in 2006–2007, tertiary teachers from across China reveal this dilemma is still a central concern even among those most involved in spreading and valuing English learning, and the polemical positions they adopt in their statements are very much those so often voiced in the past. However, some responses also reveal a shift in interpretation of the objective 'to control the barbarians' towards one which envisages a different role for English. In this chapter, the results from the survey of Chinese tertiary teachers on the benefits and dangers of the spread of English are presented (further results are presented in the following chapter). The views expressed were compared with those found in the public domain of the press, popular internet sites and scholarly publications. These wider sources supported the evident new role for the language emerging from the survey. In conclusion, this development is discussed with reference to China's original quest for Western learning and the Confucian tradition.

Survey

Profile of respondents

The views of tertiary teachers of English were gathered using an anonymous, 10-question online survey. In each case, a local contact was solicited to help spread the invitation to participate, and in all 154 volunteers responded from a variety of institutions in 10 locations across China. Figure 15.1 and Tables 15.1–15.4 provide a profile of the respondents, showing their location, the type of institution and programme they teach in and their age and gender.

Figure 15.1 Location of respondents

Respondents were from a cross section of Chinese tertiary institution type from right across the country, and were reasonably evenly distributed among these. Divided into those in cities in high urban areas and those in provincial cities, the institutions included *Normal* universities and colleges, *Comprehensive* universities, *Technical* universities, universities dedicated to the teaching of *Languages and cultures* and *Professional* colleges focused on the field of business.

Close to half of the respondents were primarily engaged in teaching students who major in English, while the other half taught students majoring in other fields, all of whom study English.

Respondents were predominantly under 40 years of age and graduates of the last 20 years. Females outnumbered males by 3:1, a ratio that reflects the dominance of women in the language teaching field.

Views

Respondents were asked to complete the following two sentences in their own words.

(1) The best thing(s) about the growth of English learning in China is. ...
(2) The worst thing(s) about the growth of English learning in China is. ...

Table 15.1 Respondents by institution type

Location/institution type	Urban		Provincial		Line total	
	Institution	Number of respondents	Institution	Number of respondents	Institution	Number of respondents
Normal	2	32	3	33	5	65
Comprehensive	2	14	1	4	3	18
Technical	1	13	4	36	5	49
Language	2	12	0	0	2	12
Professional	0	0	2	8	2	8
Not stated		2				2
Total – institutions and respondents	7	73	10	81	17	154

Table 15.2 Respondents teaching in major and non-major English programmes

Programme	Number of respondents
Majors	72
Non-majors	80
Not stated	2
Total	154

Table 15.3 Respondents by age and gender

Age	20s	30s	40s	50+	Total
Male	11	17	7	7	42
Female	46	45	18	3	112
Total	57	62	25	10	154

Benefits

As Tables 15.4 and 15.5 show, the 200 benefits listed by the 154 respondents could be divided into two almost equally favoured themes: (1) *utilitarian* benefits, achieved in the *local* domain (49%) and (2) *educational* benefits, achieved in the *international* domain (51%).

Utilitarian benefits

Echoing the age-old quest in China to learn English to serve domestic practical objectives, 22% of respondents proposed China's economic

Table 15.4 Q1 – theme 1 – utilitarian benefits

Beneficiary	Perspective and benefit	Frequency	% of total Q1 responses (N = 200)
Teaching	Professional perspective – develop the quality	35	17
Students	Practical perspective – get good jobs	20	10
Nation	Economic perspective – advance China	44	22

Table 15.5 Q1 – theme 2 – educational benefits

Beneficiary	Perspective and benefit	Frequency	% of total Q1 responses (N = 200)
Students	Humanitarian perspective – broaden their minds	39	19
Nation	Intercultural perspective – exchange ideas in English	50	25
World	International perspective – intercultural exchange + teach others Chinese	12	6

development as a major reason for accepting the spread of English in the country, writing for example: 'to strengthen China', 'to learn advanced technology'. Seventeen percent of respondents took a professional perspective on this, saying that they thought the continuing spread of English would help support the work of their colleagues and themselves by maintaining the provision of resources, training and jobs. Ten percent of respondents raised the probable financial benefits to students once they graduated, including 'to have more opportunities to work abroad'.

Educational benefits

From the broader educational perspective, the dominant view (25%) was of the benefits to the country from engagement in the international sphere: 'Strengthen the cross culture communication and help Chinese people know the world better. China can be closely connected with the outside', 'The Chinese people will find their horizon expanded through the learning of English', 'More and more Chinese people are learning English, including children and old people. They are getting more and more open-minded'. A further 18% of respondents raised the development of students through such engagement, saying, for example, 'It makes the younger generation know more about what the other nations are like', 'They have more exposure to western cultures and can read the original works of English literature'. A total of 12 respondents, making up 8% of the group, went further than advocacy of international exchange, suggesting that knowing English would allow China to spread its language and culture in the world. For example, three of them said, respectively, that the benefits would mean 'We can open our country', 'Make the world know China better, and vice versa', 'Strengthen China's influence in the world'. A fourth saw it as a way to hedge his bets: through English, he wrote, students can 'see how painfully important it is to strengthen the powers of the nation so that the people will be ready when one day English is replaced by Chinese; or alternatively, should the people fail, one can still survive under the disguise of another identity'.

As Tables 15.6 and 15.7 show, the 12 respondents who held this view work across the range of tertiary institution type, seven in high urban cities and five in provincial cities. They include a higher ratio of men, 1:2, than the 1:3 of survey participants; twice as many are teaching non-majors as majors, a proportion nearly half as many again of their proportion in the survey as a whole; and more of the younger members of the cohort. Nearly half of those who suggested this 'world perspective' also nominated China's economic development as a benefit, and the other half linked it to a more reciprocal intercultural exchange.

Table 15.6 Number of advocates of spreading Chinese: Profile (i) ($N = 12$)

Programme	Majors	4
	Non-majors	8
Gender	Male	4
	Female	8
Age	20s	7
	30s	3
	40s	2

Table 15.7 Number of advocates of spreading Chinese: Profile (ii) ($N = 12$)

Institution + No.		*Other benefits also nominated by 1 or 2 respondents*					
U Normal	2	Intercultural	1	Economy	1		
U Technical	1	Intercultural	1	Economy	1		
U Language	2	Intercultural	1	Economy	1	Teachers' English	1
U Professional	2			Economy	1	Teachers' English	1
P Normal	1						
P Technical	2			Economy	1	Teachers' English	1
P Professional	2	Intercultural	1	Economy	2	Broaden Students	2

U = Urban; P = Provincial

Those advocating taking Chinese language and culture to the world combined with economic development may have been moved simply by a desire to reverse the world situation they now perceive of English on top, with one in which Chinese is on top. But even if this is their primary motivation, it is still a very new idea, and particularly interesting when viewed in light of China's quest for modernisation. In the 19th century, the purpose of learning English was in order to repulse the foreigners so as to keep China and its culture safe for the Chinese. Although then, as in the centuries before, maverick individual Chinese, including even the occasional emperor, had made friends with Westerners, and these people had studied a great deal of each other's language and culture, sharing China's tradition and taking its language and culture outside its present borders has not hitherto been an embraced Chinese view or recognised goal.

Dangers

The 167 responses in the second completion (Tables 15.8 and 15.9) also divided into themes reflecting utilitarian concerns and educational concerns.

Utilitarian dangers

While all respondents had something to say about the benefits of the spread of English, a handful said they were unsure what dangers might follow from such a development; a tiny set made very individual comments; a minority said it was a waste of time and resources for some students to be pushed through a course they were neither interested in nor had aptitude for, and a couple claimed, 'Only a few people could really

Table 15.8 Q2 – theme 1 – utilitarian dangers

Target	*Perspective and danger*	*Frequency*	*% of total Q2 responses (N = 167)*
Unsure		7	4
Miscellaneous	4 × one-off responses (economic/political)	4	2
Students	Utilitarian perspective – a waste for all to do it	13	8
Teachers	Practical perspective – difficult to implement	8	5

Table 15.9 Theme 2 – educational dangers – percentage of responses

Target	Perspective and danger	Frequency	% of total Q2 responses (N = 167)
Students	Educational perspective – learning English = just getting a certificate	17	10
Society	Knowledge perspective – less skilled in/ignorant of classical and modern Chinese and the cultural heritage	24	14
Nation	Psychological perspective – loss of national identity, culture and tradition	17	23
No danger	Open perspective – there is nothing to be afraid of	55	33

use English in their work. The importance of English has been exaggerated'. A similar number complained of difficulties in implementing in their local situation directives from the central government to give all students access to learning oral and written English.

Educational dangers

In contrast to the small set adhering to a utilitarian perspective on dangers, nearly half the respondents (47%) were concerned about dangers to educational standards posed by the spread of English. Half of these people claimed this on grounds of psychological influence, writing that the 'ideological side effects on youth' would lead to loss of knowledge of their own culture and even the collapse of the heritage as the young came to value Western culture over Chinese culture. The great danger, said one, would be 'to actually get what you wish for – turning the Chinese into what the English once were, and what the Americans are today'. Many raised the idea of the young 'losing', 'blurring' or 'becoming less aware and less proud of' 'the essence of the beloved country' and their Chinese identity. Fourteen percent were anxious about the shrinking Chinese language skills of students who were spending less time each year on study of their own language and cultural canon, and the many who no longer studied classical Chinese. On another path, nearly one fifth of those listing educational dangers worried about a devaluing of English education itself, with students being encouraged to see English certification as the goal and 'equating language capacity with the Midas touch' rather than seeking humanistic learning in depth. One respondent wrote: 'I fear that English may be taught in the way similar to serving fast food. People learn in haste and do not sit down and appreciate it'. Some also felt that English proficiency drove a wedge between Chinese, with students 'mistaking a good command of English as a sign of their improved social status among their peers' and thus creating a new kind of snobbery.

In contrast to these 47%, a solid 33% of respondents claimed they could see no dangers at all in the spread of English in China. Indeed, several thought the very acquaintance with a second language and culture would serve only to strengthen appreciation of Chinese language and culture: 'At least that is what I feel after learning English for so many years' wrote one respondent, while another said: 'Chinese culture is so broad and profound, and it will surely become popular worldwide one day. At that time Chinese people will be proud of Chinese culture, and will then cherish it'.

As Table 15.10 shows, only one of the 12 respondents who saw being able to spread Chinese in the world as a benefit of knowing English thought there was no danger in the latter process, four had utilitarian concerns and one was worried about the loss of Chinese language skills. The remaining six respondents, representing nearly the full spectrum of institutions, were worried about loss of national identity.

Table 15.10 Number of advocates of spreading Chinese: Dangers ($N = 12$)

Danger	Institution type and number	
Lose national identity	U Professional	2
	U Technical	1
	U Language	1
	P Professional	1
	P Normal	1
Lose Chinese language	U Normal	1
English as just a certificate	P Technical	2
Hard to implement	P Professional	1
Waste of resources	U Language	1
No danger	U Language	1

U = Urban; P = Provincial

Summary

To sum up, respondents' views show that several teachers perceive English as a subject on the curriculum that uses up a great many resources, some of which might be better spent on other things, not least the teaching and learning of modern and classical Chinese. Not everyone needs to know English, they argue, so not everyone should have to learn it and, anyway, the resources to teach it well on such a scale are not available. Furthermore, it could lead to some loss of Chinese identity. While one third see no dangers, the entire group see benefits, proposing that English can broaden students' mind and help them get a good job. English is also seen to be beneficial because it provides access to science, technology and international trade, all of which are good for China's development. Through learning and using English, Chinese can communicate with the rest of the world and exchange ideas so that both sides can get to know and understand one another's culture. Some even propose that through English, Chinese can open their country and their heritage to foreigners, a move they think would be good for both sides.

Considered in light of the Chinese quest over the past century and a half, the voices heard in the views above are almost entirely familiar. The proposition put forward by one in three of the survey respondents that learning English is beneficial because it permits intercultural exchange, not simply technical and social development for China, must be seen as a modern development. Yet within the modern era, it is an objective that has been suggested by teachers in China for some time now (e.g. Gao, 1996; Hu, 1988). What is less familiar, however, is for English to be thought of as the first step in creating a relationship which could lead foreigners to explore Chinese life and thought through learning its language, with the active assistance of Chinese people, and this is true no matter whether the underlying motivation is a hope of domination or a search for mutuality. While in absolute terms, the numbers involved are far too small to have significance, in practical terms, any voice proposing this direction is salient.

Easternisation

Cultural rejuvenation

Although for most of the last century and a half the less familiar voice found in the survey has rarely been heard, seeking to locate it in the broader society reveals that it is not, in fact, a totally new voice in China.

The most ardent and articulate contemporary proponent of strengthening Chinese culture at home and seeking to take Chinese learning to the world has been Professor Ji Xianlin of Peking University, a graduate in Western literature and a world-renowned scholar in Indo–Chinese connections through Buddhism. In October 2001, he and Zhang Dainian headed a declaration of *The Great Renaissance of Chinese Culture and Efforts to Spread World Peace*, 《中华文化宣言为促进新世纪中华民族伟大复兴和世界和平与发展而奋斗》 published by 76 scholars of Chinese culture. (For this and the following texts, see Chen, 2006). In response, in May 2004, the *Recitation Book of Chinese Cultural Classics for Basic Education* (《中华文化经典基础 教育诵本》) was published, edited by Jiang Qin, and on the 2555th anniversary of Confucius' birth (28 September 2004), the first official ceremony honouring Confucius since 1949 was conducted in China, followed in 2005 by a 'Global Honouring of Confucius' ceremony (2005全球联合祭孔). Also in September 2004, at the '2004 Cultural Summit Forum' (文化高峰论坛) held in Beijing, 72 well-known scholars and authors, including Xu Jialu, Ji Xianlin, Ren Jiyu, Yang Zhenning and the author and former Minister for Culture, Wang Meng, signed the 'Jia Shen Cultural Proclamation' (《甲申文化宣言》). Called by the traditional name of the year 2004, the proclamation advocates in the context of globalisation the necessity of cultural diversity and equality in cultural communication.

More recently, in an article published in 2007 in China's intellectual daily newspaper, *Guangming Ribao*, the terms coined by Ji of 'Eastern Learning Gradually Permeating the West' and 'Easternisation' (东学西渐与 "东化" *Dong Xue Xi Jian yu 'Donghua'*) appear as the title. The first of these two phrases reverses the strategy of 'Western learning gradually permeating the East' (西学东渐 *Xi xue Dong jian*) followed by Jesuit missionaries in China in the 15th and 16th centuries, aiming to convert the Chinese over time. The actual four-character term for this process, '*Xi xue Dong jian*', however, seems only to have been coined much more recently, in 1915, when it was used as the Chinese title of a book written by Rong Hong (also known as Yung Wing), who had been the first Chinese scholar sent to study Western military learning in the United States in 1872. Originally written in English, the book had been published in the United States in 1912 under the title, *My Life in China and America*. Its selection as the Chinese title makes clear that '*Xi xue Dong jian*' was a term considered at the time to have very positive connotations.

Eastern thought in the West

In his writings, Ji Xianlin also makes it clear that he believes China has learned a great deal that is of value from the West to East process of *Xi xue*

Dong jian. But he is an advocate of 'the principle of both taking and send-ing' (拿来主义与送去主义 *nalai zhuyi yu songqu zhuyi*) in the matter of inter-cultural communication. 'A culture needs to be both continuing to develop its traditional culture and thus remain national, *and* updating itself through the influence of other cultures by communicating with other nations', he argues. The 'principle of taking' – also called 'takeism' or 'grabbism' – comes from China's great 20th century writer, Lu Xun, who urged those taking part in the vernacularisation of literature movement a century ago, as a matter of principle, to take from abroad and use as they pleased what-ever they needed in terms of genre, narrative style and so forth. Ji points out that the world today has been very powerfully dominated by Westernisation and while, of itself, this is not a bad thing, it should not, and indeed, cannot, remain the overall cultural influence everywhere. What the world needs now, he proposes, is the integrative principle of 'Easternisation' (东化 *Donghua*), in order to correct the imbalance inherent in Western culture's overly analytical essence that breaks down connectedness. Advocating that in its quest to modernise, China might also put something back into the global pool is new in recent times.

Ji, however, claims that, historically, there is nothing new in the notion of *Easternisation*. He says it was in existence in Han and Tang dynasty times (220 BC–900 AD), when the economic and cultural centre of the world was China, and continued even later in Ming and early Qing times (15–17th centuries). In these centuries, he goes on, the Chinese always had contact with other peoples, most particularly those from countries bordering China, but also from beyond, and they welcomed them into their country and treated them well [albeit, it should be noted, also seeking to isolate them from the general popula-tion (e.g. Rossabi, 1975)]. Over the course of these centuries, 'We spread a lot of our inventions and creations out into the world. And the way the world is now has a lot to do with Chinese culture', Ji says. Among contacts during the past eight centuries of Ming, Qing and Republican rule, Western missionaries and traders, including the fabled Marco Polo, have also been made welcome in China, and have been closely engaged with by Chinese scholars and emperors over philosophical and scien-tific matters (see Lo Bianco, this volume, Chapter 1). Ji concludes: 'The depth and breadth of Chinese culture have appealed to foreign mission-aries, overseas Chinese, foreign students and businessmen, who have helped to spread it all over the world'.

Views such as Ji's also have adherents in contemporary Western history circles, most notably among participants in the Sino-centric debate known as 'The California School of New World History'. Authors and works involved include, for example, Jack Goldston's *Revolution and Rebellion in the Early Modern World*, which was published by the University of California Press in 1991; Bozhong Li's *Agricultural Development in Jiangnan, 1620–1850* and André Gunder Frank's *ReOrient: Global Economy in the Asian Age*, both of which appeared in 1998; Kenneth Pomeranz's *The Great Divergence* (2000) and John Hobson's *The Eastern Origins of Western Civilisation* (2004). Their views have not been received without criticism (e.g. Deng, 2000, 2004), based largely on charges of using monofactorial methods of assessing development for comparison, and on the perceived far greater degree of Western agency involved in the uptake of inventions from China (paper, gunpowder, the compass, printing) in the course of its modernisation compared with the more submissive Chinese adoption of Western ideas.

The view proposed by some of the surveyed teachers that Chinese language and culture should be spread in the world is shown to be supported by a number of powerful leaders in the public domain. Furthermore, like the teachers, these scholars see English as the obvious vehicle for carrying out this task, while they also recognise the need to ensure students receive deeper Chinese language education at home. Furthermore, their support is already considerably more than just rhetorical. Since their 2001 proclamation, Ji and colleagues have published a fresh collection of the classics aimed at rejuvenating Chinese culture among the young at home, and some newly selected collections of major Chinese works translated into English and other languages intended to begin the process of having Eastern thinking prevail over Western culture in the world in the 21st century. One collection, by the eminent scholar Yue Daiyun, entitled *Chinese Learning Gradually Permeating the West Series* (中学西渐丛书 *Zhong Xue Xi Jian Congshu*) (Yue, 2007) is aimed at correcting misinterpretations of Chinese culture by Westerners in the past and showing the universal applicability of Chinese culture (中华文化普适性 *Zhonghua wenhua pushixing*). The five books in the series published so far show the range of thought under consideration: *Leibniz and Chinese Culture, Babbitt and Chinese Culture, Kafka and Chinese Culture, Snyder and Chinese Culture, Pound and Chinese Culture*. Ji's own collection, entitled *Chinese Learning Gradually Permeating the West, Chinese Culture in the West* (东学西渐中国文化在西方 *Dong Xue Xi Jian, Zhongguo Wenhua Zai Xifang*), comprises seven books of equally broad range: *The Influence of Chinese Culture on Europe, The Influence of Chinese Philosophy on Europe, The Spread of Chinese Science and Technology to the West and Its Influence, The Influence of Chinese Legal Culture on the West, The Spread of Chinese Military Science to the West and Its Influence, The Influence of Chinese Culture on American Literature* and *The Influence of Chinese Modernization on Western Society*.

The public view

While these movements have been getting under way, there has also been no small amount of discussion and debate using the Internet concerning the spread of English in China, some on informal sites such as blogs, others on more formal exchange sites. The contributions show the range and kind of views expressed by the surveyed tertiary English teachers are widely held across a broad spectrum of educated Chinese. Thus some rail against the vulgarity of English when compared to the beauty of Chinese, others demur, claiming it is good for China to open to the world and to engage with others, others are fearful of loss of cultural identity, or of China reaching too high too soon. A major recent site has been the *Rejuvenation Forum* (复兴论坛), which opened in October 2007 hosted by the national English language television channel, CCTV. Among the hundreds of contributions, written in English and listed on the screen by number (#numeral), the following examples are a typical selection:

The nationwide English learning is an insult to our national culture. (#6)

For all those 'education experts', it's worth thinking about how many students have wasted their time to study English instead of pursuing their real interests .... How many Chinese classics have you read? (#14)

How could we call someone who doesn't know much about his/her own traditional culture a talented person? (#48)

Chinese culture is mostly kept on the mountain, in the temple and other places of interests, all of which are visited by people as something to watch or appreciate ... Who will study and promote it? On the other hand, the western culture is in the city, on the streets, and in contact with people's life on a daily basis. As a result, people are influenced by it subconsciously, especially those kids. (#163)

First, I absolutely support the learning of English because we need to communicate with the rest of the world, not only in the economic aspect, but also in aspects of technology and education. We can't be left behind again ... Second, I want to say that learning English is not to pass the test, it is for one's own use. (#67)

Let's welcome the invasion of English. Our Chinese culture will incorporate them all. (#207)

Any language is a wealth of all human beings, instead of a particular nations' own property. Chinese is the common wealth of people around the people as well. (#7)

The day will come when the world will learn our language and the Chinese language will become international. (#106)

English is a weapon we use on our journey to the national rejuvenation ... a tool that young people have to master for the sake of the nation's rejuvenation. Our goal is to replace English with Chinese as an international language as soon as possible. At that time, young generations won't have to waste time on learning English. (#144).

In addition to these more informal outlets, similar views can be found in scholarly journals:

Chinese students already have no problems tolerating and accepting western cultures in terms of language expression, clothing, concepts and customs. In contrast, it is Chinese culture that is being unprecedentedly ignored, leading to the degradation of Chinese language, culture, and ethic values among some students. (Xu, 2004: 87)

All cultures are hybrid and mixed, and thus cultures need not be scared of being invaded, but instead complement and promote mutually in their communication and conflicts. (Huang, 2006: 106)

Chinese culture is losing its immunity and being invaded severely by the western culture, and the 'loss of language' (失语症) is the evidence of that. (Zeng, 2005: 50)

Learning English has two purposes: getting to know western culture and spreading our national culture. On many occasions, the latter is more important and meaningful. (Zeng, 2005: 51)

The most obvious characteristics of China's re-emergence is to share with the world. (Wu, 2007).

For some years, many journal articles have expressed a preference for the concept of 'English as an international language', believing it relieves Chinese of the need to adopt American or British ways of thinking and interacting, and hence removes the stigma of Chinese dependence on English-speaking societies (e.g. Wen, 2000; Zhang, 2001). In a similar vein, following the call of Wang (2002) to 'discover the East and export Chinese culture', authors continue to support 'foreignisation' as the strategy to adopt in translation so as to break the imperial status of a 'superior' culture and realise 'pluralistic cultural globalisation' (多元化的文化全球化) (e.g. Zhong *et al.*, 2005). A 2004 survey of 2278 university students from all over China found that a significant motivational factor in their study was 'helping the world to know more about China' and 'help China to go to the world' (Gao *et al.*, 2004: 32). Yang (2007: 14) sums up the position this way:

> We are studying western language and culture not to identify with or surrender to it, but to incorporate its essence on the basis of understanding it, and to use it for the promotion of our own culture so that Chinese culture and western culture could communicate equally. We need to export our excellent culture, to let the world hear China, and make our own contributions to the development of global culture.

The spread of Chinese language and culture

The above quotations show scholars and members of the general public alike expressing very much the same range of views as the surveyed teachers. There are, thus, those who bewail the waste of resources being spent on English, those who fear the loss of Chinese culture due to the spread of English, the lowering of regard for Chinese language and culture both at home and abroad and the corruption of traditional Chinese values due to Western influences on the young. And these views are often accompanied by acknowledgement of the very real individual and national benefits, both utilitarian and educational, that learning English can and does bring. A common conclusion is a call for individual patriotism and an appeal to the Chinese government to reduce the amount of time all spend on learning English and to strengthen the status of the Chinese language nationally and internationally.

In fact, the Chinese government is campaigning strongly to do just what they ask. Firstly, at home, they are supporting the rejuvenation of Chinese studies mentioned earlier by having universities re-introduce classical Chinese and by adding traditional content to textbooks; and secondly, beyond China, they are establishing a chain of Confucius Institutes throughout the world and bidding to control the teaching and learning of Chinese language internationally through accreditation of standards for teaching and assessment of learner proficiency (see their official website: http://english.hanban.edu.cn/market/HanBanE/412360. htm). The Confucius Institutes draw on several European models of an international cultural centre, such as Germany's *Goethe Institute*, Italy's *Dante Alighieri Society* and France's *Alliance Française*, all of which aim to provide language teaching and cultural information to local communities around the world, while some in recent times have also begun to involve themselves in scientific exchange and the creation of business links. By far the most powerful model for the Confucius Institutes, however, has been the British Council, which along with its various predecessors, has been a potent presence in China's quest to modernise, regarded both positively, as the affluent and often generous means to what was sought, and, negatively, as the bastion of expatriate arrogance and racism towards Chinese people and society.

It will be some time before the Confucius Institutes can command anything like the billions of pounds spent annually by the British Council in maintaining and developing the influence of English language, culture and commerce. For now the Confucius Institutes are run through the National Office for Teaching Chinese as a Foreign Language, better known in short by its abbreviated Chinese name, the *Hanban*, and their mission is primarily the enhancement and advancement of the teaching and learning of Chinese language and culture in other countries. The means envisaged are provision of short- and longer-term courses for teachers of Chinese at all levels of the education system and for all purposes (e.g. academic study, business and tourism), materials distribution and development, including film and multimedia products and testing of language proficiency.

In an article in the *International Herald Tribune* of 11 January 2008, the Chinese Director of the Confucius Institutes, Xu Lin, is quoted as saying that creating a worldwide network of Chinese language and culture was in response to 'the Chinese language craze' in neighbouring countries like Vietnam, South Korea and Indonesia, and requests by American education officials from 'several dozen states' to help them establish Chinese language programmes. 'There is a China frenzy around the world at the moment', she said. In addition to responding to demand, according to the American host of the Confucius Institute in New York City, the Chinese government 'are using Chinese culture to create a warmer, more positive image of Chinese society'. The choice to name the Institutes after the ancient Chinese scholar 'speaks volumes about the country's soft-power ambitions', concludes Howard French, writer of the article. In the same year that the Confucius Institutes were set up, General Secretary Hu Jintao instructed his fellow countrymen to speed up the promotion of Chinese language internationally by implementing the '11th Five-year Plan for Chinese Language to go Abroad'. In early 2008, there are some 200 institutes already established in some 36 countries, but the intended scope of operations and the level of implementation are impossible to ascertain.

Conclusion

The survey of tertiary teachers of English revealed a range of perspectives on the values and dangers to China of the continuing expansion of

English, from local, technical concerns to lofty educational aspirations. Checking these results in various public domain discussions shows them to be highly representative of contemporary educated Chinese opinion. Amid formidable problems facing Chinese on their path to modernisation, the use and spread of English in China have produced opponents and no small amount of concern about loss or corruption of China's cultural heritage. Yet the greater number hail it as the valuable means to national strength and personal growth and a source of enrichment for Chinese culture and language. Unharmed by this development, these must be protected as treasures and even seen as potential gifts to the world.

In an earlier discussion of Chinese success in accommodating Western learning, modernisation and Maoist rule in relation to neo-Confucian thought, Metzger (1977: 233–235) reminds us that, faced with cosmopolitan, Western influences amid problems of economic backwardness and threats to political integration, China has proved considerably more successful in its modern development than other Third World nations. He suggests that the Chinese enthusiastic embrace of modernisation may be because they came to see that it provides a meaningful way of realising an ethos rooted in their history, fully in keeping with the classical and neo-Confucian view that 'the spiritual cannot be exhaustively known unless one masters practical matter'. Thus rather than following the view so long argued for successfully by certain powerful scholars, that maintenance of the Chinese essential *ti* – the understanding of ultimate principle – should be kept separate from adoption of the Western mastery of the external world – the utilitarian *yong* – this line of thinking proposes that the two should be seen as complementary and joined. Without referring to a dialectical resolution in these terms, the views presented in this chapter have largely expressed a similar perspective and comparable optimism that it can be achieved.

This same view, that Chinese need to balance inner cultivation with concern for regulation of the outer world, including the raising of living standards, is found in the writings of neo-Confucian scholars over some centuries, and the perception that this could be realised through adoption of Western technology is a view found in the writings of a handful of 19th and 20th century reformers. Of particular significance to the discussion here and throughout this book is the proposal a century ago by journalist and reformer Cheng Guanying that, just as Ji Xianlin proposes today, this union would not be beneficial for the Chinese alone, but that East and West 'could learn from each other to achieve a perfect form of learning and civilisation', one in which material things and ultimate principle are joined (Metzger, 1977: 215–216).

The difficulties and potential for undesirable consequences confronting the Chinese on the path to modernisation are real, but from the above perspective, the fear of some that the widespread embrace of English may reflect 'a people aimlessly drifting away from their traditional moorings with no clear sense of identity' (Metzger, 1977: 235) would be incorrect. Instead, it suggests that while not all of the present outcomes may be accepted in the longer term, they are the result of having taken what will prove to be the right path, the one that leads to consolidating Chinese identity through reconciliation of the original *ti–yong* split of Confucian thought and the consequent *ti–yong* dilemma of engagement with Western learning. Moreover, it suggests that if gradually permeated by Chinese thinking, the West, too, would benefit by, as Ji Xianlin puts it, having its disconnected, utilitarian expression of essence being eventually balanced by the integrative, intuitive expression of Chinese essence.

Whether the West, and the native English-speaking world in particular, will be open to embracing the gift of Chinese tradition some now seek to offer is hard to estimate. There has been a long, if interrupted, history of engagement and sharing of thought and language between the two groups that spans centuries. Any greater involvement in the 21st century would thus be a renewal of scholarly dialogue and popular social and technical interactions, rather than the taking of a new course. Positive contemporary signs that such a renewal might be welcome are the increasing discussion in the West of cultural factors and imbalanced values as the bases of the growing economic woes and social dissonance, typified by Rosenblum (2007), the high frequency of culturally critical views of the West, especially of English-speaking societies, by Asian writers such as Mahbubani (2008) appearing in various media, and of the local endorsement of these views in articles such as Cohen (2008). The key to success in developing a more consolidated identity for both groups through mutual engagement is likely to reside in the spirit and mode of engagement. While being told what to do is a process considered normal, indeed, proper within Chinese tradition, their individualistic orientation leads English speakers to generally respond poorly to directives. It remains to be seen whether in taking their tradition abroad, a process they have barely begun, the Chinese will seek to engage interculturally with those they wish to persuade, and to integrate differences in social concepts and practices, which are particularly salient in the field of learning.

The role of language, whether English or Chinese, in this quest for mutual rectification remains constructed in Chinese rhetoric as largely that of a tool, although those who have taken the lead in attempting to present the essence of Chinese culture and thought in English must regularly be gaining insights into its actively constitutive power as they grapple with finding appropriate ways to express in a language influenced by a different set of lives and histories outside China, what has been shaped by those elements as they have unfolded over centuries within China. If, as they hope, those in the West they are aiming to reach do begin to undertake the study of Chinese language in any significant numbers, and especially if they do so open to more than purely utilitarian rewards, there is great potential as East goes West for Chinese–English dialogue over essence, identity and language to become a long series of new and very rich global conversations.

References

CCTV (2007) Forum: 术有专攻, 不能让英语教育成为民族复兴的制约 2007-10-5. [Skills should be specialized. We cannot let English education hold back the national renaissance]. On WWW at http://fuxing.bbs.cctv.com/viewthread. php?tid=11191583&extra=page%3D7. Accessed 8.12.07.

Chen, Z.B. (2006) 九十年代以来传统文化热之考察 [*Jiushi niandai yilai chuandong wenhuare zhi kaocha. A Study of the Traditional Culture Craze Since the 1990s*]. 北京: 学术中国. [Beijing: Xueshu zhongguo, Academia China]. On WWW at http:// xschina.org/show.php?id=6476. Accessed 8.12.07.

Cohen, R. (2008) The Baton Passes to Asia. *The New York Times*, 30 March 2008. On WWW at http://www.nytimes.com/2008/03/31/opinion/31cohen.html?_ r=1&ex=12078. Accessed 02.04.08.

Deng, K.G. (2000) A critical survey of recent research in Chinese economic history. *Economic History Review* 53 (1), 1–28.

Deng, K.G. (2004) Book review: The Eastern origins of Western civilisation. *Economic History Review* 57 (4), 799–800.

Feng, A.W. (2000) A canon, a norm and an attitude – ideological dimensions in foreign language education in China. Report of Annual Meeting of the Teachers of English to Speakers of Other Languages, 32nd, Seattle, WA, 17–21 March 1998. ERIC, ED424746.

Frank, A.G. (1998) *ReOrient: Global Economy in the Asian Age*. Berkeley: University of California Press.

French, H.W. (2006, 11 January) China's latest export: Language. *International Herald Tribune*. On WWW at http://www.iht.com/articles/2006/01/11/news/ china.php. Accessed 05.12.07.

Gao, Y.H. (1996) A "1 + 1 > 2" model of foreign language learning. In G. Xu (ed.) *ELT in China 1992* (pp. 417–432). Beijing: Foreign Language Teaching and Research Press.

Gao, Y.H., Cheng, Y., Zhao, Y. and Zhou, Y. (2004) English learning and changes in self-identity. In Y.H. Gao (ed.) *The Social Psychology of English Learning by Chinese College Students – Motivation and Learners' Self-Identities* (pp. 25–62). Beijing: Foreign Language Teaching and Research Press.

Goldston, J. (1991) *Revolution and Rebellion in the Early Modern World*. Berkeley and London: University of California Press.

Guangming Ribao (Guangming Daily) (2007) 东学西渐与 [*Dong xue Xi jian*. Eastern Thought Gradually Permeating the West]. Broadcast 1 January 2004. On WWW at http://gb.cri.cn/3601/2004/12/24/342@401811.htm. Accessed 05.12.07.

Hobson, J. (2004) *The Eastern Origins of Western Civilisation*. Cambridge: Cambridge University Press.

Hu, W.Z. (ed.) (1988) *International Communication: What it Means to Chinese Learners of English*. Shanghai: Shanghai Translation Publishing House.

Huang, M. (2006) On playing down foreign festivals and cultural invasion. *Journal of Chongqing Vocational and Technical Institute* 15 (4), 105–107.

Ji, X.L. (2001) "东学西渐与 "东化" ("*Dong xue Xi jian*" yu "*Donghua*" "Eastern thinking gradually permeating the West" and "Easternization"). Radio broadcast. *China On-line*. On WWW at http://gb.cri.cn/3601/2004/12/24/342@401811.htm. Retrieved 5.12.2007.

Ji, X.L. (2007) 东学西渐中国文化在西方 [*Dong Xue Xi Jian, Zhongguo Wenhua Zai Xifang. Eastern Thought Gradually Permeating the West, Chinese Culture in the West*]. Hebei: Hebei People's Publishing House.

Li, B.Z. (1998) *Agricultural Development in Jiangnan, 1620–1850*. Houndmills and London: Palgrave Macmillan.

Mahbubani, K. (2008) *The New Asian Hemisphere: The Irresistible Shift of Global Power to the East*. New York: Public Affairs.

Mao, Z.D. (Mao Tsetung) (1942) On new democracy. *Selected Works of Mao Tse-tung*, Peking (Beijing): Foreign Languages Press, 1965.

Metzger, T.A. (1977) *Escape from Predicament: China's Evolving Political Culture*. New York: Columbia University Press.

Pomeranz, K. (2000) *The Great Divergence, Europe, China and the Making of the Modern World Economy*. Princeton, NJ: Princeton University Press.

Rosenblum, M. (2007) *Escaping Plato's Cave: How America's Blindness to the Rest of the World Threatens Our Survival*. New York: St Martin's Press.

Rossabi, M. (1975) *China and Inner Asia*. London: Thames & Hudson.

Teng, S.Y. and Fairbank, J.K. (1954) *China's Response to the West – A Documentary Survey 1839–1923*. Cambridge, MA: Harvard University Press.

Wang, Y.C. (2002) Discover the East and export Chinese culture [发现东方与中国文化输出]. *Journal of Liberation Art College* 3, 5–12.

Wen, W.P. (2000) On postcolonial English and education in postcolonial context. *Journal of Sichuan International Studies University* 16 (4), 72–81.

Wu, J.M. (2007) *How to Look at the Rejuvenation of China*. [如何看待中华民族的复兴]. On WWW at http://www.hxlsw.com/Artis/20061010/2291_1.asp. Accessed 09.01.08.

Xu, K.Q. (2004) The loss of Chinese culture in bilingual education. [双语教学热中应关注中华民族文化遗失问题]. *Foreign Language Education* 25 (3), 86–89.

Yang, W.F. (2007) Chinese language and culture education and foreign language teaching. *Technological Information* 14.

Yue, D. (2007) 学西渐丛书 [*Dong Xue Xi Jian Congshu. Eastern Thought Gradually Permeating the West Series*]. 北京: 首都师范大学出版社出版 [Beijing: Shoudu Shifan Daxue Chubanshe. Beijing: Capital Normal University Press]. On WWW at http://www.gmw.cn/01gmrb/2007–01/04/content_530838.htm.

Zeng, H.W. (2005) College English education and Chinese culture education. *China College Teaching* 4, 50–52.

Zhang, M. (2001) Standard English, English varieties and international English [地道英语，英语变体与国际英语]. *Journal of Further Education of Shaanxi Normal University* 18 (2), 55–58.

Zhong, W.M., Li, Y.X. and Zhang, Y.X. (2005) The cultural input and foreignization strategies in Chinese–English translation. *Journal of Xiangnan University* 26 (3), 73–76.

Chapter 16
Being Chinese, Speaking English

JOSEPH LO BIANCO

Introduction

After adoption of free market reforms in the late 1980s and encouragement of foreign investment (Pang *et al.*, 2002) initially into the Pearl River delta and later more generally throughout its national territory, China experienced a decade of unprecedented rates of economic growth and entered the 21st century as 'the world's factory' (Kalish, 2003). Economic success has stimulated not only reconsideration of the global role of China as an economy, military power and locus of contemporary culture but also reconsideration of its traditional culture, inducing ever more students around the world to study Chinese (Liu & Lo Bianco, 2007; Wang, 2007; Ward, 2007). In the Western media the learning of Chinese is a regular feature of business pages, but also increasingly of society pages, so much so that 'Chinese is now hot in the world ... 3 million non-Chinese are learning Chinese as a foreign language, and that number is growing quickly' (Collins, 2006). Such expansion has given rise to both admiration and emulation, but in some circles it has also provoked alarm. This has been particularly noticeable in Africa, where, perversely, voices and interests created by past imperialism allege that a new imperialism is underway (Malone, 2008).

The expansion of Chinese as a foreign language is set to continue for a considerable period (College Board, 2006), highlighting a long-established pattern in which approximately a decade of economic and political success by a new power produces an elevated demand for study of its language. In this way, school foreign language choices are a reasonably reliable mirror of world events. The fortunes of the major second languages studied in schools across the world today are all closely tied to world military, economic and political events of the past century and a half (Cha & Ham, 2008). Each change is signalled by new ways of talking about the newly prominent centre of power, its language and society, evident today in changed discourse around the appropriate social, political and economic arrangements that flow from the economic success of China, as expressed in the Asia Society of New York, Press Release of 12 July 2005 (Asia Society, 2005). Even when economic success stagnates or declines as in the world recession that commenced in late 2008, it is clear that much debate centres on China's role in the resolution of the current economic crisis and the new arrangements to be instituted for world financial management when economic growth returns.

Similar discursive effects were produced by the global trade competitiveness of Japan and (South) Korea in recent decades. Both provoked a search for explanations beyond economic factors alone, interrogating 'underlying' cultural causes and meanings, such as 'Asian values', 'family cohesion', thrift and delayed consumption, Confucian 'discipline', etc., and led to expansion of the foreign teaching of Japanese and Korean.

Influencing Informally

In previous work analysing the booming interest in Chinese, the role of influence as a non-institutional and non-formal mode of language planning was highlighted (Lo Bianco, 2007). Isolating the role of influence aims to include in the discipline of language planning the often underestimated effects produced by persuasion, promotion and attraction. The undertheorisation of influence is a serious flaw in conventional accounts of language change, and the field of language planning in particular, which is often limited by an overly mechanistic characterisation of what legitimately counts as factors producing language change. Because of this deficiency, language planning theory is rarely used to inform accounts of the massive expansion of English in the world, certainly the largest language change in recent decades. Typically, explanations for the emergence of mass English language spread make recourse to critical branches of sociology, to normative political science or to branches of sociolinguistics other than language planning.

The growth of English cannot be directly attributed to formally declared policy texts, laws or regulations of government agencies, and the predilection of language planning theory to begin its accounts of language planning from such authoritative documents limits the line of questioning that language planning theoreticians have been able to pursue about one of the largest communicative transformations in history. Even when such formalisations are possible, the textual manifestation of formative ideological patterns is hardly amenable to understanding by reliance on their effects.

Instead, the wide social and cultural shaping effects that hegemonic economic and political power generate are typically accounted for by political scientists, most recently in the distinction between the imposing and palpably coercive effects of 'hard power', that is, military and economic, and the culturally attracting and persuading effects of cultural 'soft power' (Nye, 2004). Critical scholarship makes recourse to notions of hegemony as conceptualised by Gramsci (Ives, 2004) and Bourdieu's (1977, 1991, 1993) accounts of linguistic behaviour in consolidating markets in which capital accumulations, both actual and symbolic, are exchanged. All of these are efforts to understand the links between material forces like shifts in economic and military power and their linguistic and cultural manifestation.

Institutionalising Influence

Language education choices are influenced via messages and prestige that flow typically through channels of consumption of popular culture and the commodification of cultural products in various kinds of markets. However, influence over language choice also takes institutional form (Guo, 2004). The institutionalised form of influence is clearest in the establishment of state agencies entrusted to promote national languages and cultures beyond the geo-political sovereignty of national states. It is significant that one decade after Japan and Korea emerged as global trading economies, they each established external national cultural agencies. These agencies were specifically designed for foreign cultural representation with a mission to undertake language spread, inevitably to represent authorised if not official versions of culture. The Japan Foundation was established in 1972, initially as a special legal entity under the Ministry of Foreign Affairs; the Korea Foundation followed suit in 1991.

These bodies have an impressive array of cultural, linguistic and international exchange activity. China succeeded in a virtual echo of this pattern of a decade of trading success, followed by the creation of an international cultural exchange agency with a central language teaching remit. In 1987 China established the National Office of Teaching Chinese as a Foreign Language (NOCFL), known usually as the *Hanban*, with a range of activity including the development of a Chinese Proficiency Test for Foreigners (HSK), cultural exchanges and tours, support networks for foreign teachers of Chinese, and various language teaching support methods. A key focus has been the setting up of joint venture language centres with prestigious host education bodies around the world, the Confucius Institutes.

The most well-known national cultural agency is the British Council. While the British Council has been important in supporting English internationally, it has not been the primary generator of demand for English. Instead, the demand for English flows from the unique conjunction in history that a transfer of political and economic power was effected in and through the same language: post-World War II when British imperial reach declined and American economic, political and military hegemony accelerated. Some of the effects of this unique historical circumstance, retention of language hegemony despite change in the political hegemony, are revealed in China's own foreign language teaching policies (Adamson, 2002; Lam, 2005). Specifically, we can see how pre-revolution China favoured English among its foreign languages, replaced it with Russian during the Cold War period, but then restored English to foreign language supremacy after market reforms were inaugurated by Deng Xiaoping from 1989. This represents a sequence of influences from acknowledging the utility of English under British imperial reach, supplanted by Soviet allegiances during the period of Cold War rivalries, supplanted in turn by globalised capital under American sway and a return to English. Perhaps more dramatic was the post-colonial rejection of English from official state functions, and as language of instruction, in several Asian and African colonies of Britain and their progressive restoration of English under conditions of economic globalisation (Lo Bianco, 2008), indicating the indirect 'soft' power corollary of politico-economic power, and its manifestation in universalised popular culture.

As a factor in the global promotion of Chinese, influence has the additional feature of an international Chinese ethnic diaspora that pre-exists the promotion of Chinese as a 'foreign' language. The numerous dispersed Chinese minority populations around the world have long been engaged in 'community' language maintenance. As the Chinese authorities establish agencies and programmes to support Chinese teaching abroad, these communities and their language maintenance efforts enter complex and sometimes ambiguous relationships with a foreign state promoting a standardised and official version of their dialectal speech forms (Wang, 2007). Code-switching research (Li, 1994, 2005) among British Chinese children enrolled in language maintenance programmes in complementary schools established prior to China's official interest in language promotion shows how children alternate between more Chinese or more British identities in the language choices they make in informal conversations and in classroom interaction. Reflecting a local presence for Chinese and the repertoire of identities available to British Chinese children, some language switching responds to teacher use of language forms perceived to meet homeland expectations. The prior existence of vibrant Chinese-speaking communities who maintain Chinese across generations distinguishes this case of language promotion abroad from its British, French or German counterparts. Most of the language promotion undertaken by the British Council, the Alliance Française and the Goethe Institute assumes 'foreign' language promotion activities unencumbered by local communities with attachments to local forms of the language and local institutions for its promotion. Nor is the Chinese case like the promotional work of the Japan Foundation and the Korea Foundation, whose languages have not traditionally featured in curricula abroad.

However, in this respect the Chinese case and its inherent dilemmas do resemble the main features of the Italian case, namely, extended geographic dispersion, major dialect diversity and substantial pre-existing language maintenance activity. These diaspora speaker communities are then required to interact with an energetic promotion of the standard forms of the 'nation's official language' (Li, 2005) when the nation perceives these communities as a linguistic beachhead. The code switching suggests norm ambiguity through two language paradigms: one validated in community use and the other authorised formally in the homeland. In the Italian case, both of these have public and institutional form in two agencies entrusted with language promotion. A small number of prestigious Italian Cultural Institutes are formal dependencies of the Italian Ministry for Foreign Affairs and typically run programmes of literature-based standard language acquisition and 'high culture' activity centred on Renaissance studies, art history and classical civilisation. These are 'complemented' by a much vaster network of locally based Dante Alighieri Societies, loosely coordinated by a central agency (concerned neither with 'standards' nor with authorisation). The latter run programmes that reflect a hybrid mixture of immigrant diaspora population needs and communicative contexts and local foreign language enthusiasts oriented towards tourism, art and culture studies. While sociolinguistic realities mean that both bodies must negotiate aspects of foreign and dialectal connections to the national standard, the local bodies permanently and continuously manage and reconcile periphery and centre notions of identity (Totaro-Genevois, 2005).

Foreign cultural policy for Chinese faces a similar pattern of interaction as it negotiates linguistic promotion and spread. The foreign language enters contexts in which preceding, dispersed, native speaker populations are well established and whose activities of recovery and retention of the national language, or one of its varieties, must be reconciled and accommodated to authorised versions. Local institutions reflect both historical vintages and regional associations and give rise to the complex sociolinguistics classically found among emigrant communities.

This prior existence of 'Chinese' emigrants, including those whose origins are unconnected with the political sovereignty of the mainland,

and in some cases hostile to it, involves negotiating across not only linguistic adaptations and cultural identities but also institutional structures and hierarchies. Underscoring this is recent research on Chinese teaching in Australia (Orton, 2008). Of the 2716 students who took the final school exams in Victoria in 2006, 1588 were candidates who had attended a minimum of seven years of Chinese language medium schooling (comprising mostly international students), 381 were Chinese as second language advanced candidates, with between one and six years of schooling in Chinese medium institutions, and 747 were Chinese as second language candidates for whom requirements stipulate a maximum of three years residence and one year of Chinese medium education. Here we see combined the efforts of language retention, new learning and first language medium education, each very different in acceptable linguistic norms and expectations.

Language retention has been the main orientation of Chinese teaching in settings in which it is now a promoted foreign language (Liu & Lo Bianco, 2007). The total language learning effort for Chinese in foreign settings is still dominated by community institutions who have had to change their accounts of the cultural capital represented by 'Chinese' (Wang, 2007) in this new era. The existence of 'heritage' representations of Chinese among immigrant populations in which Chinese is 'home language' has rapidly adapted to being constituted as a foreign and world language of strategic importance, but longer-term accommodations are underway in relation to promotion and influence activities from China, which involve taking into consideration issues of emotional attachment, linguistic variation and diverse forms of cultural capital.

As the homeland policies of influence adapt to pre-existing language, cultural, regional and political realities, pedagogical questions also emerge. Pedagogical issues occur in classrooms where 'background' speakers' needs require acknowledgement, or accommodation, and in local schools and community cultural settings where norms of language use have already defined what it means to be Chinese and to speak Chinese (Hill, 2004). Official versions, and even prescribed forms of what it means to be Chinese, and local versions of what constitutes acceptable, or expected, Chinese lingual identity and behaviour are therefore brought into dynamic relations of contact and negotiation at both institutional and informal levels.

Influence: English in China

The foregoing discussion of how language planning influence is projected abroad on behalf of Chinese has an emergent mirror within China in relation to English. While the community dimension of English within mainland China is socioeconomically and geographically small and highly circumscribed, some of the ways in which a mass and obligatory study of English in China is described raises issues of influence, identity and cultural impact. The present discussion is also informed by survey evidence from Chinese institutions.

The following section reports data gathered in an anonymous 10-question survey of teachers of English at the tertiary level across China. Data from the survey are also analysed by Orton (this volume, Chapter 15).

Respondents

The variables built into the sample involve location and type of institution at which respondents teach, as well as the nature of the academic programme in which they are engaged, their age and gender.

The survey was administered online and elicited responses from 154 teachers in 10 institutions dispersed across China. The physical locations are 10 cities: Beijing, Changchun, Chongqing, Foshan, Harbin, Hefei, Kunming, Lanzhou, Shanghai and Shenyang. The diversity of institutional types includes *normal* universities and colleges (65 respondents), *comprehensive* (18 respondents) and *technical* universities (49 respondents) as well as universities specialised in language and culture education (12 respondents) and finally *professional* business institutes (eight respondents). Two respondents did not state their institutional affiliation.

The respondents were for the most part young, and predominantly female, with 57 aged in their 20s, 62 in their 30s, 25 in their 40s and 10 aged more than 50 years. The bulk has therefore been educated in the past 20 years, during which English became an established component of China's formal education structures. The respondents were more or less equally teaching English majors and students majoring in other disciplines but taking English in a minor academic sequence or some other arrangement.

It is perhaps worth noting that the age profiles correspond, if only roughly, with some major foreign relations eras in post-revolutionary China: the 60-year-olds more or less with the birth of the People's Republic, the 50-year-olds with the Great Leap Forward, the 40-year-olds with the Great Proletarian Cultural Revolution, the 30-year-olds with the death of Mao Zedong and the rise of Deng Xiaoping, and the 20-year-olds with the policy of openness to market economics and state capitalism that has brought about the immense economic transformation of the country. While these periods are not coterminous with language education policies

(Adamson, 2002; Lam, 2005), they broadly correspond to a move from a preference for Russian, to the ejection of Russian from Chinese education, to a transition between Russian and English, along with a small number of other foreign languages, to general encouragement of English as the first foreign language and to obligatory inclusion of English as the first foreign language and as a tool of general education services and planning (such as a tertiary selection hurdle and a language of tertiary instruction).

Responses

Below are extracts from answers to questions asking respondents to nominate positive and negative reactions to the growth of English learning in China. The first question asked about the worst aspects associated with the growth of English learning in China. Several broad categories of answer were offered from which respondents selected their preferred 'problem', grouped below in the seven dominant themes that emerged.

- *Loss of national identity, culture and tradition*: For 55 respondents, this cluster of dangers, problems and issues looms large. While there is a small bias among these respondents towards urban normal and technical institutional locations and provincial normal institutions, they are evenly distributed between English study modes. Although female respondents comprise a 3:1 ratio in the total sample, almost 4:1 of the adherents to the view that English represents a potential danger to national identity, culture and tradition are female.
- *Less knowledge of Chinese language, classical Chinese and cultural heritage*: The next largest single response, nominated by 39 individuals, addresses more specifically linguistic and literary issues. Among those who felt this concern, there was a small bias towards being located in urban and provincial non-technical institutions and a bias towards females, although not excessively. Adherents of this view were not otherwise differentiated by age or according to English majors/non-majors.
- *English as a certificate*: Twenty-four respondents felt that the mass teaching of English was regrettable because it turned English study into certificate hunting rather than a pursuit of knowledge of English in its own right. Those who felt this way were rather evenly distributed in type of institution at both provincial and urban levels and not especially differentiated by whether their students were English majors or non-English majors, and, taking account of the female dominance of the sample, rather evenly distributed on that score too.

- *Waste for students*: The idea that compulsion and mass teaching involve waste for students, since those not motivated to learn English are still required to study it, attracted 17 respondents. These 17 reveal a provincial bias, reflecting perhaps the particular difficulties that rural or non-urban areas have in accessing qualified and competent English teachers and back-up support. Also strongly holding this view were teachers of students who were not English majors, suggesting that the problem is exacerbated for those students whose courses of study are not centred on English, but for whom regulations and laws impose compulsory English study.

- *No danger*: Thirteen randomly distributed individuals refused to accept any dangers arising from the rapid and deep spread of English in China. These individuals instead cited a range of neutral, positive or very positive effects from the penetration of English deep into Chinese institutions of education. The rather even distribution across institution type, gender, form of English study and age perhaps suggests that all categories of tertiary Chinese English teachers are open to and agents of the view that English can be permitted the wide range of institutional roles it now occupies in Chinese education, that is, that English can be permitted the role of a 'basic skill' in Chinese education.

- *Difficult to implement*: Only eight respondents felt that the main problem with English language policies in China today was the difficulty of implementation. Those holding this non-ideological or practical orientation were not differentiated in any significant ways according to any of the variables assessed.

- *Miscellaneous sociopolitical consequences*: A diffuse category of various sociopolitical consequences flowing from mass and compulsory English teaching won adherence from seven respondents, the smallest number.

The second question explored the best and most positive aspects associated with the growth of English learning in China. Several broad categories of answer were offered from which respondents selected their preferred 'positive', grouped below in the six dominant themes that emerged.

- *Cross-cultural exchange (communication and understanding)*: Fifty-one respondents nominated cross-cultural exchange, and specifically communication and understanding, as the key positives and outcomes from China's English policy. These respondents were strongly represented in urban normal and provincial technical institutions. There was also a significant bias towards female adherents and among the youngest two age categories.

- *China's development*: The next largest response focused on the direct benefits to China and its national economic and technological progress. This was the view of 45 respondents well represented across all variables.

- *Broadening Chinese people's horizons*: Thirty-nine individuals in the sample, lacking any discernable differentiation except underrepresentation among male respondents, felt that the main positive to be gleaned from mass and obligatory English teaching was that it would lead to a broadening of the horizons of Chinese people.

- *Better for English learning*: For 35 individuals, however, the main benefit was to the actual teaching and learning of English. There is a dispersed and unconcentrated presence across all variables of this view.

- *Better employment prospects*: With a small overrepresentation in provincial institutions, but not in any other way differentiated, 20 tertiary English teachers considered that the main benefit of widespread English education was that it would enhance the employment prospects of graduates.

- *The world knows China/Chinese language*: With no discernable concentration among the variables, a small category of 12 respondents felt that mass English teaching and learning would assist in getting the world to know China and Chinese better. This indirect benefit of English teaching was a low-level presence in all categories.

Discussion

Chinese national discourses have long deployed a dichotomy between indigenous or native learning as the essence alongside a pragmatic, utilitarian or instrumental benefit accruing from foreign languages. This has been operationalised in the binary division between essence and utility (体–用 *ti–yong*) discernable in longstanding Confucian representations of knowledge. For more than 150 years, English has represented the principal vehicle for the application of this understanding, with the exception of the dominance of Russian in the immediate aftermath of the formation of the People's Republic after 1949. The rupture of relations between China and the USSR brought with it the associated rupture of the *ti–yong* accommodation, which had arisen for Russian and its definitive transfer to English.

Motivated by what Feng (2007) has called a Chinese 'fear of influences', English has been kept distant from the perceived zone of cultural and national essence and represented as an auxiliary vehicle facilitating access to the Western scientific skills and technological knowledge. This has been a protective mission to strengthen China's preparedness to resist foreign incursions at cultural levels but also politically. Residues of these constructions are apparent in the respondents' framing of answers to questions about the role and effects of English in China today and are inscribed in the narrative many tell of China's relations with the world. However, as we have seen, the depth of presence of English inside Chinese institutions and its increasing utilisation as a vehicle for engagement with the world are now matched by the projecting of Chinese interests abroad.

Institutionalisation of Chinese influence abroad by encouraging widespread learning of Chinese brings policy makers and educators face to face with prior definitions of what it means to be Chinese among established diaspora communities, and against images of China as it is perceived by ever more knowledgeable foreigners. The fear of influences is increasingly coming up against a desire for influence.

Tertiary teachers' responses to questions about English and its roles recirculate *ti–yong* understandings in the utilitarian, educational, national and cross-cultural prisms through which judgements are made of English teaching policies. Concerns for China and the national culture occur repeatedly. Although differentiated, there is a strong cluster of issues that reflect personalised relationships at the local, international and institutional domains with English. This suggests that English education offers a range of 'local reward systems' that attract a community of interest. Internationalism is interestingly bifurcated, with a strong receptive element (China and Chinese people knowing about others, especially English speakers, and engaging in acts of cross-cultural communication oriented towards learning about difference through English) and the world, and English speakers in particular, learning about China and Chinese through English.

Although we can identify a total of 200 benefits/problems listed by the 154 respondents, these cluster in recurring themes of utilitarian, educational, national and cross-cultural arguments and are specified at national, international and institutional domains. Table 16.1 shows those responses that epitomise these categories of interest with the interplay of official and informal influence, organised in four clusters of motivation and the three fields in which these apply. Responses are either normative or descriptive.

Table 16.1 Responses according to motivations and applications

		Institutional	National	International
Utilitarian		'To create more positions for non-native speakers of English, increase the economic investment in promotional materials'	'The great need for English in today's society'	'... economic spur from outside China and sustained economic growth'
			'The introduction of advanced sciences and technologies from the West ...'	
Educational		'That the language abilities help Chinese to gain more cultural capitals'	'That it may make young Chinese to gradually lose interest or need to study Chinese culture'.	'To let Chinese people know more things about the world'
		'English learning is not learning anymore, rather, various tests of English are viewed as a must, a certificate ...'	'Popularize the learning of English in rural areas'	
		'... students put so much emphasis on it that they ignore other subjects; quite a lot of them study English only to pass exams ...'	'A large amount of Chinese children aged between 5–10 have begun to learn English, and really they can speak fluently'	
		'To learn is to have an exam'		

(Continued)

Table 16.1 Continued

	Institutional	National	International
National	'English has become an international language, which has been recognised by Chinese'	'To lose Chinese identity' 'English learners are bold enough to open their mouth to speak English' 'It's profit driven, too much business elements in promoting the learning of English' 'Many people still can't speak freely'	'The boost of the national image ...' 'Command of the English language may offer the Chinese a better chance to articulate their cultural and ideological ...' 'Chinese culture and tradition can be known and understood by the outsiders' 'To let other cultures know China better'
Cross-cultural	'Strengthen the cross-culture communication and help Chinese people know the world better' 'To learn more about Western culture'	'To create an English communication environment within Chinese society ...' 'It makes China more international'	'It will make China more open' 'To let Chinese people know more things about the world'

Conclusion

Only a few respondents imagine a permanently or irretrievably delete-rious effect from mass English learning, although a considerable number are ambivalent or somewhat concerned, and a small number are seriously concerned, either for impact on the nation, education or its learners. Furthermore, these respondents are clear that the fortunes of China, its history, prestige and honour, let alone its language and classical literary canon, are implicated in and affected by the teaching of English to everybody.

For some this constitutes a point of weakness in the age-old China–West conversation, while for others utilitarian reasoning prevails in judgements they make about the emergence of overarching or shared norms of inter-action across national borders. In these calculations about how a future world will communicate, Chinese civilisation is absorbed into a kind of world synthesis of cultures, but the primary communicative vehicle for that synthesis remains English. For others, Chinese 'hard' power will be matched by the expansion of Chinese 'soft' power, influence attached to importance, and so China's cultural and language presence across the world will become visible in processes of both informal and institutional influence gaining. The result will be less and less Chinese accommodation to others through English and more the other way around.

In this latter vision, of course, it is English, and images of Chinese as a kind of 'new English' that are being alluded to. In discussions with teacher educators in China, such views are not uncommon, but their often vague nature and the amorphous shape any such worldwide appropriation of Chinese-ness would take underscore the provisional and evolutionary form that the 'emergence of Chinese' idea takes.

Yet, it is remarkable how frequently the question of China, Chinese and China's ancient cultural accomplishments is associated even with the learn-ing and teaching of English within tertiary institutions in China, by Chinese teachers and for Chinese learners. It is a recurring feature of the contempo-rary Chinese social imaginary (Walden, 2008) that a new world is taking shape, and this imagined emergent world order is not just a change from the past, but a change that contains and restores a part of the past.

One Chinese university lecturer expressed the view that 'we' are fortu-nate to be living at this time, because the images 'we' have inherited of 'China' and the 'west' are recognisably undergoing historic transforma-tion: 'We can see it happening'. This historic transformation, he argued, will see Asia in general, and China in particular, as full protagonists in an unprecedented interconnected global system of economics, education and culture. Unlike past social transformations, on this occasion 'we will be conscious' of the change, and will perceive it directly, rather than have it mediated by authorised texts, popular understanding or parental accounts directed at impressionable children. It will be, he said, China saying to the world 'I am back!'

We often imagine the future as a kind of conversation. Chinese, like other Asians, or indeed Europeans, Americans, Australians or Africans, cannot know the precise contours of this imagined future, nor if it will arrive, but many long for its birth and anticipate its character, some perceive its infant steps, and one or two have already heard its first words.

References

Adamson, B. (2002) Barbarian as a foreign language: English in China's schools. *World Englishes* 21 (2), 257–267.

Asia Society (2005) *Expanding Chinese Language Capacity in the United States: What Would it Take to Have 5 percent of High School Students Learning Chinese by 2015?* New York: Asia Society. On WWW at http://www.internationaled.org.

Bourdieu, P. (1977) The economics of linguistic exchanges. *Social Science Information* 16 (6), 645–668.

Bourdieu, P. (1991) *Language and Symbolic Power.* Cambridge: Cambridge University Press.

Bourdieu, P. (1993) *Sociology in Question.* London: Sage.

Cha, Y-K. and Ham, S-H. (2008) The impact of English on the school curriculum. In B. Spolsky and F. Hult (eds) *Handbook of Educational Linguistics* (pp. 313–328). London: Blackwell.

College Board (2006) New agreement will build Chinese language programs in U.S. schools. On WWW at http://www.collegeboard.com/press/releases/51453.html.

Collins, G. (2006) Can Chinese become a global language of networking and business? On WWW at http://www.ecademy.com/node.php?id=73452&seen=1.

Feng, A. (2007) Intercultural space for bilingual education. In A. Feng (ed.) *Bilingual Education in China: Practices, Policies and Concepts* (pp. 259–286). Clevedon: Multilingual Matters.

Guo, Y. (2004) *Cultural Nationalism in Contemporary China: The Search for National Identity under Reform.* New York, NY: Routledge.

Hill, A.M. (2004) Language matters in China: An anthropological postscript. In M. Zhou and H. Sun (eds) *Language Policy in the People's Republic of China, Theory and Practice Since 1949* (pp. 333–339). Dordrecht: Kluwer.

Ives, P. (2004) *Language and Hegemony in Gramsci.* London: Pluto.

Kalish, I. (2003) *The World's Factory: China Enters the 21st Century.* Deloitte Research Consumer Business Study. On WWW at http://www.deloitte.com/dtt/cda/doc/content/DTT_DR_China21Century.pdf.

Lam, A. (2005) *Language Education in China: Policy and Experience since 1949.* Hong Kong: Hong Kong University Press.

Li, W. (1994) *Three Generations Two Language One Family: Language Choice and Language Shift in a Chinese Community in Britain.* Clevedon: Multilingual Matters.

Li, W. (ed.) (2005) *Conversational Code-Switching. Journal of Pragmatics*, Special Issue, 37, 3.

Liu, G. and Lo Bianco J. (2007) Teaching Chinese, teaching in Chinese and teaching the Chinese: Australian perspectives. In J. Lo Bianco (ed.) *The Emergence of Chinese, Language Policy* (Vol. 6, Issue 1, pp. 95–117). Dordrecht, Netherlands: Springer.

Lo Bianco, J. (2007) Emergent China and Chinese: Language planning categories. In J. Lo Bianco (ed.) *The Emergence of Chinese, Language Policy* (Vol. 6, Issue 1, pp. 3–26). Dordrecht, Netherlands: Springer.

Lo Bianco, J. (2008) A friendly knife? English in the context of Sri Lankan language politics. In L. Farrell, U.N. Singh and R.A. Giri (eds) *English Language Education in South Asia: From Policy to Pedagogy*. Delhi: Cambridge University Press India.

Malone, A. (2008) How China's taking over Africa, and why the West should be VERY worried, *Daily Mail* (newspaper), 18 July, London. On WWW at http://www.dailymail.co.uk/news/worldnews/article-1036105/How-Chinas-taking-Africa-West-VERY-worried.html.

Nye, J.S. (2004) *Soft Power: The Means to Success in World Politics*. New York: Public Affairs.

Orton, J. (2008, October) *Chinese Language Education in Australian Schools*. Melbourne: Graduate School of Education and the Confucius Institute, The University of Melbourne. On WWW at http://www.asiaeducation.edu.au/public_html/reports.htm.

Pang, J., Zhou, X. and Fu, Z. (2002) English for International Trade: China enters the WTO. *World Englishes* 21 (2), 201–216.

Totaro-Genevois, M. (2005) *Cultural and Linguistic Policy Abroad: The Italian Experience*. Clevedon: Multilingual Matters.

Walden, G. (2008) China, Red in Tooth and Claw Review of *Wolf Totem* by Jiang Rong, *Standpoint Magazine*, London, Social Affairs Unit Magazines.

Wang, S. (2007) Building societal capital: Chinese in the US. In J. Lo Bianco (ed.) *The Emergence of Chinese, Language Policy* (Vol. 6, Issue 1, pp. 27–52). Dordrecht, Netherlands: Springer.

Ward, L. (2007) Never mind French and Spanish … *Education Guardian*, 4 February, Education Guardian.

Index